Cemeteries of the City of Hampton Virginia

Formerly Elizabeth City County

Compiled by
Barry W. Miles

Edited by
James H. Mero and *Joseph A. Atkins*

HERITAGE BOOKS
2007

HERITAGE BOOKS
AN IMPRINT OF HERITAGE BOOKS, INC.

Books, CDs, and more—Worldwide

For our listing of thousands of titles see our website
at
www.HeritageBooks.com

Published 2007 by
HERITAGE BOOKS, INC.
Publishing Division
65 East Main Street
Westminster, Maryland 21157-5026

Copyright © 1999 The Hugh S. Watson Jr. Genealogical Society of Virginia

Other books by the author:

Abstracts of the Wills and Administrations of Accomack County, Virginia, 1800-1860
Barry W. Miles and Moody K. Miles, III

Cemeteries of the City of Newport News, Formerly Warwick County, Virginia
Barry W. Miles and Gertrude Stead

Marriage Records of Accomack County, Virginia, 1854-1895
(Recorded in Licenses & Ministers' Returns)
Barry W. Miles and Moody K. Miles, III

Tombstone Inscriptions of Upper Accomack County, Virginia
Mary Frances Carey with Moody K. Miles, III and Barry W. Miles

All rights reserved. No part of this book may be reproduced or transmitted in any form or by any means, electronic or mechanical, including photocopying, recording or by any information storage and retrieval system without written permission from the author, except for the inclusion of brief quotations in a review.

International Standard Book Number: 978-0-7884-4462-X

FOREWORD

In 1994 the Executive Board of the Tidewater Genealogical Society approved a project to publish books on the cemeteries of the City of Hampton, City of Newport News, York County, James City County, City of Poquoson and Gloucester County.

Members of the Society appointed to accomplish this project were: James H. Mero, Special Projects Chairman, Program Manager; Co-chairmen: City of Hampton, Ernest Lee Culler; City of Newport News, Gertrude E. Stead; York County, Everett Hogg; James City County, Patricia Higgs; City of Poquoson, Jessie F. Forrest; and Gloucester County, Harry R. Jordon. Due to the time required to accomplish the project it was necessary to replace some of the co-chairmen. Jessie F. Forrest is now co-chairman of York County and Barry W. Miles is co-chairman for the City of Hampton.

By 1996 the cemetery books for the City of Poquoson and Gloucester County had been completed. The book for the City of Hampton, formerly Elizabeth City County, was near completion. Mr. Barry W. Miles accepted the responsibility to complete the Hampton Cemeteries book. He has organized and compiled information on the Hampton Cemeteries by checking the work that had been accomplished, reading and recording information from tombstones of many other cemeteries, and preparing the book for printing and typing same.

Appreciation is extended to all those who have contributed material for this book.
A special thanks to Ernest Lee Culler who spent many hours locating cemeteries and researching cemetery information in the Hampton Historical files.
All reference to the Virginia Historical Inventory (W. P. A.) are courtesy of the Library of Virginia, Richmond, Virginia.

James H. Mero
Program Manager
Cemeteries Project

TABLE OF CONTENTS

Foreword iii

Table of Contents iv

Introductions x

Abbreviations xii

First Church of Kecoughtan 1

Second Church of Elizabeth City Parish 2

Third Church of Elizabeth City Parish 6

Antioch Baptist Church Cemetery 12

Armistead Cemetery 16

Ballard Cemetery 18

Barnes Cemetery 20

Bassett Cemetery 22

Bethel AME Church Cemetery 35

Bloxom Cemetery 41

Davis Cemetery 43

Drummond and/or Messick Cemetery 44

Elmerton Cemetery 46

Good Samaritan Cemetery 61

Greenlawn Cemetery 65

Guy Cemetery 71

Hampton University Cemetery 72

Hansford Cemetery	87
Hebrew Cemetery	92
Herbert Cemetery	129
Hollier Cemetery	131
Johnson Cemetery	133
Latimer Cemetery	135
Lattimer - Hickman Burial Grounds	136
Lewellen - Moore Burial Grounds	138
Mason or Drummond Cemetery	139
Mears Cemetery	140
Morning Star Baptist Church Cemetery	141
Phillips Cemetery	143
Phillips, C. L. Cemetery	153
Rosenbaum Memorial Park	156
Rountree and/or Cedar Island Cemetery	172
Routten, Jack Cemetery	174
Routten, Richard Cemetery	176
Routten, Spencer Cemetery	178
Shelton Cemetery	180
Sherwood Burial Ground	182
Sinclair Cemetery	185
Sinclair - Johnson Cemetery	187

Smith Cemetery	190
Stores Cemetery	207
Tennis Cemetery	209
Thornton Cemetery	210
Tucker Cemetery	214
Vaughan (Cloverdale) Cemetery	216
Watts Cemetery	220
West Cemetery	222
Williams Pit Landfill	228
Destroyed Cemeteries	231
First Methodist Church	231
Asbury Cemetery	233
Fredrick Barnes Cemetery	233
William Beam Cemetery	233
Confederate Cemetery	234
Hamilton Cemetery	234
Hawkins Cemetery	234
Hubbard / Guy Cemetery	234
Lewis Cemetery	235
Mallory Cemetery	235
Massenburg Cemetery	235
Moore Cemetery (Old Moore Farm)	236

Pembroke Farm Graveyard 236

Pool Cemetery 237

Poor House Farm Cemetery 237

Post Cemetery, Fort Monroe 237

Routten, Joseph Cemetery 238

Saunder Cemetery 239

Martha Savage Burial Ground 239

Smith, James Cemetery 240

Smith, John Cemetery 240

Tents Lodge Cemetery 240

Topping, James Cemetery 240

Topping, John P. L. Cemetery 241

Topping, Robert Cemetery 242

Unknown Burying Ground 242

Wallace - Tennis Cemetery 242

Wray, C. Cemetery 242

Wood Cemetery 243

Cemeteries not in this Book 245

The Fourth Church of Elizabeth City (St. John's Cemetery) 245

Clark Cemetery 245

Ebenezer Baptist Church Cemetery 246

Hampton Memorial Gardens 246

- Hampton Veteran Memorial Gardens 246
- Hampton National Cemetery 246
- Mount Olive Baptist Church Cemetery 247
- Oakland Cemetery 247
- Parklawn Memorial Park 247
- Peninsula Chapel Mausoleum 247
- Pleasant Shade 247
- Veterans Administration 248

Slave Cemeteries 249
- Wood Plantation 249
- Downey Farm 249
- Slave Cemetery (Woodland Road) 249

Index 251

INTRODUCTION

This book covers the area of the City of Hampton. Hampton was originally part of Elizabeth City County. Elizabeth City County was larger than the present City of Hampton. Part has been incorporated into the City of Newport News.

This book is the effort of several members of the Tidewater Genealogical Society; also, records from the Work Progress Administration have been used. Acknowledgment of the efforts of these individuals are recorded with the individual cemeteries.

We have made an effort to locate any cemetery that has been brought to the attention of the Society. Many of the cemeteries have been destroyed or access has been denied. If public information is available, it has been incorporated in the cemetery data. As co-chairman, I have made an effort to visit every cemetery or burial ground. There are a few cases where this has not been possible due to the undergrowth. There have been reports of slave cemeteries, and they have been recorded even though they cannot be verified by written records. The destroyed cemeteries, cemeteries not located, cemeteries where the graves have been moved, and cemeteries without any tombstones have been entered in this book.

There are several cemeteries that have not been included in the book. These are the very large cemeteries in the City of Hampton which have from three thousand to fifteen thousand interments. These cemeteries are maintained by owner management companies and have records that can direct an individual to a particular grave site. Also, a National Cemetery is located in Hampton, which has approximately 24,000 interments, and is maintained by the United States Government. Any one of these cemeteries could be a project by itself and a book by itself.

This book will assist genealogists with ancestors in the City of Hampton and Elizabeth City county. Some historical information is included on land patents and land ownership which influenced the location of the small family cemeteries. The location of many family cemeteries and the land owned by the families can be seen on the Map of Elizabeth City County, Virginia, copyright December 22, 1892. The map is from actual surveys by E. A. Semple, Wm. Ivy and C. Hubbard and platted by E. A. Semple, Civil Engineer and County Surveyor of Elizabeth City county. This map also shows the U. S. Cemetery location.

African American cemeteries have been included in this work. In each of the cemeteries given, it has been stated if the cemeteries are known to be African American. Caution must be used, as with any research because, if the cemetery is stated to be African American it does not necessary mean that persons of another races are not buried there.

We can be sure that there are additional graves in small family burying grounds or cemeteries. Due to time and development of the property many of the stones no longer exist. Many persons buried did not have a stone because of the cost of a marker. Many families could not afford markers. Field stones were used to the mark the spot where family members were buried. When family members died, these locations were no longer known. Many fieldstones have been moved by persons who did not know their purpose. My involvement in collection of cemetery inscriptions has proved to me that the written word will most likely last longer than that etched in stone.

A note of caution. There are words that will appear to be misspelled. When information is transcribed from tombstones, the spelling is given as it is on the tombstone, to the best ability of the transcriber. Also, information has been quoted from various historical records, newspapers, and the Virginia Historical Inventory (W.P.A.), courtesy of the Library of Virginia, Richmond, Virginia. All genealogists and historians using the information in this book should follow the golden rule for genealogists. Do not accept the enclosed information as the final authority. Go to the original source and read the information for your research.

Acknowledgment for the work included in this book is given with each individual cemetery. A special thanks must be given to individuals and institutions for their contributions to make this book possible: The Library of Virginia for the Virginia Historical Inventory (W.P.A) Records, Hampton University for historical information, authorization of the owners, directors or churches to transcribe tombstones, David Routten for his knowledge of Fox Hill area cemeteries and historical information, Kenneth Quinn for historical information, Mr. Keith and Mr. Winter for transcribing some of the cemeteries, Mr. Hutchinson's Boy Scout Troop for their transcriptions, and many others that have contributed to this work. including Mr. James H. Mero and Mr. Joseph A. Atkins for editing the material and Mrs. Jill Russell for proof reading. I, Barry Miles, must thank my wife, Leslyn Miles, for the many hours I have toiled in compiling the data, inputing data and transcribing tombstones of many of the African American cemeteries in and around downtown Hampton, the Hebrew and Rosenbaum cemeteries in the Wythe area, and many others of the cemeteries in the City of Hampton. The task has been monumental but I do hope it will aid researchers in their genealogical endeavors.

The **Tidewater Genealogical Society** hopes this works will aid those in search of their ancestors.

Barry W. Miles
Co-Chairman
Cemeteries Project
City of Hampton

ABBREVIATIONS

Arty.	Artillery		
b	born	m/o	mother of
b & d	born and died	m	married
Bn	Battalion	Maj	Major
Brig	Brigade	MD	Medical Doctor
Btry	Battery	mos	months
btw	between	MP	Military Police
BWI	British West Indies	ms	months
c	circa, about	PFC	Private First Class
c/o	child/of	PH	Purple Heart
Capt	Captain	Pvt	Private
Cmbt	Combat	QM	Quartermaster
Col	Colonel	QMC	Quartermaster Corps
Cpl	Corporal	Regt.	Regiment
CSA	Confederate States of America	Rev	Reverend
d	died	s/o	son of
d/o	daughter/of	Sr	Senior
d/s	double stone	USA	United States Army
Div	Division	USAF	United States Air Force
Dr	Doctor	USCG	United States Coast Guard
ds	days	USMC	United States Marine Corps
Engr	Engineers	USMM	United States Merchant Marine
f/o	father/of	USN	United States Navy
Gen	General	USNR	United States Navy Reserve
ggd/o	great-grand-daughter	Viet	Vietnam
gs/o	grandson of	Vir	Virginia
h/o	husband of	w/o	wife of
hq	Headquarters	wid/o	widow of
inf/o	infant of	WO	Warrant Officer
inf	infant and infantry	WW1	World War 1
Jr	Junior	WW2	World War 2
Lcpl	Lance Corporal	yrs	years
Lt	Lieutenant	ys	years
LTC	Lieutenant Colonel		

being made at the Second Church 24 years after its so-called abandonment."

According to historical information, the second church was abandoned in 1667 and was demolished in 1698.

Acknowledgment: Prepared by James H. Mero, 1996.

A Commemorative Granite Cross place at Location of the Alter of the Second Church

Cemeteries of the City of Hampton, Virginia / formerly Elizabeth City County

THIRD CHURCH OF ELIZABETH CITY PARISH
Pembroke Avenue and Patterson Street (48) {I - 10}
1667 - 1727/28

The Third Church of Elizabeth City Parish was built circa 1667 on a site known as Westwoods Town Quarter, later called Pembroke Plantation, and was about a mile or more from the second church. The location of the site is at Pembroke Avenue and Patterson Street. This site is now surrounded by a brick wall erected November 1, 1950 by the Hampton Roads Garden Club. Beneath the site are foundations of the old Church. A stone commemorating Peter Heyman, Esquire, was given by His Excellency, Francis Nicholson, Esquire. His Excellency Francis Nicholson served as Lieutenant Governor, deputy to Effingham, 3 June 1690 to 20 September 1692. Some tombstones identifying early burials remain.

In 1968 Mr. M. Brummal, Jr. recorded the plaque of the Third Elizabeth City Parish Church and it is quoted below:
"Here is the site of 'The New Church of Kecoughtan' built before 1667 on Pembroke farm at the Third Church of Elizabeth City Parish, established in 1610. It was a frame building and its brick foundation and some early colonial tombstones remain. When the town of Hampton was founded in 1691, this church lay outside it, and in 1727 was ordered to be replaced by a fourth Parish Church within the town, the existent, St. Johns Church, Hampton."

Over the years, several people have read the tombstone inscriptions of this cemtery. Two transcriptions are included herein giving the dates transcribed. In many cases they are different.

In June 1964 a pamphlet was prepared by Ellen Ironmonger Pearson (Mrs. Henry A.) for the Hampton Historical Society and included information on the Reverend James W. Wallace. Reverend Wallace was rector of the Third Church of Elizabeth City Parish from 1691 - 1712. He requested that he be buried on his plantation 'Erroll" on Back River. The plantation was named for his home in Scotland. Reverend Wallace had vast holdings in Elizabeth City County, owned several slaves and was a Doctor of Medicine. Reverend Wallace was buried in a cemetery at Erroll Plantation which was later known as Hansford Cemetery. The gravestones of Reverend and Mrs. Wallace were moved first to St. John's Churchyard Cemetery and later moved to the old Churchyard Cemetery of the Third Church of Elizabeth City Parish on Pembroke Avenue. Their remains and graves are in the Hansford Cemetery on Rockwell Road, Hampton, Virginia.

Acknowledgment: Mr Brummal, Jr., 1968. Mr. Steve Keith and Tim Winters, September 10, 1989.

Historical Marker of 3rd Church of Elizabeth City Parish Church

The Grave of Reverend Mr. James Wallace

Here Lieth the body of Mary ROBINSON
born the 18th day of August 1712
and dyed the 25th day of May 1726
her text is in the final book
of the Corinthians the fifteenth chapter

Here lyes the body of M. Euphon DANDRIDGE
who was kind and charitable to all poor people
she exchanged this life for better on the __ day
of April A. D. 1717 and in the 21 year of her age
In silence let my tear make known
our dearest friend from us fled
who virtue pure was much shown
will god did take to his home
tho she lyes here she not there dead

Under this same stone lyes the body of her son
Wilson DANDRIDGE who departed this life
the 21 day of Oct 1716

Here lyes the body of the
Reverend Mr. James WALLACE
late minister of this parish he was
born AR Errod in Perrhshire____
North Brittain he was serviceable
to this Colony in a double capacity
both as a Divine and Physician
on the space of one and twenty
year he exchanged this life for
a better on_ the 3 of November AD
1712 and in the 45 year of his age
excused deceased friend ___ forbear
tarr empt_ thy praise tis far above thy phere
only in silence let me drop _reor
say virtue fled and left one temple here.

Here lieth the body of
Mr. Henry ROBINSON
born in the year 1664
and dyed the 15th day of December 1719
his text
in the twelfth chapter of the Ecclesiastes

and the fifth verse
Remember now thy creatour in the
days of thy youth while the evil days
come not nor the year drew nigh
when thou shal say I have no pleasure
in them

Ye reverend
Mr. Andrew THOMPSON
born at Stonehive, Scotland
minister of this Parish
7 years
and departed this life
ye 11 Sep 1719

John NEVILL
Vice Admiral
of his Majesty's Fleet
who died on
board ye Cambridge
ye 17 day of August, 1697

Peter HEYMAN
collector of customs in
lower district of James River
he went in pursuit of a pyrate
who greatly infested this coast
was killed
ye 29 day of April, 1700

Thomas CURLE, Gent
born November 24, 1647
in ye Parish of St Michael
in ye County of
Surry, England
and dyed May 30, 1700

The following is from the William and Mary College Quarterly Histrocial magazine, Volume XIV, Series 1, 1905 - 1907:

"TOMBSTONES IN ELIZABETH CITY COUNTY
The old Churchyard near Hampton
Tombstone of John NEVILLE, Esq.

Tombstone of John NEVILLE, Esq.

Here lyes the Body of
JOHN NEVILLE, ESQR. VICE ADMIRAL
of his MAJESTYES FLEET and COMMANDER
in chiefe of ye squadron cruising
in the WEST INDIES
Who dyed on board ye CAMBRIDGE
the 17th, day of August, 1697
in ye Ninth Year of the Reigne of
KING WILLIAM THE THIRD
Aged 53 years.

Tombstone of Thomas CURLE
in hopes of a Blessed Resurrection
Here lyes the Body of Thomas CURLE
gent who was born November 24th 1640
in the Parish of St. Michael in Lewis in the
County of Sussex in England and Dyed
May the 30th 1700
When a few years are come, then I shall
goe the way whence I shall not Return
Job. 16ch. 22v.

Tombstone of Peter HEYMAN

This Stone was given by His
Excellency Francis Nicholson
Esq Lieutenant and Governor
Generall of Virginia in memory of
Peter HEYMAN Esq Grandson
to Sir Peter HEYMAN of Sumerfield
in ye County of Kent he was
Collector of ye customs in the
Lower District of James River and
went voluntarily on board ye Kings
shipp Shoreham in Pursuit of a
Pyrate who greatly infested this
coast after he had behaved himself
seven hours with undaunted courage
was killed with a small shot ye 29th
Day of April 1700
in ye Engagement he stood Next ye

Governor upon the Quarter Deck
and was here Honorably interred
by his order

Tombstone of Rev. Mr. Andrew THOMPSON

Here Lieth the Body of
Reverend Mr. Andrew THOMPSON
who was born at Stone Blue in
Scotland and was Minister of this
Parish seven years and departed
this life the 1st of September 1719
in ye 46th year of his Age leaving
a character of A sober Religious
Man"

The Grave of John Nevill, Vice Admiral of His Majesty's Fleet
Who Died on Board the Cambridge Ye 17 Day of August, 1697

African American

Antioch Baptist Church

Antioch Church was established in 1895 and the present Church was rebuilt in 1980. (Information on a stone on the front of the church.) This is an African American Cemetery.

Transcribed by Elaine Cooke and Ruby Hale on Oct 10, 1989. Transcribed by Barry Miles on Sep. 28, 1996. Both listings have been incorporated in this book.

| Virginia E. SIMON | Apr 24, 1971 | Mamie E. GARRIS |
| Jul 30, 1893 | | Feb 18, 1922 |

Virginia E. SIMON
Jul 30, 1893
Apr 24, 1971

Mamie E. GARRIS
Feb 18, 1922

Edward PINNER
Jun 29, 1892
Jan 27, 1978

Raleigh BOONE
1949 - 1972

Theodore PARKER
Dec 17, 1934
Oct 28, 1972

Lena ANDERSON
Dec 24, 1893
Jan 28, 1976

Ernest WILSON Sr.
Aug 19, 1915
Oct 21, 1977

Martha C. BANDY
Jan 7, 1926
Nov 21, 1979

Velvet Lorriane CLAM
Mar 31, 1947
Feb 10, 1982

Bernice C. REID
Oct 3, 1933
Jun 28, 1982

Cora L. McCLOUD
Dec 25, 1892
Nov 27, 1982

Daisy FREEMAN
Jul 24, 1857
Dec 22, 1984

John M. WILLIAMS
Apr 15, 1892
Jul 1, 1975

Henry Toliver SIMON
Apr 3, 1893
Apr 4, 1984
US Navy WW1

Peter SAMPSON
Oct 22, 1875
Dec 24, 1927
Thy memory shall ever be A
guiding star to heaven.

Mary A. EVERETT
1848 - Feb 22, 1928
Aged 80 Yrs
w/o Richard EVERETT
Though thou art gone Fond
memories linger.

Richard JONES Jr.
Apr 9, 1883
Jul 22, 1924

Richard H. JONES
1842 - Oct 27, 1920

Frank JONES
1833 - Jan 17, 1897
d/s Julia JONES

Julia JONES
1822 - Jul 23, 1918
d/s Frank JONES

Margaret BOYKIN
Feb 29, 1928
w/o Jacob
stone on ground

Forest MITCHELL
Jan 19, 1912
Apr 13, 1930
Sleep one and take thy rest.
We loved you but God loves
you best
stone on ground

Isaac LASSITER
Jun 2, 1877
Mar 1, 1943

Alice Greene SIMPKINS
1897 - 1942

Martha TOWNSEND
Jan 10, 1927
aged 75 yrs
stone on ground

Garie FLEMING
Oct 28, 1862
Mar 29, 1967

June _____
cannot read

Pompie WILKINS
Nov 2, 1922
stone on ground

Patsy CORBIN
Oct 1, 1900
Jul 12, 1984

Blanche BARROW
Jun 25, 1909
Jul 17, 1983

Annie SHEARRIN
Apr 10, 1903
May 19, 1988

Albert B. JONES
Oct 5, 1878
Dec 19, 1914

Daisy B. BOYKIN
Jun 3, 1896
Dec 12, 1978

Bobbie Jean McNEAL
Mar 23, 1927
Nov 1, 1977

Daisy SIMPSON
Dec 30, 1907
Nov 23, 1972

Leanard O. CORBIN Sr.
Dec 20, 1890
Nov 1, 1967

Ruth Jackson SARGENT
Oct 26, 1902
Mar 1, 1967

Lauvinin Sykes GRAVES
Apr 2, 1883
May 23, 1944

Louise Sykes JACKSON
1875 - Jun 29, 1930

Arthur BOYKINS
Aug 3, 1877
Jul 9, 1944

Benjamin F. JONES
Jul 22, 1897
Jun 14, 1961

Garfield MITCHELL
1907 - 1960

Hattie RICHARDSON
Jul 22, 1894
Feb 21, 1970

Harold JONES
Jan 5, 1953

Patsy ISLER
1863 - 1956

Emmaline NORTHCUTT
1887 - 1953

Addie V. MITCHELL
Apr 14, 1888
Feb 29, 1980

Rosa CAREY
Sep 10, 1871
Jan 13, 1960

Clementine H. BLACKLEY
Aug 6, 1923
Jul 12, 1962

Frank BROOKER
Aug 15, 1898
Nov 7, 1961

Rosa M. BOONE
1892 - 1969

Polly BOONE
1931 - 1957

Samuel HENRY
Oct 12, 1949
sunken in ground

Junious SYKES
Jul 4, 1863
Jun 1, 1945
stone on ground

Ethel E. PINNER
1914 - 1973

Geo. D. NORTHCUTT Jr
Aug 9, 1920
Apr 6, 1984

Collins BOYD
Aug 13, 1964

Robert MITCHELL
Aug 15, 1898
Sep 23, 1964

Alphonso MITCHELL
Jan 12, 1919
Mar 4, 1971

Alfred MITCHELL
Nov 23, 1914
Feb 2, 1992

Jerome MERRITT
Mar 30, 1951
Mar 26, 1981
U S Navy

Ethel L. HUBBARD
Apr 10, 1921
Aug 25, 1981

Victor L. BOYKIN
Sep 18, 1897
Mar 7, 1971

Alice V. BOYKIN
Sep 16, 1878
May 15, 1970

James C. HUBBARD
Oct 14, 1915
Aug 25, 1962

Evelyn BOONE
1911 - 1967

Leonard O. CORBIN
Apr 6, 1920
Dec 31, 1953
S. SGT 9204 Tech
SVG Unit WW2

Nathaniel E. JACKSON
May 15, 1912
Nov 6, 1957

James SYKES
Dec 5, 1869
Jan 25, 1958

Lillie S. SYKES
Aug 26, 1878
Jan 12, 1970

Ida B. HALL
Jan 7, 1879
Feb 18, 1972

Estelle B. STANLEY
Feb 22, 1896
Mar 13, 1964

Thelma B. PIERCE
Oct 12, 1898
Nov 27, 1995

Edward H. JENKINS
Nov 14, 1956
Jul 8, 1993

Noralicia Montrose BROWN
Jan 3, 1991
Jul 17, 1992

Georgia B. BOOKER
Mar 15, 1894
Sep 12, 1986

Jennie S. LANGLEY
Mar 20, 1891
Jul 23, 1986

Daniel LANGLEY
Feb 26, 1911
Feb 18, 1991

Alvin WILLIAMS
Apr 19, 1918
Mar 9, 1994

Jessie E. MERRITT
Sep 9, 1909
Oct 25, 1990

Sallie Law LAWYLER
May 1889
Oct 1912

Mattie S. DREW
Died 1968

Gabbie HOWARD
Mar 1889
Aug 8, 1912
Age 23

John W. WINBURN
Jun 8, 1886
Aug 22, 1909

W. FOUNTAIN
Nov 1923
Apr ____

Antioch Baptist Church Cemetery

ARMISTEAD CEMETERY
Armistead Avenue across from Downy Farm Road (72) {G - 6}

This is the cemetery called the Armistead Cemetery and the Highland Farm Cemetery. The owner of the property when Mary Bullifant transcribed the information for the WPA, was Highland Farms. The cemetery is located about 300 yards on the east side of N. Armistead Avenue at Downey Farm Road. The cemetery is in extremely bad condition. There are two large table top vaults with the flat tops with writing, similar to those in St. John Church Cemetery and Burton Parish Cemetery. The vaults have been broken into, the tops with writing have been removed and are broken. There is one tombstone standing. Inscription could not be read.

From the Works Progress Administration of Virginia Historical Inventory, the following was transcribed by Mary Bullifant, January 6, 1937.

The location at that time was 2 miles north of the city limits, on Yorktown Road, 1/2 mile across fields east of the highway on Highland Farm, Hampton, Virginia.

The property where the cemetery is located belonged to the Westwood S. Armistead family when the burials took place.

Destroyed Vaults and Last Tombstone Standing in Armistead Cemetery

Sacred
To the Memory of
Westwood S. ARMISTEAD
Who for nearly 40 years was Clerk
of the Courts of this County
Born June 23, 1790
Died January 25, 1840
Also
His Grandchild
Mary Susan daughter of
James D. and Nancy COULLING
Who died July 18, 1849
Aged 2 years.

Here lies the body of
Elizabeth S. SHIELDS
Wife of S. R. SHIELDS
She left her earthly for her
heavenly home
May 24, 1858
Aged 33 yrs.

Howard
Beloved son of
Dr. S. R. and G. S. SHIELDS
Died 1849
Aged 5 years.

Sacred
To the memory of
James W. COULLING
Born July 2, 1843
Died May 19, 1851

In Memory of
Nancy Todd COULLING
Daughter of Samuel ARMISTEAD
Died August 5, 1855
Aged 39 Years
Erected by her husband.

In Memory of
Mrs. Louisa M. ARMISTEAD
Who departed this life
November 4, 1827
Aged 33, years.

BALLARD CEMETERY
Marcella Road - Behind U. S. Military Reservation (2) {F - 7}
African American

HISTORY:
On November 6, 1982, an article was in the (TIMES-HERALD) Question Line entitled "Forgotten Grave" Eleven years ago, Question Line received an inquiry about the grave. The marker was still legible then, read "Nelson Ballard, Co. I, 1st U.S.C. Cav." That signifies he was a black Civil War veteran who served in Company I, First United States colored Calvary of the Union Army.

It was determined that Ballard, a Nansemond County native, enlisted as a private in 1863. It appears that he returned to Virginia and worked as a laborer with his wife, Martha, on a farm in what was called the "Wythe" district of Hampton.

Ballard was buried on the farm in 1882, and the next year, Martha Ballard bought the 2 ½ acre lot from the owners. She died in 1899, and probably was buried there also.

The land seems to have been privately owned until 1974, when it was included in a 32 acre parcel acquired by the Hampton School Board. Since no descendants of Ballard were located, the city will provide limited maintenance for the grave site along with routine care of the school grounds."

ADDITIONAL INFORMATION:
An article by Clarence E. Brown titled "A Very Grave Story" was published in the "Kecoughtan Smoke Siginals", 26 September 1982, published by the Kiwanis Club. Mr. Brown obtained information from various sources for his article. The following are excerpts from the article:
"The Veterans Administration in Washington, states that Nelson Ballard had enlisted in Norfolk, Virginia December 11th, 1863 at the age of 25. His name appears on the muster-out rolls of this outfit February 4th, 1866 at Brazos Santiago, Texas. He died in Hampton on March 26, 1882.

The 1880 U.S. Census listed Nelson Ballard as age 40, his wife age 50. His wife, Martha, purchased 2 1/2 acres from Daniel F. and Lucy Cock on December 29, 1883. The Wythe district at the time was north of present Mercury Boulevard, west of Armistead, which is the location of the headstone at the end of Marcella Road. His wife died in 1892, and from records, evidence shows that Nelson Ballard was buried on Cock's land, which was sold to Martha Ballard the year following her husband's death".

A memorandum prepared on October 31, 1984 by Barbara Wood, Arts and Humanities of the city of Hampton states: "Received a phone call from Mr. Kenny Quinn, October 31, 1984, pertaining to the grave site of Nelson Ballard. Kenny grew up on the Downy Farm and was told by a Mr Sours, an old black man who saw people buried in old slave burial grounds, that Nelson Ballard is one of many graves in that location.

Kenny was to meet with Lee Parker, another gentleman from the school board, and Tom Daniel, Director of Parks Dept. at 3:30 today to look at the site. They were to look for burial shaft evidence since heavy equipment has been in the area removing leaves and scraping.

Kenny wanted to know the location of the property of Martha Ballard, and the reported location of the burial of Nelson Ballard. (His idea was to determine if they were the same.) Apparently, the locations are different. The burial site of Nelson is known; the property Martha purchased from Daniel F. Cock was evidently in the 'Slabtown' area. Kenny has researched the ownership of Downy Farm from 1920 back to the original land grant. Daniel F. Cock was never the owner of the property in the burial ground area.

Two slave burial grounds were supposedly located on the Downy Farm. The site of Nelson Ballard's grave is one; the other site is reportedly near the creek that drains the pond area south of Parklawn Cemetery on Armistead Road. The locations would be along the north bank of that creek, east of Armistead Road, at the rear of a brick dwelling that stands there at this time."

Acknowledgment: The inscription was read by Mr. Keith and Mr Winters on 22 July 1992, revisited by Barry Miles on 11 April 1997. At that time it was heavily overgrown, only one fence post could be seen.

Nelson BALLARD
CO. 1
1st. U. S. C. CAV.
b. 1838
d. Mar 26, 1882

Cemeteries of the City of Hampton, Virginia / formerly Elizabeth City County

BARNES CEMETERY
Woodland Road and Pembroke Avenue (4) {L - 9}
African American

Barnes Cemetery, Barnes Monument has 7 Transcriptions

Acknowledgment: Transcribed by Mr. Winter & Mr. Keith, 1992

Mary RIVERS
d. Mar 5, 1911
w/o Anthony Rivers
His beloved sleepeth

Delia HARRIS
d. May 28, 1923
w/o Ben Harris
O death where is thy sting grave
where is thy victory

Richard SARGENT
b. Mar 26, 1859
d. Dec 8, 1949

Hattie B SARGENT.
d. Apr 27, 1918

Frank CHISMAN
b. Nov 20, 1870
d. Jan 24, 1914
Masonic Symbol
our brother

J. G. TAYLOR
d. Apr 3, 1925

J. H. TAYLOR
d. Sep 15, 1954

YOUNG
we will meet again

Estelle YOUNG
b. May 20, 1884
d. Oct 14, 1967

Robert WILLIAMS
b. Oct 1885
d. Jan 27, 1923

(broken stone)
b. Jun 1874
d. May 20, 1928

Thomas GATLEING
d. Feb 18, 1925
Age 58 Yrs
He died triumphant in faith.
Erected by his sister Roxandra
Hughes Harding.

Carnelious ALLEN
d. Dec 18, 1915
Age 55 Yrs

Helen B. MARKS
b. Oct 28, 1908
d. Sep 25, 1926
Sleep on and take thy rest.

Francis JOHNSON
d. Jul 10, 1935
w/o William Johnson
thy memory shall ever be the
guiding star to heaven

Virginia B. BARNES
b. Nov 5, 1885
d. Aug 18, 1972

---

next 7 on center marker
side 1
Martha B. HAYES
b. 1867
d. Nov 16, 1927

Sarah E. REID
b. 1897
d. 1953

side 2
Col N. G. BARNES
b. Jan 25, 1855
d. Mar 10, 1909

Roscoe T. BARNES
b. 1884
d. 1950

side 3
John BARNES
d. Oct 28, 1887
Age 52 Yrs

Julia BARNES
d. Feb 27, 1885
Aged 48 Years

side 4
Agie B. JOYNER
d. Sep 28, 1939

Willie JACKSON
b. Apr 2, 1881
d. Mar 4, 1958

Jonathan B. REID
b. Oct 6, 1882
d. Jul 10, 1958

Henry TYAS
b. 1860

PAYNE
(No Date)

BASSETTE CEMETERY
Randolph Street (5) {J - 9}
African American

Bassette Cemetery

Bassette Cemetery was started by Mr. A. W. E. Bassette in the early 1900's when Elmerton Cemetery was becoming full. Ten members of the Bassette family are buried in Bassette Cemetery. The cemetery is presently taken care of by Mr. Eugene Mitchell, who has lived next to the cemetery for over 60 years. The cemetery is being cleared by Mr. Mitchell, but there are still about 150 feet of heavy growth to be cleared at the back of the cemetery. In the older section, there are only a few gravestones visible in the heavy undergrowth. Recorded are the ones that are visible. When this section is cleared, other stones may be found. There are signs that many graves may have been dug up. It is not known if they were moved or desecrated.

Acknowledgment: Transcribed by Barry and Leslyn Miles, September thru December 1996.

Adell H. TURNER
Mar 7, 1906
May 4, 1979

Jessie Marie HOLLOWAY
Mar 11, 1904
Jan 12, 1984

Maude Holloway SMITH
Sep 25, 1898
Jun 15, 1991

Emuel Holloway EMMET
Aug 31, 1911
Jul 31, 1991

Ella H. CARSON
Aug 15, 1916
May 31, 1975

Edward V. ROBINSON
Nov 11, 1966

Inez B. ROBINSON
1900 - 1962

Olivet C. ATKINS
Oct 4, 1886
Feb 26, 1964

Bertha E. ATKINS
Dec 4, 1895
Jun 11, 1990

Mildred G. TAYLOR
Mar 18, 1883
Jan 18, 1978

Frank MITCHEIL
1897 - 1969

Irene B. MITCHEIL
Oct 15, 1900
Sept 9, 1977

William H. MITCHEIL
Nov 28, 1928
Nov 3, 1995

Bruce BLUE
Jan 8, 1905
Jul 5, 1966

Helen R. BLUE
1891 - 1966

Hattie B. REED
1887 - 1973

Robert REED
Aug 16, 1889
Mar 22, 1961

Cecily C. CLAPP
Nov 30, 1907
Aug 12, 1938
d/s w/ Mary S.

Mary S. CLAPP
Oct 15, 1878
Nov 1, 1918
d/s w/ Cecily C.

Rita B. CLAPP
Mar 31, 1918
Oct 27, 1984

Henry M. CLAPP
May 14, 1872
Jan 11, 1966

Henry L. CLAPP Jr.
Jun 23, 1953
Apr 28, 1960

Clifford PHILLIPS Jr.
Oct 4, 1935
Feb 16, 1960
Virginia A2C 5010
Air Base Sq AF

Elnora P. JOHNSON
Dec 20, 1895
Nov 13, 1960

Ernestine T. CHRISTIAN
Jan 19, 1917
Apr 23, 1965

Esther HOLLARD
Feb 23, 1892
Feb 3, 1981

Roland S. HOLLARD
Aug 2, 1888
Feb 1, 1959

James E. BRYANT
Nov 17, 1915
Sept 5, 1963

Adeline V. BRYANT
Aug 28, 1915
Oct 16, 1958

Mary LATTIMORE
May 16, 1913
May 21, 1958

Harriett W. CHRISTIAN
1862 - 1958

Harry CHRISTIAN
Sept 4, 1886
June 22, 1975

Nora A. CHRISTIAN
Jan 26, 1887
March 4, 1978

Harry CHRISTIAN
May 6, 1915
Jan 26, 1957

Eva T. HOPE
Jul 15, 1894
Jan 26, 1964

Samuel SMITH Jr.
Died Oct 27, 1956
Temporary Metal Marker

Cynthia TOLIVER
Wooden Cross

Mary TAYLOR
Aug 13, 1885
Nov 22, 1956

Newton CARTER
died Oct 23, 1958

Maggie WASHINGTON
died Oct 15, 1956
Temporary Metal Marker

Kether BULLOCK
Aug 1, 1905
Aug 25, 1956

Phillip BANKS
Oct 16, 1896
Aug 6, 1956

Leon N. GOLDEN
died Jan 21, 1957
Temporary Metal Marker

Clayborn LUSTER
Aug 22, 1885
Jul 27, 1956

Merritt TUMER
May 23, 1887
June 9, 1956

Peter E. TABB
died June 12, 1956
Temporary Metal Marker

Roxanna JORDAN
August 5, 1890
May 26, 1956

Junius S. CHANDLER.
May 11, 1912
March 9, 1956

William JACKSON
died Feb 12, 1956

James T. SHIELD
died Jan 18, 1956

Dora THORTON
died Mar 13, 1956
Temporary Metal Marker

Thomas COOK
died Mar 21, 1956
Temporary Metal Marker

James S. WILLIAMS
died --- 19, 1956
Temporary Metal Marker

Cornelious DENNIS
Nov 1955
Temporary Metal Marker

Preston STEWERT
died Feb 2, 1955

Sarah BRIGHT
1868 - 1955
Temporary Metal Marker

Jessie Shadrack ROSS
May 4, 1894
June 2, 1955

Charles S. BROWN
Jan 11, 1903
Oct 7, 1954

Chaney RUSSELL
8-25-1885
9-5-(19)54
Temporary Metal Marker

Lucy HARRIS
Jun 1, 1880
Jan 17, 1965

Charles H. HARRIS
Jan 27, 1881
Aug 25, 1954

Joseph FOX
March 14, 1955
Temporary Metal Marker

Nina MAKER
4-18-1906
6-16-54
Temporary Metal Marker

Alice CHAPMAN
1886 - 1955
Order of Eastern Star

Clarence TAYLOR
No Dates
Temporary Metal Marker

Fred MILES
died July 26, 1955
Temporary Metal Marker

Elanora A. DEBRICK
May 31, 1900
Dec 15, 1960

Montre DEBRICK
died Dec 6, 1954
54 Yrs.
Temporary Metal Marker

Donald HUNTER
No Dates

Esther Burl AIKEN
1880 - 1955

Annie PEADEN
Feb 8, 1873
Jan 28, 1954

Mina MAKER
Apr 18, 1906
Jun 16, 1954
Temporary Metal Marker

Maggie WASHINGTON
Mar -- 1954
Age 60 Yrs
Temporary Metal Marker

Lucy CONEY
died Apr 24, 1954
Temporary Metal Marker

Rosa DABNEY
1875 - 1954
Temporary Metal Marker

Olara BATTEN
Nov 6, 1882
Sept 12, 1970

Albert SAVAGE
Apr 10, 1907
Nov 9, 1969

Gertrude NETTLES
June 10, 1908

George M. BATTEN
Mar 10, 1970
Temporary Metal Marker

Thomas H. WRIGHT
Mar 1, 1898
Aug 27, 1969

Evelyn OWENS
Dec 5, 1927
Dec 28, 1968

Michael HARVEY
died Nov 10, 1968
Temporary Metal Marker

Necie EDWARDS
Mar 28, 1890
July 8, 1967

Winfield BACKUS
1909 - 1976

Katie BOONE
Mar 8, 1888
Oct 18, 1966

Tony WILSON
Jan 20, 1895
Feb 23, 1967

Jessie J. WILSON
Feb 28, 1905
Jan 22, 1966

Carrie MONROE
March 22, 1900
Sept 2, 1965

Adeline W. EDWARDS
Jan 15, 1894
April 24, 1978

Willie BAKER
May 1, 1901
April 4, 1964

Rosa BRINKLEY
1884 - 1964

Albert THORNTON
July 20, 1897
Apr 28, 1964

Lena W. TOLIVER
May 9, 1909
July 16, 1964

Arthur TAYLOR
1905 - 1964

Mamie L. TOLIVER
Aug 7, 1889
Oct 7, 1964

Fleming CHRISTIAN
1882 - 1964

Mary C. BANKS
Nov 2, 1875
Aug 15, 1963

Harrison KEMP
April 4, 1892
June 11, 1963

Rufus CHANDLER
Dec 26, 1886
June 10, 1963

Isabelle JOHNSON
died Oct 5, 1963

Laura EDWARDS
died Oct 21, 1968
Temporary Metal Marker

William F. SMITH
May 31, 1963
Age 80

James WATSON
Jan 6, 1893
May 29, 1963

Carrie DAY
Mar 1898
Mar 6, 1963

Bennie BAKER
May 22, 1918
Feb 9, 1963

Josephine HOLLOWAY
died Feb 17, 1968
Temporary Metal Marker

Dora MORGAN
Aug 2, 1868
Feb 22, 1963

William SEDGEWICK
Feb 15, 1901
March 6, 1963

William THOMAS
Dec 20, 1897
March 5, 1969

Pauline TARPLET
died Mar 10, 1963
Temporary Metal Marker

Tena GREEN
Nov 16, 1902
Dec 29, 1962

Johnnie THOMAS
Dec 25, 1888
Jan 12, 1963

Dallis HILL
died Jan 11, 1963
Temporary Metal Marker

Francis BOOKER
No Dates
Temporary Metal Marker

Jennie BANKS
Oct 31, 1862
Age 72

David HARTFIELD
Sept 27, 1962

Tommie THOMAS
1805 - 1862

Hanna PATRICK
Mar 22, 1964

Henry HOWARD
died 4 - 4 - 63
(April 4, 1963)

Robert BAILEY
May 24, 1968
Temporary Metal Marker

Mary C. BANKS
May 24, 1875
Aug 15 1963

William BYRD
Dec 21, 1962
Temporary Metal Marker

Richard F. CARTER
Feb 20, 1872
July 21, 1962

Mary E. DABNEY
Feb 15, 1912
Mar 8, 1962

Oliver MITCHELL
Oct 15, 1861
April 21, 1962

Myrtle V. BLIZZARD
Dec 14, 1931
Apr 25, 1962

Marie L. MARSHALL
1885 - 1962

Albert POWELL
died Feb 17, 1962
Temporary Metal Marker

Harriett RUSSELL
Aug 23, 1892
Nov 16, 1961

Rose RICHARDSON
died 1962

Thomas HARRISON
Aug 2, 1908
Oct 26, 1961

Henley TALIAFERRO
March 11, 1954
Nov 23, 1969

J. J. TALIAFERRO
Mar 9, 1917
Nov 9, 1961

Esther SANDFORD
Mar 16, 1894
Nov 16, 1961

Arthur WRAY
Dec 25, 1900
Dec 26, 1961

Malcolm CORBIN
died Jan 25, 1962
Temporary Metal Marker

Charles BARKS
June 13, 1961
Temporary Metal Marker

Pearl HUNTHILTON
May 22, 1896
June 13, 1961

Ceorcia H. ALBOUY
Aug 20, 1875
June 2, 1961

Lewis BATTEN, III
Nov 6, 1910
Oct 21, 1973

Rosa HAMMOND
died May 5, 1961

Laura E. TABB
Feb 11, 1889
Jan 14, 1961

Harold W. THORNTON
Aug 6, 1907
Feb 26, 1961

Percy J. GREEN
April 22, 1899
March 21, 1961

Charles TUCKER
April 11, 1887
Dec 14, 1960

Christine GAYLE
Feb 5, 1933
Nov 24, 1960

Elijah CROWFORD
Dec 28, 1897
Dec 2, 1971

Pinkey CRAWFORD
Jan 26, 1900
Oct 11, 1960

Annie Austin WRIGHT
Mar 13, 1902
Jun 21, 1960

Alberta PIERCE
Dec 25, 1901
May 20, 1960

Frank Lee WATSON
Dec 18, 1895
Apr 4, 1960

Stewart BROOKS
Apr 10, 1889
Oct 8, 1959

John J. WILSON
Apr 17, 1897
Nov 24, 1959

Corodius WHITE
Jun 2, 1904
Nov 28, 1958

Cemeteries of the City of Hampton, Virginia / formerly Elizabeth City County

Emma ELLIOTT
Dec 12, 1880
Dec 17, 1959

Earl B. HARRIS
Nov 29, 1905
Dec 16, 1959

Daisy UROUHART
1904 - 1959

Vivian JENNINGS
Jul 7, 1901
Feb 13, 1960

Robert CALLIS
died Feb 21, 1960
Temporary Metal Marker

Evelyn BARKERS
Dec 20, 1903
Mar 5, 1960

Hester WHITE
Mar 12, 1890
Mar 5, 1960

Edith COMBS
died Dec 24, 1960
Temporary Metal Marker

Fred CALLOWAY
died Apr 9, 1960
Temporary Metal Marker

Mary B. LEE
died Mar 6, 196-
Temporary Metal Marker

Alexander BARLETT
Apr 14, 1909
Oct 9, 1959

Junius BARKERS
Sep 4, 1959
temporary Marker

Oliver MITCHELL
Feb 27, 1905
July 29, 1959

Bennie TOLIVER
1909 - 1959

Joseph B. KEMP
Aug 5, 1898
June 8, 1959

Charles H. MARROW
Dec 18, 1886
July 10, 1959

Elmore WATKINS
Oct 1890
July 1955

Ada E. WATKINS
Sep 6, 1898
May 8, 1959

Maddie A. WEBSTER
July 3, 1889
April 7, 1959

Emma R. PORTER
May 6, 1889
Mar 30, 1959

Samuel D. THORNTON
Sep 12, 1879
May 23, 1959

Mary T. THORNTON
Dec 5, 1883
Mar 10, 1959

Ida Cooper WASH
Jan 6, 1886
Nov 23, 1954
Temporary Metal Marker

Cecil CHANDLER
died Nov 28, 1956
Temporary Metal Marker

Willis E. FOSTER
Jul 1892
Jun 53
Temporary Metal Markers

Mary TAYLOR
died Nov 22, 1956
Temporary Metal Marker

Isaac TROY
died Aug 20, 1952
Temporary Metal Marker

Julin DAVIS
died Sep 24, 1956
Temporary Metal Marker

Ronald E. FOSTER
No Dates
Temporary Metal Marker

Alex S. BLACK
died Mar 22, 1953
Temporary Metal Marker

Raymond PEEDEN
Apr 6, 1910
Jan 16, (19)52
Temporary Metal Marker

Margta FREEMAN
Jan 4, (19)49
Nov 6, (19)56
Temporary Metal Marker

Fannie VINSON
died Jan 2, (19)54
Temporary Metal Marker

Alvin COMBS
died Aug 4, 1952
Aged 45 Yrs
Temporary Metal Marker

Mary F. JOHNSON
died Nov 27, 1956
Temporary Metal Marker

Annie McDONALD
died Dec 4, 1956
Temporary Metal Marker

Maggie CARTER
died Dec 11, 1956
Temporary Metal Marker

James Herbert WRIGHT
died June 10, 1958
d/s w/ Effie Payton

Effie Payton WRIGHT
died Dec 22, 1960
d/s w/ James Herbert

Clementine WILSON
died Aug 24, 1958

Mary E. WILLIAMS
July 15, 1895
Oct 11, 1958

Samuel S. W. WILLIAMS
Oct 11, 1884
Jun 28, 1962

Bessie S. NORTHERN
May 3, 1877
Nov 17, 1958

Ethel Frazier DAWNS
Nov 29, 1898
Dec 17, 1959

Mamie K. CAREY
Sept 18, 1884
Jan 11, 1958

Elnora BAILEY
died Feb 3, 1959

Percy L. KEMP
died Mar 27, 1960
Temporary Metal Marker

Mattie HOLLIER
Mar 22, 1880
Mar 6, 1959

Beatrice Stevens SMITH
May 25, 1934
Apr 20, 1959

Allen BARTLETT
died Oct 9, (19)59
Temporary Metal Marker

Alexander YOUNG
died Oct 15, 1959
Temporary Metal Marker

George W. MONDEN
1894 - 1959

David CHARLOT
died Sep 2, 1958

Margaret BENNETT
died Jul 29, 1958

Franklin PRESSEY
Nov 11, 1898
May 8, 1958

Lenard ASH
Feb 22, 1896
Mar 27, 1958

Joseph P. BROWN
Mar 4, 1881
Feb 28, 1958

Coleman WELLS
Oct 8, 1907
Mar 22, 1958

Orine M. PENNICK
Oct 26, 1917
May 12, 1958

Mary Florence BOLLING
Aug 31, 1887
Apr 8, 1957

Purnell ROYSTER
died Oct 27, 1957

William N. BURNELL
May 10, 1890
Mar 26, 1972

Eli PARKER
died Oct 10, 1957

Elizabeth STATEN
1856 - 1957

Daisy W. HOOKER
1879 - 1963

Cob HOOKER
Dec 12, 1881
Apr 8, 1957

Ezekiel FOSTER
Sep 20, 1908
Apr 23, 1957

John A. DABNET
Apr 8, 1911
May 13, 1957

Susie HERBERT
died June 11, 1957

Mary S. HILL
Jan 30, 1890
May 15, 1957

Josephine THOMAS
died Jun 28, 1957

Lucous RANDOLPH
No Dates
Temporary Metal Marker

Henry WISE
Jan 2, 1897
July 19, 1957

Melvin L. HUGHES
No Dates
Temporary Metal Marker

Jurline HAWKINS
died May 31, 19--
Temporary Metal Marker

John W. YOUNGER
July 4, 1880
Mar 26, 1957

Lydia A. JACOBS
Dec 12, 1874
Mar 19, 1957

George R. BARBER
Mar 22, 1885
Mar 4, 1957

Junius F. AUSTIN
Mar 1, 1876
Feb 10, 1957

Grave not marked

S. A. TALIAFERRO
May 13, 1873
Jan 2, 1957

Annie L. PORTER
Mar 8, 1878
Dec 24, 1958

Julie OMAR
Sep 2, 1905
Dec 21, 1956
Temporary Metal Marker

Rosa SMITH
Feb 14, 1883
Dec 20, 1956

James RICHARDSON
1896 - 1961

Julia H. McNAIR
Oct 25, 1907
Mar 21, 1956

Thomas BALLARD
Jan 14, 1914
July 28, 1956

Isaiah BALLARD
Mar 10, 1910
Jun 2, 1965

John E. WALKER Sr.
Oct 21, 1906
Dec 10, 1993

Edna C. WALKER
July 20, 1913
Sept 15, 1956

Elsie Simpson SHAW
1866 - 1956

Delia E. LATTIMORE
Oct 2, 1893
Feb 17, 1964
d/s w/Edward M.

Edward M. LATTIMORE
died July 7, 1956
d/s w/Delia E.

Matthews THORNTON
died Apr 30, 1956

Annie D. DANIEL
Sept 12, 1884
Mar 6, 1956

Maude Phillips CLAIR
1904 - 1953

Joseph L. BRADSBERY
Mar 3, 1891
Jan 28, 1954
Va PFC 13 Co 155
Dep Brig WW1

Mary J. WASHINGTON
Mar 4, 1889
Apr 10, 1957

Grave not marked

Grave not marked

Grave not marked

Noris B. BATTON
Aug 8, 1925
Oct 7, 1966

Walter M. REID
Feb 27, 1918
Oct 30, 1966

Mary E. MOORE
Mar 24, 1901
Dec 2, 1984

Fannie HARRIS
1878 - 1963

Grave not marked

Elnora KENNEDY
Mar 23, 1882
July 21, 1966

Celestyne ATKINS
1906 - 1940

Ida Binga ATKINS
Nov 8, 1871
Aug 15, 1958

Ella M. WRIGHT
Mar 15, 1885
Oct 21, 1963

Grave not marked

_____ PEYTON
No Dates

Albert MITCHELL
Apr 8, 1972

Richard MITCHELL
died Nov 15, 1967

James MITCHELL
Oct 23, 1909
May 28, 1965

Betty M. JOHNSON
Oct 31, 1908
Aug 17, 1962

Fannie M. STEWART
Aug 26, 1905
Oct 20, 1955

Willis H. STEWART Jr
Aug 12, 1896
May 12, 1952
Va PVT 1
Development BN WW1

Julia C. PATTERSON
b. May 1, 194-
d/s w/ Rev Jesse W.
Graves moved, only Marker

Rev. Jesse W. PATTERSON
Jul 15, 1870
Aug 11, 1954
d/s w/Julia C.
Graves Moved, only Marker

Elizabeth HAYWARD
Nov 29, 1888
Jan 4, 1975

Edward HEYWARD
May 15, 1891
Mar 22, 1960

Izie F. PERRY
died July 24, 1948

Blair B. PERRY
died Nov 30, 1959

Addie WILLIAMS
Sep 8, 1884
Jan 4, 1985

Williams CHARITY
Aug 25, 1899
May 29, 1982

Susie S. LOGAN
1922 - 1953

Sarah E. SAVAGE
1915 - 1960

SATCHELL
Marker Only

Julia Chandler SATCHELL
Dec 29, 1881
June 21, 1969

Spencer SATCHELL
Sept 28, 1880
Aug 26, 1951

Estelle J. SAVAGE
1896 - 1988

James H. SAVAGE
1888 - 1950

Clyde PRITCHETT
1912 - 1961

Rose P. DAVIS
Apr 27, 1918
Nov 12, 1995

Abraham DAVIS
Feb 6, 1894
Dec 26, 1975

George M. MINKINS
Jan 1, 1903
Oct 2, 1987

Lillian R. CHATMAN
July 31, 1922
Aug 18, 1995

Viola ROBINSON
Dec 25, 1892
Oct 9, 1979

Lillian WEBSTER
Oct 26, 1894
Jan 25, 1987

Mary L. HOPE
Feb 2, 1908
Mar 27, 1980

Cecil HOPE
Sep 3, 1888
Mar 26, 1965

Elouise Phillips TAFT
May 20, 1916
May 8, 1995

John Mallery PHILLIPS
Mar 10, 1920
Jul 19, 1988
Hampton City Council 1974-86
Vice Mayor 1982-1986

Joseph Manley PHILLIPS
"Capt Joe"
1894 - 1959

Mary Jane MOSELEY
1874 - 1852

Hattie Moseley PHILLIPS
1896 - 1951

Eleanor WILLIAMS
1907 - 1970

Ella WISE
1886 - 1958

Hattie S. DIGGS
Mar 29, 1883
July 24, 1951

Bennie CARROW
Jun 30, 1909
Nov 9, 1968

Paul J. RICHARDSON
died Jun 26, 1955

Georgia L. RICHARDSON
May 15, 1891
Mar 7, 1949

Johnnie ROBINSON
1882 - 1956

Mabel B. McCOY
Jan 12, 1907
Aug 21, 1977

Walter T. McCOY
Dec 23, 1900
Mar 17, 1987

Cemeteries of the City of Hampton, Virginia / formerly Elizabeth City County

James E. BELL Jr
Jul 18, 1892
Feb 12, 1952

Mary W. CARDWELL
June 5, 1875
Jan 26, 1963

Richard E. BROADFIELD
Nov 21, 1920
Feb 21, 1967

Janie M. BOONE
1912 - 1966

Clarence C. BOONE
1909 - 1962

Willie LIPSCOMB
Feb 3, 1902
May 9, 1959

Lucille LIPSCOMB
Mar 5, 1910
May 27, 1950

George M. MINKINS
1885 - 1959

Emma MINKINS
1888 - 1952

John W. OSBORNE
Sept 20, 1879
Dec 19, 1948

Jacob WILLIAMS
Jan 18, 1882
May 17, 1934

Frank L. SHIELDS
Nov 6, 1896
July 5, 1947

Susie D. JONES
April 17, 1883
Feb 28, 1950
w/o Walter H. Jones

Daniel ARMISTEAD
Jan 6, 1890
Apr 10, 1966

Alexina ARMISTEAD
Mar 2, 1900
Jun 5, 1960
error 1800 should be 1900

Annie C. WARD
died Dec 23, 1958
Age 79

Charles H. MOORE
Apr 18, 1880
Mar 1, 1969

Mary E. MOORE
1904 - 1948

Charles P. MILLS Jr.
Aug 26, 1900
May 21, 1946

Frances YOUNG
May 1, 1870
Nov 2, 1945

William H. MILES
Mar 3, 1877
Apr 26, 1943

John Henry DIGGS
Apr 15, 1880
Dec 31, 1942

Julia WASHINGTON
Jan 28, 1875
Mar 13, 1957

Mabel WASHINGTON
Aug 30, 1907
July 25, 1967

Evelyn L. SATCHELL
Mar 15, 1888
Apr 9, 1944

Edward W. NELSON
Aug 22, 1922
June 1, 1944

Minnie B. HENDERSON
Dec 28, 1874
Feb 8, 1946

Lucy H. ELAM
Aug 5, 1875
Jun 8, 1944

Samuel CHANDLER
Oct 4, 1904
Oct 27, 1955

Estella PONDEXTER
died Feb 19, 1953

Samuel PONDEXTER
died Feb 18, 1953

William T. SCOTT
died Sep 24, 1960

Annie R. CHANDLER
May 16, 1884
May 3, 1968

Luke CHANDLER Jr
Jan 18, 1887
May 6, 1965

John F. CHANDLER
Jun 14, 1898
Jan 23, 1945

Beulah J. DABNEY
Mar 27, 1890
Aug 26, 1970

Mollie L. SCOTT
died Jul 27, 1966

William L. SCOTT
died Aug 14, 1944

Pauline D. EPPS
1908 - 1968

Charles EPPS
1908 - 1944

Otis ASH
Jan 22, 1928
Oct 28, 1967

Sallie A. HOPSON
Oct 16, 1900
Oct 13, 1968

Hattie B. CHANDLER
Aug 15, 1885
Dec 5, 1951

Naomi E. ORR
June 5, 1904
Oct 6, 1941

Josephine JARVIS
died Jun 26, 1958
Temporary Marker

Stephen SMITH
1905 - 1974

Verlenia Sampson SMITH
Jul 6, 1900
Dec 27, 1981

Edgar HARRIS
1901 - 1985

Ophelia SIMPSON
1901 - 1963

Hattie WASHINGTON
died Jan 10, 1960

Joseph WILSON
died Oct 24, 1943

Harry R. PAYTON
Mar 4, 1904
Feb 26, 1947

Martha E. PAYTON
Sept 14, 1880
Sept 7, 1947

Charlie L. SCOTT
Jul 18, 1902
Jun 16, 1944

Eliza CHANDLER
1867 - 1948

Ruth CHANDLER
1914 - 1950

Hannah CHANDLER
1884 - 1950

Emma K. DIGGS
1891 - 1942

Rebecca WASHINGTON
Aug 25, 1903
Aug 27, 1944

Catherine WASHINGTON
died May 5, 1941

Elizabeth Sampson HOYLE
1903 - 1972

Alice Goode SAMPSON
------ - 1946

Capt. Ben SAMPSON
died Feb 3, 1941

Ida E. BASSETTE
1865 - 1940

A. W. E. BASSETTE Sr
1859 - 1940
(Owner and founder of
Bassette Cemetery)

A. W. E. BASSETTE Jr
No Dates
our devoted father

Phoebe Estella BASSETTE
No Dates
our loving wife & mother

Louise Bassette BROWN
May 5, 1890
Mar 1, 1965

Burl BASSETTE, MD
1888 - 1973

A. W. E. BASSETTE III MD
Dec 1, 1921
Sept 5, 1984

Undine Davis BASSETTE
Jun 18, 1888
Dec 4, 1983

Edward E. BASSETTE, DDS
Feb 17, 1895
July 16, 1984

George E. BRIGHT
Mar 19, 1914
Apr 12, 1968

Kate Lewis BOOTH
1879 - 1952

Charlie L. MARSHALL
Dec 22, 1888
Jan 6, 1942

Estelle MARSHALL
June 26, 1899
Feb 18, 1958

Richard WILSON
Apr 17, 1871
Apr 29, 1943

Richard WILSON
Aug 9, 1905
Jun 1, 1949

Emily H. ELLIOTT
Oct 2, 1903
Jul 28, 1937

John LONG
Jan 24, 1896
May 27, 1972

Alberta LONG
Sept 29, 1877
Jan 1, 1938

William BARNWELL
1852 - 1937

Cemeteries of the City of Hampton, Virginia / formerly Elizabeth City County

Pearl B. BASSETTE
Dec 31, 1886
Feb 28, 1973

C. S. BASSETTE, Dr.
Jan 29, 1878
May 24, 1932

Millie R. PATRICK
May 27, 1895
Sep 16, 1968

Edwards WILLIAMS
1864 - 1933

Ernest H. FOWLER
Jan 16, 1903
Feb 11, 1946

Charlie MILLS
1875 - 1938

John H. WASHINGTON
1903 - 1941

Eddie WASHINGTON
Jul 14, 1864
Jan 11, 1939

Mary A. FRANCIS
1859 - 1938

George B. ROBBINS
1875 - 1940

Margaret LEACOOK
Jun 26, 1892
Nov 6, 1977

Mrs. A. WASHINGTON
died Apr 8, 1958
Temporary marker

Clinton COOK
1898 - 1952
erected by W. J. Bradshaw

John H. CAREY
Nov 22, 1895
Sept 17, 1957
Temporary Marker

Mathaline A. WILKERSON
Oct 19, 1906
Mar 3, 1952

Sallie N. DAVIS
1916 - 1952
Temporary Marker

Fredrick DREW
1920 - 19-2
Temporary marker

James B. HARRIS
1914 - 1950

Pricilla BRAKTON
1857 - 1951
Temporary Marker

Seretha Ann DIGGS
Apr 11, 1880
Jul 13, 1949

Arthur BROOKER
1892 - 1949

Mrs. Virginia BROWN
died Feb 18, 1950
Temporary Marker

Mary Susan FRANCIS
May 16, 1867
Mar 11, 1950

Charles H. JOHNSTON
Jun 5, 1875
Aug 5, 1949

Louise H. WILLIAMS
Mar 15, 1897
Feb 13, 1949

Josephine BAILEY
1881 - 1959

Henry BAILEY
died Mar 18, 1948

Charles H. CARTER
Sept 7, 1886
Feb 26, 1948

Fannie WILLIAM
1880 - 1948

George TOLIVER
May 15, 1881
Jan 4, 1948

John SAVAGE
1884 - 1947

Woodson W. COOK
June 21, 1929
Oct 21, 1947

Sarah Parker HARRIS
died Aug 9, 1946
Age 73 Yrs

Morphelia HOWARD
1880 - 1946

Arthur N. WALLER
Aug 8, 1881
Jun 20, 1945

Hattie J. CARTER
Mar 22, 1897
Dec 5, 1944

Andrew G. CLARK
Mar 2, 1885
Nov 10, 1944

James Moses BEST
died Feb 9, 1945

Ethel Webb PAIGE
Sep 10, 1884
May 12, 1945
w/o Charles H. Paige

Christopher MORGAN
died Jul 3, 1944

Hattie S. WRAY
Oct 5, 1889
May 12, 1944

Valeria PURDY
Mar 21, 1902
Sep 5, 1943

Robert JACKSON
Sept 19, 1926
Dec 31, 1943
Joseph Jackson New York

Dora FRANCIS
Oct 3, 1901
Jan 3, 1944

Herbert L. BYRD
Dec 5, 1921
May 24, 1943

Cora HOPE
died May 6, 1943

Viola SISICO
Mar 2, 1910
Apr 19, 1947

Russell VON McREA
Oct 22, 1943
May 1, 1944

Eugene T. SMITH
Nov 15, 1940
Sept 15, 1942

Arthur W. HERBERT
Aug 22, 1880
Dec 26, 1942

David F. BATTEN
Sept 30, 1869
Jan 23, 1941

Ethel Tynes JOHNS
No Dates
Mother

Toney TYNES
No Dates
Father

Charles A. TYNES
No Dates
Son

Elizabeth A. TYNES
No Dates
Mother

Marion V. ASH
Nov 5, 1903
June 14, 1959

Ernest L. WYNN
Dec 10, 1887
Nov 4, 1958

Charles H. HILL
July 29, 1931
w/ Mary

Mary M. HILL
Jan 6, 1940
w/ Charles

Hillary _____
Apr
Aug 19

George WATTS
1868 - 1947
d/s w/ David

David WATTS
1870 - 1950
d/s w/ George

Susie BANE
Dec 2, 1885
June 23, 1943
Gone but not forgotten

Alex SHAW
July 10, 1854
July 30, 1911

Elizabeth Beth CARTER
died Sept 6, 1925
age 52 Yrs
w/o Watlter Carter

Ida M. HARRIS
1912 - 1939

BETHEL AME CHURCH CEMETERY
Lincoln Street (6) {J - 10}
African American

"In August, 1864, the small band who were to become the congregation of the Bethel A.M.E. Church, first met at Camp Hamilton, an area of Tabb's farm called "New Tabb's Field," near Hampton Institute (University today.) Brothers Merrit Thomas, James Segal, Thad Peeden, Randall Gooden and sisters Carolina Segal and Sarah Parker, under leadership of Father Peter Sheppard, formed the new church. Sheppard was a local preacher who held membership in St. John's A.M.E. Church in Norfolk.

Bethel's first house of worship was on Wine Street, then called "Oak," for some reason -- whether the original name was unknown or newcomers didn't like the connotation of wine, is not recorded. In 1871, led by Rev. James T. Morris, the worshipers brought a lot on Lincoln (near the present church) where this church was built in 1887. On Sunday, April 19th, 1972, singing "Onward Christian Soldiers" led by its three choirs, the congregation marched out of the old into the modern, air-conditioned new. Its cost of $212,000 is probably more than the combined capital of the whole town would have been in 1864."

The above is from the Lost Landmarks of Old Hampton, by Hamilton H. "Sis" Evans. Library call number V 975.541 Ev161o.
Acknowledgment: Transcribed by Barry Miles 7 June 1997.

Bethel AME Church

Mary B. LEWIS
Feb 1, 1869
Sept 27, 1928
Sleep on and take thy rest.
f/s M. B. (corner broken)

Emma S. MILLS
Feb 13, 1908
May 23, 1979

David ELEY
Jan 31, 1844
April 12, 1919

Viola B. HARRIS
Mar 26, 1889
Sept 26, 1958

Lee W. BURROUGHS
died Aug 25, 1912
age 49 yrs, 7m, 17d.
He who always waits
upon God, is ready
whenever he calls.
(Masonic)

In Memory of
Lucy
wife of
Thomas KENNEDY
died Dec 13, 1904

Parxxx
Mar 23, 1841
stone on ground
cannot read

In Memory of
Martha CARTER
died Feb 2, 1906
age 76 yrs

Pedestal no marker

Mother
Catharine GARNER
1887?
at rest
stone broken

Eliza Ann JORDAN
1873 - 1929
4 corner Markers "J"

Rebecca
Beloved wife of
Andren CHANDLER
July 4, 1891
Mar 14, 1925
Servant of God
Well Done

Emma
Beloved wife of
A. L. BROWN
July 25, 1882
Mar 6, 1920
at rest

John FORTUNE
died Feb 3, 1919
Aged 65 yrs
Asleep in Jesus
Masonic

Walter E. YOUNG
1877 - 1918
Gone but not Forgotten
Masonic

Annie TARLTON
(No Dates)

Pedestal no marker

Rev. W. TRUHART
born Mar 1, 1857
died Oct 10, 1905

Elizabeth WEAVER
died Sept 23, 1904
age 56 years

William T. NELSON
died Oct 7, 1921

Nancy YOUNG
born 1856
died 1920
Safe in the arms of Jesus
Safe on his gentle breast.

Martha MELTON
died April 17, 1903
age 62 yrs
unusual grave site
side rail outline grave of
marble

William E. LYLES Sr.
Feb 29, 1906
Oct 9, 1985
d/s w/ Iola W.
In Loving Memory

Iola W. LYLES
born Apr 27, 1909
died no dates
d/s w/ William E.

Lucy S. SCOTT
Feb 18, 1895
June 16, 1977

In Memory of
Mrs. Mary E. SUGG
born Feb 24, 1866
died Sept 23, 1920
Servant of God well done
(cannot read rest)

Ruth J. HOWERTON
Oct 16, 1900
died April 24, 1917
rest in peace

Chas BROADFIELD
born 1824
died Dec 15, 1904
Asleep in Jesus
Blessed sleep

Margaret
wife of
Chas. BROADFIELD
died Jan 1903
age 65 yrs
Asleep in Jesus
f/s M. B.

Geo R. BROADFIELD
born 1860
died 1902
Asleep in Jesus

Henry SHININGHOUSE
died June 13, 18xx
age 55 years
d/s w/ Caroline

Caroline
SHININGHOUSE
Died June 28, 1906
aged 87 years
d/s w/ Henry
Gone but not Forgotten

Oliver B. CHENAULT
1907 - 1975
Rest Blessed Servant

Frank C. WINSTON
Jan 5, 1907
Jan 16, 1976
d/s w/ Lillie B.

Lillie B. WINSTON
April 6, 1909
Feb 20, 1993
d/s w/ Frank C.

Mother
Martha V. DEAN
1914 - 1985

Saphonia JONES
July 12, 1900
Feb 1, 1989
In Loving Memory

Wife and Mother
Mary Charles MILLER
July 4, 1917
March 2, 1993

William Albert JORDAN
December 2, 1893
June 6, 1987
at rest

Mattie L. NORTHCUTT
July 8, 1910
September 18, 1986

Ogden P. BOYKIN
1905 - 1991
d/s w/Naomi

Naomi W. BOYKIN
1917 - Blank
d/s w/Ogden

Ellen MORRIS
Oct 7, 1944
June 3, 1996

Elizabeth NELSON
April 7, 1867
July 30, 1938

Lena SAUNDERS
Sept 15, 1861
March 3, 1937

Essiex BROOKS
1849 - 1937

Ethel M. HOWERTON
Left us Dec 22, 1935
f/s Daughter

Rosa BEAMON
wife of Sherman Beamon
died Feb 26, 1943

Sherman BEAMON
1878 - 1935
Faithful Husband

Josephine JORDAN
May 6, 1880
May 10, 1935

Lucy J. WYCHE
Nov 15, 1871
Nov 2, 1960

William A. WYCHE
1869 - 1934
Husband - Father
f/s W A W
Masonic

Granville T. TRUHART
Jan 20, 1877
Oct 30, 1932

Beatrice R. THOMAS
Oct 8, 1891
Aug 26, 1957
Stone laying on ground

Alfred Saunders
Jan 28, 1885
Jun 23, 1940

Georgette A. SCOTT
died Jan 2, 1934
Age 57
Asleep
f/s Mother

Vault no markings

Nettie R. NELSON
Jan 22, 1872
April 19, 1937
f/s N. R. N.
William H. BURRELL
Oct 26, 1880
Aug 23, 1944

James R. BEAMON
died March 20, 1938

George W. FREEMAN
born Jan 25, 1834
died Nov 6, 1902

Maude Pierce FIELDS
April 20, 1892
died Nov 17, 1942
at rest

Fred A. NELSON
1868 - 1942

Josephine E. JEFFRESS
Oct 14, 1895
Apr 13, 1944

Emily A. JORDAN
Oct 28, 1895
July 28, 1944

Rebecca FREEMAN
born 1845
died Dec 8, 1904
age 60 yrs
This stone given by
(cannot read) Stone lying
on ground

Sam'l JUNIFER
Co. B. 30 U.S.C.
Military stone

Vault no markings

ANDERSON monument

Thomas K. ANDERSON
Nov 22, 1888
Jan 20, 1944

LLOYD monument

D. Blanche LLOYD
July 18, 1883
Nov 5, 1961
II Tim. 4: 7 & 8

Ruppert A. B. LLOYD,
MD
Dec 15, 1885
Aug 4, 1946

Azarina L. EPPS
July 29, 1887
May 16, 1978

next four in stone border

Lizzie A. JENKINS
June 22, 1877
March 24, 1959

WILSON monument

Helen J. WILSON
January 2, 1899
October 15, 1987

Leonidas E. WILSON
Aug 22. 1898
Jan 15, 1940

William SPARKS
1853 - 1934
Honest and Faithful

Mother
Fannie TRUHART
October 22, 1857
April 20, 1934

Armistead W. TRUHART
Oct 6, 1880
June 7, 1938
at rest

Viola Collings BAKER
Dec 23, 1899
June 12, 1931

Wm. H. COPELAND
born May 29, 1873
Sept 29, 1910

Betsy Ann Hodges
SLAUGHTER
July 28, 1888
Sept 17, 1981

Rev W. R. HOWERTON
Born Nov 18, 1867
d/s w/ Mary B.

Mary B. HOWERTON
Nov 12, 1875
Sept 21, 1947
d/s w/W. R.
f/s M.B.H.

Mills PINNER
Oct 17, 1863
Oct 31, 1937
at rest

Amelia CALHOUN
died Dec 30, 1937
temporary metal marker

Lillian C. JENKINS
June 12, 1886
Feb 15, 1957
Stone lying on ground

Vault no marker

America PAYNE
Co. 1 37 U.S.C. Inf.
no dates

Alexander JENKINS
Sept 28, 1867
Mar 18, 19xx
stone broken

Mother
Nancy BERRY
died March 22, 1919
f/s N. B.

Stone broken cannot read

Vault no markings

Thaddeus H. PEEDEN
Died May 19, 1940
Virginia PVT US Army

7 vaults no markings

Our Love
Roy H. DILLARD
Aug 8, 1958
Nov 15, 1964

Bettie THOMAS
Dec 8, 1910
June 17, 1959
Stone lying on Ground

2 vaults no markings

Horace THOMAS
Jan 19, 1899
Aug 12, 1977

Stone Cannot read
in script very faint

xxxx Joseph
THORNTON
died Feb 26, 188x

Marshall Delaney
YOUNG
born September 13, 1888
died March 9, 1947
Virginia PFC
368 Inf 92 Div.
World War 1

Mary E. WILKINS
Dec 23, 1923
Dec 8, 1945

Mary E.
Dau of
W. H. & E. JOHNSON
Jan 7, 1884
May 2, 1901
stone broken

Rebecca Young
CHEATOM
1874 - 1954

Walter P. JACOBS
1855 - 1954

Vault no markings

Mother
Sadie E. BIRGE
3. 10. 1882
7. 14. 1967

Father
Grorge A. BIRGE
Oct 10, 1885
Feb 2, 1949

In Memory of
our Daughter
Mary L. BROOKS
born May 21, 1883
Nov 1, 1901
Asleep in Jesus
stone broken

Nora F. SCRIVENS
1895 - 1975
Stone lying on ground

Robert SCRIVENS
died Oct 24, 1955
Stone lying on ground

Easter JONES
May 28, 1878
Aug 15, 1955

Vault no markings

Viola M. PEEDEN
Feb 22, 1904
Mar 8, 1980

Florence A. PEEDEN
Mar 28, 1906
April 12, 1981

Ida PORTER
May 8, 1891
May 6, 1954

Edward WILLIAMS
Nov 13, 1910
May 3, 1952
Masonic
Rest in Peace

Charles Wallace CAFFEE
1881 - 1952
Father of Robert W. &
Stanley J.
d/s w/Sarah

Sarah Anne Elizabeth
CAFFEE
1883 - 1976
Mother of Robert W. &
Stanley J.
d/s w/ Charles

Stanley J. CAFFEE
1921 - 1978

Our Mother
Emma RICHARDSON
died Apr 9, 1938
Age 50 yrs.
Only asleep

George F. DRUMMOND
1896 - 1939

Clifford Ermine LYLES
Dec 17, 1910
March 15, 1950

Iron fence no grave inside

Memory of our Mother
cannot read
Mar 13, 1947
Home made marker

xxxx Johnson NELSON
(No Dates)

In remembrance
Sarah CHAPMAN
1854 - 1891
age 37 yrs
cannot read inscription

BLOXOM CEMETERY
Silver Isles Boulevard and Buffalo Road (7) {O - 6}

Tombstones of John A. Guy & Nancy P. Guy

This cemetery is situated on land that was conveyed to Major Perry Bloxom by deed dated May 16, 1836, and recorded in Deed Book G at page 261, in the Circuit Court for Elizabeth City county, (now the City of Hampton), Virginia. This cemetery was owned by Major Bloxom and his heirs during the times of the burials listed herein.

Acknowledgment: Barry Miles, 16 Nov. 1996 and Mrs. Wm. W. Wyatt (Betty Harper Wyatt).

Mary E. GUY
wife of John T. GUY
died Nov 18, 1859
in the 28 yr of her age the
deceased had been a member of
the M E Church and died in
full hope of a blessed immortality.

John BLOXOM
born Oct 22, 1836
died May 28, 1904

Appears to be two
other graves not marked

Nancy P. GUY
In memory of wife of
George W. GUY
Aug 16, 1874
aged 28 yrs
stone leaning against other stone

Susan BLOXOM
May 18, 1840
Feb 28, 1896
Stone lying on ground

"B"
Small stone lying ON GROUND

Bloxom Monument Lying on Ground

DAVIS CEMETERY
Blue Bird Gap Farm at Newmarket Creek (9) {G - 9}

Acknowledgment: Transcribed by S. Keith and T. Winters Sept. 3, 1989

Sacred
to the memory of
Margaret
wife of
Hadrach WOUTTEN
who was born
March 11th 1797
and departed this life
January 19th 1835
(unreadable inscription)

Philip P. DAVIS
Oct 12, 1845
July 22, 1913

Beula Davis
CURTIS
Nov 16, 1873
July 18, 1913

Alice West
DAVIS
April 3, 1851
Feb 14, 1922

Lilian Curtis FOX
Jan 11, 1896
Oct 12, 1918

Unknown
(stone base marked 1908
with Masonic emblem)

DRUMMOUND AND/OR MESSICK CEMETERY
Finn Point Lane / off Harris Creek Road (11) {M - 3}

From the General File Drawer, in Charles Taylor Library.
File titled "Copeland-Finn-Drummond House", is a reference to the "Lattimer-Hickman Burial Grounds", adjacent to the Lattimer-Wilson House, owned by Taylor S. Holtzclaw.

References is then made to the Drummond Burial Grounds, a small walled section of three graves, an unknown Confederate soldier and a Poquoson couple.

Thomas Drummond was the third owner of nearby Copeland-Finn-Drummond House, the oldest house in Fox Hill (now City of Hampton), reputedly the base of Blackbeard the Pirate. The house was built sometime between 1720 and 1750 and can be seen from Mears Plantation "Brittain".

A grant of 180 acres in 1632 to Thomas Bonwell/Bonnell, stayed in Bonnwell hands until 1803, when given by Makel and Elizabeth to daughter Catherine, who married Caleb Mears.

The Brick wall is still standing, the iron gate is lying on the ground. There is an evidence of graves inside the wall. There is a Confederate marker to the east and three Messick graves to the north west.

Acknowledgment: Transcribed by Jessie F. Forrest Nov 14.

Information from Mrs. Jessie F. Forrest.
Graves are unmarked, except for a Confederate Soldier marker. There is also a brick wall surrounding what apparently was a graveyard in the area. This wall was once closed with an iron gate now on the ground.

Ann Maria was the granddaughter of Elijah Linton of Somerset Co. Md. He served in the militia during the Revolutionary War, from the state of Maryland. His son, Elijah, Jr., moved to Mathews Co. and eventually to York Co. Ann Maria Linton married John Messick. This family spent most of their lives in Messick, now City of Poquoson, York County, Virginia.

Reference: Article by Anne C. Newsome, "Historical Hampton Homes" which appeared in the Dominon Magazine section of the Daily Press, February 8, 1970.

John MESSICK
Nov 24, 1804
Jun 9, 1883
(Stone is separated from grave,
leaning against tree)

Ann Maria MESSICK
Departed this life
June 19, 1875
Aged 71 Years

Custis MESSICK
May 25, 1795
Died September 14, 1867
Aged 72 y 3 m 11 d

C. S. A.
Marker no information

Two Foot Markers
C. M.
A. A. M.

Drummond and Messick Cemetery

ELMERTON CEMETERY
King Street (12) {J - 9}
African American

History - Deed Book O, page 53, Elizabeth City County. On 31 May 1858. Deed between Jefferson B. Sinclair and Georganna, his wife, to Henry C. Whiting, James Dye, and John B. Carr all of Elizabeth City County. 3 1/2 Acres on King Street, next to a ditch that runs from the front gate of J. B. Sinclair Farm. Recorded 23, 1887.

Acknowledgment: Transcribed by Barry Miles October/December 1996 and Darla B. Long, January 1997.

Rev. Y. JACKSON
Aug 17, 1887
Pastor of 1st Baptist Church
Hampton
Aged 50 Yrs.
stone on ground

Martha J. WHITE
died Mar 4, 1941

Jacob PARSON
Dec 27, 1876
Nov 22, 1929

Peter ROBINSON
died July 13, 1877
Mem.. C. P. Lodge No 1596
Aged 40 Yrs

John WHITE
died Oct 30, 1917
Aged 68 Yrs

Frances PERKINS
died Dec 17, 1890
Aged 70 Yrs

Willie PARKER
Oct 22, 1892
Oct 22, 1918

Lizzie KENNEDY
died Nov 22, 1917
Age 48 Yrs
stone on ground & broken

Bessie Luster TAYLOR
July 26, 1902
May 14, 1925

Margaret CARTER
Aug 13, 1859
Oct 27, 1926
w/ C. H. CARTER

C. H. CARTER
Jan 11, 1855
Mar 25, 1906
w/ Margaret CARTER

Richard LLOYD
died Feb 8, 1903
w/ Mary LLOYD

Mary LLOYD
died Dec 6, 1917
w/ Richard LLOYD

Martha B. WILLIAMS
died Dec 29, 1917

Mammie CARR
Jan 7, 1892
Nov 8, 1925
d/o R. H. & M. R.

Caroline SPRATLEY
died Mar 4, 1913
Age 75 Yrs
w/ Mary B. Washington

Mary B. WASHINGTON
Feb 1898
Apr 1, 1906
w/ Caroline SPRATLEY
stone on ground

Phillip TABB
Dec 10, 1892
Dec 10, 1899
stone on ground

Lina R. MASON
Jan 20, 1869
Jan 27, 1916

Nora JONES
died Nov 11, 1912
Aged 54 Yrs

John HERBERT Sr.
1818-1899

Esther A. HERBERT
1830-1899
w/o John

Lucy MARSHALL
1872
Jun 6, 1900
stone broken

Ruth MARSHALL
1888
Aug 2, 1908

Charlotte T. ALEXANDER
Sep 8, 1855
Feb 8, 1925
w/o Thos.

Mary E. KING
(No Dates)
stone broken

Elizabeth BRIGHT
died Dec 13, 1926
Age 79 Yrs
stone on ground

Maria BILLUPS
died Oct 12, 1925
Aged 80 Yrs
stone on ground

James H. FRANCES
1866
stone broken

Thomas NEADHAM
died Mar 22, 1897
w/ Lucy
stone broken & on ground

Lucy NEADHAM
died Jun 16, 1909
w/ Thomas

Ellen J. SPRIGGS
died Sep 15, 1891
Aged 56 Yrs
stone on ground

Mary Frances WASHINGTON
Apr 7, 1859
Apr 7, 1919
Aged 60 Yrs
stone on ground

Hannah BRIGHT
died Apr 26, 1900
Age 57 Yrs

Charles DAVIS
died Jul 21, 1925

Marih A. NEWMAN
Mother of
Alice E. TURNER
died Jan 3, 1928
Age 70 Yrs
Stone on ground & broken

Jennie THURGOOD
born in Hampton
Sept 3, 1877
died in New Haven, Conn
May 5, 1904

Sallie BURELL
1849
Jun 11, 1914

The PEAKE'S graves are
enclosed by an iron fence

Sarah Peake GREEN
Nov 1, 1867
Jul 9, 1917

Mary PEAKE
1823 - 1862

Thomas D. PEAKE
1824 - 1897

Sarah A. PEAKE
Mar 27, 1836
Nov 3, 1906

Sarah WALKER
1812 - 1884

Ernest T. PEAKE
Oct 31, 1876
July 17, 1898

Mary Elizabeth MELVIN
1855 - 1914

Fanny relic
of Karl RUSSCIA
died Mar 7, 1887
Age 74 Yrs
stone on ground

Infant sons of
Dr. C. S. & Pearl B.
BASSETT

Louisa PIERCE
died Oct 12, 1882
Age 20 yrs 2 mo 5 days
w/o Andrew W. BASSETT

Mary O. ORRELL
Sept 30, 1852
Oct 2, 1900
stone broken

Mrs Fanny BRYANT
Nov 2, 1862
Aged 25 Yrs

Joseph WHITE
(No Dates)

Simon BRYANT
May 11, 1868
Aged 68 Yrs

Thomas EDWARDS
died Mar 19, 1900
Aged 70 Yrs
stone on ground

Matilda ADAMS
died Sept 28, 1897
Aged 65 Yrs
stone on ground

Nannie MAYO
died Nov 18, 1902
Age 45 Yrs

Edward HILL
died Mar 4, 1920
Aged 55 Yrs
stone broken

Raymond DIGGS
May 29, 1902
Aug 1, 1914

Curtis BANKS
died Feb 28, 1925

Annie BARNES
Apr 2, 1887
Apr 10, 1898
stone broken

Agnes CR____
died Sept 15, 19xx
Age 20 Yrs
stone broken

Phil _____
died Jun __
Age 55
stone broken

_____

J. Henry ROBINSON
died Nov 25, 1918
Aged 52 Yrs.

Henry ROBINSON
Aug 6, 1888
Age 73 Yrs
w/ Lettie ROBINSON

Lettie ROBINSON
Mar 10, 1913
Age 87
w/ Henry ROBINSON

_____

Fannie E. WILSON
died Feb 21, 1922
Age 48 Yrs

Mary L. WRIGHT
died Mar 24, 1900
w/o Wm Wright
Age 34 Yrs

William WASHINGTON
1875
Jun 24, 1926
w/ Ludwool WASHNGTON

Ludwool Lee WASHINGTON
Jan 3, 1894
May 15, 1925
w/ William WASHINGTON

Sarah Janette WRIGHT
Sep 13, 1896
Sep 23, 1925
w/o H. C. Wright

Walter P. JOHNSON
died Feb 15, 1900
Age 28 Yrs

Alexander GARDINER
1839
Apr 11, 1904
stone on ground & broken

John BROWN
died Oct 20, 1907
Age 21 Yrs

James BAILEY
died Mar 10, 1899
Aged 43 Yrs

Kate J. BAILEY
died Mar 15, 1928
w/o James BAILEY

Lillie BOWEN
1884
Jul 4, 1926
w/o John
stone broken

Fannie JOHNSON
1837
May 21, 1911

Nannie L. LATTIMORE
died Apr 13, 1937
stone on ground

Rosa Celestine HOPE
Jul 24, 1911
Sep 8, 1914
stone on ground

Mary Ann CALLIS
Jul 15, 1860
Jun 16, 1910

Rebecca CHANDLER
Sep 1901
Apr 9, 1910
Aged 8 Yrs 7 Mo

Andred TOLIVER
Jan 26, 1924
Virginia PVT 542 Engrs

Chas. E. BURTON
died Mar 10, 1922
w/ Nancy BURTON

Nancy BURTON
died Jun 20, 1924
w/ Chas. E. BURTON

Eva M. JACKSON
Sep 2, 1882
stone in ground
cannot read

Wm. Elmore JORDAN
died Oct 22, 1912
Aged 36 Yrs

Laura YOUNG
Nov 6, 1846
July 7, 1911

Thomas CORNICK
Aug 15, 1850
Aug 26, 1911
stone on ground

Thomas E. MOORE
Dec 15, 1872
May 29, 1926

Dorsey DEVENPORT
born Jan 12, 1883
stone broken

George W. PRICE
Nov 18, 1868
Apr 12, 1911
Age 42 Yrs

Henry GIBBS
Jun 12, 1879
Sep 10, 1916

Edward WRAY
Jun 17, 1835
Jan 30, 1913
Aged 78 Yrs

Robert S. PURDY
Oct 7, 1888
Age 24 Yrs
stone on ground

William H. CHAPMAN
July 1863
Feb 28, 1922
stone broken

Tamer WHITE
died Mar 16, 1922

Clara B. HARRIS
Aug 1882
Apr 20, 1922

Maria LOVETTE
Nov 24, 1857
Jan 21, 1924

Sarah SAVAGE
May 5, 1860
Jun 14, 1913
w/o T. W. SAVAGE

Simon S. HILL
Mar 1857
Aug 9, 1915

Gracie A. SMITH
July 4, 1866
Apr 9, 1916

Margaret PRICE
Mar 10, 1845
Apr 26, 1914
Age 69 Yrs

Frances FRANCIS
Apr 10, 1860
Jul 5, 1924
stone broken

Maria THORNTON
died Aug 3, 1924
Age 41 Yrs

―――――――――

next 10 marking on same
stone, Ellison PARKER

Margaret PARKER
Aug 14, 1858
Feb 15, 1918

John E. PARKER

James L. PARKER

Ruth M. PARKER

Ellison PARKER

Lady A. PARKER
Nov 24, 1882
Feb 24, 1907

Rachel PARKER
died Jun 29, 1901

Margaret FIELDS
Feb 17, 1924

Rachel ADDISON
died Aug 30, 1924

Ellison PARKER
Apr 13, 1858
Feb 28, 1930

―――――――――

Susie TOLIVER
died July 8, 1924
Age 35 Yrs

Elen CAREY
Jun 6, 1866
Nov 22, 1916

Martha KIRBY
1845
Apr 14, 1917

Rosa E. DAVIS
1852 - 1913
w/ James S. DAVIS

James S. DAVIS
1876 - 1924
w/ Rosa E. DAVIS

_____ PARKER
Stone on ground
cannot read

Dean PARKER
(No Dates)

Geo. W. SIMMONS
Feb 1872
Nov 15, 1916

Benjamin F. DEAN
1876 - 1945

Julia J. DEAN
July 4, 1849
Sept 22, 1916

Emma DEAN
Dec 6, 1883
Feb 23, 1928

William S. PARKER
Aug 9, 1891
Dec 13, 1938

William CHISMAN
Aug 22, 1885
Jan 28, 1917

Marion CHISMAN
Mar 20, 1897
May 6, 1926

Sarah CHISMAN
1857 - 1928

Junius CHISMAN
1888 - 1950

Geo. F. BURKLEY
Sept 14, 1854
Jan 30, 1917
born King & Queen Co Va.
died Hampton, Va.

Samuel T. SMITH
April 11, 1870
July 26, 1950

Robert W. SMITH
Oct 11, 1861
Feb 7, 1901

Warren T. SMITH
July 30, 1830
Mar 2, 1930

Martha R. SMITH
Oct 7, 1830
Dec 23, 1923

Venus Ann BOLLING
Feb 3, 1844
Nov 9, 1916

George W. VAUGHN
Apr 1851
Nov 20, 1921

Rachel TAYLOR
1833 - Dec 29, 1914
w/o George E. TAYLOR
born Nova Scotia
died Hampton, Va.

Augustus BANKS
July 30, 1876
Sept 24, 1912

Addison PARKER
died Feb 24, 1924
Age 39 Yrs

James G. LEE
Sept 20, 1883
Jan 3, 1915

Sprigg LEE
died Jan 6, 1914
Age 68 Yrs
by wife, Jane LEE
I know that my redeemer liveth

William L. LEE
born Aug 29, 1870
w/ Ethel LEE

Ethel L. LEE
Nov 26, 1876
Mar 29, 1916
w/ William L. LEE

Charles H. LEE
Mar 6, 1865
Feb 8, 1910
s/o Sprigg LEE

Lucy A. LEE
Dec 9, 1842
Apr 30, 1895
w/o Sprigg LEE
Died in Friendship love
& truth sleep on
beloved

Alice E. DENNIS
Mar 10, 1856
Apr 22, 1906

Arlean J. MAUEN
May 27, 1900
Dec 14, 1965

Samuel J. SCOTT
died Sept 20, 1951

Otenia L. CHUDD
Sept 1, 1912
Sept 1, 1912

Alice V. BAILEY
Apr 1879
Nov 5, 1927
w/o Samuel BAILEY
stone on ground

John BOWDEN
1876 - 1939

Catherine B. WILLIAMS
died Dec 27, 1937

Nancy PARKER
died May 18, 1936

Junious SMITH
died Aug 1, 1920

George D. GARDNER
Apr 24, 1877
Mar 19, 1920

Edward GARDNER
died July 20, 1920
Age 38 Yrs

Mary E. HICKMAN
187-
July 30, 1923

Samuel E. JOHNSON
Nov 4, 1903
Sep 18, 1959

Mary DIGGS
died Dec 3, 1928
Age 80 Yrs

Mary A. SCOTT
Aug 1895 - July 25, 1919
d/o Francis Taylor
Sleep Beloved & take thy rest
we loved thee but
Jesus loves thee best

Frank H. DIGGS
June 21, 1889
Sept 2, 1957
Sleep on, we love you
but Jesus loved
you best

London SEXTON
Jan 31, 1883
May 15, 1959

Alfred SEXTON Sr
Mar 2, 1921
Dec 18, 1958

Jennie S. SEXTON
Mar 11, 1885
Nov 13, 1966

Lucie Brooks TYNES
Sept 26, 1886
Dec 17, 1918
The fairest flower we fondly
love, how soonest fades & die

Rosa ROBINSON
Oct 10, 1869
Apr 9, 1926

John Henry WRAY
Jan 22, 1865
Dec 11, 1926
w/ Bertha WRAY

Bertha WRAY
born Jan 3, 1885
w/ John Henry WARY

Rev. John H. GRAY Jr.
May 29, 1865
Feb 21, 1922
w/ Ellen F. GRAY

Ellen F. GRAY
Oct 2, 1864
Mar 8, 1935
w/ Rev. John H. GRAY

William E. ATKINS, MD
Dec 8, 1870
Aug 27, 1927
God's Nobleman

Indiana R. COMBS
1867 - 1902

Lillian R. ATKINS, MD
died Mar 21, 1934

Olive V. Stewart TONKINS
1885 - 1936

W. G. STEWART
1881 - 1928

S. E. STEWART
Jan 12, 1970

Dorothy STEWART
Jun 10, 1910
Mar 9, 1913

M. C. STEWART
1857 - 1926

W. H. STEWART
1857 - 1930

Elizabeth Harris
ROBINSON
died Nov 26, 1904
Age 62 Yrs

John H. PRICE Sr.
Apr 20, 1844
Sept 14, 1912
Age 68 Yrs
Stone on ground

Victoria Lee SWELL
died Oct 13, 1917
Sacred to the memory thy seeth
ye the living among the dead
stone on ground

_____ PARKER
Nov 20, 1877
July 1923
stone Broken

Nannie A. PENNICK
Oct 1870
Apr 1923
In loving memory of our
wife & Mother

John H. MINKING
Aug 10, 1874
Mar 16, 1923
Gone but not forgotten

Mary FREEMAN
1862 - 1917
Mother at rest

In memory of
Laural L. WILLIS
died July 12, 1921
His Beloved Sleepth

Leander CHANDLER
Aug 1, 1907
July 1, 1921

_____ HARRISON
stone in bad condition

Norah GIBBS
Nov 27, 1855
July 20, 1920
Mother

Willie J. CARTER
Dec 16, 1893
Jun 16, 1920
Mother darling
Sleep in Jesus

John Bril LAWS
(No dates)

Frank LAWS
Jan 6, 1841
Jan 14, 1921
Father

Matilda LAWS
died Oct 2, 1944
Mother
at Rest

Mary Ellen CURTIS
died Dec 31, 1944
w/o Charles H. CURTIS

John BENJAMIN
1875 - 1937
Devoted h/o Rosetta
BENJAMIN

Andrew BANKS
died Nov 21, 1919

Sarah E. ARMFIELD
Oct 24, 1856
Oct 15, 1920
w/ Peter WALLACE
rest in peace

Peter P. WALLACE
May 16, 1863
Sept 25, 1919
Sleep in Jesus

Matilda RANSOME
Mar 1847
May 27, 1918
Servant of God well done

George WILLIAMS
Mar 1861
July 8, 1921
At Rest

Pinkey WILLIAM
Nov 8, 1866
Dec 17, 1922
At Rest

Carrie B. FIELDS
Nov 2, 1930

Matilda Cooper McHERN
Jan 7, 1895
May 10, 1937
At Rest

Annie MILLER
May 15, 1857
July 25, 1922

William M. COOPER
Feb 8, 1834
Mar 1, 1910

Mittie Ann COOPER
Feb 20, 1866
Feb 19, 1961

Junius T. BATTEN
Aug 12, 1878
Mar 6, 1959

Hazel WHITE
Aug 16, 1891
Mar 30, 1957

Lucy BOOSE
1860 - 1921
At Rest

Arthur R. BAILEY
May 8, 1884
Dec 28, 1938
Husband

Sarah BATTEN
died Nov 23, 1918
Aged 60 Yrs
at rest

Eli RICKS
died Sept 28, 1925

Carrie JONES
died Dec 15, 1925
d/o John & Virginia
Age 12 Yrs

Robert H. CURTIS
1860 - 1925
w/ Mary L. CURTIS

Mary L. CURTIS
1857 - 1953
w/ Robert H. CUSTIS

Ann Lepearl HOWARD
1892 - 1973
d/o Thomas J. HOWARD

Thomas J. HOWARD Sr.
Oct 23, 1868
Jun 2, 1928

Thaddeus WILLIAMS
Mar 10, 1821
Nov 15, 1894

Hartin L. WILLIAMS
Oct 29, 1873
Jun 6, 1870
d/o T. W. & N. WILLIAM

George A. BROWN
Dec 27, 1889
Nov 11, 1905

Thomas N. BROWN
1845 - 1915

Ida H. WOODY
Dec 16, 1907
Age 50 Yrs

Jackson WEBB
Oct 3, 1856
Nov 23, 1916
stone on ground

Ann WEBB
Feb 28, 1857
Sept 7, 1894
Aged 37 y 6 m 10 d
w/o Jackson WEBB
stone on ground

Willie Anna TAYLOR
Nov 24, 1881
Jan 22, 1926
Gone but not forgotten
stone on ground

W. H. ROBINSON
1852 - 1929

Mary ROBINSON
died Jan 21, 1932
Mother

Margaret COOPER
died Sept 1890
Age 63 Yrs
w/o Wm COOPER

Rebecca WILLIAMS
died Dec 22, 1904
Age 66 Yrs

Annie B. WILLIAMS
died Apr 12, 1890
Aged 12 y 10 m

Fannie T. Ash HOWARD
Dec 25, 1869
May 3, 1897
w/o Thomas J. HOWARD

W____ HOWARD
born ___ 12, 1895
died ___

_____ HOWARD
unreadable

Louisa WHITE
Jul 1, 1863
Apr 25, 1915
w/o R. L. WHITE

Fannie L. BANKS
Apr 25, 1856
June 5, 1923

Comfort HOWARD
1866
Jan 16, 1897
Grandmother

Nat HOWARD
1831 - 1899
Grandfather

Annie S. AUSTIN
Nov 13, 1881
Feb 26, 1972
w/ Haywood L. AUSTIN

Haywood L. AUSTIN
Apr 10, 1871
Aug 23, 1963
w/ Annie S. AUSTIN

Robert T. FIELDS
1901 - 1944

James Z. PATTERSON
Feb 22, 1879
Jun 15, 1948
Father

Winnie MASON
Jul 1, 1901
Aug 7, 1921

Winnie ROY
Jun 19, 1860
Apr 19, 1925

Selena WASHINGTON
Aug 21, 1873
July 21, 1952
w/ Peter WASHINGTON

Peter WASHINGTON
Apr 7, 1869
Masonic Emblem
w/ Selena WASHINGTON

Capt. Wm. SNEED
Jan 20, 1875
Nov 16, 1942
Masonic emblem

Sadie RIDDICK
Sept 19, 1903
Aug 7, 1994

Anthony E. RIVERS
1872 - 1921

Davie W. JACKSON
1872 - 1924
w/ Florence B. JACKSON

Florence B. JACKSON
1882 - 1969
w/ Davie W. JACKSON

Olga T. JACKSON
1910 - 1985
w/ no name

Blank
w/ Olga T. JACKSON

Marcan ____
stone broken

Frances DAVIS
1866 - 1955

Andrew DAVIS
1856 - 1934

Sarah WYNN
1852 - 1936

Columbus WINN
1845 - 1922

Mary WYNN
1818 - 1898

Lucy J. WEST
1869 - 1927

Lucy A. PETHAM
1833 - 1918

William H. WEST
1860 - 1907

Althea Harris JONES
Dec 25, 1892
Mar 24, 1955

Dr. Joseph Julian JONES
died Jul 25, 1928

Robert T. FIELDS Sr.
died Oct 8, 1920
Age 58 Yrs

Belle F. PATTERSON
Apr 1878
Jan 7, 1964
Mother

Catherine W. FIELDS
1858 - 1933

Washington FIELDS
1815 - 1867
Father

Martha A. FIELDS
1813 - 1891

George W. FIELDS
1853 - 1932

Sallie B. FIELDS
1869 - 1944

Rosa WOODARD
Dec 26, 1866
Jul 18, 1890
w/o Sandy WOODARD

Thomas HARMON Jr.
Jan 12 1892
July 5, 1977

Thomas HARMON
Mar 8, 1855
Mar 15, 1924

Sarah HARMON
Aug 15, 1862
Apr 15, 1933

Royal ECHOLS
May 5, 1838
May 12, 1899

William MALLORY
died Sep 13, 1949

Peter L. RANDALL
s/o Wm. RANDALL

Agnes RANDALL
died Oct 13, 1897
d/o Wm & Mary RANDALL
stone sunken in ground

Mary RANDALL
died Jul 20, 1886
Aged 44y 6m 20d

Wm. RANDALL
Co. L. (cannot read)

William GRINSTEAD
Apr 1, 1878
Jun 1, 1896

_____
Next 5 inscriptions are on
stone of A. M. SMITH

Elizabeth SMITH
Mar 14, 1849
Sept 3, 1889

Robert S. SMITH
Jul 25, 1878
Jul 7, 1895

Robert M. SMITH
Mar 14, 1847
Feb 13, 1923

A. Mitchell SMITH
Jul 1878
Jun 8, 1900

Bettie M. SMITH
Apr 1878
Apr 1965

Beulah H. JARVIS
1888 - 1960
Mother - Eastern Star
w/ Curl H. JARVIS

Curl H. JARVIS Sr.
1874 - 1957
Masonic
w/ Beulah H. JARVIS

Curl H. JARVIS Jr.
Aug 3, 1912
Mar 29, 1962

Roxanna E. JARVIS
1914 - 1962
Daughter

Shirley S. JARVIS
Oct 31, 1933
Jun 27 1994
Beloved Mother &
Grandmother

MILLER monument
no dates

Eliza A. MILLER
died Mar 7, 1915
Mother

Samuel C. MILLER
died Nov 7, 1922

Simon BRYANT
died Aug 16, 1912
Aged 78 Yrs
Thy Trials ended
thy rest is won

Mary L. BRYANT
Jan 18, 1919
Peaceful sleep

Catharine BRYANT
died Dec 18, 1922
In God Care

Mary E. PHILLIPS
Aug 15, 1865
Oct 26, 1945

J. M. PHILLIPS
1857 - 1922

PHILLIPS Monument

BARRETT Monument

Janie Porter BARRETT
1865 - 1948

Harris BARRETT
1865 - 1915

May Porter BARRETT
1896 - 1918

CHANDLER monument

James H. CHANDLER
Dec 7, 1873
Nov 22, 1949
At Rest

Hattie E. CHANDLER
Sept 8, 1895
Jul 9, 1954

Thomas A. CHANDLER
Aug 18, 1884
Oct 4, 1857

Richard R. PALMER
Jun 9, 1849
Jun 10, 1911

Mary E. WILLIAMS
Dec 16, 1861
Apr 19, 1918
At Rest

Kate Wms. MILBURN
Sept 6, 1885
May 3, 1935

Nannie W. DAVIS
Jun 30, 1890
Jul 20, 1944
w/o Fred D. DAVIS

Rebecca TANNER
died Oct 20, 1920
w/ Lossie Tanner
ROBINSON

Lossie Tanner ROBINSON
died May 25, 1943
w/ Rebecca Tanner

Mary Z. CHISMAN
Apr 23, 1897
May 24, 1916
His Beloved one sleep on

James N. ANDERSON
1898 - 1963

R. M. ANDERSON
Mar 3, 1874
May 8, 1916
w/ no name (blank)

No Name
w/ R. M. ANDERSON

Ira ANDERSON
Feb 1900
Nov 11, 1978

Lillian ANDERSON
Feb 19, 1879
Jun 9, 1966

Mar 27, 1879
Jan 17, 1918

Mattie TALIAFEROR
died Nov 2, 1934
In Loving Memory of My
Dear Mother

---

four sides of stone

side 1
Werner SIDEL

side 2
Our Loving Father

side 3
F. __ EDRICK

side 4
blank

Charles SMITH, Jr.
born 1857
died Oct 23, 1913

Ella SMITH
died Feb 23, 1916
Age 63 yrs
At Rest

Charles SMITH
Dec 1838
Apr 14, 1918
Sleep on Father and into
thy Rest

Annie E. RILEY
born Apr 17, 1858
died Feb 23, 1916
At Rest

Chas. E. RILEY
Jan 22, 1878
Feb 21, 1903

C. H. DIGGS
1857
Jan 17, 1924
Gone but not Forgotten
Temporary stone broken

Chaney BROWN
1836
Sep 15, 1885
w/o M. C.
Mother
stone broken

Louisa V. LEVITT
Mar 1833
Aug 4, 1898
stone broken

Junious S. CHANDLER
May 15, 1885
Sept 15, 1915
stone broken

John H. CHISMAN
Dec 29, 1865
Apr 8, 1912
stone on ground

Warren TOLIVER
died Feb 26, 1904
Age 65 Yrs
stone broken

_____(Cannot read)
Born Jan 3, 1832
In loving memory of father and
mother who departed this life
in full triumph of faith
Henry ROBINSON age 73
Lettie ROBINSON
Mar 10, 1913 age 87

In loving memory of father &
mother who departed this life
in full triumph of faith
Henry ROBINSON
Mar 10, 1913
Age 87

J. Henry ROBINSON
died Nov 25, 1918
Age 52 Yrs
Gone but not Forgotten

Fannie WILSON
died Feb 21, 1922
Age 48 yrs
Rest in Peace

Thomas H. DAVIS
Stone sunken in ground

John H. MERLEY
Apr 6, 1845
Apr 18, 1891
cannot read inscription

Millie DAVIS
Dec 19, 1867
July 9, 1904
w/o Thomas DAVIS

Susan WASHINGTON
Dec 28, 1891
May 31, 1924
w/o Eugene
stone in bad condition

William _____
died March 22, 1885
Age 39 Yrs
stone leaning badly

Mary Elizabeth LEE
departed this life Sept 2, 1890,
Aged 21 yrs
Sacred in the Memory of the
Daughter
Here this the flower of our
home beloveth this codded
mound we watch we wait dear
child to come when the just
trump shall saved

De Russey ROBINSON
died Aug 28, 1892
Age 24 Yrs
w/ Mitchell B. ROBINSON

Mitchell B. ROBINSON
died Oct 28, 1900
Aged 28 Yrs
w/ DeRussey ROBINSON

John ROBINSON
died Apr 16, 1905
Age 94 Yrs

John J. ROBINSON
died Mar 27, 1901

Julia J. JOHNSON
died Dec 19, 1905
Age 81 Yrs

Andrew W. ROBINSON
July 10, 1881
Aug 22, 1912

Henry B. ROBINSON
Aug 25, 1876
Dec 16, 1920

Susan TOLIVER
died Apr 15, 1906
Age 60 Yrs
stone leaning against
a fence

Louisa CHANDLER
March 12, 1864
Sept 9, 1936
Mother

Luke CHANDLER
1863 - 1904
temporary marker

Harry C. SMITHERS
died Jan 20, 1899
Age 15 yrs

Elizabeth BANKS
Sept 7, 1926 Mother
stone leaning against
another stone

Maria SMITHERS
died Feb 13, 1906
Age 55 Yrs
At Rest

James GATHRIGHT
Sept 12, 1878
Sept 24, 1930
At Rest

(cannot read)
Oct 1, 1933
At Rest

Chas. D. GATHRIGHT
Mar 3, 1880
Mar 1, 1904

Gladys L. RUSSELL
Mar 22, 1906
July 18, 1941
Loving Memory of our
Daughter

Annie E. SMITH
died Sept 28, 1917
Age 17 yrs

In Memory
Sylvia SPRATLEY
Sept 10, 1830
Sept 10, 1903
Age 73 Yrs
Servant of God Well Done

In Memory of
Wm. BANKS
died Aug 15, 1901
h/o Rosa BANKS

In Memory of
Rosa BANKS
died Apr 11, 1911
w/o Wm. BANKS

Thy will be done
Robert John HERBERT
Feb 15, 1847
Mar 3, 1911
w/ Mary HERBERT

Mary HERBERT
Mar 14, 1857
May 24, 1905
w/ Robert John HERBERT
cannot read inscription

Mary E. WILLIAMS
born Jan 15, 1846
died Feb 11, 1900

Mary E. WILLIAMS
Jan 15, 1846
Feb 11, 1900

DAGGS monument

Harriet CARPER
1840 - 1891
Mother

Hattie Daggs LATTIMORE
1885 - 1928

Wm. H. DAGGS
1859 - 1927

Richard WATTS
Dec 1855
Sept 4, 1916
Gone but not forgotten

George THOMAS
Sept 9, 1871
Aug 5, 1915
Gone but not forgotten
stone on ground

Sadora ARMSTEAD
died Nov 28, 1918
Age 26 yrs

Elizabeth ARMSTEAD
Died Oct 28, 1918
Age 22 Yrs
At Rest

Raphael SIMON
Oct 28, 1899
in Aux Cayes Haiti W. I.
July 18, 1918
Hampton Va USA
Age 19 Yrs
stone on ground

Cornealious D. SHORTS
1853
Mar 22, 1918
Beloved w/o Rev T. H.
SHORTS D. D.
She has done what she
could

Rev. T. H. SHORTS D. D.
Pastor of Queen Street Baptist
Church 33 Years from Sept
1882 to Apr 1917
Born Sept 1850
died Apr 25, 1917
Blessed are the dead
Erected to the Memory by the
Church

George E. BOOKER
March 25, 1911
May 11, 1969

Marian S. BOOKER
July 14, 1905
Nov 28, 1962
f/s M S B

Lillie E. BOOKER
Sept 9, 1879
Sept 25, 1954
At Rest

Samuel Eugene
BOOKER, Sr.
Jan 25, 1873
Jan 9, 1947
At Rest
f/s S E B

Arthur G. SMITH
Born Jan 15, 1873
Died July 6, 1919
w/ Hattie Smith

Hattie Madison SMITH
Born Aug 16, 1877
Died April 15, 1915
w/ Arthur SMITH
stone on ground

Catharine HOWARD
and Family
No Dates
Home made stone

Catharine HOWARD
Died Jun 14, 1916
Mother
at rest
foot stone

James HOWARD
Died Aug 16, 1922
Brother
at rest
foot stone

Milton WALKER Jr.
Died April 22, 1914
Age 33 years

Rosa A. HERBERT
Born 1849
Died Mar 12, 1907
Mother
Rest in peace
Stone on Ground

in rememberence of
Arthur B. THORNTON
Born Sept 23, 1884
Died Aug 23, 1919

William B. WEAVER
1852-1929
Father of the Fatherless
d/s Blank

Blank
d/s w/ William WEAVER

Raymon B. WEAVER
Feb 11, 1898
Sept 18, 1931

Rhoda Anna WEBESTER
Born Feb 22, 1854
Died Aug 26, 1921
She Being Dead yet Speaketh
At Rest

Wesley ROBINSON
Dec 17, 1868
Jan 6, 1930
w/ Queen ROBINSON

Queen V. ROBINSON
April 5, 1877
April 17, 1936
w/ Wesley ROBINSON
Stone on ground

Sarah BROWN
Born 1855
Oct 5, 1924
w/o Nathan BROWN
Sleep on and taken thy rest
stone on ground

C. POINDESTER
Nov 15, 1920
Age 74

Thomas TABB
Born Aug 29, 1852
Died Sept 17, 1923
At Rest

Louise N. STEPHEN
"Nurse"
1886 - 1952
Departing she has left
behind her loving foot-prints
on the sand of time
husband W. D. STEPHEN

William D. STEPHEN
Died Nov 12, 1956
Son of Dr. Geo. D. Stephen

Our Darling
Ida Elaine BASSETT
Born Sept 14, 1916
Died May 12, 1918
inscription not legible

son and dear brother
W. P. REDGROSS
Born Sep 18, 1865
Died Feb 1, 1920

Farley P. HARRIS
Aug 20, 1880
Dec 6, 1938

Helena H. TOLIVER
Died Feb 21, 1956

Sadie Roberta MAJOR
May 22, 1904
October 8, 1946

Elizabeth SHIELDS
Born Oct 29, 1899
Died June 18, 1918
Stone lying on ground

Lola M. NELSON
July 27, 1880
April 2, 1934

Thomas WERNHAM
Died October 25, 1939

Sarah A. WERNHAM
Jan 16, 1860
Jan 9, 1930

In memory of
Lillian A. WERNHAM
Died June 23, 1918
Age 23 Years
Where rainbows of glory
unceasingly play
Our Lillian is singing
in heaven today

Matilda E. ANDERSON
Born Dec 1, 1856
Died June 18, 1918

Geo. D. ANDERSON
Nov 11, 1849
Mar 6, 1916
When this earthly Tabernacle
be dissolved I have a building
with God

Mother
Lucy A. BLUE
died Jul 6, 1934
At Rest

In Memory of
Martha WALKER
Died Oct 7, 1916
w/o Milton WALKER Sr.
Sleep on Dear Mother
and take thy rest

Mary A. PRESSEY
Aug 15, 1858
July 10, 1911
w/o R. C. PRESSEY

Ellen LAWSON
Died May 4, 1912
Age 80
Stone broken and
lying on ground

Chas. E. RILEY
Born Jan 22, 1878
Died Feb 21, 1903

Annie E. RILEY
Born April 17, 1858
Died Feb 23, 1916
At Rest

Ella SMITH
Died Feb 23, 1913
Age 63 yrs
At Rest

Charles SMITH
Born 1857
Died Oct 23, 1913
Brother

In loving Memory of
my Dear Mother
Mattie TALIAFEROR
Died Nov 21, 1934

Pointed stone
homemade
Warren _____

Our Little
Freddie WILLIAMS
Aug 12, 1914
April 18, 1918

In remembrance of
my beloved husband
Willie HOLMES
Born Oct 15, 1876
Died Feb 14, 1916
at rest

Frank DALE
Died May 16, 1908
age 50 yrs
Resting in God

Amanda Willis KRUGER
Died Dec 19, 1913
Age 70 Yrs
cannot read inscription

Sarah BOWEN
1876 - 1911
w/o John
Gone but not Forgotten
Homemade Marker
Broken

Cemeteries of the City of Hampton, Virginia / formerly Elizabeth City County

The following was provided by Darla B. Long. She dug through the broken tombstones stacked in a pile and some that were buried, or lying face down. She is thanked for her efforts.

Andrew E. CRITTENDON
Born Sept 1863
Died Nov 10, 1922
At Rest
Age 59 yrs.

In memory of
John H.
Beloved husband of
Amanda WHITE
Died July 1, 1887
Aged 65 years

Our father has passed away
from our sight
Our father was our pride and
delight
And this lessens our sorrow
when this life is o'vr
We hope to meet him on
Heaven's bright shore.

(was face down)
In memory of
Milie ROBINSON
Died Aug 3, 1893
Aged 70 years

(broken)
Queen E. SUTTON
xxx 4, 1884
Feb 28, 1904
At rest

(was under markers)
Margaret CLARKE
Died June 4, 1915
Age 50 yrs
Sleep on beloved sleep and
take thy rest

In memory of
Samuel HOLMES
Born Sept 1872
Feb 19, 1908
Age 36 years
Sleep on beloved and take thy
rest

(broken)
William S. HOLLOWAY

(broken)
Catharine
wife of
_____ ROBINSON
Died xxx 1925

(broken)
Cornelious GAMM
Born June 15, 1849
Died May 2, 1910
His beloved sleep xxxxx.

Willie R.
wife of
Watt D. NEWSOME
Born Feb 15, 189x
Died Jan 3, 19xx

(inside low rock wall)
George W. JONES
Born March 4, 1884
Died Aug 18, 1906

In memory of
Fanny
relict of Burl BASSETTE
Died Mar 7, 1887
Aged 74 years
Rest, rest in peace Mother
From us thy face is gone:
nor will we see each other
Till we meet around the
heavenly throne.
Erected by her son Andrew

Emma J.
wife of
P. B. STEVENSON
Born Mar 18, 1868
Died Apr 8, 1910
Gone But Not Forgotten

Cyrus H. _____
son of
Elvira
April 26, 1883
Jan 9, 1928
Gone But Not Forgotten

(broken)
Died April 6, 1909
Rest in Peace

GOOD SAMARITAN CEMETERY
Woodland Road (13) {L - 10}
In front of Hampton Golf Course
African American

History
On 14 September 1876 the trustees, Alexander Washington, James Williams and Samuel Smith, for the Good Samaritan and Israelites of Zion, purchased the land from Thomas Tabb for $200.00.
Deed Book 4, page 547.

On October 1896 the Good Samaritan and Israelites of Zion Tent #89, separated and the land was divided. The Good Samaritan received the parcel of land that is the present the site of the cemetery. Deed Book 28, page 67.

No other information on this property was given in the deeds books or the assessors office.

Acknowledgment: Transcribed by Paul L. Brown 30 and 31 Dec 1986, T. Winter and S. Keith Sep 3, 1989. Both were used in the final listing.

Annie BILLUPS
Died Oct 2, 1901
Age 80 Yrs
Gone but not forgotten

Lewis BILLUPS
Died Aug 10, 1896
Age 70 Yrs
Asleep in Jesus

Caroline BILLUPS
June 15, 1814
May 25, 1909
She died as she lived
a Christian

Mother
Edna WILSON
Dau of C. E. & S. BILLUPS
Sept 22, 1889
May 11, 1922
Gone but not forgotten

In memory of Our Mother
Sarah A. BLACKLY
Died April 5, 1921
Age 73 Years

Willie CALM
1870-1911
At rest

Mother
Annie N. CALM
June 25, 1902
April 25, 1927
Wife of Robert CALM
May the resurrection find
 thee in the bosom of thy God

Bennie CLARK
Born Aug 12, 1882
Died June 18, 1891

Robert C. CLARK
Oct 25, 1881
Sept 14, 1918
Gone but not forgotten

Nealie CLARK
Born Dec 31, 1886
Died Oct 27, 1893

My dear Husband
Keenley CHAPMAN
Born Dec 24, 1846
Died Dec 28, 1926
At rest

Mother
Louisa CORNELL
Born June 12, 1846
(Stone Buried in Ground,
unable to read rest)

Mother
In Memory of
Jane CORNEY
Born 1824
Died Jan 22, 1914
Age 90 Years
Sleep on Beloved and Take
thy rest. We loved thee, but
Jesus loved thee best. J. C.

Mariah DOWNING
Born July 17, 1865
Died Oct 27, 1910

Mamie A.
wife of
J. Arthur DANCE
1878-1918

Henry DAVIS
Died March 27, 1883
Aged 18 Years

Chery MOODY
Died Oct 6, 1889
Aged 85 Years
C. M.

In Memory of
Bettie E. HARRIS
Born 1869
Died Dec 3, 1907
Gone but not forgotten
B. E. H.

To the memory of
Laura E. HARRIS
Born Dec 17, 1869
Died April 10, 1901
At rest

In memory of
Diana HARRIS
Born 1833
Died Nov 19, 1908
Age 75 Yrs.
At Rest
D. H.

Jas. HENRY
U. S Navy

My beloved son
Thomas HOLMES
May 25, 1886
Jan 8, 1915
Only sleeping

Wm. T. HOLMES
Died April 21, 1906

Wm. S. HOLMES
Born Sept 7, 1883
Died Sept 12, 1902
At Rest

Sister
Martha JACKSON
1881-1932

Father
William H. JOHNSON
May 22, 1851
April 5, 1924
At rest

Sarah JOHNSON
April 10, 1811
April 11, 1911
Age 100 Yrs.

Husband
Romeo C. HALL
Jan 28, 1882
June 21, 1932
Asleep in Jesus

Cemeteries of the City of Hampton, Virginia / formerly Elizabeth City County

Beloved Daughter of
Joseph H. & Lucy J. HALL
Born at Fort Monroe Va.
Aug 7, 1872
Died at Providence, R. I.
March 2, 1902
K. M. H.

Mother
Lucilla J. HALL
Born July 3, 1839
Died May 25, 1906

Isabella Daughter of
Lucy & Joseph H. HALL
Born at Fort Monroe, Va.
July 3, 1866
Died June 7, 1876
A member of the Daughters of
Zion. Safe in the arms of Jesus

Father
Joseph H. HALL
Born Oct 13, 1835
Died July 15, 1904
J. H. H.

Mother
Daisy M. HALL
Dec 18, 1881
Sept 3, 1961

In Memory of Mother
Percilla KING
Died Jan 23, 1900
Aged 76
Asleep in Jesus

Mary E. KING
Jan 1, 1833
May 15, 1926
(a low marble wall surrounds
grave and stone)

Elizabeth
Dau of
W. M. & Eliza JOLLY
Born Nov 20, 1917
Died Feb 21, 1919
We will meet again

To my beloved son

Alfred C. MASON
Born Mar 3, 1874
Died Jan 6, 1905
Asleep in Jesus

In memory of my Mother
Georgie MASON
Died April 27, 1906
Age 49 Years
Sleep on Beloved and take
thy rest.

To beloved wife
Sarah McHERN
Born Nov 30, 1878
Died Feb 9, 1920
Sleep on and take
thy rest

Rachel PAIGE
Died May 26, 1914
at rest

Aurther PAIGE
Died 1919
(Homemade concrete)

In memory of
William PRESSEY
Died Aug 15, 1884
Age 55 Yrs.
Father of Mary E. SMITH
Peaceful be thy
silent slumber

Buster PAIGE
Died Dec 2, 1921

Betty REYNOLDS
June 26, 1862
Sept 1, 1921
At rest

Susan ROBERTSON
Born 1829
Died 1897
Aged 68 Years

In memory of my wife
Bettie SCOTT
Died June 20, 1920
Aged 59 Yrs.
Sweet thoughts will always
linger around the grave where
you are laid
no one knows I miss you, no
one knows the tears I shed

In memory of
Marcus SMITH
Died Jan 28, 1906
Age 68 Yrs.
Father of Claiborne A.
Sleep on and take thy rest

SMITH
Died Aug 16, 1915
Age 65 Yrs.
Mother of Mary E. SMITH
Asleep in Jesus
Blessed Sleep
(Top of stone broken off)

James THOMAS
Died Feb 20, 18-5
Aged 25 Yrs, 1 Mo.

Mary E. SMITH
Died Feb 13, 1933
(Double Stone)

Claiborne A. SMITH
Died Feb 16, 1949
(Double Stone)

Agie Chapman TUCKER
Oct 16, 1895
Aug 30, 1928
At rest
A. C. T.

Elijiah WEBB
Died Dec 27, 1922
Aged 65 Yrs.
Gone but not forgotten
E. W.

In memory of
Caleb WIGGEON
Died Nov 11, 1894
Age 74 Years
Asleep in Jesus

Comfort WIGGEON
Born 1824
Died Jan 30, 1903
At rest

Stone Embedded in tree
top part unable to read
Jan 28, 1903
Age 71 Yrs.

Views of Good Samaritan Cemetery

GREENLAWN CEMETERY
Shell Road (14) {E - 14}

This is a very large cemetery with over 10,000 interments. Greenlawn Cemetery has not been transcribed for this book. It is well managed and locations of grave sites can be researched in the cemetery office.

For the purpose of this book, we will record only the Confederate Prisoners of War Soldiers buried in Greenlawn. The introduction (author unknown) to the listing of the Confederate Soldiers buried at Greenlawn is quoted:

"I was asked to locate the Parker West farm in Newport News, Virginia, by a family in North Carolina who were notified by the War Department their Great Grandfather, a Confederate Soldier, was taken prisoner and died in Newport News in 1865 and was buried on the Parker West farm.

I learned a memorial service had been held honoring some prisoners of war who died in Newport News and were later moved to Greenlawn Cemetery in that city. A trip to the cemetery office lead me to the cemetery register which showed the names of 164 prisoners of war were moved to the cemetery on March 7, 1900. I also learned a book had been written about the Parker West farm.

Subsequently I learned 'When The Yankee's Came' by Parke Rouse was the story of the landing of the Yankees in Newport News May 27, 1861, following Virginia voting to secede from the Union, April 17, 1861. Mr. Rouse edited the memoirs of George Benjamin West, the son of Parker and Mary West, who at the age of 22 sat in the yard of the P. West farm on Newport News Point, where the waters of Hampton Roads and the James River came together, and watched the landing. He described how they took over the farm, later tore down the house and all the buildings and built Camp Butler to launch their attack on Richmond, The Capital of the Confederacy.

Fighting in the area is expertly described by Mr. and Mrs. Charles Hunter in their articles of Williamsburg in the 1800's. They say, 'fighting reached Williamsburg on May 5, 1862 and lasted only one day'. 'For many the battle of Williamsburg was a sort of a free circus with fireworks; the townspeople strolled in the battlefield and stood under umbrellas to watch the fighting'.

Mr. West stated, 'where his father's farm had been, a prison camp had been established about the last of March 1865 and was used until about July 4, 1865'. In 1900 Mr. West requested the list of names from the War Department which was placed at the cemetery when the bodies were reinterred there. A monument was erected by the Confederate Veterans of Hampton. Recently a marble marker bearing the name, rank and organization of each of the 164 prisoners was placed in the cemetery by Mr. and Mrs. Thomas Duncan, and a Memorial service was held on Memorial Day in 1979 to dedicate the marker."

Monument in Greenlawn to the Confederate Soldiers Who Died at Camp Butler

Cemeteries of the City of Hampton, Virginia / formerly Elizabeth City County

Confederate Prisoners of War, who died at Newport News, Virginia and are buried at Greenlawn.

NAME	RANK	CO.	REGIMENT	DATE OF DEATH
James MERCER	private	A	18th Virginia Battalion	April 27, 1865
James F. HOLLINS	private	B	59th Alabama	April 30, 1865
Charles BOYLE	private	F	11th Virginia	May 1, 1865
J. TAYLOR	private	K	54th North Carolina	May 2, 1865
J. J. LASSITER	private	F	11th Florida	May 2, 1865
Booker SMITH	sergeant	C	46th Virginia	May 3, 1865
F. BATES	corporal	E	11th Virginia	May 3, 1865
John TANNER	private	F	11th Florida	May 4, 1865
G. BLOXOM	private	E	32nd Virginia	May 5, 1865
T. L. VIA	sergeant	H	57th Virginia	May 5, 1865
H. J. CHISWELL	private	C	11th Florida	May 6, 1865
S. SIMMS	private	D	20th North Carolina	May 6, 1865
B. BECKHAM	private	F	1st South Carolina Arty.	May 6, 1865
John A. WHITMAN	private	K	57th North Carolina	May 6, 1865
J. P. WILLOUGHBY	private	C	Hampton Legion	May 7, 1865
C. E. HAYNES	private	H	13th Georgia	May 7, 1865
Benjamin HUNT	private	A	Cobbs Legion	May 8, 1865
L. J. CHAPMAN	private	G	37th North Carolina	May 8, 1865
Daniel RARIDAN	private	C	32nd North Carolina	May 9, 1865
D. CARROLL	private	C	53rd North Carolina	May 9, 1865
Abner SHIVER	private	F	11th Florida	May 9, 1865
G. H. HOLTSCLAW	private	C	22nd South Carolina	May 9, 1865
J. S. REYNOLDS	private	C	46th Virginia	May 10, 1865
F. HASSEBANK	private	B	Hugers Batt'n Arty.	May 11, 1865
Peter McGEE	private	A	25th Virginia	May 11, 1865
J. C. YOUN	private	I	22nd South Carolina	May 12, 1865
Samuel WOOD	private	B	10th Virginia	May 12, 1865
J. CLAYTON	private	F	1st South Carolina Arty.	May 12, 1865
A. MINTER	private	A	1st Eng. Regt.	May 12, 1865
W. C. LEE	private	I	43rd North Carolina	May 13, 1865
R. S. RHODES	private	D	45th North Carolina	May 13, 1865
W. S. SHAW	private	K	45th North Carolina	May 14, 1865
J. B. McGINNIS	private	H	35th North Carolina	May 14, 1865
J. W. HOLLAND	private	A	18th Virginia Artillery	May 14, 1865
J. F. McCOY	private	K	6th South Carolina	May 15, 1865
E. KELLY	private	E	2nd South Carolina	May 16, 1865
H. W. BREWERTON	private	A	7th South Carolina	May 17, 1865
J. D. CLARK	private	K	54th North Carolina	May 17, 1865
Jacob RUDISIL	private	B	54th North Carolina	May 17, 1865
A. B. SMITH	private	C	46th Virginia	May 18, 1865
W. O. FIELDS	private	B	10th Virginia Battalion	May 19, 1865
John KALBFLEISH	private	D	22nd Georgia	May 20, 1865
B. WILKINSON	private	G	18th Virginia	May 20, 1865
Michael PLASTER	private	I	24th Virginia	May 20, 1865

Name	Rank	Co.	Unit	Date
Wm. ELKINS	private	I	5th South Carolina	May 20, 1865
S. R. DONAHUE	sergeant	H	6th North Carolina	May 21, 1865
Thos. H. ANDREWS	private	C	10th Virginia Artillery	May 22, 1865
John McCLENAHAN	private	K	30th Virginia	May 22, 1865
Thos J. MILFORD	private	A	26th Mississippi	May 22, 1865
A. H. TUNSTILL	private	E	44th Virginia Battalion	May 23, 1865
H. PICKERING	private	H	6th Georgia	May 23, 1865
J. M. DIXON	private	D	18th Virginia Artillery	May 23, 1865
G. W. WRIGHT	private	B	34th North Carolina	May 23, 1865
A. P. ALLEN	private	H	8th Georgia Battalion	May 23, 1865
W. W. KNIER	private	F	49th North Carolina	May 24, 1865
Marcellus GOODWIN	private	E	19th Virginia Battalion	May 24, 1865
W. L. SHELTON	private	H	38th Virginia	May 25, 1865
J. FOWLER	private	F	18th South Carolina	May 25, 1865
G. W. CUNDIFF	private	B	10th Virginia Battalion	May 25, 1865
J. W. REED	private	G	13th Georgia	May 27, 1865
C. J. GRADY	private	H	46th Virginia	May 27, 1865
J. McEWEEN	private	B	1st Eng. Regiment	May 27, 1865
Henry HOLMES	private	E	64th Georgia	May 28, 1865
James GEARY	private	G	Hampton's Legion	May 28, 1865
J. S. GIBBS	private	D	34th North Carolina	May 28, 1865
L. W. ROBERTSON	private	A	20th Virginia Battalion	May 29, 1865
Thomas PARISH	private	D	48th North Carolina	May 29, 1865
Geo. BROCKWOOD	private	C	18th Virginia	May 29, 1865
V. A. PALMER	private	E	Cobb's Georgia Legion	May 30, 1865
James F. MARTIN	private	I	54th North Carolina	May 31, 1865
Jas. OAKLEY	private	I	Hampton's Artillery	May 31, 1865
M. McAULEY	private	E	48th North Carolina	June 1, 1865
T. W. JOHNSON	private	H	46th Virginia	June 2, 1865
Luther YOUNT	private	C	Pogue's Artillery	June 2, 1865
M. JONES	private	D	18th Virginia	June 2, 1865
M. P. DUDLEY	private	H	57th Virginia	June 2, 1865
A. CAMPBELL	private	B	18th South Carolina	June 3, 1865
A. E. WILLIAMS	private	A	18th Virginia Battalion	June 3, 1865
J. W. WOODEN	private	E	5th North Carolina	June 4, 1865
J. M. WHITE	private	A	18th Virginia Battalion	June 4, 1865
Sam'l SPICKARD	sergeant	H	24th Virginia	June 4, 1865
W. D. WRIGHT	private	K	11th Virginia	June 4, 1865
B. B. BAYKEN	corporal	A	15th North Carolina	June 4, 1865
R. McMURRAY	private	K	1st S. C. Eng. Regiment	June 7, 1865
M. A. ELLIS	private	G	48th Georgia	June 7, 1865
J. M. CHAPMAN	private	E	6th North Carolina	June 8, 1865
Thos. GOODWIN	private	A	30th Georgia	June 9, 1865
M. C. HOUSE	private	I	3rd Arkansas	June 9, 1865
C. SLATER	private	H	11th Florida	June 9, 1865
B. B. JACKSON	private	-	Jeff. Davis Arty	June 10, 1865
W. S. CRUISE	private	E	13th Alabama	June 10, 1865
J. LINDSAY	private	I	11th Virginia	June 10, 1865
Louis KNETTEL	private	K	30th Virginia	June 10, 1865
David SWEET	private	E	7th Tennessee	June 10, 1865
William ROUSLEY	private	E	4th North Carolina	June 10, 1865

D. RAY	private	E	57th Virginia	June 11, 1865
J. D. RICE	private	C	6th North Carolina	June 11, 1865
W. G. ANDREWS	lieutenant	C	10th Virginia	June 11, 1865
E. W. LANE	private	C	18th Virginia	June 11, 1865
C. J. FOX	private	F	11th Virginia	June 12, 1865
J. L. DAVIS	sergeant	C	18th Georgia	June 12, 1865
R. M. HUDSON	private	D	19th Virginia	June 12, 1865
Andrew WELLS	private	B	9th Florida	June 12, 1865
S. L. NUNN	private	K	34th Virginia	June 12, 1865
F. M. STONE	private	D	Hampton's Legion	June 12, 1865
E. L. SMITHSON	private	A	56th Virginia	June 13, 1865
W. J. WATERS	private	K	66th Georgia	June 13, 1865
Jacob FRUZELAND	private	A	30th North Carolina	June 14, 1865
W. REDDING	private	H	56th North Carolina	June 14, 1865
J. E. KENT	private	E	Cobb's Legion	June 14, 1865
E. A. MERRELL	private	C	11th Virginia	June 14, 1865
M. F. WELLS	private	B	10th Virginia	June 14, 1865
J. D. REYNOLDS	private	B	38th Virginia	June 15, 1865
James M. CLOUTZ	private	B	11th North Carolina	June 14, 1865
J. R. HARMICLE	private	K	32nd North Carolina	June 15, 1865
David FOLEY	private	A	57th Virginia	June 16, 1865
J. R. DENNIS	private	F	11th South Carolina	June 16, 1865
Jas. L. GUTHRIE	private	D	19th Virginia Battalion	June 16, 1865
J. R. HUFFMAN	private	I	1st Virginia	June 16, 1865
W. L. MANLEY	private	E	25th North Carolina	June 17, 1865
Andrew LEE	private	D	41st Alabama	June 17, 1865
David GREGORY	private	F	41st Alabama	June 17, 1865
W. RAWSEY	private	H	38th Georgia	June 18, 1865
J. B. COOK	private	A	34th Virginia	June 18, 1865
C. SIMMONS	private	K	30th North Carolina	June 18, 1865
A. JACOBS	private	F	11th Florida	June 19, 1865
Wm. MONEGHON	private	H	57th North Carolina	June 19, 1865
Wm. NIXON	private		3rd North Carolina	June 19, 1865
G. A. ANDERSON			Madison Artillery	June 19, 1865
S. I. CRODELL	private	A	1st North Carolina	June 19, 1865
J. BROWN	private		Stribling's Va. Battery	June 19, 1865
M. O. OGLESBY	private	B	10th Florida	June 20, 1865
J. H. VINYARD	private	B	10th Florida	June 21, 1865
W. H. JONES	private	B	30th North Carolina	June 22, 1865
R. BARNES	private	C	16th Georgia	June 23, 1865
P. M. JOHNSON	private	I	41st Alabama	June 23, 1865
Edward M. COX	private	H	Hampton's Legion	June 23, 1865
J. DAVIS	private	F	9th Georgia	June 23, 1865
B. LUCIOUS	private	F	28th Georgia Battalion	June 23, 1865
Wm. SHOEMAKER	private	A	24th Virginia Cavalry	June 23, 1865
J. D. PLUNKETT	private	F	3rd Georgia	June 24, 1865
James E. LANE	private	A	11th Virginia	June 24, 1865
J. H. HOPKINS	private	B	22nd South Carolina	June 24, 1865
R. G. THOMAS	private	H	3rd North Carolina	June 24, 1865
J. WILSON	private	H	2nd North Carolina	June 24, 1865
C. H. KEY	private	G	34th Virginia	June 24, 1865

Name	Rank	Co.	Unit	Date
W. J. BEAN	private	F	23rd North Carolina	June 24, 1865
O. W. MORRIS	private	H	34th Virginia	June 26, 1865
S. BLANKENSHIP	private	C	56th Virginia	June 26, 1865
Alexander BRITT	private	K	3th North Carolina	June 27, 1865
W. C. ALEXANDER	private	B	13rd North Carolina	June 27, 1865
J. E. SIMONS	private	I	2nd Louisiana	June 28, 1865
W. BURGEN	private	A	18th South Carolina	June 28, 1865
Wm S. CUTHBERTSON	private	K	5th North Carolina	June 28, 1865
James M WOOLDRIDGE	private	B	46th Virginia	June 29, 1865
A. J. YOUNGER	private	E	45th North Carolina	June 29, 1865
John HARRIS	private	E	Navy Battalion, N. C.	June 30, 1865
A. K. RICHARDSON	private	B	18th Georgia	June 30, 1865
Samuel HUDGENS	private	A	10th Virginia	July 2, 1865
N. P. BRISTOE	private	A	34th Virginia	July 2, 1865
Wm. SLAUGHTER	private	F	9th Virginia	July 2, 1865
T. D. TRENT	private	C	18th Virginia Battalion	July 3, 1865
Charles GUILL	private	F	53rd Virginia	July 4, 1865

GUY CEMETERY
Hall Road (15) {O - 5}

The Guy Cemetery is situated on a parcel of land that was part of a tract of land acquired by William Hopkins Guy, circa 1817. There are only a few markers existing today. Mr. David Routten and Mr. Barry Miles visited the site together. Mr. David Routten provided the following information: Some from the existing markers, some from past markers and some from information provided to him by persons who lived in the area and are related to the family.

Acknowledgments: Mr. David Routten, Mr. Barry Miles, and Mrs. Betty Harper Wyatt.

Mary A. GUY
wife of Jno. T. GUY
died May 2, 1874
age 33 yrs.

John Thomas GUY
Nov 26, 1828
Oct 19, 1896

Lucy Belle GUY
Dec 26, 1878
July 2, 189?

William M. GIDDINGS
born December 31, 1831
died November 14, 1899
at rest

McGee GIDDINGS
born August 25, 1879
died September 10, 1883

Benjamin F. ROWE
Son of Thomas & Louisa ROWE
died June 17, 1891
at age 26 yrs, 1 month, & 8 days

The following without tombstones

William Hopkins GUY
born 1804
died May 26, 1878

Catharine Snead GUY
wife of William Hopkins GUY
born June 1809
died 1882

Charles GUY
son of Adolphus GUY

Thomas GUY
son of Smith GUY

Parents of
Joseph COLE
and
Mary Cole LEWIS

Jane LEWIS
daughter of
Martin Luther LEWIS
and
Mary Cole LEWIS

Mary Elizabeth Cooper GUY
1st wife of Smith GUY, Sr.

Margaret Ann GUY
daughter of Adolphus &
Sophia GUY

Martha Ann GUY
daughter of Adolphus &
Sophia GUY

HAMPTON UNIVERSITY CEMETERY
Hampton University {19) {K - 11}

- 1867 - Wood Farm purchased. October 1, ground was broken for a temporary building.
- 1868 - With two teachers and fifteen students, General Samuel Chapman Armstrong founded a school for young freedmen who would "go out and teach and lead their people from slavery to economic and social freedom."
- 1870 - Charter granted by the General Assembly of Virginia.
- 1878 - Wigwam, dormitory for Indian boys, built. First party of Indian students arrived April 13. Indians received government aid until 1912.

The above courtesy of the Hampton University Library Archives.

Of principal interest are the Cemeteries on the grounds of Hampton University. The above history explains why American Indians came to be buried on the grounds of Hampton University. Please note the transcriptions of tombstones of the international faculty and students at the School.

The Map of Elizabeth City Co. Va. from actual surveys by E. A. Sample, Wm. Ivy and C. Hubbard and platted by E. A. Sample, Civil Engineer and County Surveyor, copyright Dec 22, 1892, shows the Cemetery by the Normal School.

Acknowledgment: Researched by James H. Mero and transcribed by Barry Miles, May 1997.

Ethel D. Wainwright
CLAIBORNE
Aug 26, 1898
Sept 8, 1980

Helena M. Wainwright
JOHNSON
Jan 7, 1898
Nov 11, 1984

Jessie Cornelia
WAINWRIGHT
Jan 11, 1902

Edith Elizabeth SMITH
Nov 13, 1921
Dec 8, 1992

Frederick D. INGE, PHD
1896 - 1977

Victor Hugo FIELDS
July 11, 1907
Nov 1, 1977
A Servant to his Creator
and to Man Kind ?

"Ace" Henry Lewis LIVAS
Apr 20, 1912
Jun 10, 1979
d/s w/ Alice

"Coke" Alice Smith LIVAS
No Dates
d/s w/ Henry
In Loving Memory

Mildred T. FREEMAN
Mar 30, 1913
Nov 17, 1992
d/s w/ William A.

William A. FREEMAN
July 2, 1900
Oct 8, 1979
d/s w/ Mildred T.

Charles ROBINSON
1908 - 1978
d/s w/ Blanche
"Peace"

Blanche ROBINSON
1909 - no date
d/s w/ Charles
"Peace"

Angle B. OWENS
Sept 17, 1922
Jan 14, 1994
d/s w/ Mattie B.

Mattie B. OWENS
Apr 19, 1921
Aug 4, 1994
d/s w/ Angle B.

Johnelle K. MELVIN
Oct 14, 1909
no date
d/s w/ Horace

Horace W. MELVIN
July 5, 1913
March 23, 1976

John Francis LaCROSSE
Dec 5, 1852
April 12, 1928

Lillian Wallace LaCROSSE
Feb 20, 1858
March 28, 1936

Frederick Jay ROBINSON
Dec 11, 1865
Dec 18, 1930

Adrianna Williams ROBINSON
April 12, 1862
May 20, 1949

Jennie Freeland HARRIS
1900 - 1927
d/s w/ Margaret Booth
fm/ J. F. H.

Margaret Booth FREELAND
1899 - 1928
d/s w/ Jennie
fm/ M. B. F.

Albert A. FREELAND
April 16, 1865
Jan 13, 1927
fm/ A. A. F.

Fred D. WHEELOCK
May 13, 1863
April 23, 1926

Matilda T. WHEELOCK
August 24, 1872
March 23, 1959

Margaret Loring BLODGETT
April 4, 1888
July 22, 1922
Little Daughter
July 17 - 25, 1922
Stone with Metal Plaque

Infant DUTTON
June 16, 1942
June 17, 1942

Isaac HOWE
Dec 13, 1841
June 28, 1919

Lena Jason WHITE
January 1, 1896
March 22, 1979

Laura BETTS
w/o Frederick Williams Dichtel
Aug 19, 1879
Jan 25, 1967

Jennie HOUGHTON
w/o Frank K. Rogers
Aug 3, 1860
April 28, 1915

William H. COLE
died July 16, 1945

Frederic D. GLEASON
born Feb 13, 1867
died July 5, 1910

Eunice Congdon DIXON
born at Leicester, Mass
Jan 11, 1821
died at Hampton Institute
February 27, 1907
A Beloved Friend and
Teacher of the Freedmen
and Their Children in
Loving and Grateful
Remembrance
This Stone is erected by
her old pupils

Sarah K. FELTHAM
w/o Chas. L. Goodrich
Dec 29, 1849
Nov 17, 1901

Mary Elizabeth WINDHAUS
w/o William H. Wittle
died Jan 6, 1907
aged 40 Yrs.

Charles Robert
VAN HORN
June 8, 1913
Dec 14, 1918
Our Darling

Anna Laura CROSS
born July 22, 1856
died June 7, 1924
w/o John W. Cross
at rest

My Husband
John W. CROSS
born December 11, 1849
died September 18, 1909
Aged 59 years at rest

Catharine E. AERY
1859 - 1909

Charlotte FAIRFIELD
born Feb 1864
died March 22, 1917

Stonewall Jackson SCOTT
died Jan 29, 1920
aged 57 years

Clarence Oscar SCOTT
Born Sept 1, 1899
died Nov 28, 1923

Eliza G. RIX
born in Newbern N. C.
died July 28, 1922

Alta G. SPENNIE
born March 22, 1901
died March 24, 1923

Mother
Josephine Elizabeth
SMITH
born Feb 27, 1862
died May 30, 1923

Albert E. F. VAN
BEVERHOUDT
born Jan 5, 1906 Bunker Hill,
St. Thomas, Virgin Islds., USA
died July 26, 1924

Susie Rix SPENNIE
born in Raleigh N. C.
June 1, 1866
died in Hampton, Va.
Nov 7, 1927

Henry Bailey JORDAN Jr.
born March 20, 1909
died Sept 20, 1929

Eliza QUICK
born in Stanfordshire
England, January 13, 1868
died in Hampton Virginia
February 7, 1948
In Service of Hampton
Institute 1906 - 1934

Edward H. SPENNIE
April 1, 1866
Oct 2, 1950

Renaud BROWN
June 13, 1922
Sept 15, 1952

Eliza S. MOORE
June 5, 1903
June 4, 1924
d/s w/ Reginald Q.

Reginald Q. MOORE
Jan 20, 1902
Feb 8, 1975
d/s w/ Eliza S.
In Loving Memory

Harold L. RUGGLES
1896 - 1933
d/s w/ Ruth T.

Ruth T. RUGGLES
1889 - 1975
d/s w/ Harold L.

Dr. Herman N. NEILSON
December 21, 1907
September 14, 1978

Dr. Thomas Wyatt TURNER
1877 - 1978
d/s w/ Laura Miller

Laura Miller TURNER
died 1934
d/s w/ Thomas Wyatt

Jessie S. STINNEFORD
1893 - 1985

Leroy H. STINNEFORD
1897 - 1933

Harold Curtis BLANTON
born July 4, 1913
died March 18, 1933
a short but complete life

Doris C. McNICHOLS
July 1, 1910
Feb 13, 1933

George J. DAVIS
died April 30, 1932
Age 83 Years
d/s w/ Charlotte F.
Foot Mkr. G. J. D.

Charlotte F. DAVIS
died Feb 9, 1937
Age 76 years
d/s w/ George J.
Foot Mkr. C. F. D.

William O. GIBSON
Sept 20, 1957
Nov 27, 1930

Allen WASHINGTON
1866 - 1930
d/s w/ Annie

Annie WASHINGTON
1878 - 1957
d/s w/ Allen

Frank Dean BANKS
Nov 15, 1855
Aug 28, 1930

Susie T. BANKS
June 11, 1868
June 5, 1947

Frederica WALTHER
w/o Charles W. Betts
Oct 12, 1854
Feb 19, 1930

Charles Wilson BETTS
June 8, 1851
Feb 16, 1939

Emma Booth FREELAND
July 7, 1873
Nov 11, 1966
at rest

A. F. EIBELL
Aug 2, 1934

Bessie Hawkins GREEN
1943

Ida Cooke GILBERT
d/s Alf. D. G. & Amelia C.
died July 4, 1915
Age 7 days

Son of F. A. & G. W. BUCK
1904 - 1905

Ida Estelle LaCROSSE
died Feb 5, 1904
Aged 7 Yrs

Sarah A. GOFF
died October 11, 1901
Aged 56 yrs.

Bishop BROWN
born May 16, 1888
died Aug 29, 1918

Theodore V. VANISON
died Nov 10, 1899
Age 14 Years

Missouri F. WHITE
died July 10, 1902
Aged 29 Years
Infant Daughter of
Barton & Missouri
WHITE
died July 22, 1902

Frederick HALE
died July 26, 1903
Aged 20 Yrs.

James Egbert COLES
born Sept 12, 1910
died (Stone sunken in ground)

Eva Roberta COLES
born Nov 17, 1908
died Nov 21, 1908

Estella M. EVANS
Beloved w/o John H.
died July 12, 1919

John H. EVANS
Beloved h/o Estella M.
died December 29, 1910
Asleep

Esther B. AIKEN
born May 31, 1913
died June 9, 1913

Alfred HORTON
Nassau N. P. Bahama Islands
died Sept 29, 1913
Aged 21 Yrs.

Dennis CROELL
born June 5, 1896
died March 10, 1916

Edith BROWN
Dixie Nurse
died Jan 19, 1920

Our Darling
Mary Louise HOWARD
born Jan 11, 1920
died March 29, 1921
Age 1 Yr 2 Mos 18 Days
at rest

Scott G. SIMS
s/o Asa C. Sims
died April 7, 1921

Rosco Howard BOLLING
Jan 9, 1924

Oliver Joshua HUBBARD
born Nov 27, 1922
died Feb 29, 1924

William Little CROW
Sioux, South Dakota
died Oct 28, 1886
Aged 19 Yrs.

Alexander ESTES
Sioux, South Dekota
died Feb 2, 1887
Aged 24 Yrs.

Obed PHELPS
Sioux
born at Hampton
died Mar 21, 1887
Infant

James C. READ
died July 30, 1887
Aged 19 Yrs.

Daniel COOK
died Sept 23, 1887
aged 20 Yrs.

Isham SMITH
died Jan 16, 1888
Aged 23 Yrs.

Frank DOOR
Sioux, South Dakota
died June 28, 1888
Age 19 Yrs

Camaliel ROBERSON
Sioux
born at Hampton
died May 10, 1889
Aged 6 Weeks

James McCOY
Pawnee, Oklahoma
died July 18, 1889
Aged 21 Yrs.

Charles H. FLAX
May 22, 1904
May 1, 198?
A bell is not a bell
until you ring it
A song is not a song
until you sing it
and love is not love
until you share it

Musician, Humanitarian,
Teacher-Founder-Director,
Crusaders, Minister of Music,
Memorial Church, Hampton
Institute;
Directory, Choir Director
Organists Guild of the
Hampton Institute,

Minister Conference.

Tyrrell POLE-ANT
Kiowa, Oklahoma
died Mar 15, 1890
Age 14 Yrs.

Joseph P. WHITE
died June 2, 1890

Children of Frank D. &
Dixie C. BANKS
Frank Gibson
1892 Aged 6 Mo.
Orpheus Marshall
1893, Aged 3 Yrs.
both on one stone

Walter Little EAGLE
Sioux, South Dakota
died July 12, 1892
Aged 16 Yrs.

Sarabheterson VANISON
died Nov 18, 1893

Mary SAMPSON
died Jan 14, 1894
Aged 74 Yrs.

Hattie KELLOGG
Apache, Arizona
died Feb 24, 1895
Aged 15 Yrs.

Samuel HUGHES
died May 10, 1895
Aged 13 Yrs.

Isabella DAVIS
died July 21, 1895
Aged 27 Yrs.

Calixta SANTA CRUZ
of Cieneuegos, Cuba
died April 22, 1899
Aged 51 yrs.

Carl McClellan HILL
July 27, 1907
April 4, 1995
11th President Hampton
Institute - 8th President
Ky State University
Educator - Research -
Administrator

_____
next 3 on same stone

Harriette W. HOWE
D/O Albert & Lydia F. D.
Dec 3, 1867
March 31, 1917
Foot Mkr. H. W. H.

Lydia F. DRESSER
w/o Albert Howe
Dec 28, 1843
Feb 1, 1896
Mother

Albert HOWE
Born Dorchester Mass.
Dec 14, 1836
died March 18, 1925
Foot Mkr. A. H.

_____

Harry Dresser HOWE
s/o Albert & Lydia Howe
born January 12, 1872
died December 27, 1943
a beloved Physician
d/s w/ Elizabeth his wife

Elizabeth Wingate
HOWE
born May 21, 1876
died August 27, 1966
d/s w/ Harry Dresser
Foot Mkr. E.W.H.

Hollis Burke FRISSELL
1852 - 1917
d/s w/ Julia Dodd

Julia Dodd FRISSELL
1853 - 1948
d/s w/ Hollis Burke
f/s J. D. F.

George Perley PHENIX
1864 - 1930
d/s w/ Maria

Maria Stevens PHENIX
1866 - 1966
d/s w/ George

M. S. P.
born in Rangoon, Burma
July 29, 1866
died Feb 26, 1966

Samuel Chapman
ARMSTRONG
born in Hawaii
Jan 30, 1839
died in Hampton
May 11, 1893
Stone with Bronze Plaque

Daniel W. ARMSTRONG
March 12, 1893
July 16, 1947

Edith Armstrong TALBOT
Aug 30, 1872
May 14, 1941
"Songs have replaced the strife
Morning has banished night and
where was death, is life"
E.A.T.

Daniel FIRE-CLOUD
Sioux, South Dakota
died Sept 3, 1886
Aged 14 Yrs

Armstrong FIRE-CLOUD
Sioux, born in Hampton
died Aug 6, 1886
infant

Virginia MEDICINE-BULL
Sioux, South Dakota
died Jan 30, 1896
age 17 years

Louisa BANKS
Sioux, South Dakota
died July 23, 1886
age 11 years

Elizabeth KENNEDY
Sioux, South Dakota
died Jun 21, 1886
Aged 22 Yrs

Simon MAZAKUTE
Sioux, South Dakota
died Mar 26, 1884
Aged 18 Yrs.

Benjamin BEAR-BIRD
Sioux, born in Hampton
died Aug 4, 1885
Age 2 Yrs.

Edith YELLOW-HAIR
Sioux, South Dakota
died Nov 26, 1885
Aged 9 Yrs.

Emma WHIPS
Sioux, South Dakota
died May 25, 1895
Aged 2 yrs

Lora BOWED-HEADSNOW
Sioux, South Dakota
died Mar 20, 1885
Aged 22 Yrs

Mary TURNER
died Jan 18, 1885

Mary PRETTY-HAIR
Sioux, South Dakota
died Jan 6, 1885
Aged 14 Yrs.

Eva GOOD-ROAD
Sioux, South Dakota
died Jan 4, 1884
Aged 17 Yrs.

Lucy Ida BLACK
Sioux, South Dakota
died Dec 23, 1884
Aged 15 Yrs.

Belany SAYON
Zululand, So. Africa
died Dec 10, 1884
Aged 22 Yrs.

Jesse HAWLEY
died Nov 21, 1884
Aged 15 Yrs.

Helen SCOTT
Sioux, South Dakota
died Nov 18, 1884
Aged 7 Yrs.

Edward BUCK
Sioux, South Dakota
died Dec 2, 1884
Aged 1 Year

Mary RED-BIRD
Sioux, South Dakota
died May 30, 1884
Aged 17 Yrs.

CRACKING-WING
Mandan, South Dakota
died Apr 21, 1884
Aged 17 Yrs.

Saluda HUGHES
died Oct 8, 1883
Aged 24 Yrs.

Francesoa RIOS
Papago, Arizona
died Aug 21, 1883
Aged 15 Yrs.

Henry Kendall
ACOlEHUT
Yuma, Arizona
died Aug 13, 1883
Aged 22 Yrs.

LASUTE-WHITE-BACK
Grosventre, North Dakota
died Jan 24, 1882
Aged 15 Yrs.

John BLUE-PIPE
Sioux, South Dakota
died May 3, 1885
Aged 20 Yrs.

Robert C. GREEN
died April 8, 1885
Aged 19 Yrs.

John T. MORRISETTE
died Dec 29, 1885
Aged 29 Yrs.

George BANKS
born Elizabeth City N. C.
died May 3, 1876
Aged 26 Years

Alphonsus HOLLY
s/o Jan. & M. J. Holly
born in Lexington Va.
Jan 1, 1855
died Mar 27, 1871

Joseph ROYAL
died Oct 6, 1873
Aged 18 Yrs.

Thomas NOBLE
died May 28, 1873
Aged 21 Yrs.

Lucy MAYS
died Aug 14, 1875
Aged 16 Yrs.

Infant Daughter of
Don A. DAVIS Jr
May 1955

Olive MADISON
died Mar 1877
Age 21 Yrs.

MAHPLYA-MANI
Sioux, South Dakota
died June 2, 1879
Aged 26 Yrs.

George SHARP-HORN
Arickaree, North Dakota
died Jan 21, 1879
Aged 20 Yrs.

Nick PRATT
Cheyenne, Oklahoma
died May 30, 1879
Aged 18 Yrs.

Francis R. ENCONTRE
Sioux
died Dec 26, 1879
Aged 18 Yrs.

E. CORUPTAHA
Mandan, North Dakota
died June 18, 1880
Aged 20 Yrs.

Grorge Norcross HIPOYA
Mohave, Arizona
died Sept 1, 1881
Aged 18 Yrs.

Enoch Conklin SAVARPKS
Pima, Arizona
died Oct 11, 1881
Aged 17 Yrs.

Joseph TASUNKA-WASTE
Sioux, South Dakota
died Nov 6, 1882
Aged 17 Yrs.

Children of James &
Sarah MILLS on same
stone
In memory
May Aged 3 Mo.
died 1875

Lucy Aged 5 Yrs
died 1876
Susie MILLS
died Oct 16, 1878
Aged 4 Mos.

Lucy Ann SEYMOUR
Sept 24, 1827
died April 12, 1881
cannot read
Foot Mkr. L.A. S.
From WPA records

L. Dwight SEYMOUR
born in Hadley, Mass
April 26, 1819
died in Hampton, Va.
November 12, 1873
Our Beloved Physician
Foot Mkr. L.D.S.

Large stone by cedar tree.
Janette Copeland DAEZIEN
Foot Mkr. J. C. D.
Cannot read any more

Carl A. HABITHAN
s/o of McHarthan
died July 14, 1899
Age 10 mo.

Harriet B. BARTLETT
January 21, 1849
July 23, 1918
at rest with Jesus

Capt. Clearington
Augustus BARTLETT
died Feb 26, 1890
Age 52 Yrs.

Harriet Mason STEVENS
born in Tavoy, Burma
Nov 24, 1841
died in Hampton Va.
Feb 14, 1948
They that turn many to
righteousness shall shine as the
stars for ever and ever.

(cannot read name)
died Dec 30, 1881
Aged 3 Yrs. 2 Mo.
Stone in poor condition

Robert R. MOTON
1867 - 1940
Hampton - Tuskegee

Jennie Dee BOOTH
w/o Robert Rossa Moton
1880 - 1942

Sacred to the Memory of
Georgia A. BOLLING
died May 23, 1946
only asleep

Scared to the memory of
Edward A. BOLLING, Sr.
June 25, 1884
May 20, 1958
only asleep

John Henry WAINWRIGHT
1867 - 1954

Mary Chaney WAINWRIGHT
1872 - 1960

Juliet E. STONEY
died Nov 28, 1987
d/s w/ Ralph S.

Ralph S. STONEY
died March 10, 1974
d/s w/ Juliet E.

Dr. Henry Adam McALISTER
March 16, 1892
March 23, 1967
d/s w/ Mary Brandon

Mary Brandon McALISTER
Aug 16, 1892
Nov 29, 1963
d/s w/ Henry Adam

William Stephen HART
Oct 29, 1894
Sept 13, 1980
d/s w/ Helen Santa Cruz

Helen Santa Cruz HART
Jan 16, 1907
July 5, 1981
d/s w/ William Stephen

Lucy C. COLES
Aug 23, 1867
June 5, 1964

Robert Allen COLES
Aug 12, 1873
Feb 6, 1956

Rosa Belle COLES
Oct 9, 1876
Sept 1, 1946
Foot Mkr. R.B.C.

Gesien M. TESSMANN
1873 - 1941
d/s w/ William M. O.
Foot Mkr. G.M.T.

William M. O. TESSMANN
1869 - 1940
d/s w/ Gesien M.
Foot Mkr. W.M.O.T.

Susie J. HAYES
Oct 5, 1892
d/s w/ Truly W.

Truly W. HAYES
Nov 12, 1891
Sept 21, 1937
d/s w/ Susie J.

Mary Alston
SANTA CRUZ
Dec 14, 1870
July 28, 1959

Alexander SANTA CRUZ
Cientueges Cuba
April 24, 1870
Hampton, Va.
Oct 6, 1936
Foot Mkr. Father

Leigh Richmond MINER
1864 - 1935
"Beautifier of the Campus"

Mildred Jeanette WHITE
Daughter of L. C. &
Z. P. White
July 27, 1920
Aug 29, 1944
Foot Mkr. M.J.W.

John H. JINKS
Oct 21, 1858
Jan 14, 1932
d/s w/ Nancy Mather

Nancy Mather JINKS
June 9, 1865
July 8, 1942
d/s w/ John H.

Clara T. AERY
1871 - 1934

William A. AERY
1882 - 1963

Emily Chadsey DEANE
September 10, 1862
February 24, 1940
fm/ E.C.D.

Marion Colvin DEANE
February 9, 1890
July 2, 1953

Zula Patterson WHITE
w/o Lorenzo C. White
March 9, 1894
Aug 25, 1945
Stone is off pedestal
Foot Mkr. Z.P.W.

Robert B. MILLER
1876 - 1940

Ada N. MILLER
1880 - 1976

William H. KEFFIE
died May 9, 1941

Elaine Evans KEFFIE
Jan 24, 1885
Aug 24, 1981

John B. PIERCE
Aug 9, 1875
Aug 2, 1942
d/s w/ Beatrice J.

Beatrice J. PIERCE
Oct 28, 1881
Aug 3, 1974
d/s w/ John B.

Albert J. CARTER
May 30, 1867
Dec 19, 1942
Husband
Asleep in Jesus
Foot Mkr. A.J._.
broken

Martha S. CARTER
Feb 21, 1873
Jan 3, 1951

Daniel E. TRENT
May 1, 1874
Sept 30, 1944
Erected by USN.T.S.
Hampton, Va.
Foot Mkr. D.E.T.

Baby Boy SCOTT
died Dec 18, 1966

Oscar H. HOUSER
Mar 6, 1913
Aug 25, 1935

John Minor BOTTS
Sept 29, 1889
Feb 24, 1947

BOTTS monument

John Minor BOTTS
principal of George P.
Phenix Training School

Ella Lockhart EVANS
January 24, 1885
January 26, 1948

John Scott EVANS
Feb 27, 1873
Sept 28, 1967

Don A. DAVIS Jr.
Aug 9, 1913
June 20, 1989
d/s w/ Lennie S.

Lennie S. DAVIS
No Dates
d/s w/ Don A.

Martin H. THOMAS
Feb 23, 1901
Feb 7, 1955
Beloved Husband
& Father
Masonic Emblem

Violet HOWARD
September 30, 1859
January 2, 1955

Mary J. MILES
1866 - 1952
Mother

Phoencie L. TULL
Jan 26, 1890
June 26, 1982

John W. B. TULL
July 17, 1885
July 23, 1952

Sara LANE
1869 - 1952

CHENG-YANG
H S U
1897 - 1951
Oriental Rights

Myrtle Palmer JACKSON
June 22, 1892
June 9, 1972
"The world is a better place
because she lived in it."

Lutrelle Fleming PALMER
September 25, 1888
November 18, 1950
"Greater integrity hath no man,
than this, that he gave his life
for an ideal"

Marim D. MANN
July 25, 1907
May 9, 1967

William S. MANN Jr.
June 5, 1903
August 27, 1950

Archer F. CANNADY
Dec 26, 1874
Jan 30, 1950
d/s w/ Mary Lelia

Mary Lelia CANNADY
July 8, 1884
March 16, 1953
d/s w/ Archer F.

Mae Beamon REID
1894 - 1972
d/s w/ William Thaddeus

William Thaddeus REID
1887 - 1950
d/s w/ Mae Beamon

Caroline S. ISHAM
April 1, 1878

Charles S. ISHAM
Jan 4, 1878
Aug 25, 1948

Fannie M. GIBSON
March 7, 1875
Mar 14, 1948

William S. HART Jr.
November 21, 1927
Feburary 12, 1949

Hamlin NELSON Sr.
Aug 28, 1878
June 25, 1949

Maceo A. SANTA CRUZ
July 20, 1898
February 6, 1951

Peter E. BOWMAN
May 12, 1874
Aug 8, 1955
Masonic
d/s w/ Mayme V.

Mayme V. BOWMAN
Aug 10, 1897
Jan 13, 1978

Louise Barbour DAVIS
1905 - 1955
d/s w/ Collis Huntington

Collis Huntington DAVIS
1900 - 1974
d/s w/ Louise Barbour

Eleanor A. GILMAR
Aug 20, 1896
Feb 14, 1975

Joseph Shafter
HIGGINBOTHAM
1898 - 1968
d/s w/ Volena Gale

Volena Gale
HIGGINBOTHAM
1898 - 1963
d/s w/ Joseph Shafter

Julin W. NELSON
May 7, 1900
March 1, 1973

Charles A. NELSON
August 30, 1898
October 15, 1963

Walter C. DOUGLAS
1885 - 1961

Mary S. GRADY
1895 - No Date
d/s w/ Frank L.

Frank L. GRADY
1890 - 1966
d/s w/ Mary S.

Lawson S. RANDALL
1890 - 1983
d/s w/ Niza L.

Niza L. RANDALL
1892 - 1991
d/s w/ Lawson S.

Mamie Latimer RAYSOR
died June 17, 1995

Lorenzo C. WHITE
Feb 28, 1890
Jan 5, 1981

Queen A. COTTON
died Aug 28, 1963
d/s w/ Nannie B.

Nannie B. COTTON
died Aug 19, 1961
d/s w/ Queen A.

William Louis FIELDS
August 28, 1913
May 29, 1960

Charles William YOUNG
September 27, 1903
October 29, 1959

Roscoe E. LEWIS
1904 - 1961
With Bias Toward None

Ednora Mae COOPER
1902 - 1960
Wife

Paige Irving LANCASTER
Virginia 1st Lieutenant
367 infantry World War 1
October 16, 1890
September 20, 1958

Virginia W. TAYLOR
Aug 8, 1910
Oct 31, 1957
Mother

Alpha B. HOLLAND
Oct 4, 1908
Jan 17, 1957

Viola Goin PALMER
August 6, 1912
March 13, 1991

Edward Nelson PALMER
January 30, 1917
August 10, 1956

Bettie V. M. MINKINS
November 5, 1914
December 4, 1994

Bickford E. MINKINS
October 19, 1872
March 11, 1956

Cora Miller BEAMON
1866 - 1955

Janie I. TERRY
April 20, 1882
Oct 25, 1971
d/s w/ Davis H.

David H. TERRY
Aug 1, 1879
Aug 18, 1955
d/s w/ Janie I.

Geraldine Lewis RIDDICK
February 23, 1930
August 14, 1955

TAYLOR _____
No Dates
d/s No Names

Amanda Peele CHEATHAM
Jan 10, 1903
Apr 10, 1978
d/s w/ Ludd Nelson

Ludd Nelson CHEATHAM
Mar 25, 1900
Nov 10, 1974
d/s w/ Amanda

Harriett M. HILL
April 17, 1902
April 17, 1986

Maceo T. WILLIAMS
Dec 5, 1896
March 19, 1968

Rosa Hutchins MAY
1887 - 1971
Jemmies Mother

Mildred George SMITH
May 13, 1888
Sept 3, 1967
Wife & Mother
d/s w/ Gideon Edward

Gideon Edward SMITH
July 13, 1889
May 6, 1968
d/s w/ Mildred
Husband & Father

Annie Laura Fleming
STROUD
Aug 10, 1900
Sept 30, 1966
Mother
d/s w/ Lamar A.

Lamar Alexander STROUD Jr.
Nov 2, 1897
June 27, 1970
d/s w/ Annie Laura

Fred T. WHEELOCK
July 9, 1902
Aug 21, 1966

Alphonso WARREN
1903 - 1966
Stone shape of a bowl

William Hale THOMPSON
June 1914
Jan 1966

Pauline WARREN
April 12, 1913
January 16, 1966

Kay R. LATIMER
May 26, 1894
November 6, 1987

Walter R. BROWN
Nov 21, 1884
July 19, 1968
d/s w/ Lois Sheppard

Lois Sheppard BROWN
Apr 2, 1892
Feb 9, 1981
d/s w/ Walter R.

Virginia Brown CORBIN
June 10, 1919
Dec 21, 1965

Norma Boisseau Armistead
SCOTT
October 24, 1884
August 6, 1977

Lillian P. SMITH
May 22, 1900
May 20, 1965
d/s w/ Clarence A.

Clarence A. SMITH
Oct 4, 1906
No Dates
d/s w/ Lillian P.

Willie McALLISTER
June 22, 1890
Nov 16, 1964

Margaret S. JONES
Feb 13, 1909
No Dates
d/s w/ Walter T.

Walter T. JONES
Feb 2, 1915
Feb 18, 1987
d/s w/ Margaret S.

Clarence A. YOUNG Sr.
1906 - 1982
d/s w/ Adelaide B.

Adelaide B. YOUNG
1908 - 1964
d/s w/ Clarence A.

Mary T. M. SMITH
Oct 8, 1882
March 25, 1964

Elmo Saylor CHRISTY
May 4, 1886
Feb 15, 1966

Nellie Pierce CHRISTY
July 2, 1884
Oct 18, 1870

Marion Grant THORSTON
Feb 20, 1897
Aug 31, 1973

Charles H. WILLIAMS
1886 - 1978
d/s w/ Alma M.

Alma M. WILLIAMS
1899 - 1988
d/s w/ Charles H.

Thomas White YOUNG
1908 - 1967

Lillian B. JONES
Jan 29, 1891
June 10, 1968

Llewellyn M. BERRY
Sept 5, 1906
Oct 17, 1968

Ethel D. DAVIS
1889 - 1973
d/s w/ Don Andrew

Don Andrew DAVIS
1890 - 1969
d/s w/Ethel D.

Wendell L. THOMPSON Sr.
May 10, 1897
March 27, 1969
d/s w/ Ida B.

In Loving Memory
Ida B. THOMPSON
March 16, 1900
April 15, 1968
d/s w/ Wendell L.

Asa C. SIMS
Nov 4, 1888
May 3, 1972
d/s w/ Ethel C.

Ethel C. SIMS
April 24, 1896
June 5, 1969
d/s w/ Asa C.

Louise G. ARMSTRONG
Nov 26, 1910
Aug 29, 1973
In Loving Memory

Aubrer E. COLES
Virginia CM2 USNR
World War 2
Feb 9, 1917
Jan 20, 1970

Addie WYCHE
May 21, 1904
Jan 31, 1989
d/s w/ Elliott

Elliott WYCHE
July 5, 1906
Jan 27, 1986
d/s w/ Addie

William H. MOSES
1901 - 1991
d/s w/ William & Julia

William H. MOSES 3rd
1938 - 1991
d/s w/ William & Julia

Julia M. MOSES
1913 - 1993
d/s w/ William & William

John Wesley LEWIS
March 23, 1898
Oct 7, 1985
d/s w/ Ursula Fleming

Ursula Fleming LEWIS
Jan 5, 1903
Nov 1, 1976
d/s w/ John Wesley

Ada S. TAYLOR
June 15, 1898
Apr 25, 1987
d/s w/ Oliver G.

Oliver G. TAYLOR Sr.
Apr 4, 1892
Apr 17, 1975
d/s w/ Ada S.

Sadie Lee Marchant
PERKINS
Sept 20, 1905
Feb 3, 1992
Spirited and well
Loving and Beloved

Herbert A. PERKINS
LCDR US Navy W W 2
Oct 9, 1900
Aug 31, 1992
Professor of Mathematics

Annie Hamm WALKER
May 29, 1907
Sept 11, 1975
d/s w/ Frissell C.

Frissell C. WALKER
Oct 3, 1905
d/s w/ Annie Hamm

Inez Fields SCOTT
March 13, 1900
Aug 9, 1978
d/s w/ Frederick

Frederick Conklin
SCOTT
Nov 2, 1887
Sept 6, 1974
d/s w/ Inez Fields

Maretha "Marie" R.
EBB
April 10, 1893
July 4, 1974

Laura V. BILLUPS
Daughter No Dates

Mary B. JOHNSON
July 7, 1883
March 19, 1974
Mother

Amanda N. ADAMS
May 26, 1904
Sept 24, 1978

James M. ADAMS
March 10, 1906
July 27, 1981

John RIDDICK
Dec 23, 1889
Feb 4, 1986
d/s w/ Mamie

Mamie RIDDICK
Mar 20, 1886
Dec 15, 1983
d/s w/ John

Beulah W. HOWARD
w/o Thomas J. Howard
Sept 19, 1876
May 10, 1973

Dr William R.
STRASSNER
Jan 2, 1900
May 4, 1994
d/s w/ M. Frances

M. Frances STRASSNER
Mar 31, 1902
No Date
d/s w/ William R.

Warren Thomas
JONES
February 26, 1916
September 20, 1972

James T. ALTON
Feb 15, 1907
July 14, 1972
At rest

Lucile W. WILLIAMS
June 27, 1894
Jan 25, 1975

William H. ROBINSON
July 20, 1908
July 11, 1990

Waders Jack TYGER
July 16, 1907
June 6, 1978
d/s w/ Eva Session

Eva Session TYGER
No Dates
d/s w/ Wader Jack

Ethel Harrell FOXX
Dec 15, 1919
Oct 10, 1971

Vera E. PERRY
No Dates
d/s w/ Isaiah B.
In Loving Memory

Isaiah B. PERRY
Aug 17, 1920
Sept 24, 1971
d/s w/ Vera E.

Frances M. EAGLESON
July 17, 1898
May 18, 1987
Her voice was ever
low and sweet

Josephine B. DUTTON
1913 - No Date
d/s w/ Benson L.

Benson L. DUTTON
1910 - 1992
d/s w/ Josephine B.

Graves on Left side
of driveway

Edward N. JONES
July 25, 1914
Dec 6, 1996

Maurice S. JACKSON
July 6, 1921
No Date
d/s w/ Jules F.

Jules F. JACKSON
Aug 5, 1920
Nov 1994
d/s w/ Maurice S.

Eleanor J. MOORE
1912 - 1992
d/s w/ Sylvius S.

Sylvius S. MOORE
1912 - No Date
d/s w/ Eleanor J.

Verdell W. CHATMAN
Aug 6, 1925
March 19, 1992
In God Trust

Ivy M. BURDEN
Jan 17, 1924
Nov 6, 1990
Stone shape of heart
In Loving Memory
the family

Dorothy P. COTTON
died July 12, 1993
d/s w/ James Alton
Into thy hands I
Commend my spirit

James ALTON
Feb 14, 1902
May 10, 1990
d/s w/ Dorothy P.
Cotton

Nancy B. McGHEE
Mar 19, 1908
Feb 10, 1995
Wife
d/s w/ Samuel C.

Samuel C. McGHEE
Aug 1, 1917
Apr 9, 1990
Husband
d/s w/ Nancy B.

Russell L. HARRISON
Dec 11, 1922
Apr 14, 1986

Vivien Lipscombe SMITH
July 8, 1943
In Loving Memory

Edward T. LIPSCOMBE
March 15, 1913
No Date
d/s w/ Louise H.

Louise H. LIPSCOMBE
May 7, 1912
Oct 27, 1986
In Loving Memory
d/s w/ Edward T.

Theresa Sims SMITH
March 9, 1920
Feb 23, 1987
A Delicate Flower

Ruth DICKINS
December 12, 1912
January 4, 1988

Robert L. ANDERSON
1917 - 1987
d/s w/ Jeanette H.
Memory is the only thing
that grief can call her own

Jeanette H. ANDERSON
1917 - No Date
d/s w/ Robert L.

Willie T. GLOVER
Oct 13, 1934
July 26, 1987
In Loving Memory

Ruby M. BURKE
May 10, 1913
Sept 25, 1988
In Loving Memory

Julian H. LIPSCOMBE
June 29, 1911
d/s w/ Lucy S.

Lucy S. LIPSOCMBE
July 23, 1918
Oct 4, 1984
In Loving Memory
d/s w/ Julian H.

Joseph W. GILLIARD
1914 - No Date
d/s w/ Bertha L.

Bertha L. GILLIARD
1910 - 1990
Humanity and art

through the ages
d/s w/ Joseph W.

Robert Aaron RICE
Dec 24, 1915
Nov 2, 1985
d/s w/ Eleanor Lundy

Eleanor Lundy RICE
Dec 10, 1921
Apr 16, 1993
I will say of the
Lord he is my refuge
and my fortress
d/s w/ Robert Aaron

Sylvester W. BANKS
Sept 23, 1909
April 4, 1985
In Loving Memory

Katrina L. BANKS
Aug 14, 1902
Jan 7, 1992
Beloved Mother
& "Auntie"

Clinton R. PARKS Sr.
Jan 4, 1906
April 24, 1984

J. Stanley CARTER
1908 - 1984
d/s w/ Julia T.

Julia T. CARTER
No Date
d/s w/ J. Stanley

James S. CARTER Jr.
Virginia PVT 3441 SVC
Comd Unit
Sept 28, 1932
Dec 26, 1959

Rev. Seymour J. GAINES
May 4, 1919
March 23, 1983
Pastor of 1st Baptist
Church, Hampton
1967 - 1983

Allie L. GAINES
April 4, 1919
No Date

Fredinand V. JOHNSON
1911 - 1983
d/s w/ Alma L.

Alma L. JOHNSON
No Dates
d/s w/ Fredinand V.

Audrey B. COOPER
Mar 7, 1941
d/s w/ William M.

William M. COOPER
Nov 22, 1892
Aug 12, 1979
A great humanitarian
Together Forever
d/s w/ Audrey B.

Mary Anne COOKE
Jan 28, 1907
March 23, 1980
d/s w/ Garland A.

Garland A. COOKE
Aug 22, 1913
Oct 6, 1979
d/s w/ Mary Anne

Clarissa D. BANKS
No Dates
d/s w/ Lewis E.

Lewis E. BANKS
June 1, 1912
Oct 25, 1979
Together forever
d/s w/ Clarissa D.

Montrose T. BROWN
No Dates
d/s w/ John W.

John W. BROWN Sr.
Aug 10, 1914
March 7, 1982

Cornelius W. SHERMAN
Jul 26, 1934
No Dates
d/s w/ Shirley C.

Shirley C. SHERMAN
Apr 1, 1935
Nov 29, 1982
If we have no Dreams
d/s w/ Cornelius W.

Stone Covered
with wood

Howard S. KEMP
August 1, 1927
November 10, 1898

Christopher M. KEMP
June 8, 1890
Jan 7, 1981
d/s w/ Lillian W.

Lillian W. KEMP
April 13, 189-
April 8, 1989
d/s w/ Christopher M.

Dowling M. BOLTON
1915 - 1981
d/s w/ Lorraine W.

Lorraine W. BOLTON
1917 - 1979
d/s w/ Dowling M.

Types of tombstone in
Hampton University Cemetery
Botton is on of the
American Indian Tombstone

Cemeteries of the City of Hampton, Virginia / formerly Elizabeth City County

HANSFORD CEMETERY
Rockwell Road (83) {K -4}

On 19 April 1997, Barry Miles went to the see the Wallace/Tennis Cemetery and the Hansford Cemetery on Rockwell Road. Both cemeteries are on the same private property and the owner refused the Genealogical Society's request to record the tombstone data, and no pictures could be taken. Mr. Miles was allowed to visit the sites. There is only one stone in the Wallace/Tennis with two inscriptions, and only one tombstone in the Hansford Cemetery. The owner's request is here by granted and no pictures or address is given.

The following information is from the Hampton Public Library the information on the Hansford - Tennis (Graveyard) Cemetery is one Confederate soldier.

"James HANSFORD
Co D. 9 Va. Inf.
C.S.A.
1842 - 1905

WALLACE FAMILY

"**Rev. James W. WALLACE**

Evidence has been found that the Indians enjoyed hunting and fishing in this area. A number of arrow-heads and Indian artifacts have been found on the property, but the earliest colonist to own this property was the Rev. James W. WALLACE, who was The Rector of St. John's Church from 1691-1712. he was born about 1667 in Scotland. In his will he requested that he be buried on his plantation "ERROLL" on "BACK RIVER".

He named his plantation "ERROLL" from his home "Enroll" in Perthshire, Scotland. "Back River" was called Back River because it was at the back of a number of beautiful plantations along this River.

The Rev. WALLACE has vast land holdings in this area of Elizabeth City County. He owned many slaves. He was also a Doctor of Medicine and was a very clever business man. Rev. WALLACE had a grandson named, Capt James W. WALLACE, who was a Burgess from 1769-1772, a Justice of the Peace, a Vestryman at St. Johns, and a member of the Committee of Safety during the Revolutionary War. The actual plantation home of the WALLACES was not right her, but farther up the River on this same side where the old Shelton Farm was. There are many Descendants of this family still living in Hampton and the Fox Hill area.

As almost all the old large plantations were divided among heirs and some portions sold; so it was with this one, and we find a large portion of the WALLACE Plantation "ERROLL" was sold to Thomas HANSFORD of York County."

The following paper was prepared June 1964 for the Historical Society, Second Annual Historical Tour by Ellen Iromonger Pearson (Mrs. Henry A.).

HANSFORD FAMILY

"The HANSFORD family is an old and very interesting family, and I might, say, a very famous Family.

John HANSFORD, The immigrant, settled in York County before 1630.
His son:

1. Thomas HANSFORD was very prominent during Bacon's Rebellion; he was very loyal to Bacon, and if you remember your history, he was one of Bacon's trusted Captains! After Bacon died suddenly many of his men were captured including Thomas. Gov. Berkeley ordered him hung to make him an example. Thomas HANSFORD has gone down in history as the "FIRST MARTYR FOR AMERICAN INDEPENDENCE".

2. Another son of John HANSFORD, the immigrant, Charles HANSFORD, was the great-great-grandfather of the HANSFORD who bought this property. Charles HANSFORD married Elizabeth FOLIOTT, the daughter of the Rector of Hampton Parish of York County, Virginia. This Elizabeth FOLIOTT was a direct descendant of King EDWARD I of England, through his daughter, JOAN.

3. At another time, before the Revolutionary War, one of the HANSFORD wives was arrested and tried in a York county court and fined for 'singing a Song against the King'.

Thomas HANSFORD Our Thomas HANSFORD who purchased a portion of the WALLACE Plantation (the great-great-grandson of Charles who married Elizabeth) was a very influential citizen and had vast property holdings. In addition to this property, he inherited 75 acres from his father, Richard HANSFORD, in York county; through his wife, Hannah DAVIS, he acquired another 311 acres that she had inherited from her Father. He owned land in the Town of Hampton and land joining the Town of Hampton. His land in Hampton was situated on the "Old Hospital" site.

The Thomas HANSFORD home was located down this lane, close to the water. He operated an Ordinary or Store on the same site, and Sea Captains and Boatmen came to his Store for provisions and supplies.

As Rev. WALLACE had divided his plantation, so, many years later, Thomas HANSFORD divided his land among his heirs. The records show that he and Hannah DAVIS had five (5) children, but this property was divided among three (3) of them:

James D. HANSFORD
John HANSFORD
Missoura HANSFORD

James and John HANSFORD inherited this property which included the **Cemetery**. James built the first house on this site. James later sold his interest to his brother, John, and later John sold to Mr. James TENNIS.

Missouri HANSFORD Missoura HANSFORD inherited the old Thomas HANSFORD home, the ordinary, slave quarters, barns, etc. She married Horace JETT. The old Thomas HANSFORD home burned in the late 1890's and Missorua's son, Robert JETT and his wife Mary Virginia UNDERWOOD, built this present home in the early 1900's-before World War 1. Their son, John JETT lives there now. He showed me the old well, the bricks of the foundation of the old Thomas HANSFORD home and slave's quarters."

TENNIS FAMILY

Three generations of the TENNIS Family have lived right here on this property that was later owned by Mr. and Mrs. W. E. Cheyne (Happy Cheyne).

James and Casandra Bunting TENNIS (She was from the Eastern Shore).
Their son:

Benjamin and Angelina Watkins TENNIS and their children.
The widow of Benjamin TENNIS married Callie KRATZER. He survived her many years, and lived right here until his death.

Nell Hudgins PRICE (Mrs. Claude O.), the granddaughter of Benjamin TENNIS, said the WATKINS family lived directly across the River, where Langley Air Force Base is now located, in a large white house that was situated on a point. The TENNIS and WATKINS families were very friendly. In the summer they visited back and forth by boat, and in winter the River froze so solid they drove back and forth by horse and buggy. So, the TENNIS son, Benjamin, and the WATKINS daughter, Angelina, fell in love and married. They lived here and raised their family right here.

Mr and Mrs W. E. CHEYNE

As I said, this property was more recently owned by Mr. and Mrs. Happy CHEYNE. This is the third home on this site. The first was built by James HANSFORD. It Burned. The second was built by James TENNIS. It was partially burned. Benjamin TENNIS built the present house. The CHEYNES have added extensive repairs inside and out since they purchased the property.

Cemeteries of the City of Hampton, Virginia / formerly Elizabeth City County

THE HANSFORD CEMETERY

I have given you a little background of the people who have lived and died here on this property and are now resting in this Cemetery. It has been called the HANSFORD CEMETERY for many, many years, and dates back to the early 1700's. It was a Family Cemetery many years before the Revolutionary War.

This huge Sycamore Tree is said to be about 500 years old. It was over 80 feet tall during the Revolutionary war. For many years Sea Captains and Boatmen coming in Back River would take a bearing on this Tree and set their course to come in the River without any difficulty. It was called the "LOOK OUT" tree. You can tell it is aged old, and they say it was a very beautiful tree until 20 years ago - lightening struck it and knocked the top out of it. I think it is still beautiful!

SOME OF THE PEOPLE BURIED HERE

1. **The Rev. and Mrs. James Wallace.** About 50 or 60 years ago, when the Rev. Carter Brackston BRYAN was Rectory of St. Johns, he was very historical minded, and because Mr. WALLACE had also been a St. John's Rector, he was influential in having the stone from Mr. and Mrs. WALLACE'S graves moved to St. Johns; they were later moved to the old Pembroke Cemetery on Pembroke Avenue. But their bodies and graves are still here.

2. **Thomas and Hannah Davis HANSFORD** are buried here. Their son:

3. **Mr. James HANSFORD** is buried here. He was a Confederate Veteran. He was badly wounded at Drury's Bluff. He had a confederate marker on his grave for many years, and for years the Daughter of the United Daughters of the Confederacy visited his grave and brought flowers and flags each Memorial Day.

4. **Missoura Hansford JETT** and her husband, **Horace JETT**, are resting here.

5. **James and Casandra Bunting TENNIS** are buried here.

6. **Benjamin TENNIS** is buried here. The large English Box shrub marks Benjamin's grave. Angelina Watkins Tennis KRATZER is buried in St. John's with her second Husband, Callie KRATZER.

7. A number of children are known to be buried here:

   a. The daughter of Mr. and Mrs. Joseph TENNIS. Her name was "**Tribulation TENNIS**".

   b. A baby girl of the **STACEY** Family. (Mrs STACEY is the granddaughter of

Missouri Hansford JETT.)

 c. **William JETT**, a small son of Mr. and Mrs. Robert JETT. (Robert JETT was the son of Missoura Hansford JETT.)

8. The last person to be buried here was:

 a. Mr **Paul A. TENNIS**, the son of Benjamin and Angelina Watkins TENNIS. This was after World War 1. John JETT was a pallbearer.

Elizabeth Jett OLDFIELD, Robert JETT'S daughter, said this Cemetery was many times larger than it is now. She knows it was originally a very large Cemetery, and can remember it being larger than it is today when she was a little girl. It is owned by the Robert JETT heirs. As the years went by and the fields were plowed and crops planted, the Cemetery became smaller and smaller until it is as you see it today. Three stones are visible on the side, and Mrs. CHEYNE says there are about 5 graves clearly visible during the winter on the other side. The Cemetery is located in the yard of the Cheyne property.

REFERENCES
 Records: Elizabeth City County
       York County
 Interviews with:
      Mrs Taylor Ransone, historian of St. John's Church.
      Mrs Thelma Ironmonger Hansford, author of the Book: "History of the HANSFORD Family", pages 170-173.
      Mrs Nell Hudgins Price (deceased)
      Mrs Elizabeth Jett Oldfield
      Mr. John Jett (deceased)
      Mr. and Mrs Cheyne died without issue and left their estate to VMI, Lexington, Va."

HEBREW CEMETERY
Kecoughtan Road (38) {G - 13}

This Cemetery is well maintained and compact, but some tombstones are overturned. There are a variety of types of tombstones, and many different and unique stones in this cemetery. We have chosen not to put long inscriptions in the book, as that would greatly extend the transcription time and extent the length of the book. There are about thirteen hundred interments with markers. As with the Rosenbaum Cemetery, this cemetery uses mostly a family monument and a small stone at the foot of the grave to document the personal data. With this method of documenting the interment, We used the same system in both the Hebrew and Rosenbaum Cemeteries. If there is a family monument with only the family name, it was entered in the data in capital letters and the data from the smaller stone followed. If the data was from a headstone, then it is followed with (h/s). If there is no notation, then the data came from a foot stone.

There will be entries from this cemetery which will say "Books". When Hebrew Books containing the word of God are worn out they are not destroyed, but buried according to custom.

OSER

Abe E. OSER
Oct 28, 1895
Jan 7, 1981
Beloved Husband & Father

OSER

Louis E. OSER
Nov 28, 1893
May 6, 1968
Beloved Husband & Father

Dorothy Dora OSER
Dec 25, 1892
Jan 10, 1978
Beloved Wife & Mother

OSER

Harry OSER
May 8, 1896
Jan 9, 1980
Beloved Husband & Father

OSER

Sylvan OSER
April 30, 1900
Jan 21, 1967

Edith G. OSER
March 2, 1902
Jan 12, 1976

SCOLL

Irvin L. SCOLL
Sept 25, 1900
Nov 27, 1956

Ruth E. SCOLL
Jan 1, 1908
March 30, 1970

Julius FINK
March 17, 1899
Jan 23, 1936
Husband - Father h/s

Alfred D. PELTZ
died Feb 3, 1930
w/ Henry M. h/s

Henry M. PELTZ
died June 29, 1929
w/ Alfred D. h/s

Marvis (in Hebrew) h/s

Infant son of Sam and
Mary SIEGEL
died Nov 1, 1943 h/s

Infant son of Maurice
and Rose C. ERLACH
July 17, 1932 h/s

Norma R. SHERR
Born April 18, 1938
died Dec 14, 1936 h/s

Neil Morton BALSER
Born June 23, 1933
died Dec 14, 1936 h/s

Marvin Tubin BALSER
died Oct 27, 1950 h/s

Miriam MALNICK
died Dec 28, 1928 h/s

Julius HOLZSWEIG
died Aug 21, 1927
age 12 years h/s

Bernard MOSKOWITZ
born July 4, 1922
died Jan 16, 1927 h/s

FRANK

Nettie FRANK
died June 20, 1948
Mother

Joe FRANK
died Feb 19, 1925
Father

Leo Ike
son of Ben & F. B.
GORDON
born dec 6, 1900
died Dec 15, 1909
Rest in Peace
stone off pedestal h/s

Berna LEE
died 2 Jun 1900 h/s

Myer LIRMAN
died May 16, 1900
stone off pedestal h/s

Frances daughter of
Ben & F. B. GORDON
born Jan 15, 1900
died March 10, 1900
Rest in Peace h/s

Abraham AUSTRAIN
died March 20, 1922 h/s

Sarah S. PELTZ
w/o H. M. Peltz
aged 49 years h/s
Mother f/s

Goldie PELTZ
born Oct 29, 1893
died June 23, 1911 h/s
daughter f/s

Max SHAFFER
died Jan 16, 1958

Abraham AURBACH
Dec 4, 1901 h/s

Annie I. LINKRAMM
died Dec 20, 1901 h/s

Florance LEVY
born Sept Aug 29, 1897
died July 4, 1903 h/s

Bernard son of
Wm. & Bertha GORDON
born Aug 12, 1919
died Sept 15, 1919 h/s

Anna F. LEVY
died Oct 24, 1905 h/s

Books

Rose SAMET
died June 28, 1904 h/s

Jacob ROSENBLOCH
died April 8, 1905 h/s

Our Darling
Alfred AKERMAN
born July 12, 1897
died Dec 27, 1905
aged 8 yrs 6 mos h/s

Rachel daughter of Dave and
Sarah DAVIDSON
born Nov 13, 1895
died Dec 7, 1906
May her soul rest in peace

Hadaso POLISH
died Nov 25, 1907 h/s

Lena BERGER
born Dec 20, 1889
died Dec 3, 1907 h/s

My Sister
Fannie E. COHEN
died Dec 1907
age 2 years h/s

Our Beloved Mother
Annie COHEN
died Dec 17, 1907 h/s

Irvin CARMEL
born Oct 20, 1918
died Feb 15, 1920 h/s

_____ POLISH
died Nov 9, 1908
w/ Davis h/s

Hyman Davis POLISH
died Nov 4, 1908
w/ Hyman h/s

Rose E. MOREWITZ
died Mar 15, 1917 h/s

Rosie SHARF
born July 26, 1913
died Nov 5, 1920 h/s

Sarah E. SIEGEL
died Nov 5, 1920
age 5 years h/s

Charles POMERANZ
New York
PFC US Army
World War 1
September 26, 1893
July 17, 1961
h/s Military

Morris ODIS
Virginia
PVT Btry B 4 TM BM Cac
World War 1
December 5, 1982
March 12, 1962
h/s Military

Morton Isaac HOLZSWEIG
born Aug 2, 1917
died Mar 28, 1918 h/s

Bessie M. EPSTEIN
died May 31, 1921 h/s

infant son LAZARUS
born Feb 27, 1939
died Mar 2, 1939 h/s

Louis HERZEKOW
died Aug 16, 1936
age 75 years h/s

Joseph FRANKLIN
died Feb 4, 1918 h/s
stone laying on ground

Esther SNITZ
no dates h/s

Celia BERMAN
died Oct 8, 1918 h/s

S. WILKS
born Nov 7, 1906
died April 22, 1918 h/s

Mother
Eva COPPEL
died Jan 26, 1961 h/s
Mother f/s

David GOLDBERG
died June 8, 1916
aged 28 years h/s

William SIMON
New York
PVT US Army
World War 1
July 15, 1886
April 6 1971
Military h/s

Books

Dora MOREWITZ
died Feb 5, 1929
d/s w/ John A. h/s
Mother f/s

John A. MOREWITZ
died Feb 6, 1918
d/s w/ Dora
Father f/s

Nayton WHITE
born 1887
died March 24, 1914 h/s

Julius SMITH
1891 - 1913 h/s
Brother f/s

Hirsh GLASSMAN
1893 - 1912 h/s

A. H. MOREWITZ
1852 - 1912 h/s

Benedict SILVER
died Feb 1, 1912 h/s

Jacob LENETSKY
born Feb 22, 1861
died Nov 2, 1910
age 49 h/s

Max LEIBOWITZ
died April 12, 1907 h/s

Samuel WHITE
died Aug 10, 1905
aged 51 years h/s

Morton Emanuel
WEINBERGER
New Jersey
S2 USNR
World War 2
Feburary 20, 1920
September 7, 1968
Military h/s

Harry E. PELTZ
born Aug 7, 1895
died June 22, 1911 h/s

Meyer ROTHSCHILD
PVT 111 PA INF
February 23, 1910 h/s

Belle AUSTRAIN
died Dec 27, 1904 h/s
stone off pedestal

Fannie GRONER
died May 29, 1904
Aged 19 years h/s
Sister f/s

Sarah LEVINSON
died Nov 14, 1903 h/s

Freidel S. PELTZ
died July 15, 1901
Aged 64 years h/s

Annie T. LEIBOWITZ
died Nov 1, 1900
aged 26 yrs 6 mos h/s

Sarah LEVINETZKY
died Feb 4, 1899
aged 37 years h/s

Moses DRELICK
died Nov 23, 1902 h/s

Moses AUSTAIN
died Jan 14, 1902 h/s

Jacob SOLOMON
born Oct 10, 1846
died Jan 5, 1902 h/s

Louis MANN
died April 27, 1900 h/s

MIRMELSTEIN

Etta Beck MIRMELSTEIN
Oct 31, 1884
June 4, 1958
Beloved wife & Mother

Samuel A. MIRMELSTEIN
March 12, 1881
Nov 30, 1981 h/s
Beloved Husband & Father

Rebecca MIRMELSTEIN
died Jan 15, 1912
age 59 yrs h/s
Mother f/s

Stone on ground
face down

I. LEVY
born 1877
died April 14, 1911 h/s

Meyer SCOLL
born Sept 25, 1872
died Jan 10, 1935 h/s
Father f/s

W. SCOLL
died May 29, 1919 h/s
Father f/s

Ray FRIEDBERG
died Sept 25, 1922 h/s
Mother f/s

Dora SCOLL
born Dec 14, 1879
died Aug 1, 1943 h/s
Mother f/s

Rev. Abraham Benzion
MIRMELSTEIN
died April 28, 1920
age 72 yrs. h/s
Father f/s

B. M. OSER
died Sept 6, 1920 h/s
Father f/s

Hannah R. OSER
died 29, 1945 h/s
Mother f/s

Beryl Morton OSER
born Dec 31, 1922
died March 26, 1935
Thus died a Saint
To us who loved him
He is not dead but ever lives.
h/s
son f/s

Bertha Fisch SPIGEL
died Feb 10, 1925
age 29 years h/s
Darling we miss thee
Sister f/s

COHEN

Ida COHEN
died Dec 5, 1926

Isaac COHEN
died July 8, 1931

Louis FISCH
died Nov 8, 1931
age 90 years h/s
Father f/s

Sarah M. BRAVERMAN
died Jan 7, 1929
age 67 years h/s
d/s w/ Isaac

Isaac BRAVERMAN
died Aug 27, 1928
age 72 years h/s
d/s w/ Sarah M.

FRIEDMAN

Mollie FRIEDMAN
born Dec 25, 1895
died Dec 22, 1970

Samuel FRIEDMAN
born Nov 24, 1891
died April 28, 1949

BLECHMAN

Eva BLECHMAN
born March 15, 1876
died Aug 28, 1943
Mother

Julius BLECHMAN
born March 25, 1873
died July 24, 1965

NACHMAN

Sadye C. NACHMAN
born Nov 26, 1898
died Nov 11, 1944

Harry L. NACHMAN
born Aug 29, 1895
died Feb 24, 1972

MIRMELSTEIN

Fannie Binder
MIRMELSTEIN
June 6, 1892
June 5, 1945
Mother

Louis B. MIRMELSTEIN
Oct 28, 1889
April 7, 1960
Father - Masonic

MASSELL

Fannie M. MASSELL
June 20, 1875
June 17, 1963
Beloved Mother

Herman MASSELL
Aug 15, 1872
April 11, 1947
Beloved Father

NACHMAN

Sarah NACHMAN
Oct 21, 1977

Harry J. NACHMAN
May 26, 1984

Abe NACHMAN
Feb 1, 1895
Feb 8, 1972

Robert LAZARUS
died Sept 10, 1929 h/s
Father f/s

Fannie GREENSPON
died Dec 23, 1928
age 75 years h/s
Mother f/s

Hannah MORRIS
died March 8, 1928
age 71 years h/s

Abraham MORRIS
died June 17, 1925
age 69 years h/s

LEVINSON

Elizabeth M. LEVINSON
born October 16, 1890
died March 24, 1977

Isaac J. LEVINSON
born August 21, 1883
died June 6, 1956

LEVINSON

Celia LEVINSON
born March 10, 1878
died Dec 6, 1946

Max LEVINSON
born April 15, 1872
died June 17, 1956

LEVINSON

(in Hebrew) h/s
Father

Rosa LEVINSON
died Nov 14, 1955
age 93 years h/s
Mother f/s

Beckei SHAPIRO
died Aug 12, 1921 h/s
Mother f/s

Rebecca MEYER
died Sept 22, 1910
In loving Memory of our
Mother May her soul
rest in peace h/s

Sarah HOLZSWEIG
died March 22
1910 - 5670

Samuel SCHAIRWITZ
(No Dates) h/s
Stone face down on ground

Books h/s

Riska COOPER
died July 13, 1906
aged 50 years h/s

Sarah E. SHERMAN
born 1867 - died 1907 h/s
stone off pedestal

Kreine LEVY
born Jan 24, 1839
died Sept 25, 1907 h/s

Rachel M. LUKOWITZ
born 5598 - died 5668
March 1, 1903 h/s

Annie FELSTERN
died Jan 20, 1909 h/s
Wife f/s

Charles FISH
Feb 22 1881
Jan 30, 1920 h/s
Brother f/s

Hannah Pika FISH
died Dec 24, 1903 h/s
Mother f/s

(In Hebrew) h/s

Our darling
Sarah NACHMAN
died Nov 12, 1897
aged 28 years h/s

Chave Esther NACHMAN
died Sept 13, 1900
age 62 years h/s
C. E. N. f/s

Joshua NACHMAN
died April 13, 1904
aged 69 years h/s
J. N. f/s

B. NACHMAN
died Nov 28, 1905
aged 43 years h/s
B. N. f/s

Sarah NACHMAN
died Dec 3, 1911 h/s
S. N. f/s

David ROSENBALT
died Aug 20, 1898 h/s
D. R. f/s

Joseph J. BERMAN
1864 - 1899 h/s
Father F/s

Head stone missing
J. K. f/s

Joseph MICHAELSON
died April 12, 1900
d/s w/ Roaa h/s
J. M. f/s

Rosa MICHAELSON
died April 13, 1900
d/s w/ Joseph (stone broken)
R. M. f/s

David BAKER
died Sept 11, 1900
age 35 years h/s
D. B. f/s (stone broken)

L. MAYER
died July 6, 1902 h/s

Norman AURBACH
died March 1, 1908 h/s

Moses KAPLAN
died March 9, 1911-5671
(stone broken) h/s

Ida LEVY
died May 23, 1919 h/s
Sister f/s

Bennie SMITH
died May 23, 1919 h/s
Son f/s

Hyman SMITH
died May 23, 1919
age 31 years h/s
Husband f/s

Tena SMITH
died Dec 2, 1921
age 38 years h/s
Mother f/s

E. S. HALPERIN
Aug 9, 1912 h/s
E. S. H. f/s

Hanna Rebecca KIRSNER
died Dec 13, 1912
h/s broken

Grunne FRIEDLAND
1855 - 1913
h/s stone off pedestal
f/s Mother

Ida EPSTEIN
March 23, 1913 h/s
f/s Mother

Yetta RUBENSTEIN
born 1849 died 1914
May her soul rest in peace
h/s

Esther Rebecca SOLTZ
died Jan 2, 1915 h/s
f/s E. R. S.

Goldie MEYHR
died Dec 16, 1915 h/s

Rebecca GROSS
May 16, 1881
July 23, 1916 h/s

Sarah T. SILVER
born May 22, 1886
died May 6, 1917 h/s

Fanny SANDLER
died Oct 13, 1918 h/s

Sarah HALPERIN
Oct 1903 - Oct 14, 1918 h/s
f/s Daughter

SOLOMON
h/s on ground

Max SOLOMON
born Dec 7, 1883
died March 25, 1920
Son

Cemeteries of the City of Hampton, Virginia / formerly Elizabeth City County

Susan SOLOMON
born July 12, 1857
died Feb 17, 1934

Rose SAMUEL
died July 25, 1943 h/s

Goldier RITAER
died Jan 11, 1928 h/s
f/s Mother

Nissim Raphael
TARRAGANO
died Jan 22, 1928 h/s

Our Baby
Delores Daughter of
James & Florence GRAINE
Nov 11, 1925 Jan 11, 1928 h/s

Minnie GLUCKSTEIN
born March 22, 1900
died Nov 16, 1922 h/s
f/s Mother

Morris CAPPEL
died July 28, 1920 h/s
f/s Father

Aaron MEYHR
no dates h/s
f/s Father

Rachel SHWERDLOFF
died Nov 27, 1923
age 62 years h/s
f/s Mother
stone laying on ground

Bertha REICHMAN
wife of Edward Marcus
died May 22, 1926
age 26 years h/s
f/s Daughter

Alex SHARF
died July 7, 1929 h/s

Abraham COHEN
born April 10, 1900
died Sept 3, 1924 h/s
f/s Son

Issac MICHAELSON
9 Oct 1961
Stone face down on ground

Fanny MICHAELSON
23 Nov 1923
Stone face down on ground

Jacob HALPERIN
died Aug 22, 1921 h/s
f/s Brother

Books

Alec ABRAHAM
born May 25, 1880
died June 15, 1923 h/s
f/s father

Kate KAPLAN
1864 - 1923 h/s
f/s Mother

Sarah R. SNITZ
(no dates)

Mauachia BLACKMAN
born Jan 14, 1846
died May 9, 1921 h/s
f/s Mother
stone on ground

Pearl GROSS
died May 1, 1920
age 72 years wife h/s
f/s Mother

Sarah BAKER
born March 25, 1873
died February 2, 1913 h/s
f/s S. B.

SHIMKOWITZ
iron fence encloses next 3

Simon SHIMKOWITZ
born Aug 4, 1891
died Feb 23, 1949 h/s

Morris SHIMKOWITZ
Beloved Father of his children
born in Hasenpoth, Russia
Dec 25, 1864
died Feb 11, 1925
rest in peace h/s
f/s Father

Esther Kemp SHIMKOWITZ
Beloved wife of Morris
Shimkowitz
born in Wreschen Germany
Jan 20, 1865
died April 4, 1919
rest in peace h/s
f/s Mother

Isaac NACHMAN
died Jan 24, 1912

Solomon GREENSPON
died Feb 13, 1918
Age 65 years h/s
f/s S. G.

Mina Devera SCOLL
died Oct 5, 1915 h/s
f/s Mother

Rev. Tobias H. SCHWARTZ
died Oct 9, 1913 h/s
f/s Father

Sarah SCHWARTZ
died Dec 19, 1948
age 82 h/s

Molly Esher SIEGEL
died 8 July 1926
f/s Mother

Rose BRENER
died Dec 27, 1918 h/s
f/s Wife

Henry LEWCOVITZ
born 1877
died Feb 10, 1917 h/s
f/s Brother

Sarah Ida LEVINSON
July 8, 1899
Feb 1, 1920 h/s
f/s Mother

Abraham M. REISFIELD
died May 8, 1916
aged 65 years d/s h/s
w/ Millie
f/s Husband

Millie REISFIELD
died Jan 28, 1933
aged 67 years d/s h/s
w/ Abraham
f/s Wife

Israel HOLZSWEIG
died Oct 1, 1914
age 79 years h/s

H. L. CAPLON
died April 27, 1919
age 51 years h/s

Rose CAPLON
died Oct 15, 1937
age 71 years h/s
f/s
Mother

Jacob KIRSNER
March 12, 1920
age 86 years h/s
f/s Father

Sarah WEGER
died June 14, 1948 h/s
f/s Mother

Meyer L. WEGER
died Nov 9, 1922 h/s
f/s Father

Solomon BROWN
died Feb 27, 1924
age 71 years h/s
f/s Father

Mordechai Heshil NEWMAN
born Aug 1856
died Oct 9, 1924 h/s
f/s Father

Meyer J. BINDER
died June 9, 1925
age 61 d/s h/s w/ Katie D.
f/s Father

Katie D. BINDER
died July 22, 1933
age 64 d/s h/s
w/ Meyer J.
f/s Mother

Abraham LEVITT
born Oct 1856
died Jan 21, 1929 h/s
f/s Father

NACHMAN

Myer NACHMAN
July 14, 1987 h/s

Ella C. NACHMAN
March 27, 1992 h/s

Ben D. NACHMAN
February 8, 1989 h/s

FRANK

(In Hebrew) h/s

SHAPIRO

David Herman SHAPIRO
19 Apr 1944 h/s

Max Bernard SHAPIRO
30 Jan 1968 h/s

Lena Fisch BESKIN
born Jan 10, 1877
died Nov 12, 1946 h/s

Joseph BESKIN
born Jan 9, 1874
died Nov 9, 1944 h/s

EPSTEIN

Jacob Robert EPSTEIN
Nov 26, 1902
July 9, 1968

Etta Leah EPSTEIN
died Feb 18, 1936

Monnie EPSTEIN
died June 23, 1931

MORRIS

Lillian C. MORRIS
born March 29, 1896
died Dec 31, 1975

Phillip MORRIS
born April 26, 1887
died June 30, 1936

Abraham CONN
born Nov 15, 1895
died Jan 27, 1929
d/s h/s w/ Sarah Bertha
f/s Son

Sarah Bertha CONN
born 1871
died Dec 4, 1928
d/s h/s w/ Abraham
f/s Mother

Jacob GROSS
died Oct 10, 1924
age 70 years h/s
f/s Father

Ethel SEGALIN
died Jan 2, 1934
age 65 years h/s
f/s Mother

Rose Bess WEGER
born May 19, 1924 h/s
f/s Sister

Harriet Weger KIRSNER
Dec 24, 1926
Oct 27, 1980 h/s

Leah SKIMKOWITZ
born Oct 16, 1921
age 36 years h/s
f/s Wife

Mary A. SENSTEATER
died Sept 29, 1923 h/s
f/s Mother

Dora S. SATISKY
died May 17, 1920 h/s
f/s Mother

Isidore BARGER
born 1852
died Sept 17, 1919
d/s h/s w/ Sarah
A God fearing, devoted
Husband & Father
f/s Father

Lovely and pleasant in their
lives
Even death did not separate
them

Sarah BERGER
born 1863
died July 22, 1919
d/s h/s w/ Isidore
A God fearing, devoted Wife &
Mother
f/s Mother

Ida GOLDBERG
died Feb 19, 1920 h/s
f/s Blank

Israel B. GOLDBERG
died Jan 21, 1929 h/s
f/s Father

Rose BRAVNSTEIN
died Sept 23, 1924
aged 47 years h/s
f/s Mother

Bernard Z. GRAFF
Beloved Father & Husband
died Aug 28, 1925
age 77 years h/s
f/s B. Z. G.

GRAFF
To live in Hearts
we leave behind is not to die

Ellis Joseph GRAFF
born Nov 3, 1877
died May 24, 1943 h/s
His works live after him

Jeannette Mintz GRAFF
born Jan 13, 1879
died Jan 16, 1960 h/s
Her memory is ever Blessed

William A. GRAFF
Beloved h/o Leona H. Graff
born March 22, 1887
died Oct 5, 1918 h/s
f/s W. A. G.

Nellie ROSENBAUM
born July 23, 1891
died March 21, 1915 h/s
This is a very large head stone

Mother
Zeporah FRIEDMAN
1872 - 1964 h/s

Morris M. HANDELSMAN
died Dec 25, 1920 h/s

Mary HANDELSMAN
born 1845
died 1924 h/s

Nathan BALSER
died Feb 7, 1922 h/s
f/s Father

Mollie BALSER
died July 17, 1940
age 63 years h/s

Max BALSER
born Feb 22, 1902
died Jan 7, 1927 h/s

Our beloved Mother & Sister
Celia BROMBERG
died March 16, 1929 f/s
f/s C. B.

Augustus LEVIN
died April 8, 1926 f/s

Ida KULMAN
died Sept 21, 1932 h/s

Margaret Ethel RICE
Beloved w/o Ben Jamin S.
Rice
April 23, 1886
April 20, 1932
at rest h/s
f/s Mother

Dearly Beloved Wife, Mother
& Grandmother
Rose LICHTENBERG
born April 15, 1886
died Feb 14, 1931
Peace h/s
f/s Mother

Dearly Beloved Father,
& Grandfather
Henry LICHTENBERG
born Aug 23, 1872
died Feb 14, 1931 h/s

Joseph M. KAPLAN
1864 - 1929 h/s
f/s Father

Wolfe LEVY
died Jan 31, 1932 h/s
f/s Father

Harry OXMAN
born Nov 20, 1882
died Aug 2, 1932 h/s

Jennie HALPERIN
died May 26, 1932
age 81 years h/s
f/s Mother

Daughter
Ester SAMUELS
Apr 15, 1900
Aug 6, 1926 h/s

Fannie FRIED
died Nov 13, 1934
age 62 years h/s
f/s Mother

Morris COHEN
1870 - 1935
d/s h/s w/ blank

Molly STEIN
died Feb 1, 1941
age 79 years h/s
f/s Mother

Benjamin STEIN
died May 28, 1931
age 70 years h/s
f/s Father

Joseph STEIN
died Oct 8, 1936
Age 34 years h/s
f/s Brother

Mother
Anna DIAMOND
died Dec 4, 1937 h/s
f/s Mother

Hayman WERBLOW
died Nov 17, 1939
age 60 years h/s

MALNICK

Abraham MALNICK
Aug 1, 1893
April 23, 1940

Rose MALNICK
Aug 5, 1893
Sept 14, 1973

Raymond D. MALNICK
July 28, 1923
June 14, 1995

LEVY

Samuel LEVY
March 15, 1887
Oct 23, 1950

Anna E. LEVY
March 18, 1888
Jan 22, 1961

Susan Roth STEIN
Jan 15, 1948
July 5, 1985

Robert STEIN
Feb 2, 1911
May 12, 1985

Sarah STEIN
Nov 4, 1908
Sept 19, 1973

Bertha WARD
Nov 4, 1910
June 28, 1969

Louis WARD
died May 20, 1942
age 60

Nathan COHEN
June 15, 1888
Sept 15, 1946
d/s w/ Thelma

Thelma ABRAMS
June 17, 1912
Dec 16, 1941

REICHMAN

Jennie REICHMAN
Jan 1, 1878
Nov 8, 1962

Nathan REICHMAN
Aug 19, 1874
July 2, 1940

Ethel GOLDBERG
died Sept 13, 1941
age 33 years
f/s Mother

Rebecca GOLDBERG
died Feb 10, 1940
age 50 years
f/s Mother

Helen COHEN
died May 8, 1953
76 years

Flora KAPLIN
died Dec 27, 1941
age 55 years
f/s Mother

Harry KAPLAN
died Dec 21, 1936
age 50 years
f/s Father

Herman FRIEDMAN
died May 17, 1936
aged 69 years
f/s Father

Abraham COHEN
died July 4, 1935
age 59 years
f/s Father

Bessie SEAR
died June 22, 1952
age 71 years
f/s Mother

David SEAR
died June 7, 1935
age 58 years
f/s Father

Nathan TOUBERT
died Jan 5, 1934
age 36 years

A. J. ASENSTEATER
died Jan 21, 1933
f/s Father

Sam JACOBS
died Jan 21, 1933
age 57 yrs
f/s Father

J. B. LEVY
died Jan 2, 1933
age 60 years
d/s w/ Sophie
f/s Father

Sophie LEVY
died May 17, 1952
age 73 years
d/s w/ J. B.
f/s Mother

Yetta JACOBS
died Sept 7, 1945
age 67 years

Benard NACHMAN
born Oct 9, 1898
age 29 years
f/s Son

Next three in iron fence

Josephen GREEN
died March 3, 1941
age 63 years
f/s Husband

Harry Aaron GREEN
Beloved Son of
Joseph & Sarah Green
born Oct 17, 1905
died April 29, 1926
He is not dead He will
ever be with us
f/s Son

Sarah GREEN
died March 20, 1955
age 70 years
f/s Wife

GRAFF

Dorothy GRAFF
born Jan 27, 1901
died Dec 22, 1974
Her love is forever in
our hearts

Alan Myron GRAFF
born April 3, 1911
died Nov 15, 1960
His love is forever in
our hearts

Isaac COHEN
died Sept 29, 1925
age 59 years
f/s Father

Benjamin A. PEAR
died Nov 4, 1930
age 52 years
f/s Father

Wolfe LEVIN
died Feb 18, 1931
age 87
f/s Father

LEVIN

Father
Abraham J. LEVIN
born Aug 15, 1875
died Aug 31, 1962

Mother
Pauline LEVIN
born April 21, 1880
died 12, 1946

GORDON

William GORDON
born July 15, 1875
died Oct 23, 1926

Bertha GORDON
born July 25, 1884
died Feb 20, 1971

Charles NACHMAN
died July 12, 1931
aged 60 years

Ida Richman NACHMAN
died Nov 28, 1951
age 72 years

Rossye Nachman BECKER
died Oct 23, 1939
Age 38 years

Helen Nachman FRANKEL
born Nov 14, 1909
died July 15, 1948

NACHMAN

Anna Nachman LUDWIG
1897 - 1979

Esther Scoll NACHMAN
died Nov 2, 1964

Louis NACHMAN
born April 14, 1869
died Dec 10, 1945

Louis SATISKY
died Feb 26, 1944
age 78 years
f/s Father

FISCH

Benjamin FISCH
died Aug 15, 1957

Goldie Epstein FISCH
died May 22, 1970

Mollie E. TUCHMAN
died June 5, 1989

BESKIN

Theodore H. BESKIN
April 25, 1902
May 27, 1959
Mizpah

Esther Felstein BESKIN
January 1, 1906
September 27, 1986

REYNER

Harry REYNER
died Aug 1, 1978
age 88 years
Son

Sarah REYNER
died July 26, 1949
age 84 years
Mother

Joseph REYNER
died Jan 16, 1933
age 72 years
Father

Rose Nachman GOLDSTEIN
born Aug 24, 1887
died Oct 23, 1953 h/s

Albert Maurice GOLDSTEIN
born April 19, 1891
died Feb 22, 1960 h/s

NACHMAN

Rachel NACHMAN
born Sept 15, 1874
died July 12, 1964

Marx NACHMAN
born Sept 14, 1872
died Nov 1, 1947

Benjamin NACHMAN
born May 1, 1898
died Jan 7, 1946

KERBEL

Sarah Nachman KERBEL
died Jan 27, 1946

Rudolf KERBEL
died June 16, 1945

Bennie Bernard GORDON
died Oct 8, 1932
age 37 years
Husband

GORDON

Narris GORDON
died Feb 17, 1946
age 74 years

Rachel GORDON
died July 3, 1958
age 82 years

BLACKMAN

Benjamin BLACKMAN
born July 14, 1866
died May 8, 1936

Dora BLACKMAN
born Dec 25, 1866
died Dec 27, 1932

Rebecca COHEN
born Aug 27, 1900
died Mar 28, 1936 h/s
f/s Mother

Sarah COHEN
born Dec 20, 1878
died Dec 30, 1945 h/s
f/s Mother

Mary ROSENBLOTH
died Nov 18, 1937
A woman of Valor h/s
f/s Mother

Mollie SHAPIRO
died Dec 6, 1937
Blessed be her memory h/s
f/s Mother

Fannie SNITZ
died Jan 23, 1936
d/s h/s w/ Isidore
Mother

Isidore SNITZ
died Oct 6, 1935
d/s h/s w/ Fannie
Son

Elsie S. PERRY
Dec 22, 1904
July 22, 1935 h/s
f/s Mother

Minnie BERMAN
April 19, 1934
age 60 years h/s
f/s Mother

Sol BERMAN
died April 19, 1951
age 85 years h/s
f/s Father

Ann MILLER
18 Feb 1976
stone on ground

Nathan GORDON
died Nov 9, 1935
age 56 years h/s

Pauline GORDON
born March 15, 1887
died Aug 1, 1933 h/s
f/s Gordon

Our beloved Mother
Sarah AROTZKY
1881 - 1933 h/s
f/s Mother

LEVIN

Sarah LEVIN
born July 28, 1866
died Feb 9, 1945

David LEVIN
died April 23, 1933
age 65 years

Esther Rachel GOLDBERG
died Nov 15, 1933 h/s
f/s Mother

Ethel NEWMAN
died Jan 26, 1934
age 45 years h/s
f/s Mother

Bertha ROSENSTEIN
died March 29, 1936
age 62 years h/s

Chanah LEVIN
died July 13, 1936 h/s

Minnie KINLAND
died Jan 6, 1937
age 48 years h/s

Herman LEVINE
born Oct 31, 1895
died Nov 3, 1938 h/s
f/s Brother

Ida LEVIN
born Dec 27, 1891
died July 27, 1974 h/s

RUBIN

Rachel RUBIN
Nov 23, 1885
March 2, 1940
Wife

Joseph RUBIN
died March 8, 1952
age 68
Husband

Goldie SAMUEL
4 Nov 1941
Stone on ground

Harris SAMUELS
died Jan 31, 1959
age 84 h/s

Joseph KLEIN
April 30, 1942
age 41 years h/s

Joseph LEDERMAN
died Sept 6, 1943
age 63 h/s

Issac KULMAN
died Mar 9, 1944
age 72 years h/s

Jake BINDER
born Sept 24, 1906
died June 26, 1945 h/s

Israel BINDER
died March 22, 1946
age 68 years h/s

ABRAHAM

Morris ABRAHAM
died June 10, 1954
age 69 years

Sophie Brady ABRAHAM
(No Dates)

KOPLON

Charles M. KOPLON
January 16, 1988
Beloved & Devoted Husband,
Father & Grandfather

Esther L. KOPLON
March 29, 1984
Beloved & Devoted Wife,
Mother & Grandmother

CRAMER

Sol CRAMER
Oct 20, 1900
Nov 5, 1957

Jennie DAVINSON
July 15, 1887
July 31, 1969 h/s

Betty STREET
died Dec 29, 1955
age 79 years h/s

Helen Ray WHITE
December 10, 1890
September 24, 1955
Your devoted little Mother
was a Saint force uniting us
h/s

Maurice MORGAN
died Dec 7, 1954
Age 63 Years h/s
f/s Father

Fannie J. SHARF
Dec 27, 1908
Jan 13, 1981 h/s
f/s Mother

Max SHARF
April 14, 1904
Jan 9, 1954 h/s
f/s Father

Sophia H. SAVILLE
November 4, 1895
February 6, 1972 h/s
f/s Mother

Harry SAVILLE
March 1, 1881
August 30, 1953 h/s
f/s Father

I. SIEGEL
died Dec 10, 1953 h/s

Fannie SIEGEL
died Nov 12, 1951
age 72 years h/s

FRIEDMAN

Vivian FRIEDMAN
March 23, 1899
Feb 21, 1964
Mother - Wife

Sol FRIEDMAN
March 25, 1899
June 11, 1951
Father - Husband

ABELKOP

Sarah ABELKOP
died March 27, 1953

Benjamin ABELKOP
died August 26, 1947

SHARF

Yetta SHARF
died July 26, 1953
age 72 years

Thomas SHARF
died Nov 19, 1946
age 66 yrs

Louis BALSER
died Jan 7, 1957 h/s

Sarah A. LEVIN
Oct 25, 1899
Feb 15, 1985 h/s
Mother

Benjamin LEVIN
died Dec 10, 1945
age 49 years h/s
f/s Father

Joseph M. LEVIN
Nov 1, 1930
Feb 10, 1961 h/s

David L. NEWMAN
July 3, 1891
July 4, 1964 h/s

RUBEN

Frank RUBEN
died Feb 16, 1948
Father

Sarah RUBEN
died Feb 6, 1954
Mother

Pauline FOLKOWITZ
May 19, 1896
Nov 14, 1963 h/s
f/s Wife

TURK

Ray TURK
Jan 9, 1889
July 22, 1951

Philip TURK
May 18, 1888
April 30, 1950

Hebert TURK
April 6, 1919
Nov 24, 1981

Thelma TURK
Oct 23, 1990

Minnie Fisch AAROW
died Dec 2, 1946
age 68 years h/s

Isaac RUBEN
born Oct 9, 1895
died Sept 29, 1955 h/s

Rebecca RUBEN
born Oct 1, 1896
died Oct 14, 1946 h/s

CARMEL

Sarah K. CARMEL
died Aug 3, 1962
age 80

Harry A. CARMEL
died Jan 16, 1944
age 68

Frank Joseph CARMEL
died Sept 21, 1944
age 67

CARMEL

Sarah Lena CARMEL
died Oct 10, 1967
age 88

Miriam Belle CARMEL
died Apr 11, 1981

Percy CARMEL
died April 10, 1984
age 83

ZILBER

William M. ZILBER
died Feb 26, 1977

Gertrude M. ZILBER
died Aug 11, 1947

ARONOW

Issac ARONOW
died March 25, 1955

Fannie ARONOW
born Sept 12, 1882
died Aug 7, 1947

GORDON

Annie GORDON
died Sept 24, 1946
age 63 years

Charles GORDON
died Feb 9, 1955
age 77 years

GORDON

Sam GORDON
Feb 10, 1906
Oct 28, 1950

Ida Ester BROWN
died Jan 6, 1944
age 80 years h/s
f/s Mother

MORRIS

William MORRIS
born Sept 14, 1884
died April 5, 1944

Anna MORRIS
Jan 15, 1885
Sept 13, 1974

Eva MICHAELSON
June 15, 1878
Nov 28, 1942
d/s w/ M.

M. MICHAELSON
died Oct 18, 1947
d/s w/ Eva

Yetta KESSLER
died Jan 27, 1940
age 81 h/s
f/s Mother

Amelia MORRIS
Nov 17, 1884
May 2, 1940
d/s w/ Mark
f/s Brother

Mark MORRIS
Sept 27, 1896
June 5, 1941
d/s w/ Amelia
f/s Sister

BECKER

Louis BECKER
July 14, 1888
May 9, 1980

Jennie BECKER
July 14, 1888
March 28, 1952

ACKERMAN
John ACKERMAN
died July 4, 1934
age 66 years

Fannie ACKERMAN
died July 5, 1949
age 70 years

COOPER

Sara R. COOPER
born Dec 27, 1897
died Oct 7, 1989

Isadore W. COOPER
born March 15, 1891
died Nov 27, 1943

Morris Samuel COOPER
born March 25, 1885
died Oct 14, 1968

Rose Harris COOPER
born Dec 30, 1888
died Oct 25, 1971

MORRIS

Sadye Meyhr MORRIS
Oct 12, 1888
Oct 29, 1963

Alfred MORRIS
May 14, 1881
Sept 24, 1944

Mary MEYHR
died Sept 7, 1944
age 76 years h/s
Mother

Aaron H. HARRIS
March 15, 1875
Jan 27, 1943
d/s w/ Eva

Eva L. HARRIS
March 15, 1882
Nov 19, 1968
d/s w/ Aaron

MORRIS
Sophia MORRIS
born Dec 18, 1901
died March 24, 1946

PESKIN

Annie PESKIN
died Oct 23, 1953
age 64 years

Philip PESKIN
born July 19, 1887
died Feb 9, 1944

Frank FRIEDLAND
April 18, 1875
Dec 31, 1938

Ida FRIEDLAND
Oct 11, 1874
Aug 15, 1956
d/s w/Frank

Frank FRIEDLAND
April 18, 1875
Dec 31, 1938
d/s w/ Ida

Samuel Solomon MOREWITZ
died April 23, 1936
age 67 years
d/s w/ Rachel

Rachel MOREWITZ
died March 29, 1940
age 69 years
d/s w/ Samuel Solomon

KIRSNER

Raymond B. KIRSNER
1905 - 1953

Fannie B. KIRSNER
1880 - 1976

Isaac KIRSNER
1874 - 1953

Sade Kirsner RICHMAN
born Aug 11, 1903
died Oct 5, 1934 h/s
f/s S.K.R.

M. J. CARMEL
died Sept 28, 1937
age 98 years h/s
d/s w/ Ethel

Ethel CARMEL
died July 5, 1937
age 96 years h/s
d/s w/ M. J.

Bessie HOLZSWEIG
died March 16, 1937
d/s w/ Meyer
f/s Mother

Meyer HOLZSWEIG
died March 20, 1934
age 64 years
d/s w/ Bessie
f/s Father

SILVER

Son & Brother
Hyman SILVER
died June 4, 1936
age 51 years

Father
Abraham SILVER
died Sept 15, 1939
age 89 years

Mother
Minnie SILVER
died Jan 21, 1933
age 80 years

(In Hebrew) h/s

Abraham SIEGEL
died Nov 16, 1933
aged 65 years h/s
f/s Father

Benjamin KRAMER
died April 24, 1976
age 67 years h/s
f/s Father

Rachel KRAMER
died May 12, 1949
age 79 years h/s

Lena ERLACH
died Dec 28, 1951
age 80 years h/s
f/s Mother

Elias ERLACH
died May 30, 1937
age 62 years h/s
f/s Father

Beloved wife of
Lou FELDMAN
Shirley L. FELDMAN h/s
f/s born April 10, 1904
died Dec 24, 1946

LEVY

Ida LEVY
died July 2, 1938
age 62 years

Jacob LEVY
died Oct 14, 1945
age 77

Abraham SEAR
22 Sep 1943

Ludwig MORITZ
born July 10, 1889
died May 11, 1890 h/s

Selma MORITZ
died 5 Jam 1944 h/s
stone on ground

Daniel UNGER
born Jan 10, 1893
died Feb 11, 1950 h/s
stone on ground

Harry HERZEKOW
died Jan 22, 1945
age 74 years h/s
stone on ground

Sarah PERZEKOW
died 19 Sept 1962, h/s
Stone on ground

Nalalie FALK
Feb 26 1879
Feb 17, 1945 h/s

Rita Faye KOPLON
April 1, 1933
June 7, 1952
May her soul be bound up in
the Bond of Life. h/s
f/s Our darling Daughter &
Devoted Sister

Stone face down on ground

BRENNER

Rose BRENNER
Aug 15, 1884
April 10, 1971

Jacob BRENNER
Feb 15, 1881
Oct 15, 1948

Mother
Mollie FURST
1878 - 1948 h/s

FRANK

Jacob FRANK
born April 17, 1876
died Oct 29, 1948

FRENKEL

David FRENKEL
died Feb 13, 1955

Flora FRENKEL
died April 6, 1953

Arthur POLAN
Jun 16, 1911
Dec 4, 1953 h/s

Robert M. POLAN
Jan 4, 1913
Aug 17, 1969 h/s

Sadie M. POLAN
July 1, 1888
Mar 28, 1983
In memory of my
Mother h/s

Dora R. LOWE
Sept 23, 1906
Aug 12, 1956 h/s
f/s Beloved Mother

Celia TARRAGANO
Dec 25, 1886
Nov 6, 1960 h/s

GOODMAN

Mollie J. GOODMAN
died Sept 20, 1962
age 71 years

Morris J. GOODMAN
died July 2, 1957
age 72 years

Joan Goldie Levy STREET
April 10, 1908
March 28, 1984
wife of Milton
Beloved Mother h/s

Abe ARENOV
died April 14, 1953
age 64 years h/s

HOLZSWEIG

Rose HOLZSWEIG
died May 23, 1955
age 69 yrs.

Louis HOLZSWEIG
died May 26, 1954
age 75 yrs.

Fannie B. HOLZSWEIG
born Sept 26, 1903
died Feb 27, 1990 h/s
f/s Mother & Grandmother

Philip HOLZSWEIG
born May 5, 1920
died Jan 16, 1953 h/s
f/s Father

BANKS

Sol Harry BANKS
age 75
died January 7, 1961

Jennie Polan BANKS
January 15, 1893
December 18, 1952

HALPERIN

Anna HALPERIN
Died October 16, 1956
age 69 years

Joseph L. HALPERIN
died August 29, 1952
age 77 years

HOFFMAN

Tillie HOFFMAN
May 17, 1881
Sept 24, 1975

Michael HOFFMAN
May 5, 1877
July 23, 1952

SCHER

Joseph Frank SCHER
Dec 20, 1895
Oct 8, 1980

Josephine SCHER
Jan 17, 1901
Feb 22, 1957

Benjamin SIEGEL
born Sept 19, 1898
died Aug 27, 1951 h/s

Irwin "Teasy" SIEGEL
Nov 15, 1897
Feb 24, 1954

DIAMOND

Joseph Bernard DIAMOND
died October 21, 1947

Tillie Rebecca DIAMOND
died March 20, 1947

Minnie SHIMKOWITZ
Oct 13, 1894
April 12, 1980 h/s

Sam SHIMKOWITZ
Jan 3, 1890
Sept 10, 1943

MEYER

Annie Levy MEYER
Feb 2, 1896
March 9, 1969
Loving Wife & Mother

Adolf MEYER
died July 19, 1950
age 61
Beloved Husband & Father

David Aaron MOSKOWITZ
born Feb 2, 1894
died May 7, 1942 h/s
f/s Father

Belle Brenner RUBEN
born Aug 12, 1899
died Nov 18, 1985 h/s
f/s Mother

Leon FORMAN
died December 28, 1949
age 30
Beloved Husband & Father h/s

Milton HOLZSWIG
died March 3, 1942
age 45 years

PELTZ

Sarah Rifka PELTZ
died Nov 15, 1953
age 79

Abraham J. PELTZ
died Jan 31, 1949
age 84

RADIN

Sarah Rebecca RADIN
died April 1, 1943
age 70 years
Mother

Benzion RADIN
died Nov 30, 1939
age 67 years
Father

Harry COHEN
born Oct 8, 1893
died July 31, 1940 h/s
f/s Son

Simon COHEN
died Feb 20, 1938
age 70 years h/s
f/s Father

Mollie COHEN
died July 12, 1943
age 73 years h/s
f/s Mother

CONN

Simon CONN
died Feb 12, 1941
age 69 years

Minnie CONN
died Feb 3, 1966
age 85 years

Joseph BLOOM
Nov 28, 1884
March 1, 1941 h/s
d/s w/ Leba
f/s Father

Leba BLOOM
Nov 15, 1883
April 12, 1978 h/s
d/s w/ Joseph
f/s Mother

Rose SPOONER
born Aug 10, 1879
died Oct 5, 1945 h/s

Ida PHILLIPS
died June 21, 1938
aged 80 years h/s
f/s Our Blessed Mother

Ethel NEVIAS
died April 21, 1941
age 49 years h/s
f/s Mother

Lillian RESNICK
died April 18, 1973
aged 77 years h/s

LEVY

Theodore Barney LEVY
Oct 15, 1877
May 24, 1941
Father

Racheal Lena LEVY
July 15, 1878
Sept 15, 1942
Mother

GOLDSTEIN

Bertha Heimlich
GOLDSTEIN
Feb 15, 1880
March 21, 1965
Wife - Mother

Myer Joseph GOLDSTEIN
Oct 17, 1879
Feb 7, 1951
Husband - Father

Jacob OFSA
Nov 15, 1894
April 3, 1943 h/s

Minna Schugam OFSA
August 25, 1899
August 7, 1950 h/s

SCHUGAM

Rose Segal SCHUGAM
Nov 19, 1895
March 7, 1985

Jack SCHUGAM
Oct 8, 1894
Jan 16, 1977

Irving SCHUGAM
Feb 6, 1900
Nov 19, 1957

Albert Mintz SCHUGAM
Jan 1, 1903
Mar 23, 1980

BINDER

Rose K. BINDER
born May 21, 1898
died June 18, 1992
Temporary Metal Marker
Rose Keiser BINDER
age 94

Robert D. BINDER
born Jan 7, 1894
died May 10, 1946

Edwin Jacob BINDER
born April 6, 1901
died Jan 26, 1965

Deborah Gellman BINDER
born Oct 31, 1904
died Sept 2, 1965

BARON

Dr. Edgar BARON
Aug 23, 1910
July 9, 1957

BROWN

Monroe Reyner BROWN
born July 14, 1920
died June 25, 1977

Leon D. BROWN
born Feb 10, 1887
died Nov 21, 1946

Bessie Reyner BROWN
born Oct 2, 1887
died May 26, 1963

SAMET

Lotta Reyner SAMET
born April 2, 1883
died Jan 6, 1961

Michael SAMET
born Sept 12, 1879
died March 23, 1948

Jean Lazarus MORGAN
Oct 4, 1900
May 16, 1971 h/s
f/s Mother

SIEGEL

Nathan SIEGEL
April 15, 1895
Dec 30, 1970

Sarah SIEGEL
Dec 27, 1894
Jan 7, 1980

UNGER

Rose UNGER
died Sept 26, 1959

William UNGER
died Aug 8, 1946
age 60 years

GREENSPON

Rose Shimkowitz
GREENSPON
died June 14, 1990
age 96 years

Max William GREENSPON
died Oct 28, 1946
age 60 years

Etta LAZARUS
died April 29, 1947
age 71 years h/s
f/s Mother

GREENSPON

Minnie GREENSPON
died Feb 19, 1948
age 65
Mother

Isaac GREENSPON
died April 5, 1961
age 77

COHEN

Sigmund COHEN
born Jan 1, 1904
died Nov 16, 1949

Simon SNITZ
died March 3, 1951 h/s

Max E. SNITZ
Oct 31, 1915
Oct 17, 1979 h/s

CONN

Archie M. CONN
July 17, 1903
Oct 16, 1971
Beloved Husband & Father

Rose J. CONN
Oct 7, 1908
Aug 8, 1995
Beloved wife & Mother

COHEN

Milton COHEN
Nov 5, 1891
Aug 20, 1955
Husband

Minnie Meyhr COHEN
Sept 1, 1896
Mar 24, 1983
Wife

Esther Meyhr CONNON
April 13, 1892
April 16, 1961
Mother h/s f/s In Hebrew

Morris GOLDBERG
died Nov 9, 1956
age 90 years h/s

ELLENSON

Harry ELLENSON
born Nov 15, 1884
died Oct 20, 1946

Mary D. ELLENSON
born Jan 5, 1886
died April 16, 1963

ASTOR

Julius ASTOR
Dec 25, 1893
Dec 5, 1949
Husband - Father

Rae ASTOR
Jan 15, 1896
April 25, 1980
Wife - Mother

HERMAN

William HERMAN
died April 7, 1964
age 72 years

Sadie Rubin HERMAN
died Nov 2, 1960
age 57 years

Jennie Klesmer SHAPIRO
Oct 12, 1883
Feb 3, 1955
h/s
f/s Mother

Rose Klein NEVIAS
May 22, 1901
Feb 18, 1977

SACFAN

Leon SACFAN
March 4, 1886
Dec 26, 1955
Father

Rose Mirmelstein SACFAN
June 20, 1887
Dec 20, 1955
Mother

Jean C. SEIGEL
Jan 22, 1902
Jan 18, 1978

KULMAN

Harvey Joel KULMAN
March 29, 1938
July 24, 1954

Bertha J. KULMAN
Aug 12, 1910
Feb 25, 1974

David KULMAN
Jan 15, 1904
Aug 1, 1995

GOLDSTEIN

Isadore GOLDSTEIN
died Oct 15, 1954

Sadie F. GOLDSTEIN
died Nov 28, 1959

Morris GOLDSTEIN
Sept 29, 1913
Oct 29, 1980
Son

Sam RITNER
died Oct 21, 1954 h/s

Sidney HOLZSWEIG
died Feb 15, 1957 h/s

Philip KURZER
Virginia TSGT US Army
World War 2 h/s
f/s July 23, 1926
Oct 3, 1972

MILLER

Katie MILLER
died October 22, 1954

GOODMAN

Abe F. GOODMAN
Aug 20, 1898
Jan 19, 1955

Ellis I. WEINSTEIN
Nov 25, 1885
Dec 21, 1955 h/s

Bessie WEINSTEIN
Oct 25, 1894
March 3, 1970 h/s

LEVI

Harry LEVI
January 31, 1888
March 24, 1956

Goldie M. LEVI
January 26, 1890
June 23, 1969

Charles COHEN
died Feb 19, 1946 h/s

P. CORTELL
died Aug 19, 1934 h/s

Max Herman MALINA
October 5, 1890
December 6, 1964 h/s

Shirley SPOONER
Dec 25, 1911
Nov 3, 1956 h/s

KOVACS

William KOVACS
Aug 10, 1905
Oct 30, 1956
Beloved & Devoted Husband

PERZEKOW

Henry PERZEKOW
Oct 15, 1912
Sept 17, 1975

EPSTEIN

Ida K. EPSTEIN
died Oct 5, 1977
beloved Wife & Mother

Charles EPSTEIN
died Nov 18, 1957
Beloved Husband & Father

EPSTEIN

Benjamin Louis EPSTEIN
died Feb 22, 1970

EPSTEIN

Sarah Carmel EPSTEIN
died May 4, 1973

Morris Aaron EPSTEIN
died Sept 8, 1956

ROSENSTEIN

Samuel ROSENSTEIN
July 9, 1864
Sept 20, 1965
beloved Father

Nathan ROSENSTEIN
Sept 7, 1895
Nov 13, 1961
beloved Son & Brother

Joseph FRIEDMAN
died Jan 30, 1956
age 52 years
beloved Husband & Father
May his soul rest in peace, h/s
f/s Husband

FISCH

Dora Goodman FISCH
Oct 13, 1889
Oct 17, 1977

Jacob FISCH
April 13, 1886
Jan 25, 1956

WEGER

Jenny F. WEGER
Dec 25, 1897
Feb 25, 1988

Maurice A. WEGER
Dec 10, 1896
Dec 27, 1955

KAPLAN

Reba Morewitz KAPLAN
April 29, 1897
Sept 22, 1983

Edwin I. KAPLAN
Sept 5, 1892
May 10, 1960

RICHMAN

Family group in 2 rows.

Lillian Senie RICHMAN
July 12, 1897
August 8, 1983
beloved Wife & Mother

Abraham RICHMAN
March 12, 1895
April 23, 1979
a devoted Husband & Father

Louis Joseph RICHMAN
Oct 16, 1900
Jan 10, 1972
Beloved Husband & Father

Sarah RICHMAN
April 18, 1906
June 13, 1994
a devoted Daughter

Gertrude RICHMAN
June 15, 1872
April 15, 1954
Mother

William RICHMAN
June 13, 1871
March 31, 1956
Father

Sheri Gayle RICHMAN
Sept 21, 1966
June 7, 1988

To live in hearts left behind is
not to die.
Dedicated to the Honored

Memory of our loved ones who
so nobly gave their lives for
freedom and Democracy
in World War 2 and Korea

Lt. Irvin E. NACHMAN
US Field Arty Korea
born May 29, 1928
died Jan 29, 1951

PVT Nathan LOREN
US Inf. World War II
born Aug 1, 1928
died Sept 18, 1944

Lt. Sidney BECKER
AAF World War II
born Nov 12, 1919
died Jan 7, 1944

PVT William BINDER
USMC World War 2
born Oct 17, 1924
died Mar 12, 1945

Harry A. MEYHR
April 21, 1902
August 29, 1987

POTTS

Husband & Father
Michael POTTS
Oct 25, 1893
Dec 30, 1971

Wife & Mother
Fannie Oser POTTS
Nov 15, 1892
Oct 21, 1961

Husband & Father
Julian T. POTTS, MD
Jan 28, 1914
Jan 16, 1951

Rebecca Carmel
GREENBERG
April 2, 1890
March 20, 1955 h/s

WESSERMAN

Eva Gordon WESSERMAN
May 9, 1901
July 22, 1962

Joseph WESSERMAN
Aug 29, 1896
Oct 5, 1953

LEVINSON

Bessie Lazarus LEVINSON
February 20, 1899
June 11, 1992
Beloved Wife & Mother

Charles Abraham LEVINSON
January 15, 1896
April 9, 1959
beloved Husband & Father

SHIMKOWITZ

Annie SHIMKOWITZ
Dec 24, 1890
June 3, 1963

Louis SHIMKOWITZ
Oct 14, 1886
Dec 18, 1950

Jennie PEAR
died Sept 28, 1948
age 64 years h/s

Katie GORDON
died Nov 17, 1951
age 65 years h/s
f/s Wife

RUBIN

Husband
Dr. David B. RUBIN
March 9, 1887
Sept 19, 1971

Wife & Mother
Yetta Fisch RUBIN
June 21, 1891
Aug 5, 1969

BLACKMAN

Mother
Sarah BLACKMAN
died March 11, 1987
age 93 years

Father
Leon M. BLACKMAN
died Oct 15, 1949
age 59 years

WILKS

Rosalie S. WILKS
Aug 19, 1907
Jan 9, 1990

Abe M. WILKS
July 18, 1908
Apr 3, 1994

Rachel WILKS
died Jan 23, 1972

Joseph W. WILKS
died April 26, 1947

ARCH

Benjamin ARCH
Jan 18, 1950
Father

Kenneth ARCH
Nov 11, 1965

Eva ARCH
May 6, 1948

GELLMAN - WILDHORN

Bertha GELLMAN
died April 13, 1957
Mother

Louis WILDHORN
died Feb 27, 1950
Son

NACHMAN

Max E. NACHMAN
died Nov 2, 1952

SATISKY

Aaron SATISKY
March 15, 1907
Feb 1, 1954

GOLDBERG

Solomon H. GOLDBERG
Dec 24, 1904
April 18, 1986

Ida T. GOLDBERG
Feb 13, 1886
Feb 16, 1950
Wife & Mother

Isaac Morris GOLDBERG
Nov 3, 1881
July 6, 1956

GOLDBERG

beloved Wife & Mother
Sara Levy GOLDBERG
May 10, 1908
Jan 27, 1983

(In Hebrew)

Etta Toby ABRAHAM
August 15, 1885
April 19, 1955

Father
Rev. Israel Kaiman FISHER
died May 25, 1969
age 87 years h/s

Mother
Ida FISHER
died Jan 17, 1857
age 72 years h/s

FRIEDLANDER

Sarah FRIEDLANDER
Feb 16, 1902
Aug 10, 1951

FAMILANT

Sophia FAMILANT
died Dec 22, 1962

Davis FAMILANT
died March 23, 1949

David Gershom SMITH
died May 12, 1960
age 82 years h/s

Yetta Gross SMITH
died April 10, 1956
age 74 years h/s

Marcus SMITH
beloved Husband & Father h/s
f/s died Feb 4, 1956
age 48 years

Jack E. SMITH
beloved Son & Brother h/s
f/s died Sept 7, 1984
age 50 years

SMITH

Joseph SMITH
Oct 10, 1918
July 17, 1994
beloved Husband, Father &
Grandfather

PERZEKOW

Goldie PERZEKOW
beloved Wife & Mother
April 15, 1892
Aug 6, 1959

Harry PERZKOW
beloved Husband & Father
July 15, 1888
May 24, 1967

ROBERTS

Ida Gordon ROBERTS
Beloved Wife
June 16, 1913
April 10, 1985

Robert ROBERTS
beloved Husband
June 17, 1909
Sept 28, 1988

SHRIBER

Martin SHRIBER
beloved Husband & Father
Feb 8, 1912
April 2, 1957

Dora Gordon SHRIBER
beloved Sister
May 3, 1907
Mar 31, 1977

LEVY

Nathan Joseph LEVY
Feb 9, 1901
June 12, 1959
He possessed love and
compassion for his
fellowman

GOLDSTEIN

Gertrude Klaft GOLDSTEIN
Aug 19, 1904
Oct 9, 1995
Wife - Mother

GOODMAN

Simon GOODMAN
April 12, 1888
April 13, 1954

Benjamin LEVY
October 14, 1902
February 26, 1960 h/s

OLSHANSKY

Charles OLSHANSKY
1913 - 1985 h/s

Emma ROBERTS
June 23, 1886
July 22, 1971 h/s

SCHEINMAN

Gertrude SCHEINMAN
Aug 14, 1898
Feb 23, 1993
beloved Wife, Mother &
Grandmother

Morris S. SCHEINMAN
Dec 17, 1903
Apr 12, 1979
beloved Husband & Father

BLOCK

Ethel Fox BLOCK
Jan 6, 1906
Nov 23, 1983
beloved Wife & Mother

Maurice L. BLOCK
beloved Husband & Daddy
Jan 13, 1906
July 28, 1989

BLOCK - SPIRN

Irving BLOCK
Husband & Father
Nov 1, 1915
Sept 8, 1956

Sidney SPIRN
Lt Col US Army Air Corps
World War 2
May 16, 1910
Oct 27, 1984

Mary Rose RICE
August 20, 1909
June 15, 1980

Julian Meyer RICE
beloved Brother
November 19, 1907
May 28, 1967

Benjamin Solomon RICE
beloved Father
June 14, 1879
Aug 17, 1959

Goldye ANKER
July 13, 1919
Feb 21, 1959 h/s

Samuel ANKER
May 30, 1912
May 9, 1968 h/s

KRAMER

Daniel KRAMER
Nov 11, 1905
Dec 12, 1970

Florence H. KRAMER
Sept 4, 1906
Nov 19, 1961

KRAMER

Ida Berman KRAMER
May 7, 1902
March 1, 1965

Mike L. KRAMER
March 15, 1902
Dec 29, 1969

Frances L. RICE
April 13, 1921
March 23, 1985 h/s

LOREN

Rebecca LOREN
April 10, 1885
April 4, 1958

Sam LOREN
Sept 10, 1881
Sept 11, 1966

LEWIS

Louis LEWIS
April 5, 1896
Feb 15, 1958

ERLACH

Lewis H. ERLACH
beloved Husband & Father
July 3, 1904
March 17, 1959

KURZER

Rose S. KURZER
July 1, 1893
Oct 7, 1957

Morris KURZER
Jan 5, 1890
Nov 24, 1961

Harry B. FRIEDLAND
April 30, 1902
May 10, 1981 h/s

Morris B. FRIEDLAND
April 30, 1902
February 5, 1959 h/s

Razel KRUZER
April 4, 1900
July 31, 1973 h/s

BRENNER

Dorothy Kruzer BRENNER
beloved Wife & Mother
Dec 15, 1896
April 19, 1959

Hyman BRENNER
beloved Husband & Father
March 8, 1893
Oct 4, 1983

ARONOFF

Isidore ARONOFF
beloved Husband & Father
Dec 5, 1891
Jan 9, 1981

Bertha Newman ARONOFF
beloved Wife & Mother
Feb 27, 1893
June 12, 1980

ROGERS

Frances ROGERS
beloved Wife - Mother
December 25, 1898
December 21, 1975

Hyman ROGERS
beloved Husband - Father
New York PFC 311 GD
& Fire Co QMC
World War 2
January 7, 1893
April 18, 1958

NACHMAN

William NACHMAN
died Jan 21, 1958
age 51 years

Goldie Greenspon
NACHMAN
died Sept 11, 1983
age 73 years

This completes all the tombstones in from of the driveway in front of the maintenance building.

The following listing gives stones on the left side of the maintenance building, as you face the building

HERSHFIELD

James M. HERSHFIELD
Nov 30, 1891
May 22, 1961

Miriam Scoll HERSHFIELD
Jan 15, 1902
June 11, 1959

ELLENSON

Hilda Scoll ELLENSON
Dec 31, 1909
June 9, 1967

Louis ELLENSON
Aug 10, 1913
Aug 10, 1992

STERN

Joseph STERN
Jan 3, 1900
Sept 1, 1970

Clara B. LICHT
Sept 15, 1893
April 8, 1982

Bertha SCHONFIELD
Jan 20, 1909
April 4, 1960 h/s
f/s beloved Wife, Mother &
Grandmother

SPINDELL

Sam SPINDELL
beloved Husband
June 2, 1897
Oct 4, 1959

Mary SPINDELL
May 15, 1891
Dec 6, 1977

Alfred COHEN
beloved Husband & Father
May 8, 1906
Aug 18, 1969

Florence Kapp COHEN
beloved Wife & Mother
Dec 5, 1922
Dec 20, 1959

BLACK

Father
Joseph G. BLACK
1900 - 1978
d/s w/ Rebecca L.

Mother in loving memory
Rebecca L. BLACK
1902 - 1989
d/s w/ Joseph G.

GREENBERG

Arthur S. GREENBERG
Sept 4, 1889
Nov 15, 1959

Anne P. GREENBERG
Sept 15, 1907
June 4, 1988

SUMMERS

Husband & Father
Milton SUMMERS
Oct 16, 1899
March 1, 1960

Wife, Mother & Grandmother
Mary Erlach SUMMERS
Feb 12, 1903
May 10, 1985

Hannah A. BINDER
April 29, 1909
July 10, 1966 h/s

Toby KRAMER
Dec 15, 1905
Feb 2, 1964 h/s

Abraham BLACK
June 10, 1906
Nov 17, 1959 h/s

MATAN

Zelda MATAN
Dec 27, 1912
Sept 17, 1962 h/s

Morris PEKARSKY
July 10, 1909
Dec 19, 1960

Leah Peltz PEKARSKY
May 28, 1914
June 24, 1960

LEVIN

Florence P. LEVIN
Feb 22, 1902
Nov 19, 1985 h/s
d/s w/ Leo W.

Leo W. LEVIN
Nov 4, 1986
July 8, 1988 h/s
d/s w/ Florence P.

LEVY

beloved Wife
Goldie Peltz LEVY
Jan 4, 1911
Jan 19, 1990

beloved Husband
Maxwell LEVY
March 25, 1910
Dec 14, 1973

GOLDSTEIN

Ruth Cohen GOLDSTEIN
beloved Wife & Mother
Apr 13, 1916
Feb 1, 1995
Rest in Peace

BECKER

Jack A. BECKER
May 25, 1913
May 9, 1985

Seymour FRIEDMAN
March 24, 1922
May 8, 1960 h/s

FAMILANT

Leon Albert FAMILANT
Oct 31, 1903
Dec 30, 1959

Morris Jacob NEVIAS h/s
born July 30. 1890
March 13, 1960 f/s

William FINE
Dec 3, 1902
July 31, 1960
beloved Husband & Father h/s

Ludwig STERN
July 27, 1892
April 2, 1961
d/s w/ Emma Moritz

Emma Moritz STERN
April 27, 1891
Nov 26, 1970
d/s w/ Ludwig

SAUNDERS

Isadore A. SAUNDERS
Aug 15, 1884
Aug 28, 1963

Rose Hattie SAUNDERS
Feb 14, 1888
Aug 30, 1966

FRANK

Eugene FRANK
March 21, 1915
July 19, 1981

GOLDSTEIN

Emanuel GOLDSTEIN
April 16, 1889
Dec 31, 1961

Esther GOLDSTEIN
Oct 20, 1889
Jan 24, 1961

PELTZ

Morris B. PELTZ
Dec 25, 1899
July 28, 1960

Mollie B. PELTZ
April 6, 1904
Dec 2, 1987

PELTZ

Walter L. PELTZ
Aug 16, 1923
Jan 24, 1962

PELTZ

Anna PELTZ
Jan 27, 1898
Jan 30, 1987

Nathan PELTZ
Oct 21, 1895
Aug 21, 1976

PELTZ

Harry PELTZ
Oct 13, 1908
Aug 25, 1970
Beloved Husband & Father

Donald B. KRAMER
Jan 10, 1958
Jan 28, 1961 h/s

Bessie L. TESSLER
Oct 28, 1898
March 10, 1922 h/s

LEVINE

Isadore I. LEVINE
Sept 25, 1893
Aug 20, 1961

Sarah R. LEVINE
June 16, 1896
Oct 26, 1989

Lena HANKIN
1892 - Jan 25, 1968
beloved Mother &
Grandmother h/s

Henrietta KURZER
September 16, 1923
November 15, 1960 h/s

Julius KURZER
Sept 22, 1922
Oct 30, 1979 h/s

GREEN

Marian Morewitz GREEN
May 6, 1903
Jan 11, 1993
beloved Wife

Jack GREEN
May 24, 1902
March 25, 1968
beloved Husband

FRANK

Lilyan M. FRANK
July 6, 1905
June 8, 1992
beloved Wife & Mother

Harry FRANK
Aug 17, 1904
April 22, 1961
beloved Husband & Father

ABEL

Rosa R. ABEL
April 15, 1892
Aug 3, 1982

Morris E. ABEL
Oct 10, 1892
April 3, 1961

SHAWEL

Annie R. SHAWEL
died Aug 12, 1979
age 92 years

Max W. SHAWEL
died Jan 8, 1963
age 79 years

Simon DEYONG
Aug 4, 1880
Jan 21, 1964 h/s

Betty P. BLACK
Jan 17, 1914
Oct 26, 1977
h/s & f/s

GOLDSTEIN

Ethel Conn GOLDSTEIN
April 18, 1906
Nov 10, 1975

Milton Stanley GOLDSTEIN
born 1908
died 1996
age 88
Temporary Metal Marker

FENIGSOHN

Sol FENIGSOHN
Sept 11, 1908
Sept 20, 1995
A Kind and Gentle Man

Esther H. FENIGSOHN
Oct 28, 1907
Mar 5, 1989
beloved Wife & Mother

Julias S. FENINGSOHN
Jan 14, 1903
Mar 10, 1989
Beloved Husband & Father

Eva FENIGSOHN
May 8, 1877
Aug 15, 1965
beloved Wife & Mother

David FENIGSOHN
Oct 29, 1873
May 26, 1961
beloved Husband & Father

Joe BALSER
Aug 20, 1907
Nov 9, 1966

GOLUB

Samuel Keva GOLUB
April 6, 1900
April 18, 1962
Virginia PVT
US Army
World War 1
beloved Husband, Father &
Grandfather

Celia Lavender GOLUB
Mar 16, 1802
Nov 5, 1967
Beloved Wife, Mother &
Grandmother

SIEGEL

Isaac SIEGEL
Aug 4, 1905
June 7, 1964

BALSER

Ben B. BALSER
March 25, 1900
June 7, 1963

Miriam D. BALSER
August 14, 1908
May 20, 1984

SANDERS

Sam SANDERS
died Aug 30, 1963

Sarah Levy SANDERS
died April 21, 1980

MARKOFF

Bessie E. MARKOFF
Sept 2, 1911
Oct 17, 1963

BROMBERG

Samuel BROMBERG
May 15, 1889
April 10, 1964
beloved Husband, Father &
Grandmother

Rebecca BROMBERG
Jan 15, 1899
May 6, 1975
beloved Wife, Mother &
Grandmother

ARROLL

Herman ARROLL
Nov 25, 1906
Dec 2, 1970

Sarah Farnk ARROLL
Oct 25, 1906
April 14, 1996
beloved Mother of
Jean & Helen

NACHMAN

Hilda M. NACHMAN
April 7, 1904
July 28, 1966

Simon NACHMAN
Feb 4, 1904
Dec 2, 1964

FRANK

Irvin FRANK
Mar 5, 1911
Apr 27, 1971

BOOKBINDER

BOOKBINDER

Hyman J. BOOKBINDER
Oct 15, 1890
March 11, 1982
beloved Husband & Father

Minnie M. BOOKBINDER
Apr 2, 1893
Dec 17, 1964
Beloved, Wife & Mother

VOGEL

Benjamin VOGEL
Nov 21, 1916
April 29, 1965
A Giant once lived in
this body
beloved Husband & Father

BERMAN

Jack BERMAN
Nov 19, 1909
Jan 31, 1965
beloved Husband

GREENSPON

Reuben GREENSPON
1894 - 1973

Lillian S. GREENSPON
1900 - 1973

Zilpa DIAMOND
(No Date)
beloved & devoted Mother

Zilpa Greenspon DIAMOND
July 30, 1898
Aug 31, 1979

Edna M. LEVIN
July 24, 1902
Sept 10, 1981

Fannie RUEGER
April 18, 1889
July 23, 1972 h/s

Samuel Jacob STREET
died March 21, 1965
age 79 years

LEVINE

Meyer LEVINE
Feb 10, 1898
Feb 19, 1966
beloved Husband & Father

Yetta C. LEVINE
March 4, 1898
Aug 28, 1971
beloved Wife & Mother

Celia H. BINDER
Jan 5, 1912
Oct 8, 1964 h/s

Charles BINDER
Oct 14, 1908
Aug 22, 1966 h/s

Rose M. BINDER
Dec 3, 1885
Oct 12, 1964 h/s

Morris H. FLAX
Sept 18, 1894
June 8, 1965
d/s Jennie Gold

Jennie Gold FLAX
Aug 10, 1895
April 13, 1977
d/s w/ Morris H.

Minnie KULMAN
Nov 15, 1897
Aug 14, 1967

SIEGEL

Henry SIEGEL
March 15, 1903
Dec 17, 1964 h/s

Jennie Berger SIEGEL
March 15, 1903
July 28, 1976 h/s

SERASKY

Phillip SERASKY
July 17, 1887
Jan 14, 1968

Estelle T. SERASKY
May 25, 1889
July 1, 1964

SCHWARTZ

Nathan SCHWARTZ
Mar 15, 1911
Aug 3, 1989

Julia Roslyn SCHWARTZ
May 7, 1918
May 24, 1991
Dear Mother

GORDON

Sam GORDON
July 28, 1914
June 14, 1965
beloved Husband & Father

GORDON

Joseph GORDON
July 6, 1908
May 8, 1975
beloved Husband, Father &
Grandfather

Al Abe SUGERMAN
Oct 8, 1895
April 26, 1966
beloved Brother & Uncle

FRIEDMAN

Louis FRIEDMAN
Oct 26, 1895
Oct 28, 1965

Stanley R. FRIEDMAN
Oct 16, 1938
Sept 17, 1974

Ernest FRIEDMAN
Oct 31, 1908
May 22, 1980 h/s

WERBLOW

Rebecca WERBLOW
died Nov 18, 1974
age 89 years

Isadore WERBLOW
died Nov 1, 1965
age 60 years

Alfred WERBLOW
1911 - 1990
d/s w/ Hilda

Hilda WERBLOW
1913 - -----
d/s w/ Alfred
together forever

STEIN

Morris N. STEIN
Nov 17, 1892
July 1, 1965

Samuel HENDIN
Sept 26, 1922
Aug 19, 1971

Raymond J. ARROLL
Jan 5, 1914
Jan 22, 1980
beloved Father

GREENSPON

Emanuel GREENSPON M. D.
Sept 5, 1908
April 24, 1969

COHEN

Irvin COHEN
Jan 15, 1907
July 6, 1969
beloved Husband & Father

Katie Kurzer COHEN
April 18, 1915
Oct 9, 1984
beloved Wife & Mother

COHEN

Harold "Dooley" COHEN
June 8, 1914
June 14, 1995
beloved Husband

BECKER

Milton S. BECKER
May 5, 1912
Nov 3, 1972
in loving memory of Husband
& Father

Isadore E. NACHMAN
Aug 11, 1903
Aug 8, 1975 h/s

Marion M. MARKOWITZ
Aug 3, 1895
Apr 7, 1875 h/s

Estol W. FOX
June 12, 1896
June 22, 1974 h/s

FAMILANT

Milton J. FAMILANT
Oct 31, 1911
April 16, 1985
His delight was in the teaching
of the Lord PS. 1:2
Husband, Father & Grandfather

Lillian Newman FAMILANT
Oct 13, 1915
Mar 14, 1983
The Teaching of Kindness Won
Her Life Proverb 31 - 26
Wife, Mother & Grandmother

PERZEKOW

Julian Newman PERZEKOW
March 15, 1920
May 14, 1972

Nathan Louis PERZEKOW
June 14, 1916
Aug 2, 1989

Joseph Milton RUBEN
Aug 17, 1919
June 18, 1971 h/s

Alma Ray Ruben FREEMAN
Act 9, 1922
Feb 26, 1983 h/s
beloved Mother

RUBEN

David H. RUBEN
Feb 21, 1924
Feb 18, 1995
A man of pride, integrity
and love

SAVILLE

Raphael A. SAVILLE
May 6, 1925
Oct 8, 1978
"My Heart Remembers"

TANNEN

Joseph S. TANNEN
Nov 29, 1914
May 15, 1988

GREEN

Daniel GREEN
Dec 9, 1918
Sept 26, 197x (illegible)
beloved Husband & Father

KIRSNER

Hattie KIRSNER
Feb 21, 1900
Sept 13, 1980

NOARD

David NOARD
Sept 10, 1918
Oct 21, 1974
Gone but not Forgotten

Benard L. LIVINSON
Feb 29, 1920
Dec 2, 1976 h/s
Capt US Army
World War 2
Korea

KLESMER

Irving KLESMER
Nov 27, 1904
May 5, 1980

GITLES

Pearl L. GITLES
October 27, 1921
May 21, 1987

SIEGEL

Sam SIEGEL
June 22, 1910
Feb 22, 1985

Mary SIEGEL
Feb 22, 1908
Feb 15, 1986

BRENNER

Benjamin Fred BRENNER
Sept 28, 1919
Feb 19, 1985

SCHTAMF

Frank SCHTAMF
June 16, 1916
Oct 7, 1975

Rosalind Stern ELLENSON
November 3, 1925
December 12, 1980 h/s

Samuel Leon ELLENSON
Aug 16, 1921
Jan 25, 1977 h/s

RICHMAN

Joe RICHMAN
May 15, 1904
May 8, 1981
beloved Husband, Father
& Grandfather

RICHMAN

Esther RICHMAN
Jan 17, 1917
Oct 8, 1985
beloved Wife, Mother
& Grandmother

Anshal I. NEIHOUSE
Oct 18, 1908
Feb 17, 1981 h/s
beloved Husband, Father
& Grandfather

CARMEL

Melvin M. CARMEL
Nov 13, 1916
Feb 22, 1993

CARMEL

Macy Milton CARMEL
Sept 2, 1909
Oct 16, 1976

Rose Lee CARMEL
died June 14, 1992

KANTER

Max Joseph KANTER
Aug 15, 1897
Sept 8, 1975

Celia Epstein KANTER
July 4, 1899
Feb 24, 1988

SEAR

Kieve SEAR
May 1, 1906
Sept 4, 1979
beloved Husband & Father

Edyth Arch SEAR
born March 19, 1916
died Oct 27, 1996
age 80 years
Temporary Metal Marker

COHEN

Minnie COHEN
Feb 23, 1886
Oct 11, 1981

KRADITOR

Charles KRADITOR
April 25, 1900
Oct 13, 1978

Shirley S. KRADITOR
Dec 23, 1905
June 27, 1976

FLAX

David Edward FLAX
June 8, 1915
April 22, 1989

BASS

Milton (Johnny) BASS
Aug 2, 1904
April 30, 1986

Sarah C. BASS
March 12, 1916
Oct 3, 1983

Sarah Fox SHAWEL
Aug 19, 1928
Sept 30, 1978 h/s
beloved Wife & Mother

Benjamin GORDON
1901 - 1981
d/s w/ Jennie

Jennie GORDON
1898 - 1983
d/s w/ Benjamin

FINK

Sidney J. FINK
Jan 7, 1921
Oct 30, 1986
beloved Husband, Father
& Zaide

FINK

Sophia FINK
June 11, 1898
June 30, 1987

Israel FINK
April 15, 1894
March 26, 1977

ELLENSON

Polly D. ELLENSON
Dec 25, 1911
July 6, 1982

Robert ELLENSON
Jan 16, 1917
July 6, 1987

DIAMOND

Phyllis L. DIAMOND
Aug 23, 1924
Dec 14, 1982
beloved Wife, Mother &
Grandmother

Harry Charles DIAMOND
Sept 15, 1921
Feb 16, 1995
beloved Husband, Father &
Grandfather

SHEMER

Lillyan A. SHEMER
Jan 10, 1914
Sept 15, 1990

HARRIS

Leonard P. HARRIS
March 8, 1916
October 17, 1985

ROSENWASSER

Hyman ROSENWASSER
March 25, 1911
Feb 1, 1987
Loving Husband, Father &
Grandmother

SNYDER

Esther N. SNYDER
Aug 25, 1909
Mar 4, 1995

Albert R. SNYDER
July 14, 1906
Mar 26, 1993

Edythe Nachman SLOANE
June 2, 1915
March 17, 1987 h/s

COIN

Shirley Nachman COIN
Jan 13, 1933
Sept 9, 1990
beloved Wife, Mother &
Grandmother

Anna A. SEIDMAN
Mar 16, 1908
Feb 20, 1997 h/s
beloved Wife, Mother &
Grandmother

EPSTEIN

Marlel Phillip EPSTEIN
Aug 19, 1913
Nov 11, 1992

CRUM

Robert Eugene CRUM
June 11, 1928
Feb 24, 1993

SCHWAB

Joanie SCHWAB
died Aug 30, 1994
A Joyous Spirit
beloved Daughter, Sister
& Aunt

Florence (Folla) SCHWAB
died Dec 3, 1990
A woman of Valor
beloved Wife, Mama & Bubby

SMITH

Leon Morris SMITH
Oct 27, 1908
Jan 24, 1995
Loving Husband, Father &
Grandfather

BRENNER

Milton David BRENNER
Oct 17, 1921
June 13, 1994
beloved Husband

HALPERIN

Morris Herbert HALPERIN
Mar 31, 1919
Nov 26, 1995
beloved Husband, Father &
Grandfather

The following stoner are on
the right side of the
maintenance building.

BELL

William David BELL
Oct 19, 1918
Feb 8, 1973

Leon WILKS
July 12, 1912
Oct 9, 1991

Karen Wilks HIRSCH
July 1, 1940
July 23, 1976

LIEBERMAN

Morris H. LIEBERMAN
April 24, 1893
Mar 27, 1976

Anna S. LIEBERMAN
Oct 14, 1895
May 1, 1993

ZWERDLING

David ZWERDLING
Jan 1, 1907
June 5, 1991
Scholar, Artist, Humanitarian
Husband, Father &
Grandfather

Reuben SILVERMAN
June 13, 1906
June 26, 1976

Freda SILVERMAN
Dec 28, 1907
Apr 19, 1995

Alfred H. SANDLER
July 24, 1911
Feb 19, 1993 h/s
beloved Husband, Father &
Grandfather

Bessie M. SANDLER
July 16, 1913
Nov 8, 1994 h/s
beloved Wife, Mother &
Grandmother

CAPLAN

Arthur B. CAPLAN
Jan 2, 1903
Aug 9, 1982
Teves 3, 5663 - Av 20, 5742

Rose F. CAPLAN
Feb 8, 1904
April 18, 1975
Shevet 22, 5664
Tyar 7, 7335

Joseph SNYDER
February 14, 1916
September 4, 1973
beloved Husband, devoted
Father & Grandfather
h/s d/s w/ Dorothy

Dorothy SNYDER
March 12, 1917
September 13, 1991
beloved Wife, Daughter,
Mother & Grandmother
h/s d/s w/ Joseph

Minnie S. COHEN
July 19, 1910
March 29, 1974 h/s

Harry Sol SMITH
Sept 23, 1904
July 18, 1994 h/s

MANTEL

Judah MANTEL
Aug 11, 1907
May 9, 1989

LEVINSON

Julian Leonard LEVINSON
Dec 1, 1922
Dec 16, 1990

DIAMONDSTEIN

Leon Elias DIAMONDSTEIN
July 21, 1901
Apr 16, 1975
beloved Husband & Father

Tillie S. DIAMONDSTEIN
March 27, 1904
May 17, 1995

SHAPIRO

Charles SHAPIRO
Aug 3, 1907
July 20, 1973

MINKOFF

Ida MINFOFF
Dec 31, 1900
March 29, 1994
beloved Mother &
Grandmother

Jack MINKOFF
May 15, 1897
March 31, 1968

KANTOR

Emma Satisky KANTOR
March 12, 1903
Nov 19, 1979

Murray KANTOR
April 2, 1902
Dec 28, 1969

SAMUELS

Fred Edward SAMUELS
May 9, 1896
March 4, 1980

Tillye Satisky SAMUELS
March 22, 1902
July 23, 1974

SATISKY

Elsye SATISKY
March 9, 1898
Dec 14, 1968

SATISKY

Dave SATISKY
Jan 9, 1895
Dec 14, 1968
Beloved Son & Brother

SATISKY

Maurice SATISKY
Apr 19, 1899
Apr 3, 1967
beloved Husband & Father

Ida SATISKY
July 12, 1905
Aug 26, 1989
beloved Wife & Mother

WEGER

Lenp Sinker WEGER
Aug 23, 1904
Oct 3, 1993

A. Sol WEGER
Aug 16, 1894
Dec 21, 1967

ABRAHAM

Rose I. ABRAHAM
Aug 22, 1905
Nov 12, 1990

Meyer ABRAHAM
April 6, 1904
Jan 19, 1971

PREVILLE

Mildred Samuels PREVILLE
Aug 15, 1904
Oct 16, 1991

Arthur Joseph PREVILLE
Feb 18, 1904
May 16, 1969

CAPLON

Michael CAPLON
Oct 15, 1894
May 14, 1969

Joseph CAPLON
April 9, 1888
Aug 2, 1976

SOLTZ

Esther Gillel SOLTZ
July 3, 1897
April 4, 1966

Soloman SOLTZ
July 6, 1888
Feb 17, 1987

Rachael CHAIET
Sept 15, 1891
Oct 12, 1966 h/s

Ethel B. SPAPIRO
Mar 28, 1906
Sept 27, 1990
beloved Wife, Mother &
Grandmother
h/s d/s w/ Saul

Saul SHAPIRO
May 15, 1901
Mar 18, 1993
beloved Husband, Father &
Grandfather
h/s d/s w/ Ethel B.

GOLDBERG

Virginia B. GOLDBERG
June 17, 1918
Jan 8, 1985

Jacob GOLDBERG
Oct 7, 1911
Oct 8, 1968

Harry SPOONER
Aug 12, 1912
Feb 29, 1968 h/s

COHEN

Hyman COHEN
Feb 2, 1912
Oct 31, 1988

Rose Gordon COHEN
Jan 15, 1897
Nov 10, 1971

ABEL

Rebecca ABEL
July 10, 1892
Mar 19, 1976

Joseph Alex ABEL
May 20, 1882
Jan 23, 1969

Martin D. FRIEDLAND
Feb 18, 1910
Jan 9, 1971
beloved Husband & Father h/s

Sidney FRIEDLAND
Sept 4, 1906
Feb 17, 1966 h/s

Abraham Louis BARON
1907 - 1973 h/s

DAMSKY

Rosa B. DAMSKY
March 28, 1905
May 4, 1971
Mother

Father
Jacob B. DAMSKY
Feb 14, 1900
March 26, 1952

SCHLEY

Herman SCHLEY
May 12, 1900
Jan 23, 1971
beloved Husband & Brother

BURLOCK

Carl Linwood BURLOCK
Dec 5, 1951
June 10, 1970

FRENKEL

Eva Rosenstein FRENKEL
April 2, 1908
March 25, 1989
beloved Wife & Sister

Siegfried FRENKEL
Oct 2, 1911
Jan 27, 1995
beloved Husband & Brother

Jacob FRENKEL
Oct 1, 1907
April 14, 1977
Brother

Alexander BURNS
May 5, 1918
Nov 1, 1971 h/s

SANDLER

Jacob SANDLER
Nov 25, 1886
March 29, 1966
beloved Husband & Father

Rosa Fega SANDLER
March 25, 1888
Dec 4, 1978
beloved Mother & Grandmother

FISHER

Kate Weger FISHER
August 18, 1907
February 24, 1989

Jack David FISHER
February 22, 1904
September 15, 1987

SAUNDERS

Ida Warren SAUNDERS
Dec 25, 1945
Sept 24, 1967

Louis CHERNOCK
January 17, 1897
March 27, 1988
in loving memory h/s

Goldie J. SHERMAN
Feb 22, 1917
June 29, 1983
Always in our Hearts h/s

Joseph SAMUELS
May 10, 1907
Feb 11, 1972
Virginia 81
US Coast Guard Res.
World War 2

Morris S. GOTTLIEB
Aug 15, 1901
Dec 26, 1970
beloved Husband & Father h/s
f/s Father

Ethel Gottlieb ROGATZ
Sept 28, 1909
Sept 20, 1993
beloved Wife & Mother h/s
f/s Mother

Harry JACOBS
Aug 6, 1902
Dec 29, 1972 h/s
f/s Father

Sadie Hochman STEINBERG
January 22, 1911
June 13, 1987 h/s

Harry HOCHMAN
September 15, 1903
November 12, 1972 h/s

BLUESTONE - FRIEDMAN

Gladys Helene _____
Dec 6, 1935
Jan 15, 1971

beloved Wife, Mother, Sister,
Daughter & Speaker for the
animals h/s
d/s w/ Sandra Atalie

Sandra Atalie _____
Oct 2, 1949
Jan 15, 1971
beloved Daughter & Sister h/s
d/s w/ Gladys Helene

Reda Samuels DAVIS
Sept 17, 1910
Nov 19, 1983
devoted Wife & Mother h/s

WOLSHIN

Israel WOLSHIN
Feb 2, 1888
May 29, 1977
Papa Artist

Rose G. WOLSHIN
July 26, 1893
March 5, 1972
beloved Wife & Mother

DAVIS

Bob Davis nee WOLSHIN
July 16, 1908
Feb 8, 1975
devoted Son, Father & Brother

STADLIN

Frances E. STADLIN
Aug 28, 1930
May 25, 1989
beloved Wife, Mother & Grandmother

Sol FRIEDMAN
1900 - 1992
d/s w/ Minnie

Minnie FRIEDMAN
1905 - 1984
d/s w/ Sol

Joseph Aaron GOLDEN
Nov 5, 1908
Jan 22, 1976

beloved Husband
Sam FLAKOWITZ
1907 - 1987
d/s w/ Sara

Sara FLAKOWITZ
1916 - 1987
d/s w/ Sam

GOLOMBIK

Leonard GOLOMBIK
June 10, 1920
Jan 29, 1994
beloved & devoted Husband
of Lillian GOLOMBIK

Lillian GOLOMBIK
May 14, 1923
May 5, 1988
Beloved & Devoted Wife of
Leonard GOLOMBIK

Irving ROSENFELD
Dec 29, 1912
Oct 23, 1976
Maj. US Army h/s

SHARF

Julia Reichman SHARF
Feb 19, 1911
Aug 8, 1992

Macy Morris SHARF
May 18, 1911
Aug 8, 1988

Max A. GOLDSTEIN
Oct 14, 1906
Feb 5, 1985 h/s

Theodore H. WOODMAN
Nov 11, 1912
Dec 18, 1983 h/s
Mosonic

RICE

William S. RICE
Jan 6, 1912
Dec 7, 1980

Helen I. RICE
April 24, 1915
Oct 2, 1994

Max STEIN
Oct 7, 1904
Feb 28, 1981
beloved Husband, Father &
Grandfather h/s
f/s 1904 - 1981

MILLER

Samuel MILLER
died Jan 2, 1984
age 83 years

ELLIS

Bernard ELLIS
Nov 22, 1911
Jan 20, 1987

Sally S. ELLIS
Sept 20, 1908
March 18, 1981

SAUNDERS

Beryl Leon SAUNDERS
Dec 21, 1913
July 3, 1981

Sophie Samet SAUNDERS
Oct 8, 1920
Nov 29, 1981

Jonas GRANNICK
February 19, 1920
October 22, 1981
beloved Husband & Father h/s

LEIFER

Leo LEIFER
Jan 25, 1920
May 31, 1982
loving Husband, Father &
Grandfather

Albert SHAWEL
January 17, 1909
December 31, 1984
beloved Husband h/s

Benjamin HOFFMAN
born Mar 1, 1904
died Jan 13, 1985
WO US Air Force
World War 2
Korea

HOFFMAN

Bella A. KURZER
May 16, 1916
Apr 29, 1986 h/s

Bernard W. KURZER
Oct 9, 1920
Aug 2, 1991 h/s

Milton KAPLAN
Oct 10, 1918
Nov 24, 1988

GOLDSTEIN

Jacob Henry GOLDSTEIN
April 1, 1919
Sept 15, 1984
beloved Brother

Sadie FISHER
October 28, 1906
June 11, 1993
Our Loving Sister

Anne WEINSTEIN
Feb 6, 1931
May 13, 1997
age 66
Temporary Metal Marker

David ROTHMAN
May 23, 1907
June 25, 1991
Humanitarian, wonderful
Father and devoted Husband
d/s w/ Esther Jacob

Esther Jacob ROTHMAN
Jan 7, 1906
Dec 1, 1992
Loving devoted & Caring Wife
& Mother
d/s w/ David

Corinne Jacobs SHAUITT
April 11, 1909 Sept 26, 1991
In loving memory of my wife

Maxine SHAVITT
Apr 27, 1924
Sep 1, 1993
TEC 5 US Army
World War 2 h/s

Pearl Neustein BERGER
December 30, 1992
Loving Mother &
Grandmother h/s

Harry LAZARUS
March 6, 1906
Jan 17, 1992
In loving memory h/s

Mary Stein PELTZ
1899 - 1995
age 96
Temorary Metal Marker

FINEMAN

Charles FINEMAN
July 4, 1912
Aug 15, 1989

David CARMEL
Jan 11, 1914
June 14, 1986 h/s

Maurice B. LEVY
1939 - 1986 H/S

FOX

Hannah M. FOX
Jun 4, 1912
Jan 6, 1990

Phillip FOX
Nov 1, 1907
April 15, 1986

Phyllis Goodman KEMACK
Aug 9, 1923
Feb 3, 1986 H/S
d/s w/ Daniel Leon

Beloved Parents

Daniel Leon KEMACK
Mar 24, 1925
Sept 25, 1985
d/s w/ Phyllis Goodman

Samuel PODOFF
Dec 9, 1909
Feb 23, 1993 H/S
Husband, Father &
Grandfather

EPSTEIN

Jack Kanter EPSTEIN
April 28, 1915
June 25, 1986
beloved Husband, Father &
Grandfather

PELTZ

Phillip W. PELTZ
Aug 9, 1906
June 23, 1985

Beatrice S. PELTZ
Dec 31, 1908
Dec 26, 1983

Mrs Mollie Paster GETSUG
March 6, 1915
Nov 23, 1996
age 81
Temorary Metal Marker

Jerald WEINSTEIN
Feb 9, 1918
Feb 10, 1989 H/S
"the Heart man"

Kate Sarah KRESSEL
Nov 20, 1912
Mar 5, 1989 H/S
beloved Sister & Aunt

ANKER

Irving ANKER
June 11, 1918
Feb 7, 1991
beloved Husband, Father &
Grandfather

RECANT

Ethel H. RECANT
May 2, 1914
Aug 9, 1992
beloved Wife & Mother

Dorothy Jane SCHY
May 30, 1924
July 31, 1995 H/S
beloved Wife, Mother &
Bubby
May the Radiance of your
spirit ever Shine on us.

Edythe S GLAZER
July 13, 1919
Nov 23, 1990

ANKER

Moses ANKER
March 18, 1916
Oct 9, 1989
beloved Husband, Father &
Grandfather

HEBREW CEMETERY

Acknowledgment: Transcribed by Barry Miles, February and March of 1997. Also, a special thanks to Barry Nachman for review and additional information.

HERBERT CEMETERY
Armstrong Point (75) {J -11}

LOCATION: On the right side of Armstrong lane, half way between N. N. Highway (Kecoughtan Road) and Armstrong Point. One thousand feet back of and on the land of "Joy Home", owned by Fred Cock. This information is from the W P A Administration of Virginia Historical Inventory.

There were several graves at this site, but only one stone was standing.

This is the grave of a descendant of Thomas Curle, and grandfather of the owner of "Joy Home". in 1937.

Acknowledgment: Transcribed by Mary Bullifant, Hampton, Virginia. January 4, 1937 and Barry W. Miles, 12 April 1997.

In memory of
Pascow HERBERT

Who departed this life
in the 60 year of his age
on the 21 May 1801

Sacred to the memory of
Jas. Henry C. FINCH
only child of
Jas. H. and Laura F. FINCH
Died Dec 28, 1847

Barry Miles visited the site of the marker on 12 April 1997. The only marker today is the tombstone of Pascow Herbert. I was told by one of the local residents that the marker is not at its original site. When Capt. Fred Cock was in the process of building a residence, the tombstone was found broken in two different places. Capt. Cock had a brick foundation built and the tombstone was laid horizontal on this foundation. Capt. Fred Cock came to Virginia after the Civil War and purchased land on Armstrong Point. Capt. Cock was a member of the Virginia Pilots Association. The tombstone reads as Mrs Bullifant had recorded, except the last two lines are reversed. The tombstone is several hundred yards from the Herbert House. This is said to be the second oldest house in the City of Hampton, built sometime in the late 1700's.

In 1968 the Hampton Chapter, Daughter of the American Revolution, placed a plaque on the tombstone showing that Pascow Herbert was a Lieutenant in the American Revolutionary Navy. The plaque reads:

REVOLUTION
NAVY
Lieut. Pascow Herbert
1741 - 1801
Presented by Hampton Chapter
Daughters of
The American Revolution
May 21, 1968

HOLLIER CEMETERY
Harris Avenue and McNally Street (77) {I - 2}
Langley Air Force Base

These graves are located on land (formerly an old farm) now part of Langley Field. They are almost on the waterfront of the Eastern Branch of Back River, a short distance from the old Sherwood house, now used as a school for the Field children. This is from the W P A of Virginia Historical Inventory, by Mary F. Bullifant, December 22, 1936. The following inscriptions by Mary Bullifant:

Gravestones on the Old Moore Farm.

Here lieth
Ann HOLLIER
daughter of Simon and
Ann HOLLIER
Died the 16 day of March
1796 Aged 12 years
She sleeps nor can the
lovely Angel hear the
mourning voices of friends
so dear.
The pangs of Keenest woe
their swoll'n hearts may rend.
Alas her disembodied soul
can not amend.

Here Lieth
Frances HOLLIER
the daughter of Simon and
Ann Hollier
she died the 4th day of Jan'y 1798
age 16 years
Her soul is fled and gone to rest
far from this world
of grief and pain
among the good and righteous
forever to remain
Stop reader stop! Let Nature claim
a Tear, A Mother's last and
Only child lies here.

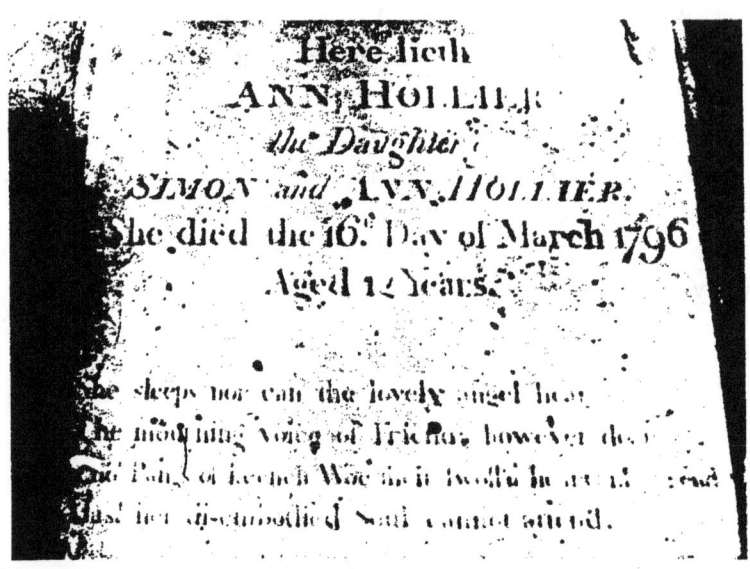

Ann Hollier, the daughter of Simon and Ann Hollier, who died age 12 on March 16, 1796, lies next to her sister, Frances, in a small cemetery in the present Lighter-than-Air area. The epitaph reads:

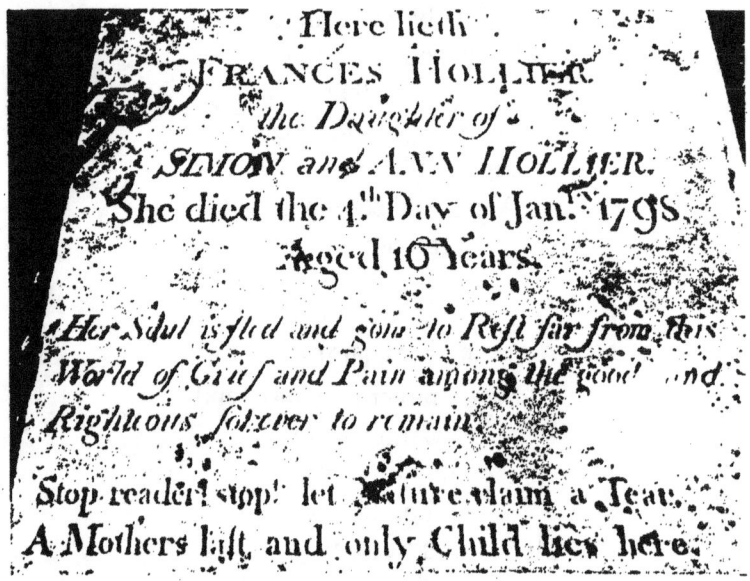

Frances Hollier, the daughter of Simon and Ann Hollier, who died age 16 on January 4, 1798, lies next to her sister, Ann, in a small cemetery in the present Lighter-than-Air area. The epitaph reads:

Pictures from Langley Field Early Years V 975.541 C946l

Cemeteries of the City of Hampton, Virginia / formerly Elizabeth City County

JOHNSON CEMETERY
Grundland Road (23) {O - 3}

Tombstone of Samuel R. Johnson

Johnson Cemetery is located in a clump of trees on the west side of the last house on Grundland Road before the old Nike site. The land was owned by Theo (Thaddeus) Johnson, this is why the cemetery is a Johnson Cemetery.

Acknowledgments: Transcribed by Mr. Steve Keith and Mr. Tim Winters, Mary P. Strup and Mrs Wm. W. Wyatt (Betty Harper Wyatt). The information in parentheses is from Mrs Wm. W. Wyatt, and is not inscribed on the tombstones. Pictures by Barry Miles.

Sacred to the memory of
Roseanna (FITCHETT)
(2nd wife)
wife of David WALLACE
Born 1802
Died Dec 1882
rest in peace

In memory of
David WALLACE
Born in Somerset Co.
Maryland
Aug 10, 1799
Died in the county
Elizabeth City, Virginia
July 8, 1875

James C. WALLACE
Born Dec 20, 1828
Died Mar 10, 1911
d/s w/ Mary J.

Mary J. (Jane) WALLACE
Born Oct 12, 1825
Died May 10, 1882
d/s w/ James C.
Farewell

Mary E.
wife of B. F. JOHNSON
Born Dec 1878 (1876)
Died Jul 1894
inscription unreadable

Samuel R. JOHNSON
Apr 7, 1842
Jan 28, 1919
Dearest loved ones thou hast
left us our loss so deeply felt
but it is God that has benefited
us. He can all our sorrows
heal.

Sallie L(Lee). J.(Johnson)
ABIDELL
July 18, 1876
May 30, 1906

Artelia C. (Clyde) JOHNSON
May 18, 1879
July 18, 1886

Annie E. BARNES
born Feb 9, 1881
died Nov 4, 1903
at rest

Mother
Mary Susan LEWIS
Dec 20, 1849
Oct 19, 1918
f/s M. S. L.
d/s with John Lewis

Father
John LEWIS
July 18, 1838
Nov 12, 1923
f/s J. L.
d/s with Mary Sue Lewis

David JOHNSON
Born July 10, 1817
Died June 9, 1859
d/s with Catherine

Catherine (Eliz.) (STORES)
JOHNSON
Born Feb 18, 1813
Died Jan 31, 1890
d/s with David

Tombstone of David & Catherine Johnson

LATIMER CEMETERY
Oakville Road (61) {J - 5}
C. L. Phillips Estate

On 28 December 1996, Barry Miles, spoke with Mr. Morgan, a resident on Oakville Road for 41 years, remembered the graves on Mr Phillips farm. He remembered the graves on Mr. Phillips farm, but said that after the Phillips family died (Mr. Phillips at about age 83 years and Mrs. Phillips in her 90's), the land was sold, and the graves removed. From the records of Mr. Luther L. Alexander, six graves were moved to Oakland Cemetery, on Pembroke Avenue. Inscriptions of four of the graves are listed below, as the appear in the book, "Identified Gravesites of Oakland Cemetery," Section 5. Hampton Public Library, V975.5412 Id2g.

The following information was transcribed by Sadie A. Anderson of Hampton on March 19, 1936.

Martha (Marina)
Daughter of Elizabeth LATIMER
Died Oct 10, 1800
Aged 7 Yrs. 6 Mos.

In memory of
(Judge) George LATIMER
Who died Nov 3, 1832
Aged 44

Matthew
Son of George and
Elizabeth LATIMER
Died March 1, 1831
Aged 3 Yrs.

In memory of
Almora S. (Almira)
Daughter of George
and
Elizabeth LATIMER
Died Sept 3, 1854
Aged 21 Yrs. 5 Mos.

The information in parentheses are from the William and Mary Quarterly Volume 14, Series 1.

LATTIMER - HICKMAN BURIAL GROUNDS
Harris Creek Road (Shore Crest) (25) {M - 4}

The following information is taken from a file entitled "Copeland - Finn - Drummond House" in the General File on the second floor of the Charles Taylor Arts Center on Victoria Blvd., Hampton, Va. This file covers the "Lattimer - Hickman Burial Grounds" adjacent to the Lattimer - Wilson House (owned by Taylor S. Holtzclaw: and the Drummond Cemetery on Harris Creek Road. Which contains a small walled area of 3 graves, an unknown Confederate soldier and a couple from Poquoson, Va.

Thomas Drummond was the third owner of nearby Copeland - Finn - Drummond House, the oldest existing house in Hampton, and base of Blackbeard the Pirate. House can be seen from Mear's Plantation "Brittain", which was given to Catherine, wife of Caleb Mears, by her parents, Makel and Elizabeth Bonnwell.

A grant of 180 acres in 1632 to Thomas Bonwell/Bonnell, stayed in the Bonnwell hands till 1803, when deeded to Catherine (Bonwell) Mears.

There is a close relationship between the Drummond and Lattimore-Hickman Cemeteries and lands.

Revisited by Barry Miles 2 February 1997 a stone was found that had not recorded. Only three stone are standing. Thoes of Thomas Latimer, Nannie Hickman and Susan Hickman. The remainder of the stone are lying flat on the ground and some are nearly covered by earth and grass.

Gone Home
Nannie HICKMAN
Daughter of
William and Sarah HICKMAN
Born 1861 - Died 1931

in thee, O Lord have
I put my trust
Foot Marker N. H.

Martha HICKMAN
Daughter of William and Sarah HICKMAN
Oct 22, 1853
Oct 29, 1927

Home where no storm or
no tempest raves
In the light of the calm
Eternal day when no willows weep
over lonely graves
and the tears from our eyelids
are kissed away

Loolah
Daughter of William and Sarah HICKMAN
Born June 23, 1865
Died May 13, 1867

Yet again we hope to meet her
when the day of life has fled
then with joy in heaven to greet thee
where no farewell tear is shed

William HICKMAN, Sr.
b. Nov 23, 1777
d. June 7, 1861
Till the day breaks
here let him be
Then shall he wait
glorious and free

Thomas LATIMER
Born Dec 31, 178-
Died Sept 14, 1859

Poem not legible

William I
son of William and Sarah HICKMAN
Born Dec 16, 1856
Died Jan 18, 1859

Little _____ Little lamb
said he
and place them on my breast
Protection they shall find in me
In me be ever Blest

William HICKMAN
Born Dec 7, 1825
Died xxx 30, 1908

keeping _____
We leave our loved one sleeping

H. M.
(not recorded)
Born 1857
Died Oct 23, 1913

Susan L.
Daughter of
William and Sarah HICKMAN
Born March 10, 1852
Died Dec 31, 1915

Sleep dear sister
Sleep and take
they rest, We loved
thee well,
But Jesus loved
thee best
Foot Marker S. L. H.

William LATIMER
Born June 15, 1789
Died Nov 5, 1859
inscription not legible

Sarah
beloved ---- of
William HICKMAN
Born January 3, 1828
Died June 30, 1894
inscripton not legible

Foot Markers
M. E. H.
W. H.
W. L.
L. H.

LEWELLEN - MOORE BURIAL GROUND
Radford Drive (26) {B - 7}

All four sites here are above ground crypts constructed of brick and concrete. The cemetery is heavily overgrown, but that has probably protected it from tampering over the years. The Hayes family, current owners, purchased the property in 1937. The Hayes property deed includes the cemetery site for protection. The gravesite is shown on the E. A. Semple map of the 1880's and shows the land owned by B. Lewellen.

Acknowledgment: Transcribed by W. S. Keith and T. W. Winters, June 9, 1990.

Fannie D. LEWELLEN
Died June 10, 1885
Aged 63 years
We miss you at home
dear mother

Mary E. MOORE
Died Nov 7, 1880
Aged 53 years
Rest in peace
Dear mother

(two crypts unmarked)

MASON or DRUMMOND CEMETERY
East of 121 1/2 Windmill Road (28) {N - 2}

Julia Ann DRUMMOND
born Jan 18, 1855
died December 24, 1892
aged 37 yrs 9 mo and 6 days
stone is leaning against a tree.

small stone
cannot read
may be a misplaced footstone

Additional information from David Routten. The following are known to be buried at this burial site.

Two or more childern
of John T. MASON

George MELSON
age about 14 years
died before 1915

Acknowledgment: David Routten for locating burial site, and information of burials in this graveyard. The name of this cemetery is not know certainty.

MEARS CEMETERY
Brittain Lane (29) {L - 3}

Edward MEARS
CO. B. 3 Va. Cav.
C. S. A.
1835-1891
C.S.A. Marker at foot

James L. MEARS
Born Sept 5, 1830
Died April 20,1891
Closed are thy sweet eyes
From this world of pain
But we trust in God
To meet thee again
Foot Marker J.L.M.

C.S.A. Marker
1861-1865
Deo Vindice

Our dearly beloved child
Albert MEARS
Son of
Tha--t & Sally L. MEARS
born April 22, 1861
Died Aug 1, 1864
A fair bud, too young for death
transplanted to the perpetual
bloom of heaven

Edward W.
son of
J. L. & G. J. MEARS
Born May 28, 1890
Died Sep 22, 1890
A little bud of Love
In bloom with God above.
Foot Marker E. W. M.

It is possible that the CSA markers are not properly placed today.
Acknowledgment: Transcribed by Thelma Savage April 1968.

MORNING STAR BAPTIST CHURCH CEMETERY
N. Armistead behind Gardners Trailer Court (74) {G - 5}
African American

Hampton Librarian, Jerry Lassiter, states that the Cemetery behind Gardner Trailer Park is the Morning Star Baptist Church Cemetery, at 2717 N. Armistead Ave.

"Daily Press" newspaper May 30, 1990. Jim Spencer's article on this cemetery.

In 1990 the condition of the cemetery was recorded by Mr Keith and Mr Winters. This cemetery is heavily overgrown with briars and trees up to 4" in diameter and is about 3" above water level. Numerous grave sites are scattered about and several have been dug up near the headstones in an apparent attempt to remove skulls and one large hole contained ashes. It is likely that other tombstones are buried or hidden by the undergrowth.

Acknowledgment: T. Winters and W. S. Keith transcribed June 5, 1990.

Eliza CHANDLER
Sept 7, 1888
Apr 4, 1926
at rest

Rosett B. LIVELY
wife of E. J. Lively
Sept 29, 1880
July 20, 1942

Mother
Kisiah LIVELY
Born 1802
Died Dec 19, 1896

Henry SMITH
Born 1830
Died Sept 23, (?) 1904

Brother
Evan WALTER
Dec 1881
Dec 7, 1921
at rest

infant son of
C. L. DANIEL
Born & Died
August 18, 1916
in rest

Father
Lymas CHANDLER
Jul 4, 1877
Jul 19, 1915
at rest

Father
John PEYTON
1850 - 1910
at rest

Nymrod CHANDLER
Born Dec 5, 1840
Died Aug 27, 1911

Colonett
wife of Nymrod CHANDLER
Born Aug 2, 1842
Died Aug 6, 1906

Marker
CASHES & WATFORD &
Family

Husband
Cashes WATFORD
Died Apr 2, 1902

Thomas WATFORD
1890 - 1907

Julia WATFORD
Born 1880
Died Oct 16, 1908
resting in peace

Elnora WATFORD
1900 - 1902

Bettie WATTS
Died April 1, 1916
Aged 38Yrs
at rest
(inscription unreadable)

Janne Estelle WATTS
Born Oct 4, 1887
Died May 28, 1913
sleep on and take thy rest

Albert WATTS
Born 1862
Died May 18, 1916
at rest

Dollie WATTS
Born May 19, 1854
Died Jan 30, 1922
at rest

D. W.
(on footstone)

Wallace SEAY
Born Aug 21, 1925
Died Apr 27, 1946

Robert James CHRISTIAN
Born Mar 6, 1873
Died Nov 1, 1890
He was the youngest child.
both were workers in the
Sabbath School and beloved by
all.

William E. CHRISTIAN
son of Edward and Laura
CHRISTIAN
Born Jan 31, 1870
Died Nov 24, 1890
He was an obedient child
to father and mother

Margaret RICHARDSON
Born March 1865
Died Sep 9, 1940
James RICHARDSON
Born March 1862
Died May 13, 1921
Gone but not forgotten

Laura Louise GOODEN
Born Feb 17, 1905
Died Jun 23, 1910

L.L.C

Lousiana PRITCHETT
Born Aug 5, 1885
Died Jun 20, 1904
Honored beloved and wept
here mother lived

Son of J. and Maggie
PRITCHETT
Henry PRITCHETT
Born Mar 29, 1917
Died Oct 16, 1917
at rest

Dau. of J. and Maggie
PRITCHETT
Carrie PRITCHETT
Born Mar 28, 1909
Died Oct 27, 1920

James STEPHENSON
Born Oct 9, 1872
Died Apr 10, 1936

Father
William HARRIS
Born 1874
Died May 7, 1918

Nancy
wife of A. L. BOWMAN
1881- 1913
at rest

Braxton BILLUPS
Born Nov 17, 1871
Died Nov 14, 1911

Mother
Laura BILLUPS
Born 1865
Died Oct 20, 1916
at rest

View of the Destruction of Morning Star Baptist Church Cemetery

PHILLIPS CEMETERY
Union and Lincoln Streets (35) {J - 10}
African American

This Cemetery was recently cleaned up by the Olde Hampton Community Association. Miss Sadie M. Brown, is the president of the Association and was instrumental in this project. The community offers thanks for this effort. There is still more work needed in this cemetery. It is very difficult to walk around, and the growth looks like it will be a problem again this year. Also, the layout of this cemetery makes it extremely difficult to transcribe. The graves are not in even rows.

Miss Sadie Brown has provided the Tidewater Genealogical Society with a history and a listing of the tombstone inscriptions.

144   Cemeteries of the City of Hampton, Virginia / formerly Elizabeth City County

HISTORY

In 1885 to 1890 the Cemetery was located on Union Street near Back River Road. The Cemetery has been registered at Hampton City Hall as Phillips, Pleasant, Rising Star, Bethlehem and Queen Street Cemetery. The land at one time belonged to the Sinclair estate and was acquired by J. Landsberg for sale as cemetery plots for $200.00. The plots or lots were sold to people living in the neighborhood, because of limited transportation.
There are some elaborate grave markers and family plot markers. Some of the local residents that purchased lots were Mr J. L. Lively, A. W. Bassett, A. T. Ransom and Segar Whiting Trust. In the early 1900; land in the area south of Union Street, known as Queen St. Baptist Church Cemetery, was being bought through the Peoples Building and Loan.

Acknowledgment: Transcribeb by Miss Sadie M. Brown in the fall of 1996, giving names and years. During March 1997, Barry W. Miles revisited the cemetery adding additional information.

Lopers Family Plot, No Graves

QUEEN STREET CEMETERY
Lincoln Street Side

Pleasant DENNIS
died Apr 11, 1914
age 64 years
at rest

Hyrm YEARBY
died June 22, 1895

Charlett YEARBY
died ----

Mary COLEMAN
1863 - 1913

Martha W. NURSE
Sept 20, 1888
Aug 19, 1961

Harold NURSE
1884 - 1946

Margaret PRESCOTT
(No Dates)

Martha COX
Jan 15, 1875
Mar 8, 1942
G. B. N. F.
Stone on ground

Lucinda MASON
1873 - 1946
Sister
In loving Memory as a
Testimonial of Regard
for her efficient work
as a founder & Mother
of St. Mary's household
No. 29.
Servant of God well done

William H. MASON
May 10, 1865
May 11, 1946
rest in peace
P. G. M. of G. U. O.
Seven wise men

_____ COLEMAN
1895

Albert ELLIOTT
Oct 29, 1924
Husband
at rest
Stone is off pedestal

Laura BROWN
w/o C. Brown
born 1887
July 19, 1926
at rest

Laura SWAN
died Oct 4, 1943
Asleep in Jesus

Eliza SPARTLEY
died Jan 2, 1928
Mother
Rest in peace

Mary E. SPARTLEY
died Aug 16, 1938
Age 49 years
At Rest

Sallie BURRELL
d/o R. & C.
1910 - 1926
G. B. N. F.

Caroline BRIGGS
Dec 1863 - 1919
Stone sunken in ground

Saria E. ROBINSON
died 1912

Ida Bell JOHNSON
1888
died Nov 5, 1916
Aged 28 years
G. B. N. F.

Robert DENNIS
died 1923

Tiberis WASHINGTON
Aug 7, 1892
July 11, 1943
at rest

Aug 29, 1939

Elizabeth HORNIS
1932

Moses DILLARD
Dec 25, 1861
Nov 12, 1938
Stone on ground

Horsit LIVELY
1905 - 1937

Elizabeth CHANDLER
died 1911

Albert KEMP
July 10, 1885
Oct 2, 1943
Husband
at rest

Mary J. SCOTT
died April 25, 1911
Mother
G. B. N. F.

George T. OLIVER
1854
died Jan 1, 1915
His beloved sleepeth

Willis BRATCHER
Jan 27, 1887
June 12, 1945
Stone sunken in ground

Sarah BAILEY
1893 - 1942

Rose E. NEWSON
Apr 8, 1892
June 22, 1918
at rest

Stone on ground

Russell BROWN
Aug 20, 1895
April 21, 1941
A faithful Friend

Alva L. MASON
1918 - 1935

Mary A. MINKINS
1877 - 1943
at rest

Eunice Minkins
COLEMAN
Oct 18, 1895
Oct 26, 1933
At Rest
In memory of our beloved
daughter
Stone off pedestal

Ellen CARY
w/o Larkin
born Dec 18, 1840
died Mar 14, 1923
Honored, Beloved
& Wept
Here Mother lies

Mary NEWSON
1923 9 yrs old

Two tin markers
unreadable

Mary REDWOOD
Feb 22, 1872
June 21, 1919
Simply to thy cross
I cling
Stone shaped of a cross

Amy REDWOOD
died March 14, 1923
Age 72 years
Asleep in Jesus
Blessed Sleep

Deller DABNEY
Jan 19, 1919
Age 50 yrs
G. B. N. F.

Phillips PERKINS
born Dec 25, 1882
died Dec 11, 1916
G. B. N. F.

Sarah BATTEN
died Nov 5, 1919
My Beloved Mother
Peaceful rest

Rebecca SYKES
died Dec 19, 1908
age 60
at rest

Thaddeus WILLIAMS
died Oct 19, 1940
Faithful assistance to
Smith Bros. Undertakers

Lillie ASKEW
Dec 12, 1885
Oct 25, 1914
G. B. N. F.
Stone on ground

Alice JOHNSON
1893 - 1940

Mary J. NEWSON
1854 - 1912

Hattie HOPE
(No Date)

Ernest NOTTINGHAM
born May 5, 1936
died cannot read
Hand Painted

Harry DAVIS
Virginia
Sgt. 538 Serv. BN QMC
February 15, 1935

Josephine DAVIS
Jan 15, 1895
Jan 3, 1944
Sister
Only asleep
Stone on ground

Susan WASHINGTON
April 16, 1939
July 1, 1939

Frank PRESLEY
Sept 4, 1885
June 7, 1938

Horace A. LIVELY
1905 - 1937

Eliza RANDALL
born 1831
Aug 13, 1921
at rest
Stone Broken

Peter T. CHATMAN
1874 - 1942
at rest

Anna MALONE
w/o John Malon
Stone sunken in ground

Mary JOHNSON
born 1854
died Nov 1, 1912
Aged 58, yrs
G. B. N. F.
Stone on ground

Lillie JACKSON
Born Nov 6, 1896
died July 19, 1918
at rest

Elizabeth CHANDLER
died Apr 12, 1911
Stone on ground

There are 8 unnamed vaults
The rear portion, 109 feet by 212 feet running back, fronting on Lincoln Street (being lots 49 and 50) used by Queen Street Baptist Church. Deed from John Luther Carter and Rebecca Carter, 24 Oct 1973. Landsberg.

Landsberg Plat -- part 104 and 103 -- 384 Lincoln Street rear. (legal Description)
Pleasant Cemetery Owner, Union Street, Deed Book --- p ---
Landsberg Plat-- L 108 part 107 (legal Description)

Rising Star Society Owner -- Union Street Deed Book 79, page 116, Landsberg Plat 109 (legal Description)

UNION STREET CEMETERIES
PLEASANT, RISING STAR SOCIETY
BETHLEHEM LODGE CEMETERY

PLEASANT plots

Robert VINSON
born Dec 21, 1895
died Sept 7, 1924
Gone but not
Forgotten

Matilda TURNER
1835
Mar 15, 1905
Gone but not
Forgotten

Richard PLESANTS
Nov 25, 1884
Jan 12, 1967

James PLESANTS
Feb 17, 1895
Dec 26, 1968

Lucy PLESANTS
Feb 19, 1900
Apr 1, 1959

Sherman PLESANTS
April 30, 1959
Age 57

Sadie PLESANTS
July 12, 1891
May 6, 1956

Curley PLESANTS
Dec 7, 1891
March 3, 1976
In Loving Memory

Georgiana BROWN
died Feb 8, 1964

Samuel RANDAL
Nov 16, 1901
Age 85 yrs
He was Deacon of
Queen
St. Baptist Church

Louisa RANDAL
w/o Samuel
June 15, 1899
Age 75 yrs

Richard A. SKINNER
USN
Aug 19, 1889
died Apr 21, 1909
Soldier fighting,
fighting for Christ as
well as for his country

Louise SKINNER
Born Mar 6, 1897
died Aug 1, 1907

Beatrice P. YOUNG
Sept 10, 1916
Apr 25, 1996

Inez B. ROY
Sept 16, 1918
May 2, 1975

Mancil R. FAISON
Aug 9, 1908
Mar 30, 1964

Robert HOWARD
died Mar 28, 1910
Aged 71 years

Queen Victoria
SKINNER
1905

_____ CLARK
Nov 21, 1925
May 29, 1926
at rest
Stone top broken off

4 CORBIN graves

James CORBIN
1867
died March 7, 1926

Wardell CORBIN
Jan 27, 1887
May 16, 1972

Alfonso CORBIN
born Feb 15, 1896
died Sept 24, 1918
Gone but not
Forgotten

Mary V. CORBIN
born Oct 6, 1871
died Oct 29, 1932

MAJOR - PHILLIPS Plot

Mary MAJOR
w/o J. O. Major
born Jan 6, 1840
died Apr 12, 1913
R.I.P.

Joseph MAJOR
born Demerara
British Guinea S. A.
Nov 9, 1848
died March 9, 1926
R.I.P.

Helena G. PHILLIPS
1881 - 1962

Solomon PHILLIPS
1883 - 1953

Baby ____
born Feb 17, 1911
died Nov 14, 1911

Elizabeth HORNIS
1932

Gladys M.
WILLIAMS
Sept 25, 1902
April 28, 1928
A sleep in Jesus

Dr. John H.
ROBINSON Jr.
born May 26, 1887
1927

Lillian PARKER
February 23, 1905
August 25, 1945
at rest

Baby Girl SMITH
died June 11, 1955
Temporary Metal
Marker

Barney WALKER
born Aug 10, 1875
died Oct 3, 1928

Estell Rollins COLE
born Oct 18, 1884
died Jan 17, 1928
inscription unreadable
Stone on ground

Nannie ROLLINS
(No Dates)

John H. BROWN
Mar 28, 1897
June 8, 1965

2 unmarked vaults

Lenora BROWN
Mar 14, 1896
Dec 23, 1975

Katte WILSON
1879 - 1964

LIVELY plots

Susie J. LIVELY
Mother
June 4, 1873
Oct 16, 1946

Araham J. LIVELY
Nov 28, 1874
May 11, 1929
Asleep in Jesus

Georgiana JOHNSON
March 15, 1855
May 20, 1925
G . B. N. F.

unmarked vault

Bland Family Marker
surrounded by iron
fence
only one grave

Harry BLAND
Mar 18, 1882
Apr 17, 1972

HOPSON Plot

Clemetine H.
JOHNSON
June 26, 1922
Jan 24, 1969

Sgt Albert TAYLOR
1st USC Cav. Co. P
1864 / 65

Walter PARKER
Va. Cook 338 Serv
BQMC 1935
Stone sunken in
ground

Elnora H. CLARK
Sept 1881
Oct 11, 1909
Aged 27 yrs

____ JOHNSON
1960

Susan MATTHEWS
died Apr 30, 1906
Aged 60 years
at rest

Elizabeth PEELE
w/o Joseph H.
born Mar 10, 1885
died Mar 16, 1928
Thy memory shall
ever be a guiding star

____ ALEXANDER
1834
Temporary Metal
Marker

William PARKER
1945

Peter CHATMAN
1942

Joseph L. WILSON
born Dec 19, 1862
died May 11, 1915
Age 53 yrs
at rest

Blanche D. HAWKINS
June 2, 1895
Feb 12, 1932
Daughter

Edith REDWOOD
April 27, 1935
at rest

Martha LEE
died Aug 23, 1927
Age 65 yrs
Faithful to her trust
Ever unto Death

Mary M. BARMER
Jan 20, 1902
March 31, 1993
By Her Sons

Curtis BANKS
Feb 12, 1916
Mar 13, 1927
Our Darling
at rest

Earnest BANKS
born Sept 22, 1875
died Sept 9, 1916
Gone but not
Forgotten

Rev. Joseph W.
BROWN
born Dec 10, 1833
died Feb 4, 1917

Reaver ANDERSON
July 7, 1904
June 4, 1921
at rest

Gertrude ANDERSON
Dec 15, 1881
Sep 9, 1921
At Rest

Button PONTON
March 4, 1870
Feb 19, 1921
Gone but not
Forgotten

LUPER Plot
surrounded by iron
fence
18" high
No Graves

Rev. J. W. CORBIN
1857 - 1908

Harold RIDDICK
Son of John & Mamie
RIDDICK
March 29, 1909
June 6, 1913

Edna A. CHIRSTIAN
June 29, 1908
April 15, 1934
G. B. N. F.

Envie ROLLINS
died April 3, 1955
Temporary Metal
Marker

Katie WILSON
Feb 10, 1871
Mar 17, 1927
A sleep in Jesus
Mother

Rosa JONES
d/o Edmond & Bettie
born Apr 13, 1872
died July 19, 1927
In love she lived
In peace she died
Her life was craved
But, God Denied

WINSTON Plot

Martha Hill
WINSTON
Jan 10, 1908
June 15, 1935

Infant BOYKIN
s/o Mr & Mrs O. P.
BOYKIN
July 31, 1951

Hattie H. W. BOAZ
Dec 22, 1904
Feb 21, 1987

Melvin S. WINSTON
May 2, 1902
Dec 2, 1984
d/s w/ Lillian

Lillian W. WINSTON
Dec 19, 1904
Sept 22, 1989
d/s w/ Melvin

Etts SCOTT
1877 - 1962

Emily Jane WINSTON
Dec 19, 1878
Dec 17, 1962
d/s w/ Frank

Frank C. WINSTON
Sr.
1871 - 1948
d/s w/ Emily

Agnes PIGROM
1930

COURTNEY Plot

Vernon M.
COURTNEY
Nov 21, 1882
April 20, 1952
d/s w/ Myrtle

Myrtle B.
COURTNEY
Feb 25, 1888
April 14, 1969
w/ Vernon

Ernest HENDERSON
May 8, 1969
w/ Lillian

Lillian C.
HENDERSON
No Dates
w/ Ernest

Ernest Courtney
HENDERSON
Age 11 years
Son

Josephine Toliver
LUPER
born Mar 15, 1864
died May 19, 1932

J. BAILEY
(No Dates)

William T.
COLEMAN
1845 - 1908
Stone on ground

Glender N.
COLEMAN
1936 - 1945

Melcon B. HOPSON
Family

Leon T. M. HOPSON
s/o M. B. & D. A.
HOPSON

Mattie M.
BRAXTON
1917 - 1963

Robert BRAXTON
1908 - 1966

Vault unmarked

J. W. TAYLOR
(No Dates)

Frenchie ROY
1896 - 1927

Joseph PERKINS
1885 - 1928

Violet ROBERTS
Mother
Dec 1, 1886
Feb 16, 1934

Coleman
WASHINGTON
1870

Clara BAILY
1932

---

surrounded by stone
& iron fence.

Osborne CHIRSTIAN
born Dec 2, 1898
died Feb 6, 1929
G. B. N. F.

———————

Anna MALONE
1903 - 1922

Americus PAYNE
1902 - 1936

Raymond DENNIS
1932 - 1933
Stone Sunken

Emmal WALKER
died Feb 26, 1928
Age 41
at rest

Rose E. NEWSON
1893 - 1918

Ben. J. W. GASKINS
born Dec 1857
died Dec 16, 1908
Age 51

C. L. PHILLIPS CEMETERY
Sandpiper Court (34) {M - 5}
on the original C. L. Phillips Estate

The Phillips Cemetery is located on the C. L Phillips estate. Information was from Mr C. L. Phillips, Harris Creek Road, Hampton, Virginia. Source: Works Progress Administration of Virginia Historical Inventory, research by Sadie A. Anderson, 17 and 18 March 1936.

Acknowledgments: Transcribed by Sadie A. Anderson, Mary P. Strup in Jun 1967, Steven Keith (date unknown), Ernest Lee Culler, January 14, 1995 and Barry Miles on 2 February 1997. The information is a combination of the data collected by each visit. The following tombstones were missing in 1995: F. B. Phillips, Joseph Phillips, Sarah E. Phillips, Elijah Phillips and Rebecca Phillips.

In memory of
George PHILLIPS
Born October 18, 1785
Died September 24, 1856
Aged 71 Years

To the memory of
Elijah PHILLIPS
Died March 5, 1848
Aged 58 Years
Marked the perfect man and beheld
the upright for the end of _____
in peace.

In memory of
F. B. PHILLIPS
Born Oct 13, 1798
Died Jan 2, 1852
Aged 54 Years

To the memory of
Mrs Rebecca PHILLIPS
Wife of Elijah PHILLIPS
Who died Jan 9, 1845
In the 65th year of her age
Blessed are the dead which die in the
Lord from whenceforth; ye saith the spirit
that they may rest from their labor and
their works do follow them.

In memory of
Joseph PHILLIPS
Born June 18, 1804
Died August 11, 1851
His purity and integrity of character
His manly independence and slow honest
were admired and believed by a large circle
of friends. By one of whom this monument
has been erected as a lasting testimony
of devoted attachment.
Note: His townhouse corner, of Queen and
Locust, survived the burning of Hampton.
(Twin of Ben)

Mary C. PHILLIPS
wife of Joseph PHILLIPS
Born September 16, 1801
Died January 12, 1847
To whose memory this stone is erected
as a testimony of love and veneration of
her children.

Benjamin PHILLIPS
Born June 14, 1804
Died August 19, 1890
("Uncle Ben" see Home
Bn 8-23-90 was in Old
Dominion Dragoons)

Colonel Jefferson C. PHILLIPS
Born Sept 30, 1821
Died June 6, 1910
13th Va. Calvary, CSA
(Commanded Old Dominion Dragoons.
As a Captain under orders from
Magruder burned Hampton
during Civil War.
See Daily Press 19 May 1901
for an account of the burning.)

Caroline E. PHILLIPS
Beloved wife of
Col. J. C. PHILLIPS
Dec 31, 1827
July 12, 1900

E. Curle PHILLIPS
Son of Caroline and
Colonel Jefferson C.
PHILLIPS
Born December 13, 1856
Died September 15, 1934

Margaret
4th daughter of E.C.
and M. E. PHILLIPS
Born February 27, 1887
Died June 6, 1910

Carlton Latimer PHILLIPS
son of Samuel Watts
PHILLIPS and Mary Jane
LATIMER
Born September 15, 1868
Died April 11, 1950

Eva Sidney PRINCE
wife of
Carlton L. PHILLIPS Sr.
Born June 10, 1875
Died April 11, 1943

Charles W. LATIMER
September 6, 1831
September 10, 1903
("Uncle Charlie" is on footstone)

Virginia R.
his wife
November 7, 1824
October 4, 1904

Sacred to the memory of
Sarah E. PHILLIPS
Born Aug 15, 1841
Died Jan 18, 1860

The following children of Samuel W. and Mary Jane (Lattimer) PHILLIPS died of Scarlet Fever and are buried in Portsmouth, Virginia.

Lola PHILLIPS born September 6, 1854 and died August 20, 1861.
Samuel Latimer PHILLIPS born January 31, 1861 and died Aug 21, 1861.
Cora PHILLIPS born March 10, 1859 and died October 9, 1861.
James Mitchell PHILLIPS born April 19, 1857 and died September 8, 1861.

Source: Phillips Family Bible - information included in Works Progress Administration of Virginia Historical Inventory.

Col. J. C. Phillips and Caroline E. Phillips, his wife

ROSENBAUM MEMORIAL PARK
Kecoughtan Road (84) {G - 13}

A deed from A. Rosenbaum to William Morgenstern, et als Trustees for Rodef Shaolem Hebrew Congregation. Verified: January 26, 1937. Original to: M. J. Kaster February 18, 1937.

This Deed, made this 11th day of October, 1935, by and between A. Rosenbaum, widower, party of the first part, and William Morgenstern, Israel Siegel, Nathan Rosenbaum, Harry J. Aaron and Alan M. Graff, Trustees for the Use and Benefit of the Rodef Sholom Hebrew Congregation parties of the second part, all of the City of Newport News, Virginia.

WITNESSETH: That for and in consideration of Five Dollars, ($5.00) cash to him in hand paid, the receipt whereof is hereby acknowledged, and other good and valuables consideration, the said party of the first part doth hereby grant, bargain, sell and convey, with General Warranty of Title, unto the said parties of the second part, the following described property, to-wit:

All that certain lot, piece or parcel of land, lying and being in Wythe Magisterial District, Elizabeth City County, Virginia, and known and described as Lot 16, in Block Two (2), on the "Plat of South River-view, owned by Rowland Hill and Albert W. Cornick," which plat is recorded in Deed Book 23, at p. 473 in the Clerk's Office of Elizabeth City Court, Virginia, and (the remainder describes the parcels of land.)

recorded in Deed Book 23, at p. 473 in the Clerk's Office of Elizabeth City Court, Virginia, and (the remainder describes the parcels of land.)

This is copied from the deed which Mr. A. Rosenbaum sold the congregation of Rodef Sholom the land now used for the Rosenbaum Memorial Cemetery. This gift was a generous act by Mr Rosenbaum.

The three main branches of Judaism maintain divergent customs and practices. Concerning burial, the Orthodox branch is definite in its beliefs and methods, while the Conservative and Reformed branches of Judaism allow some deviations. Rosenbaum Memorial Cemetery is owned by Rodef Sholom Temple, a Conservative congregation; whereas the Hebrew Cemetery next to it is owned by Adath Jeshurum, an Orthodox congregation.

The Rosenbaum Memorial Park is governed by the BY-LAWS OF THE CEMETERY committee OF RODEF SHOLOM TEMPLE.

The following was transcribed by Barry Miles, April 17 and 18, 1997. A comment for clarification of the information recorded. In most cases there is a headstone or large stone with the family's name, then there are individual markers at the foot of the graves, with the individual data. For clarification I have recorded the family markers by themselves in capital letters, then the individual information from the markers surrounding the family marker. Sometimes there are markers on both sides of the family markers. In this case the individual marker information will only be recorded when the next row was recorded. If the headstone has the individual data on the stone, it will be followed by (h/s), for headstone.

Rosenbaum Cemetery

WATERS

Sylvia B. WATERS
May 28, 1919
June 26, 1993

Leonard R. WATERS
Nov 15, 1924
Aug 20, 1979

PARKER

Pearl Lewis PARKER
Sept 7, 1903
June 25, 1994

Sidney Zalak PARKER
Aug 14, 1912
June 29, 1993
U. S. Army World WAR 2

ERLACH

Maurice ERLACH
Feb 12, 1907
May 6, 1987
Beloved Husband, Father
and Grandfather

DAVID

Goldie Rubin DAVID
March 17, 1916
February 1, 1996
Her love Nurtured us
Protected us
And inspired us
His strength engulfed us
And his indomitable spirit
Guides us

Their Support for one
another
And family established
The foundation

William Rice DAVID
January 19, 1914
October 7, 1982

LEADER

Earl D. LEADER
July 10, 1904
Dec 3, 1979

Herbert MOREWITZ
Aug 17, 1914
Mar 17, 1997
Age 82
Temporary Metal Marker

Martin A. GOLD E. H. G.
Dec 23, 1920
Oct 6, 1984
Beloved Husband, Father
Adored Grandfather
Your Humor Brightens
All our Lives
Shalom

WIESEN

Marvin Arthur WIESEN
Oct 2, 1929
July 19, 1993
Loving Husband, Father &
Grandfather

WILKS

Seymour I. WILKS
Aug 18, 1929
Apr 4, 1993
Beloved Husband, Father
and Grandfather

WEINSTEIN

Allen D. WEINSTEIN
1910 - 1997
Temporary Metal Marker

Zelda E. WEINSTEIN
March 1, 1913
October 9, 1989
Beloved Wife and Mother

SATISKY

Marcus SATISKY
Feb 11, 1909
May 24, 1983
Col. U.S.A.F. (Ret.)

CONN

Allen S. CONN
Mar 12, 1909
Dec 12, 1995
Beloved Husband, Father
and Grandfather

MOREWITZ

Louis MOREWITZ
July 15, 1910
Nov 1, 1981
A Gentle, Caring Man

Samuel DORN
1918 - 1996
Age 78
Temporary Metal marker

ROSENFELD

Lisa U. ROSENFELD
July 15, 1904
June 3, 1955
Strength and dignity are her clothing
Her Family praises her saying "you excel them all"

Boris ROSENFELD
Aug 15, 1896
May 12, 1979
In your glory I am Honored in your sorrow
I am grieved in your eternity I have life eternal

ARNER

Fannie Brown ARNER
April 16, 1890
June 9, 1988

Selma Elsie ARNER
February 11, 1920
July 26, 1988

David M. ARNER
May 7, 1923
October 2, 1992

GRUNWALD

Eugene John GRUNWALD
August 14, 1905
June 18, 1986
Beloved Husband, Father, Grand Father and GG Father

TEICHMAN

Sylvia Marian TEICHMAN
Mar 4, 1910
Feb 24, 1985

Sol Gilbert TEICHMAN
Mar 7, 1911
Aug 17, 1995

Dorothy CHESNEAU
1898 - 1996
Temporary Metal Marker

LOWENSTERN

Lee LOWENSTERN
March 31, 1907
Jan 12, 1993
Beloved Wife and Mother

Sidney LOWENSTERN
Nov 26, 1906
Feb 2, 1993
Lt. Col. US Army

Eva S. BUTLER
Born Sept 20, 1890
Died Mar 4, 1982

FLICK

Anita Butler FLICK
July 17, 1920
July 14, 1992

Walter FLICK
Jan 5, 1917
Nov 1, 1995

ARONOW

Louis B. ARONOW
April 3, 1908
Feb 21, 1982

BRASLOW

Myrtle Blanche Shoaf BRASLOW
Jan 13, 1922
Mar 16, 1994

WEINSTOCK

Bernard M. WEINSTOCK
Jan 9, 1921
Aug 13, 1989
Bernie, always a smile and a kind word for everyone

BREGMAN

Dorothy Kruger BREGMAN
Jan 2, 1919
Jan 24, 1995

Irwin BREGMAN
Oct 17, 1919
Dec 18, 1991

ELSBERG

Edward ELSBERG
February 28, 1905
May 24, 1973
Forever in our Hearts

Blanche S. ELSBERG
August 25, 1907
February 9, 1980

Sonya Binder HUNSHER
Nov 10, 1899
Dec 31, 1975

BINDER

Monte L. BINDER M.D.
Nov 10, 1919
Mar 30, 1986
Husband, Father & Gfather

CHESLER

Sarah CHESLER
May 25, 1914
June 4, 1988

Esther G. KATZENBERG
Feb 12, 1904
May 10, 197x
age 93

SANDERS

Sara W. SANDERS
Mar 1, 1917
Jan 30, 1987

SELTZER

Dr. Hyman SELTZER
born April 23, 1911
died May 5, 1997
age 86

Dora W. SELTZER
Feb 1, 1913
June 23, 1992
Beloved Wife, Mother & Grandmother

DAVIDSON

Maxwell Mickey
DAVIDSON
March 27, 1907
September 15, 1986

RUTKIN

Maynard Leroy RUTKIN
June 3, 1931
March 19, 1967

GROSS

Harry David GROSS
Jan 15, 1884
May 2, 1964

Faye G. GROSS
Jan 18, 1890
Jan 27, 1965

LEVINSON

Sol Phillip LEVINSON
Aug 9, 1902
March 6, 1975
Beloved Husband and Father

Gilbert Ben LEVINSON
June 29, 1900
Jan 22, 1995
Beloved Husband and Father

Belle Reva LEVINSON
July 9, 1902
May 21, 1989
Beloved Wife and Mother

Harriet L. WHITECOTTON
Aug 4, 1924
Nov 9, 1993
Beloved Wife and Mother

Rose Mae LEVINSON
May 1, 1913
Sept 28, 1981

LEVINSON

Jerome LEVINSON
June 20, 1908
Nov 7, 1977
U. S. Army World War 2

Sylvia Sevy LEVINSON
March 2, 1917
Oct 23, 1970

FOX

Joseph R. FOX
Aug 26, 1904
Oct 15, 1985

Sada L. FOX
Feb 23, 1906
March 4, 1980

Aubrey Abraham
RUBENSTEIN
January 1, 1923
January 28, 1989
Beloved Husband and Father

Ada GOLDMAN
Dec 19, 1909
Oct 12, 1981

Jack David GOLDMAN
June 12, 1938
July 17, 1976

Mary Farber POLLACK
July 20, 1888
Jan 31, 1985

FARBER

Barney FARBER
Dec 20, 1914
May 11, 1992
Iluatiitwwoe

SAGMAN

Sidney SAGMAN
December 1, 1923
March 5, 1977
Sid a man who loved life
Loved People and was
loved
Shalom

CONN

Lillian CONN
Aug 3, 1912
July 3, 1989
Beloved Sister, Aunt and
Friend

Eva CONN
July 21, 1902
Feb 16, 1992
Devoted Sister and Friend

KATZ

Rudolph Aaron KATZ
Oct 30, 1912
Dec 7, 1991

Albert BERK
1920 - 1997
age 76
Temporary Metal Marker

GOLDSTEIN

Irving F. GOLDSTEIN
January 23, 1917
June 1, 1995
Beloved Husband and
Father

Esther G. GOLDSTEIN
October 6, 1918
November 4, 1985
Beloved Wife and Mother

LERNER

Robert W. LERNER
May 25, 1923
March 25, 1993

Shirley Kruger LERNER
Feb 28, 1924
Nov 20, 1988

Robert Allen
BOOKBINDER
Nov 8, 1950
Feb 17, 1990
Beloved Son

Fae M. BOOKBINDER
Sept 1, 1924
Oct 30, 1996
Loving Wife, Mother and
Grandmother

Gertrude BLOCH
December 2, 1889
November 26, 1973
Devoted Mother and
Grandmother

Charles KATES
Born Nov 25, 1895
Died June 9, 1974

Rena Nachman KATES
Born Dec 25, 1898
Died Dec 30, 1992

Edith Nachman LEGUM
Born ----
Died March 1, 1997
Age 92
Temporary Metal Marker

NACHMAN

Abe NACHMAN
Oct 19, 1907
March 2, 1974
Devoted Husband and
Father

Jules R. FRANK
Sept 10, 1931
July 22, 1974
In loving memory of
Husband and Father

Lynn LEVITT-KRUGER
MD.
Oct 13, 1954
May 10, 1987
Beloved Wife, Mother and
Sister
Loving Kindness Healing
Good Deeds she gave

Moses MELAMED
Sept 14, 1920
Dec 3, 1990
Beloved Husband and Father

RUBIN

Gertrude RUBIN
Oct 4, 1995

Jack RUBIN
Nov 30, 1983

NACHMAN

Sol NACHMAN
Died May 18, 1929
Father

Ida Solomon NACHMAN
Died Jan 24, 1954

Herbert NACHMAN
Died Nov 29, 1954
Son

ROSENBAUM

A. ROSENBAUM
Born Feb 27, 1853
Died Jan 16, 1944
Those immortal dead who live again in minds made better by their presence

Tall stone monument in center of cemetery dedicated to the founder of the cemetery

AARON

Harry J. AARON
May 12, 1894
Jan 2, 1951

Lillian B. AARON
May 26, 1896
May 8, 1994

SIEGEL

Cecella SIEGEL
July 5, 1892
Jan 4, 1963
Beloved Wife and Mother

Israel SIEGEL
Sept 8, 1888
July 22, 1959
Beloved Husband and Father

SCHWARTZ

Bessye Solomon SCHWARTZ
Aug 21, 1894
July 5, 1984

Morris Wolf SCHWARTZ
Jan 15, 1884
Nov 2, 1956

MORGENSTERN

Rosaline L. MORGENSTERN
Aug 23, 1905
Dec 27, 1993

William MORGENSTERN
Oct 29, 1891
Feb 6, 1957

GORDON

Bernice Slavin GORDON
Nov 9, 1915
Dec 16, 1990
In loving memory

MOUND

Milton Norman MOUND
Dec 28th 1904
May 5th 1993

Kenneth MORGENSTERN
May 12, 1956
Sept 27, 1956

Sol ELLENSON
Feb 9, 1909
Feb 1, 1975

SOLDINGER

Harold SOLDINGER
July 21, 1917
Mar 24, 1996

EISENMAN

Louis EISENMAN
Aug 27, 1883
Feb 16, 1955

Hattie W. EISENMAN
Sept 7, 1886
Oct 16, 1979

Arthur F. EISENMAN
Feb 19, 1886
Jan 8, 1961

COOPER

Mary Wilkins COOPER
Died Nov 28, 1944
Age 73 years

Benjamin E. WILKINS
Died Jan 26, 1968
Age 73 years

Ruth B. WILKINS
November 26, 1986

ROSENBAUM

Dora W. ROSENBAUM
Jan 1, 1895
Jan 24, 1965

Nathan ROSENBAUM
June 9, 1878
March 2, 1938

ROSS

Roy ROSS
June 15, 1898
May 27, 1980

Rose W. ROSS
Feb 12, 1898
Feb 8, 1977

EISENMAN

Brunette E. KAUFMAN
July 27, 1888
Sept 1, 1978

Maurice C. EISENMAN
July 29, 1878
Oct 26, 1970

PELTZ

Gertrude D. PELTZ
Oct 31, 1901
Jan 4, 1988

H. David PELTZ
Dec 25, 1897
Oct 20, 1972

DRUCKER

Irvin R. MASSELL
December 8, 1900
February 10, 1990
Devoted Son and Brother
May his heart and soul rest
in peace

DIAMONSTEIN

William DIAMONSTEIN
Sept 24, 1907
Oct 3, 1985

SCHLOSSER

Daniel SCHLOSSER
December 14, 1915
January 5, 1977
Beloved Husband and
Father
He loved life and shared his
joy

BLECHMAN

Frank O. BLECHMAN
June 20, 1905
October 7, 1986
Loving and Beloved
Husband and Father

Wise counselor
compassionate
friend his was the way of
"Honor and Truth and the
way to work for Men"

E. David BLECHMAN MD.
January 21, 1903
August 27, 1953

Benjamin BLECHMAN
October 23, 1900
June 28, 1984
Beloved Husband and
Father

DRUCKER

Loraine Blechman
DRUCKER
July 31, 1899
February 3, 1968
Where she walked, Beauty
Followed

A. Louis DUCKER
August 16, 1898
June 27, 1995
Where he walked, love
followed

MIRMELSTEIN

Betty Joanne
MIRMELSTEIN
October 16, 1948
July 27, 1951

Robert MIRMELSTEIN
November 15, 1951
November 9, 1954

Grace B. MIRMELSTEIN
April 4, 1913
Sept 20, 1967
Beloved Wife and Mother

Dr. Samuel H.
MIRMELSTEIN
Jan 17, 1907
June 30, 1977
Devoted Husband and
Father

MOREWITZ

Beloved Parents
Samuel Maurice
MOREWITZ
Feb 9, 1884
Oct 28, 1947
d/s w/ Reba B. Dorf

Reba B. Dorf MOREWITZ
June 12, 1890
Aug 8, 1967
Married Jan 6, 1914
"Their lives were an
adventure in faith"
d/s w/ Samuel Maurice

Kay Andrea SCHER
Oct 11, 1955
May 21, 1957

Thomas D. MOREWITZ
MD.
February 20, 1893
September 5, 1957

GARNER

Edgar B. WERTHEIMER
January 13, 1880
July 16, 1951

Maud Garner
WERTHEIMER
June 6, 1887
July 24, 1927

Selwyn C. GARNER
Dec 26, 1924
Sept 7, 1944
Who died in the
performance
of his duty in the service of
his county.

William GARNER
Nov 15, 1860
April 24, 1940

GARNER

Stanley Solomon GARNER
Feb 23, 1892
Oct 4, 1970

Lillie Baskin GARNER
Sept 28, 1900
Oct 28, 1980
His banner over me is love
Song of Solomon

Jennie GARNER
Jan 24, 1879
Dec 15, 1947

Dora G. TAUSIG
June 26, 1889
July 31, 1975

Louis ROTGIN
June 27, 1907
Aug 18, 1975
Beloved Husband, Father
and Gfather

LIPMAN

Man Greatest Heritage is
his good name

Isaac LIPMAN
Died July 13, 1943
Age 73

Annie S. LIPMAN
Died September 30, 1948
age 78

Harvey SPIGEL
Aug 10, 1890
Sept 30, 1944
d/s w/ Goldie Garner

Goldie Garner SPIGEL
Oct 18, 1895
Jan 27, 1946
d/s w/ Harvey

LIPMAN - LEVIN

Minnie L. LEVIN
Nov 28, 1890
Jan 4, 1979
May her soul be bound up
in the Bond of eternal life
d/s w/ Bernard L.

Bernard L. LIPMAN
Sept 1, 1907
Dec 4, 1982
Man's Greatest Treasure is his
love for his fellow Man
d/s w/ Minnie L.

LIPMAN - EPSTEIN

Maurice EPSTEIN
Born September 13, 1892
Died August 22, 1965

Rose Lipman EPSTEIN
Born February 11, 1895
Died December 18, 1981

LIPMAN FAMILY

AUSTIN

Clare Lipman AUSTIN
Dec 23, 1904
Feb 18, 1991
Cherished wife, Mother
& Grandmother
d/s w/ Harry Jac

Harry Jac AUSTIN
May 15, 1900
Feb 20, 1995
A gentleman eternally
youthful Beloved by Family
Liked by all
d/s w/ Clare Lipman

MIRMELSTEIN

Ellis B. MIRMELSTEIN
Sept 13, 1902
Sept 10, 1994
Beloved Son and Brother
Quiet Dignity
Selfless Devotion

Isaac MIRMELSTEIN
Dec 25, 1878
Feb 4, 1958
Beloved Husband and
Father

Dora B. MIRMELSTEIN
Sept 1, 1878
Aug 26, 1959
Beloved Wife and Mother

Florence B.
MIRMELSTEIN
May 12, 1901
Jan 19, 1987
Devoted Daughter and
Sister

ALBERT T. BROUT

Albert T. BROUT
May 20, 1907
Jan 27, 1984
And the builders laid the
foundation of the Temple
of the Lord (Ezra 3:10)

Sara F. BROUT
Dec 10, 1909
Jan 16, 1988
"Give her of the fruit of
her hands, and let her
works praise her in the
Gates" (Proverbs 31:31)

Sylvia Freed MOONVES
January 19, 1914
March 21, 1966
Beloved Wife and Mother

LICHTENSTEIN

GODUTI -
MIRMELSTEIN

Kathy Mirmelstein GODUTI
April 7, 1933
January 2, 1975
Adored Wife, Daughter &
Sister
Our Bitsy - "A Cup of Sun"

Rona Becker
MIRMELSTEIN
March 30, 1925
November 17, 1992
Beloved Wife, Mother &
Gammy
She looked up,
Laughed and Loved

GOLDBERG

Marlyn Levin GOLDBERG
Jan 4, 1939
Oct 26, 1970
Beloved Wife and Mother

LEVIN

Esther Garfield LEVIN
Oct 9, 1919
Oct 17, 1976
d/s w/ Harry
Beloved Parents &
Grandparents

Harry LEVIN
Nov 28, 1911
Feb 16, 1977
d/s w/ Esther Garfield

RABINOWITZ

David Michael
RABINOWITZ
Feb 21, 1950
Feb 23, 1994
Shalom

DIAMANT

Abbot Robert DIAMANT
March 27, 1907
October 28, 1977

Lesliebeth Diamant
ROTHENBERG
August 29, 1942
August 10, 1974
Beloved Daughter & Wife

SCHOENBAUM -
SILVERMAN

Ray SCHOENBAUM
September 27, 1948
January 21, 1968
Beloved Son and Brother

Samuel Jerome "Nubby"
SILVERMAN
July 23, 1903
December 7, 1992
Forever Loved

Lena G. SILVERMAN
May 4, 1907
September 23, 1992

UNGER

Allen N. UNGER
Dec 1, 1912
June 2, 1970
A Kind and Gentle Man

SEGALOFF

Anne Burack SEGALOFF
Sept 20, 1893
Nov 5, 1984

William SEGALOFF
Aug 27, 1892
Feb 13, 1980

Charles L. SEGALOFF
Nov 22, 1896
May 8, 1989
Sholom

Bess M. SEGALOFF
March 18, 1907
Aug 12, 1968

HEILBERG

Sybil HEILBERG
Died Feb 5, 1986
We Loved You So

MOREWITZ

Jacob L. MOREWITZ
Born Feb 11, 1896
Died Jan 7, 1983

Sallie Rome MOREWITZ
Born Jan 14, 1897
Died Aug 8, 1974

BERLIN

Edward GARRICK
Mar 3, 1910
Dec 18, 1981

Daniel BERLIN
infant Son
Died Sept 11, 1950

Fannie M. BERLIN
Died November 21, 1964

Daniel BERLIN
Born June 16, 1882
Died March 26, 1944

Ruth August MOREWITZ
Born April 24, 1922
Died Dec 6, 1978

Frederick A. SPIGEL
Sept 5, 1954
May 26, 1960

Morton W. SPIGEL
July 10, 1915
Feb 23, 1985

JACOBSON

Joseph W. JACOBSON
1910 - 1989
Husband

Gitela L. JACOBSON
Ga - Ga
1912 - 1990
Wife and Sister

SPIGEL

Leroy M. SPIGEL
June 28, 1917
Jan 30, 1994

STERN

Walter STERN
1927 - 1972
Father

SPIGEL

Jack S. SPIGEL
June 1, 1911
Aug 28, 1984

Helen J. SPIGEL
July 18, 1917
Jan 1, 1975

SACHS

Melvin L. SACHS
Mar 13, 1909
Jan 8, 1973

Ida Sear SACHS
Mar 3, 1912
Mar 18, 1971

FOX

Bernard "Bucky" FOX
Nov 10, 1913
Oct 5, 1995
Beloved Husband, Father & Poppy

CRAWFORD

Ida J. CRAWFORD
1885 - 1963

GERBER

Florence S. GERBER
1917 - 1960

Esther N. POPPER
Aug 26, 1904
May 25, 1970

Nathan N. POPPER
Nov 1, 1896
May 21, 1978
US Navy World War 1

WEINSTEIN

Julius WEINSTEIN
Jan 14, 1915
Sept 8, 1993
Beloved Husband Father & Grandfather

WEINSTEIN

Morris WEINSTEIN
Dec 15, 1885
Dec 19, 1958
Beloved Father

Sophia WEINSTEIN
March 27, 1886
July 30, 1958
Beloved Mother

FRIEDMAN

Ben F. FRIEDMAN
July 18, 1909
Feb 11, 1965

Henry R. SACHS
January 5, 1897
April 18, 1972
headstone

Kate W. SACHS
February 22, 1900
March 10, 1953
headstone

COPLAND

Moses Peter COPLAND
May 27, 1882
July 5, 1957

Bessie Rose COPLAND
Dec 18, 1900
Sept 1, 1960

Samuel I. KAPLAN
April 15, 1907
July 10, 1951

SACHS

Louis SACHS
Sept 25, 1872
Dec 17, 1956

Bertha SACHS
Aug 25, 1877
Nov 14, 1941

Leopold RIIBNER
Born Aug 10, 1863
Died April 28, 1941
d/s w/ Cillie

Cillie RIIBNER
Born Sept 2, 1862
Died Sept 28, 1941
d/s w/ Leopold

Alex LIPSITZ
Born Sept 12, 1885
Died May 3, 1938
d/s w/ Rose Schwartz

Rose Schwartz LIPSITZ
Born Sept 18, 1889
Died Jan 31, 1941

Harry WANT
March 18, 1898
March 3, 1965
Loving Father

SPIGEL

Bertha Stern SPIGEL
Dec 26, 1889
April 13, 1947

Isaac A. SPIGEL
May 24, 1885
June 22, 1953

ADELSON

Phillip ADELSON
Died December 30, 1963
Age 66 Years

Eva Levine ADELSON
Died March 5, 1954
Age 67 years

Siegfried STERN
Dec 13, 1894
March 30, 1951
Father
d/s w/ Rachel

Rachel STERN
Feb 25, 1901
Oct 30, 1966
d/s w/ Siegfried

Harry A. MOREWITZ
Nov 3, 1881
Feb 20, 1962
headstone

Sarah W. MOREWITZ
Mar 14, 1890
Apr 27, 1982
headstone

Gertrude WASSERMAN
Died Nov 19, 1936
Age 66 years

Samuel B. SCHUSTER
Nov 16, 1898
Nov 5, 1955
headstone

Elizabeth Lichtenstein
JAFFEE
Jan 27, 1913
Jan 1, 1966
headstone

Cecelia MOREWITZ
Feb 13, 1913
March 29, 1974
headstone

SCHNEIDER

Shulamith SCHNEIDER
Aug 2, 1894
Sept 10, 1983
In Loving Memory
Daughter

Rose SCHNEIDER
Sept 1869
June 30, 1963
In Loving Memory

Moses SCHNEIDER
May 2, 1894
Mar 14, 1981
In Loving Memory

Eugenie Spingarn NEISSER
April 13, 1878
Dec 2, 1963
headstone

William BROWN
Jan 7, 1900
March 4, 1975
headstone

Robert Lee AARON
Oct 6, 1899
Jan 24, 1968
headstone

Pearl Franklin AARON
Feb 9, 1898
Dec 15, 1979
headstone

WEINER

Benjamin WEINER
Sept 18, 1908
May 1, 1970

Isabel C. WEINER
March 31, 1910
March 17, 1992
Beloved Wife, Mother &
Grandmother

Louis S. WEINER
Oct 12, 1910
July 20, 1970
Virginia PFC US Army
World War 2
headstone

Richard L. ZERNES
Dec 1, 1925
May 13, 1972
Illinois CPL US Army
World War 2

Sheldon KOPELSON
Jun 25, 1929
Aug 22, 1970
headstone

Pearl Lichtenberg KNEIP
Jan 5, 1892
Sept 23, 1962
Beloved Wife, Mother &
Grandmother

RICHMAN

Paul RICHMAN
Dec 25, 1895
Sept 16, 1959
Beloved Husband, Father &
Grandfather

Ruth RICHMAN
Jan 5, 1899
Jan 13, 1973
Beloved Wife, Mother &
Grandmother

William S. WOLF
July 21, 1887
July 14, 1973
Beloved Husband & Father

Dora Rosenthal WOLF
Dec 23, 1898
Oct 24, 1956
Beloved Wife and Mother

WACHTEL

Joseph WACHTEL
March 12, 1881
Aug 17, 1954
Husband and Father

Hattie WACHTEL
Oct 3, 1891
March 10, 1965
Wife and Mother

BECKER

Maxine Daniels BECKER
May 2, 1908
Feb 13, 1981

Benjamin BECKER
Sept 23, 1901
Feb 22, 1985
A Loving Heart and
Loving Spirit

BERMAN

Phillip BERMAN
May 22, 1882
May 19, 1947

Yetta S. BERMAN
Feb 2, 1882
May 18, 1957

SCHWARTZ

Ben SCHWARTZ
Feb 5, 1905
Aug 15, 1953

STURMAN

Sol STURMAN
November 6, 1886
January 8, 1964

Lena F. BATTERSON
Died July 30, 1965
headstone

Sidney A. BATTERSON
July 11, 1916
March 9, 1970
headstone

Zella M. BATTERSON
Dec 7, 1914
Aug 5, 1965
headstone

Mynne F. PRIMAKOW
July 17, 1890
Jan 18, 1981
headstone

LERNER

Margaret Ann LERNER
1955 - 1976

Simon LERNER
May 14, 1902
Dec 16, 1959

Elizabeth Gordon MALINA
June 13, 1894
July 17, 1958
headstone

Esther KAPLAN
Aug 13, 1905
April 29, 1960
headstone

Jake ERLACH
Jan 20, 1908
July 14, 1969
headstone

Harry MARKS
April 7, 1891
Sept 25, 1969
headstone

Charles HURWITZ
Aug 6, 1885
June 19, 1976
d/s w/ Sadie

Sadie HURWITZ
Oct 20, 1895
Jun 9, 1970
d/s w/ Charles

REVIER

Vincent L. REVIER
Jan 7, 1931
Oct 14, 1963

ROGATZ

Nathan ROGATZ
March 15, 1901
April 29, 1991

Lillian ROGATZ
June 27, 1904
April 19, 1975

GORDON

Jack A. GORDON
Feb 10, 1903
Nov 29, 1982

Hanna Cohen GORDON
Born June 15, 1905
Died July 22, 1996
age 91
Temporary Metal Marker

GOLDBERG

Mollie Fingerman
GOLDBERG
Oct 29, 1924
July 20, 1966

CONN

Julius CONN
October 21, 1904
September 17, 1983

CONN

Ellis CONN
Oct 27, 1910
May 17, 1972
He Fed Our Spirit
From His Own

Julius CONN Jr.
August 15, 1932
March 4, 1986

Esther LICHTENSTEIN
April 13, 1885
Jan 27, 1977
d/s w/ Julian

Julian LICHTENSTEIN
Dec 22, 1886
Feb 2, 1981
Beloved Parents,
Grandparents
& Great Grandparents
d/s w/ Esther

Footstone
Julian & Esther
LICHTENSTEIN

PERLOWITZ

Wilma Roberts
PERLOWITZ
December 31, 1911
April 4, 1974

Sol A. PERLOWITZ
April 12, 1899
July 12, 1972

LEVIN

Milton LEVIN
June 27, 1904
Sept 20, 1971

Mamie Levin CROSS
Dec 27, 1892
Jan 28, 1979
Beloved Mother &
Grandmother
headstone

Anna KHIGER
April 1, 1912
July 10, 1991
Beloved Mother &
Grandmother

Adam Shawn
HANDFINGER
Dec 22 - 24, 1968

Matthew B.
FELTMAN
Sept 8, 1968

Elisa Faye BENEN
1960 - 1961

Baby FOX
1964

Zachary Dane
MAZZEL
Nov 5, 1987

A. Rosenbaum, Founder of Cemetery

ROUNTREE and /or
CEDAR ISLAND CEMETERY
Harris Creek Road (66) {M - 5}

On 11 April 1997, Mr. Barry Miles spoke with Mrs Rountree, who told of a cemetery in back of her house. There were no tombstones. She said she had talked with a relative of the last person buried there who said that the cemetery did not have a name. Therefore, we have listed the cemetery under Rountree and/or Cedar Island Cemetery as in the list compiles by Mr. Luther L. Alexander.

On 5 June 1997, Mr. Kenneth Quinn provided the following information on this cemetery. The land was owned by the Avera family, circa 1695 to 1795, the Howell Family, 1798 to 1856, the Drummond family, 1798 to 1855, and the Willis family, 1859 to 1929. The list of graves and the plat of the cemetery was provided by Mr. Sours, surveyor of the property in 1981. From the names of the interments in the cemetery there are several choices for the name of the cemetery. Because it is located on Cedar Island and no one is sure of the name, We have chosen to list it as Rountree and/or Cedar Island Cemetery. Below is a layout provided by Mr. Sours.

This is a Plat of the Cemetery by Mr. Sours

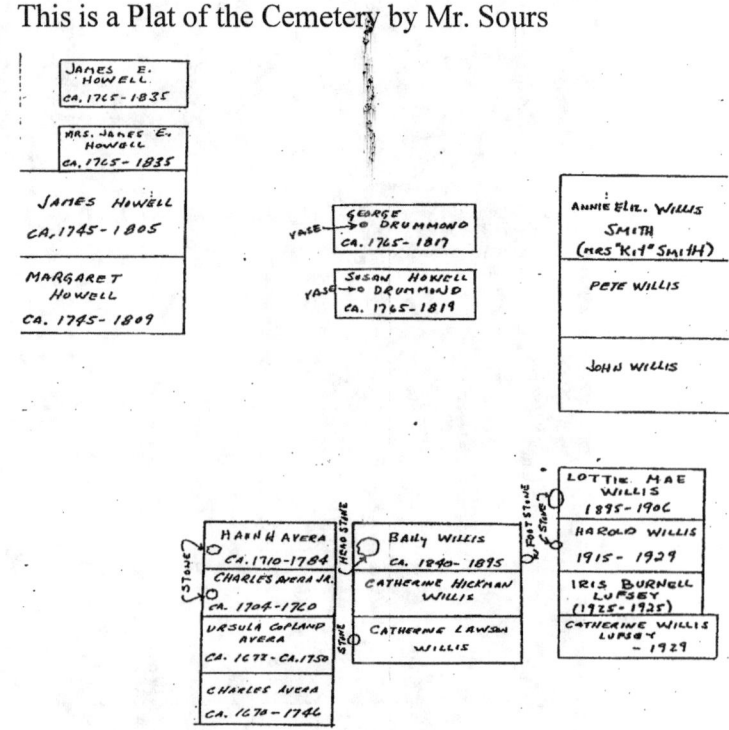

James E. HOWELL
ca 1765 - 1835

Mrs James E. HOWELL
ca. 1765 - 1835

James HOWELL
ca. 1745 - 1805

Margaret HOWELL
ca. 1745 - 1809

George DRUMMOND
ca. 1765 - 1817

Susan Howell DRUMMOND
ca. 1765 - 1819

Annie Eliz. Willis SMITH
Mrs "Kit" SMITH

Pete WILLIS

John WILLIS

Lottie Mae WILLIS
1895 - 1906
h/s

Harold WILLIS
1915 - 1929
h/s

Iris Burnell LUFSEY
1925 - 1925

Catharine Willis LUFSEY
xxxx - 1929

Baily WILLIS
ca. 1840 - 1895
h/s

Catharine Lawson WILLIS

Hannh AVERA
ca. 1740 - 1784
stone

Charles Avera Jr.
ca. 1704 - 1760

Ursula Copland AVERA
ca. 1672 - ca. 1750

Charles AVERA
ca. 1660 - 1746

JACK ROUTTEN CEMETERY
Beach Road and Holston Lane (21) {N - 4}

The three Routten Cemeteries at Beach Road and Holston Lane are part of what was a tract of 25 acres that was conveyed to Richard Routen (Routten) from Richard and James Walter Williams by deed dated January 26, 1797, and recorded in **Old** Deed Book 34 at page 329, in the Clerk's office of the Circuit Court for Elizabeth City County, (now City of Hampton), Virginia. Several of the Routten heirs still own and reside on parts of the original parcel.

Acknowledgment: Transcribed by T. Winters May 16, 1990 and, Barry and Leslyn Miles 28 September 1996.

The Cemetery is enclosed in a cement wall.

First three names on same marker

Louisa E. ROUTTEN
b. Nov15, 1827
d. Aug 2, 1894
Asleep in Jesus

Wm. C. ROUTTEN
Sept 2, 1820
d. Apr 15, 1897
Gone Home

Thaddeus L. ROUTTEN
b. Oct 25, 1855
d. Aug 24, 1905

J. J. ROUTTEN
Dec 12, 1846
Jan 9, 1930

Annie Laura ROUTTEN
Oct 14, 1857
Feb 12, 1945

Elizabeth HENNESS
April 17, 1870
Feb 11, 1943

Harvey DIXON
Nov 13, 187-
Sep --, 1883

two foot markers
W. C. R.
T. L. R.

The cement wall was erected by William C. Routten's son, John J. Routten (also buried in the cemetery), and the iron gate was probably made by Melvin S. Holston, a blacksmith in Fox Hill.

RICHARD ROUTTEN CEMETERY
Beach Road and Holston Lane (37) {N - 45}

The three Routten Cemeteries at Beach Road and Holston Lane are part of what was a tract of 25 acres that was conveyed to Richard Routen (Routten) from Richard and James Walter Williams by deed dated January 26, 1797, and recorded in **Old** Deed Book 34 at page 329, in the Clerk's office of the Circuit Court for Elizabeth City County, (now City of Hampton), Virginia. Several of the Routten heirs still own and reside on parts of the original parcel.

Acknowledgment: Transcribed by W. S. Keith on May 16, 1990 and Barry Miles on 28 September 1996.

James E. ROUTTEN
Aug 27, 1864
Jan 25, 1942

Sarah L. ROUTTEN
Apr 6, 1876
Jul 14, 1955

Henry P. ROUTTEN
March 5, 1898
July 16, 1900

Clifton E. ROUTTEN
Feb 13, 1900
July 10, 1900

Richard P. ROUTTEN
Born Jan 4, 1819
Died Apr 14, 1898
Call not back the dear departed anchored
safe where storms are o'er on the border
land we left him soon to meet and part no
more when we leave this world of change
when we leave this world of care we
shall find our missing loved ones in our
fathers mansion fair.
(footstone R. P. R.)

Matha A. ROUTTEN
June 1, 1840
Dec 17, 1901
(footstone M. A. R.)

Richard and Matha on same stone.

SPENCER ROUTTEN CEMETERY
Beach Road and Church Lane (45) {N - 4}

The three Routten Cemeteries at Beach Road and Holston Lane are part of what was a tract of 25 acres that was conveyed to Richard Routen (Routten) from Richard and James Walter Williams by deed dated January 26, 1797, and recorded in **Old** Deed Book 34 at page 329, in the Clerk's office of the Circuit Court for Elizabeth City County, (now City of Hampton), Virginia. Several of the Routten heirs still own and reside on parts of the original parcel.

Acknowledgment: Transcribed by W. S. Keith on May 18, 1990 and Leslyn Miles on September 28, 1996.

All three names are on same stone.

Edward T. ROUTTEN
Born Sept 26, 1856
Died Mar 10, 1882
Gentle readers as you pass by as you
are now so once was I
as I am now so you must be
prepare for death and follow me

Missouri F. ROUTTEN
Born Jan 9, 1839
Died Dec 29, 1903
A precious one from us has
gone her voice is hushed and
still, a place is vacant in our
home which never can be filled

Spencer S. ROUTTEN
Born May 14, 1835
Died May 28, 1892
Sleep on Beloved Sleep
on take thy rest
lay down thy head upon the
saviors breast
we love thee well but Jesus
loves thee best
good night, good night
good night

There are two graves between the Spencer and Jack Routten cemeteries, to the rear.

William D. BURGE
born 1844
died 1913

Susan A. BURGE
born 1850
died 1908

SHELTON CEMETERY
North Mallory (41) {N - 9}

Acknowledgment: Transcribed by Thelma Savage April 1968 and Steven Keith June 20, 1990.

Claud B.
son of
C. B. and J. SHELTON
Born Feb 11, 1860
Died April 17, 1893

Confederate Marker

Charles C. SHELTON
Feb 28, 1827
Dec 12, 1901

Jane E.
his wife
April 22, 1832

Liliee
daughter of C. C. & J. SHELTON
Born June 13, 1861
Died Nov 24, 1881

In memory of
Mrs J. SHELTON
Aged 35 Yrs. 10 months 22 days

Rest in peace
Susan R.
wife of Joseph CARNES
Born May 21, 1821
Died June 4, 1894

J CARNES
Husband
J. CARNES
Son
J. R. CARNES
Daughter

In memory of
James SHELTON
and
Mary COOPER
his wife
who died respectively
Dec 2, 1841
and Nov 26, 1841
remember me as you.....
as you are now so...

Nannie S. WILLIAMSON
May 1, 1833
Sept 16, 1903
to Sister
E. SHELTON
N. SHELTON
M. SHELTON
V. GRAVES
to brother
C. S. SHELTON
daughter
L. V. SHELTON
to father and mother
James & Mary G. SHELTON
Husband
J. WILLIAMSON
(To Brother
W. N. SHELTON
his wife
G. S. SHELTON
son
W. N. SHELTON
daughter
L. V. SHELTON
To father and mother
James and Mary G. SHELTON
Husband
J. WILLIAMSON)

Information in parenthesis is from the William and Mary Quaterly, Volume 14, Series 1.

BURIAL GROUND OF SHERWOOD
Langley Air Force Base at Officers Club (42) {1 - 4}

The Sherwood Cemetery was researched four times by the Works Progress Administration of Virginia Historical Inventory: First by Sadie A. Anderson on March 16, 1936, second by Mary Bullifant on December 4, 1936, third by Mrs Eleanor S. Jacobs on March 26, 1937, and fourth by Mary Bullifant on August 18, 1937.

The following information is a combination of the four reports. The information does vary between reports.

Location: First - About 1/4 mile past the guard house to right, on entering Langley Field. Formerly Sherwood Farm; Second - Government Reservation, Langley Field, to right of northern end of bridge, three hundred yards east of Main Drive overlooking the Southern Branch of Back River; Third - from Hampton, Virginia, you take the road leading to Langley Field, and as you enter the Base to the east about a block, is this cemetery; and Fourth - On United States Government Reservation of Langley Field to right of the northern end of the bridge, on waterfront of the Southern Branch of Back River, 4 1/2 miles north of Hampton, Virginia.

Sherwood Farms, where this burial ground is located, is a part of the land which was brought by the Government. Due to state laws, the cemetery remained a family burial ground. Money was solicited to build a brick wall around this cemetery. This money was secured from the heirs, and a brick wall enclosed the old Booker burial ground at Langley Field.(March 16, 1936).

This property was formerly called the Sherwood Farm, and was owned by the Bookers until the Government bought it. It is said that this was the original burying ground of the Booker family of Hampton, Virginia, and they owned this entire Government Reservation, with an exception of a small amount owned by the Hudgins (March 23, 1937).

The following is from the different reports and gives the dates information was recorded.

March 16, 1936

In Memory of Elizabeth M. ARMISTEAD
Wife of Moss ARMISTEAD
Who departed this life
Nov. 25th, 1803
Aged 23

Sacred to the Memory of
William Albert HAUSMAN
of the State of New York
who died Nov 1st, 1834
Aged 22 years, 10 mo & 10 days

Dec 4, 1936

In memory of
Elizabeth M. ARMISTEAD
Wife of Moss ARMISTEAD
born 1780
died November 23, 1803

Sacred to the memory of
William Albert HOOSMAN
of Staten Island
born 1812
died 1834

This plot also contains several
graves of BOOKERS and JONESES
dating back to the 1700's
without any stones standing.

March 23, 1937

In
Memory of
Elizabeth M. ARMISTEAD
Wife of Moss ARMISTEAD
of Norfolk
who departed this life
Nov 23rd, 1803
Aged 23 years
The stone at the foot has
E. M. A.
1803
This stone is concrete.

Sacred
to the
memory of
William Albert HORSALEY
of Staten Island
State of New York
who died
Nov 1st, 1834
Aged 22 Years
10 months and 10 days
The stone at the foot has
W. A. H.
This stone is Beautiful
white marble.

From the William and Mary Quarterly volume 14, Series 1

Location: On Langley Air Force Base near Officers' Club.

In Memory of
Elizabeth M. ARMISTEAD
Wife of Moss ARMISTEAD
of Norfolk
Who departed this life
November 25, 1805
Aged 23 years

William _____
of Staten Island
State of New York
Died November 1, 1834
aged 22 years
10 months and 10 days

Burial Ground of
"SHERWOOD"
An estate of 950 Acres
A Grant from the English Crown

TO THE PURFOY FAMILY

In the Early 17th Century
Heired by their kin
THE MARSHALL AND BOOKER
FAMILIES

The last owners by inheritance
George BOOKER 1806 - 1868
and his wife
Ann MASSENBURG 1816 - 1897

Miss Thelma Savage of Syms-Eaton Museum, Hampton, Virginia, submitted the foregoing tombstone inscriptions, for publication in the William and Mary Quarterly.

From the E. A. Semple of the late 1880's a large area where the cemetery is located was called "Sherwood."

Barry Miles visited the site on 2 May 1997. The following omission was noted.

The inscription below William Albert Hosueman:

> When Blooming youth snatched away
> By deaths resistless hand
> Our hearts the mournful tribute pay
> which pity must demand

Old Records list the following individuals buried in the Sherwood Plot.
George BOOKER died 1805
Elizabeth M. ARMISTEAD died 1805
George BOOKER died 1817
William A. HOUSEMAN died 1834
John BOOKER died 1842
Emily Booker SEMPLE died 1858
Betty BOOKER died 1872
Nannie Von SCHILLING died 1875
Ann MASSENBURG date unknown
Richard BOOKER date unknown
Mary Booker JONES date unknown

SINCLAIR CEMETERY
Kove Drive (76) {I - 7}

From the W P A of Virginia Historical Inventory, November 9, 1936. Research by Sadie A. Anderson.

The Sinclair family is one of the oldest families in Elizabeth City County. The men in the family took an outstanding part in the War Between the States and have always been prominent in the various activities of the community.

We find in this cemetery two graves that are important for their dates and historical value. The inscriptions read as follows:

George Keith SINCLAIR
Son of
Jefferson B. and
Georgianna WRAY
Born Mar 22, 1847
Died June 10, 1929
Company B. 3rd
Va. Cav. C.S.A.

Ida Elizabeth PHILLIPS
Daughter of
Col. J. C. & C. P. PHILLIPS
Wife of
George Keith SINCLAIR
Born Nov 26, 1848
Died Feb 16, 1905

The Sinclair Cemetery was revisited on 28 December 1996 by Barry Miles and the following was transcribed. Authorization was received from Mr. James J. Sinclair.

Thomas A. SINCLAIR
son of Carrie & T. A. SINCLAIR
Aug 26, 1900
Sept 30, 1907

Carrie P. SINCLAIR
Dec 30, 1870
Sept 6, 1946

Roy Lee SINCLAIR
son of G. K. and
Ida Phillips SINCLAIR
1873 - 1935

George Keith SINCLAIR
son of Jefferson B. &
Georgianna Wray SINCLAIR
Mar 22, 1847
June 10, 1929
Co B, 3rd Va Cav C S A
A "C S A" marker in front
of marker

Ida Elizabeth PHILLIPS
Dau of Col J. & C. PHILLIPS
wife of G. K. SINCLAIR
Born Nov 26, 1845
Died Feb 16, 1906

Jefferson B. SINCLAIR
Sept 30, 1868
Aug 19, 1941

Mamie E. SINCLAIR
Oct 28, 1870
Sept 30, 1938

Atwell E. SINCLAIR
June 1, 1898
June 2, 1933

Chetwyn E. SINCLAIR
Sept 28, 1909
June 16, 1947

Elizabeth S. SINCLAIR
Wife of James C. SINCLAIR
March 31, 1916
Dec 15, 1922
Bore Fruit of old age

SINCLAIR
Marker only

SINCLAIR-JOHNSON CEMETERY
Armistead Road and Westminster Drive (43) {H - 8}
African American

This cemetery continues to be used by descendants, 1997.

From "A Journey into the Past". "Can't be sold or moved bodies-only members of JOHNSON'S, PATRICK'S and WARD families can be buried there. On property formerly owned by the SINCLAIR family- (Martha Sinclair FIELD, dead").

Acknowledgment: Transcribed by S. Keith and T. Winters 1990. A well kept family cemetery surrounded by a low brick wall with an iron gate.

Eugene WARD
Sept 11, 1898
July 15, 1982

Lavina WARD
April 8, 1902
August 23, 1966

Richard T. WARD
April 20, 1888
Feb 22, 1957

Pearl. L. WARD
June 25, 1887
Jan 22, 1957

Florence WARD
Wife of
Johnson WARD
Sept 10, 1886
Sept 4, 1953

Johnson WARD
1884-1948

Esther DOWE
Aunt of Clara JOHNSON
(Loose stone laying
against wall)

Rosetta M. COOKE
June 7, 1922
Sept 6, 1987

Leon E. WARD
Aug 1, 1924
Oct 26, 1968

Leola Johnson JONES
1910-1936

Tainma V. WARD
1917-1936

Harrison W. JOHNSON
1904-1936

Mary R. WARD
Feb 14, 1900
Oct 14, 1977

Mary R. WARD
1911-1928

Samuel JOHNSON
His Beloved Wife
Eliza JOHNSON
In memory of
Grandparents of
Isaac JOHNSON

Carrie L. HOPSON
Feb 26, 1920
Feb 11, 1978

Hollis F. JOHNSON
Virginia
PVT 1 CL 44 Serv CP
Ord Dept.
January 9, 1920
March 19, 1944

Isaac JOHNSON Jr.
Born Jan 9, 1917
Died Nov 23, 1948
His memory is blessed

Isaac JOHNSON Sr.
Nov 26, 1883
May 22, 1966

Clara B. JOHNSON
March 12, 1891
Sept 20, 1973

Arlene H. PACKER
Oct 23, 1924
June 4, 1962

Lewis JOHNSON
Brother of
Isaac JOHNSON Sr
(No Dates)

Alanda R. O'HARITY
Nov 3, 1911
April 2, 1976

Montaque JOHNSON
1897-1917

Samuel JOHNSON Jr
Son of
Samuel & Eliza
JOHNSON
Died 1927
He has done what he
could

Isabell Johnson STARKS
Born Feb 10, 1865
Died Nov 24, 1936
She done her best
Asleep in Jesus

Alberta JOHNSON
Sept 3, 1884
Jan 4, 1960

Priscilla JOHNSON
Died April 20, 1893
Age 42 Yrs
Mother of Isaac
JOHNSON, Lewis
JOHNSON, Edward
JOHNSON, Rebecca &
Frances

Eliza JOHNSON
Grandmother of
Isaac JOHNSON, Sr
(No Dates)

Frances Johnson
BANRIDGE
July 10, 1879
Nov 19, 1953
Gone but not forgotten

Willie JOHNSON
July 23, 1902
Jan 31, 1970

Rebecca HAWKINS
Nov 26, 1888
June 5, 1972

Johnny SMITH
March 3, 1910
Aug 16, 1988
("Smith Brothers" at
Footstone)

A Flat Stone of Isabell Johnson Starkes

SMITH CEMETERY
Woodland Road behind Woodland Park (44) {L - 9}
African American

Charles Riddick and Martha A. Riddick, his wife, received from Thomas Tabb, 2.5 acres for $250.00 on 26 Nov. 1878. City of Hampton (Elizabeth City Co.) Deed Book 5, page 521.

On 12 June 1906, John Riddick, Charles Riddick, Minnie Riddick, his wife, Josephine Bolling and _____ Bolling, her husband, and Martha A. Riddick, widow of Charles Riddick, deceased, to George W. Smith, Sr. and George W. Smith Jr. for $225.00, 2.5 acres.
This is where the cemetery got its name. The first burial took place during the 1910's by tombstone information.
On 5 September 1969, Fred H. Smith, Ruth H. Smith, husband and wife, Clarence Smith, single, heirs of George W. Smith Sr. and George W. Smith Jr. to Geneva Smith Wilkerson and Lewis Wilkerson, her husband, for $10.00.
On 1 November 1972, Geneva Smith Wilkerson and Lewis Wilkerson, wife and husband, to Old Buckroe Heights Corp.
On 29 July 1975 Buckroe Heights Corp. conveyed the land to the City of Hampton except the cemetery, which appears to be in the existing tract of the Wilkerson family.

Acknowledgment: The tombstone inscriptions were read in December 1996, and Jamuary - February 1997 by Barry Miles.
Acknowledgment: Barry W. Miles transcribed Dec. 1996, Jan. and Feb 1997

Minnie A. MATTHEWS
Nov 25, 1894
July 17, 1988

McClellan R. MATTHEWS
Jan 15, 1928
Feb 28, 1994

Clara M. MILES
Nov 25, 1894
March 28, 1989

Corrine M. TURNER
Nov 2, 1914
Feb 9, 1988

M. Elizabeth ANTHONY-JONES
Sept 25, 1926
Jan 22, 1988

Mary GLENN
Sept 19, 1919
May 16, 1988

Clara S. RICHARDSON
Apr 14, 1881
Dec 4, 1981

In low cinder block wall

Ernestine RUFF
July 6, 1916
Nov 24, 1959

Helen P. RICHARDSON
Sept 7, 1898
March 13, 1969

Lawrence E. DENNIS
Aug 19, 1915
Jan 5, 1975

Grace E. SELDON
June 24, 1905
Oct 19, 1974

James T. SELDON
Aug 12, 1895
Aug 6, 1974

Louise CANNEY
Jan 12, 1903
Nov 15, 1974

Mary E. WASHINGTON
Sept 17, 1916
July 28, 1975

Emily BLAND
Jan 12, 1896
Sept 5, 1975

Elizabeth SELDEN
June 15, 1877
Sept 27, 1975

Robert C. FITCHETT
Dec 29, 1890
Oct 25, 1976

Victoria DAVIS
Dec 5, 1907
Nov 12, 1975

Mary E. FLEMING
Jan 24, 1920
Nov 17, 1975

Hugh FLEMING
Feb 16, 1916
Nov 12, 1987

David D. ASKEW Jr.
Sept 7, 1915
Aug 20, 1976

David J. VANN
June 26, 1914
June 29, 1976

James W. DENNIS
June 10, 1916
Jan 16, 1976

Harrison GOODMAN
July 22, 1896
June 12, 1978

Josephine D. BROWN
May 7, 1928
Feb 26, 1978

Walter M. OSBORNE
Nov 6, 1933
July 27, 1995

Clara WILLIAMS
Oct 13, 1903
Dec 8, 1987

Leolia MARSHALL
Aug 4, 1910
Oct 5, 1987

Claudis JENNINGS
1952 - 1983
Temporary Metal Marker

Willie L. OSBORNE
Aug 31, 1925
Sept 21, 1987

Clara V. DREW
Aug 11, 1904
Sept 11, 1987

Ellen ARBS
July 22, 1943
April 1, 1987

Raymond JENKINS
Jan 31, 1937
March 28, 1987

Raymond SAUNDERS
Temporary Metal Marker

No Name
Temporary Metal Marker

Ora W. JACKSON
May 18, 1901
Jul 18, 1994

Robert JACKSON
Jan 7, 1895
June 10, 1974

Nannie HARRISON
Dec 28, 1977
Age 77

Jack COOPER
Jan 12, 1922
June 12, 1979

Gwendolyn BENTHALL
Jan 27, 1923
Sept 16, 1973

William LINDSEY
July 26, 1910
April 17, 1974

Kate HARMON
Sept 21, 1915
Mar 17, 1974

Walter B. BAKER
Sept 16, 1901
April 2, 1977

John C. WARREN
Apr 11, 1923
Sept 5, 1977

Percy C. BOONE Jr.
Aug 16, 1931
Sept 11, 1977

Elizabeth SIMPSON
July 12, 1904
Nov 4, 1977

Ulysses E. WALKER
w/ Mary Walker

Mary M. WALKER
w/ Ulysses WALKER

Sunken in ground
cannot read

Edith Laura SYKES
June 8, 1888
Nov 7, 1973

Hattie L. LANCFORD
March 14, 1885
May 4, 1974

Wilton HARRELL
May 2, 1911
July 22, 1974

Mamie Lee CLARKE
Mar 8, 1910
Jan 30, 1963
In low cement fence

Thelma JENKINS
June 2, 1942
June 4, 1982

William RANDALE
Mar 31, 1923
Feb 21, 1987

Martha HARRELL
Aug 19, 1913
Feb 10, 1987

Louise B. NEWSOM
Oct 19, 1919
Dec 11, 1986

Lillian MORROW
Sept 5, 1921
Oct 25, 1986

Alonzo GRIFFIN
Nov 2, 1926
Sept 22, 1986

Sarita E. BLACKLE
Aug 12, 1951
Aug 26, 1972

Leroy LIPSCOME
April 29, 1958
July 16, 1976

George L. JONES
Sept 30, 1904
Oct 29, 1973

George P. ALLEN
March 26, 1940
Jan 1, 1972

Solomon HILTON
March 12, 1895
Aug 2, 1972

Agnes H. QUIVERS
March 17, 1904
April 23, 1972

Rosa S. LEE
1887 - 1972

Rosetta TYSON
Nov 22, 1884
Oct 21, 1973

Alfred H. RAY
Nov 27, 1925
May 28, 1973

Victoria GROSS
June 15, 1883
July 23, 1972

Mary E. SPRATLEY
Feb 16, 1898
Oct 5, 1972

Florence V. JULIUS
Feb 14, 1910
Feb 15, 1972

Eliza A. SARGENT
Sept 21, 1894
March 4, 1989

Julia Thelma PRITCHETT
1926 - 1987
Shining all the way

Dorothy MONTAQUE
Sept 10, 1908
June 30, 1986

Mattie WESTBROOK
March 11, 1886
Nov 28, 1970

Esther M. MOORE
Aug 16, 1949
June 11, 1971

James A. ROY
Jan 12, 1934
Aug 29, 1971

Emma T. TRAVIS
Feb 22, 1888
Dec 20, 1970

Minnie L. COLEMAN
May 19, 1887
April 26, 1971

Alice M. TAYLOR
Born Feb 1876
Died Mar 1971

Jefferson LOVE
March 22, 1897
Sept 24, 1971

Beatrice WILLIAMS
Aug 30, 1916
April 8, 1971

Paul A. SMITH
1903 - 1971

Charles SPRATLEY
Aug 13, 1893
Aug 19, 1971

Elmer A. BAKER
Oct 13, 1904
April 5, 1971

Artelia V. HARRISON
1886 - 1972

Margaret TAYLOR
July 31, 1914
July 1, 1986

Oscar E. NEWBY
Aug 12, 1909
Jan 29, 1986

Sylvester EVERETTE
Nov 1, 1931
Dec 24, 1985

Henry S. BLACK
March 28, 1898
Oct 1, 1985

John CHANDLER
March 22, 1940
Aug 30, 1985

Lloyd ATKINS
June 22, 1923
Nov 25, 1982

Samuel C. MILES
Oct 10, 1932
Oct 11, 1982

Luster JENKINS
Oct 28, 1897
Aug 28, 1972

Harver H. BENTHAL
June 9, 1921
August 11, 1970

Lena B. WILSON
Jan 20, 1970

Annie L. CLINE
May 10, 1928
Nov 16, 1970

Nora BURTON
Feb 12, 1920
June 18, 1978

Phyllis E. NEELY
Oct 7, 1927
May 6, 1970

Marion L. ALSTON
Sept 27, 1915
Oct 8, 1969

Ora V. CLAYTOR
1914 - 1978
Temporary Marker

Prince E. NICHOLS
Sept 9, 1892
Jan 9, 1978

Juanita C. ASH
April 1, 1929
Jan 1, 1969

Sarah Knox PHILLIPS
February 4, 1881
March 10, 1966
Sister & Aunt

Addie FITCHETTE
Aug 23, 1897
April 18, 1968

John LANCFORD
Died Feb 8, 1967

Alice J. MANN
Apr 13, 1895
Jan 12, 1977

Virginia CALLIS
1916 - 1986
Temporary Marker

Bessie G. HOGES
Aug 30, 1915
April 22, 1986
Dear Mother we love
you Daughter & Family

Maggie HARDY
July 20, 1914
Aug 20, 1985

Theadore A. WARD
1911 - 1985
Temporary Metal Marker

Anna WARD
Reserved
Temporary Metal Marker

Jessie M. BOONE
May 5, 1913
Oct 17, 1968

W. Herman JONES
1890 - 1969
Rest in Peace

Martha A. PRITCHETT
April 1, 1901
June 8, 1969

William A. PRITCHETT
June 29, 1897
Feb 9, 1968

Lavinia BOYKIN
June 1, 1901
Jan 28, 1968

Alva CONEY
July 22, 1900
Oct 6, 1967

Mary J. VANN
Dec 18, 1874
Feb 20, 1965

Howard MATTHEWS, Sr.
Aug 14, 1885
Aug 17, 1963
Husband & Father

Mary Ann SMITH
1878 - 1963

Alice H. MARTIN
July 23, 1920
May 23, 1963

Hattie W. PRESTON
June 20, 1905
Feb 14, 1963

Washington SHIELDS
June 6, 1901
July 24, 1962

Minnie B. SHIELDS
May 12, 1906
June 17, 1976

Russell T. MORRIS
September 16, 1907
November 12, 1984

Elizabeth CHRISTIAN
Feb 11, 1905
Aug 28, 1961

Charles BEACH
June 30, 1899
March 25, 1961
Gone but not Forgotten

Ella ASKEW
June 18, 1882
Jan 21, 1961

William A. OSBORNE
May 13, 1927
April 8, 1960

Lena F. TARLTON
Feb 25, 1881
Jan 23, 1960

William H. SYKES
1878 - 1960

Arleann M. WEBSTER
Jan 22, 1900
Oct 3, 1959

Liza DAVIS
Oct 1, 1879
Dec 25, 1958

Callie M. PAGE
Nov 15, 1873
July 8, 1958

Laura E. DRUITT
June 15, 1892
Aug 11, 1977

Walter T. DRUITT
Mar 12, 1889
Sept 3, 1957

Madeline WILLIAMS
Mar 27, 1893
May 22, 1983

Margaret BANDY
June 24, 1925
April 22, 1987

Roland BANDY Sr.
Sept 1, 1917
Mar 23, 1983

Grace JENKINS
May 18, 1927
Mar 27, 1983

James R. LANGLEY
Sept 18, 1935
Dec 21, 1982

Sallie CASEY
Died Apr 21, 1982

Leon CASEY
Jan 8, 1911
April 26, 1961

Bessie L. PRITCHETT
1923 - 1961
in Loving memory

Hattie V. DEAN
April 17, 1891
July 14, 1959

Ella HARDY
Sept 12, 1895
Sept 23, 1957

George HOLLOWAY
Aug 28, 1881
July 1, 1957

Bernard DENNIS
Died Aug 13, 1956

Charles TOLIVER
1913 - 1980
Temporary Metal Marker

Daisy FRANCIS
Mar 3, 1903
Sept 26, 1982

Clarence A. DAVIS
Nov 21, 1904
Oct 1, 1964

Goldie CHAVIS
Aug 10, 1906
Mar 2, 1984

Martha Knox ALLEN
Died Sept 16, 1955

Colia B. YOUNG
June 17, 1880
Aug 20, 1955

Grave Unmarked

Grave Unmarked

Grave Unmarked

Charles W. CAMPBELL
1874 - 1963

Eleanor CLAIBORNE
July 4, 1894
Sept 16, 1990

Lena Young JONES
April 12, 1898
Sept 19, 1988

Allen M. KEMP
Sept 18, 1945
April 2, 1985

George M. KEMP
April 2, 1947
May 20, 1986

Marie J. CALLIS
April 16, 1888
Oct 14, 1988

Mabel BEACH
Sept 3, 1901
Aug 9, 1984
"Momabel"

William HAMPTON
Reserved

Elnora HAMPTON
April 14, 1944
Oct 11, 1983

Delores SCALES
Sept 14, 1933
Aug 31, 1983

Mr. BLACKLEY
Died Apr 27, 1963
Temporary Metal Marker

Walter T. BOONE
Sept 18, 1883
Mar 8, 1961

Samuel H. WEST
Jan 11, 1917
March 18, 1960

David N. BARRER
August 19, 1986
Temporary Metal Marker

Mrs Josephine Booker
WILLIS
Born July 12, 1893
Died Nov 22, 1958

Otis S. THRUSTON
Born Nov 16, 1952
Died Feb 12, 1956

Frances M. PEAKE
Nov 16, 1876
June 22, 1955

Ethel ROBINSON
June 7, 1912
April 16, 1982

Agnes E. YOUNG
Oct 10, 1894
Aug 14, 1977

Jamie CARTER
Died April 25, 1953
Temporary Metal Marker

Grave Unmarked

Grave Unmarked

Grave Unmarked

Elva Mae NEWBY
Sept 7, 1891
July 28, 1988

Roscoe STROUD
Aug 26, 1898
May 13, 1964

Vivian W. CARTER
May 22, 1924
March 25, 1964

Martha JETT
Died Dec 29, 1957

Grave Unmarked

Elizabeth J. DANIELS
1893 - 1953
Sleeping in Jesus

William M. LANCFORD
Died Dec 29, 1951

Grave Unmarked

Sarah JENKINS
August 15, 1906
October 14, 1988

Nathaniel WHITE
May 15, 1940
May 30, 1969

William WARREN
Oct 5, 1917
July 11, 1964

Willie E. ROBINSON
Mar 15, 1895
Apr 9, 1964

Josephine ROSE
Sept 12, 1894
Oct 28, 1963

Franklin SARGENT
April 24, 1889
Aug 25, 1963

Effie L. BOONE
Feb 28, 1910
Dec 22, 1980

Effie Jo ARCHIE
Dec 12, 1907
Sept 28, 1980

Ettrula R. MANN
May 19, 1898
Aug 12, 1980

Walter S. MANN
July 17, 1897
Nov 25, 1953

Corrine MINNS
1909 - 1981
Temporary Metal Marker

Mary A. PRITCHELL
1929 - 1982
In Loving Memory

Minnie COSBY
1932 - 1981
Temporary Metal Marker

Alice M. MERCEY
1908 - 1981
Temporary Metal Marker

Mrs Maggie RAY
1907 - 1981
Temporary Metal Marker

Edgar A. SARGENT
1932 - 1989
Temporary Metal Marker

Grace BRISCO
1912 - 1989
Temporary Metal Marker

Harold R. CHARITY
1916 - 1988
Temporary Metal Marker

Mary SIMPSON
1917 - 1988
Temporary Metal Marker

Florine JACKSON
March 13, 1922
Oct 31, 1988

Lucy LOWE
1924 - 1988
Temporary Metal Marker

Dercy FLEETWOOD
1910 - 1988
Temporary Metal Marker

Leona TERRY
Jan 16, 1897
Aug 18, 1988

Rosa L. STROUD
Feb 18, 1918
Feb 19, 1972

Elizabeth WARREN
May 2, 1890
Mar 18, 1965

Lewis SARGENT Sr.
1907 - 1964

Ruth SARGENT
1908 - 1964

Celestine A. MANN
March 11, 1917
Feb 28, 1964
Gone but not Forgotten

Lulan JACKSON
Sept 3, 1875
July 14, 1962

Riley BRASWELL
Sept 8, 1931
June 24, 1962

Rosetta SMITH
Born 4 - 8 - 1907
Deceased 2 - 13 - 1961
In Loving Memory

Ruth J. BARR
April 17, 1916
July 9, 1961

David BARR
Oct 6, 1910
July 9, 1961

Baby Boy JOLLIE
Died Aug 23, 1979
Temporary Metal Marker

Baby Boy JOLLIE
Died Sept 6, 1977
Temporary Metal Marker

Mary Ann FURLOW
Died Nov 3, 1961
Temporary Metal Marker

Eli MITCHELL
June 7, 1883
July 2, 1962

William E. TERRY
Died Jan 7, 1963
Temporary Metal Marker

Grave Unmarked

H. S. _____
Home made Marker
cannot read

Lewis RICHARDS
May 14, 1902
Apr 5, 1968

Morris W. HUDGINS
Apr 28, 1901
Jan 30, 1966

Lillie E. PATERSON
July 14, 1885
Jan 22, 1968

Jesse J. JORDON Jr.
July 19, 1915
June 9, 1968

Nellie R. ATKINS
Mar 31, 1899
Nov 27, 1967

Blannie V. COOPER
July 4, 1894
June 7, 1986

Joseph T. COOPER
Dec 8, 1889
Dec 14, 1964

Raymond B. ANTHONY
Sr.
Feb 6, 1892
Oct 11, 1963
Father

Beatrice N. Hill
ANTHONY
July 14, 1894
February 4, 1987

Oscar DENNIS
April 15, 1894
June 27, 1960
Small Cement wall
surrounds 1 vault

Walter J. BLAND
April 10, 1901
May 7, 1968

Mary C. PURCELL
1890 - 1965

William S. MANN
July 23, 1874
Nov 8, 1964

Sallie B. TAYLOR
July 4, 1880
Sept 20, 1962

Beatrice H. HARRIS
June 9, 1915
Nov 26, 1981

Beatrice MITCHELL
March 17, 1920
Jan 1, 1961

Rita Armstead ECHOLS
MARSHBURN
June 25, 1889
January 2, 1960
Sister & Aunt

Grave unmarked

Grave unmarked

Laura Alice EVANS
Jan 21, 1910
Sept 23, 1988

Grave unmarked

Lena W. COOPER
Aug 12, 1900
Nov 14, 1982

Nicholas C. WHITE
Nov 9, 1889
Feb 2, 1962

Alice B. CARLTON
Died Oct 28, 1960

Samuel WESTBROOK
Feb 16, 1882
June 19, 1959

Amada B. BLAKE
Aug 18, 1872
May 9, 1958

Addie BLAND
Dec 12, 1877
Feb 19, 1958

Katie LANGSTON
Born Oct 6, 1884
Died Sept 24, 1955

Jesse T. BUTLER
June 27, 1892
Oct 29, 1967

Irene BUTLER
1892 - 1949

Marjorie GRIFFIN
Dec 13, 1913
May 11, 1979

Susie G. PEARSON
April 13, 1915
Jan 1, 1990

Charles GRIFFIN
Sept 10, 1907
Dec 9, 1996

James GRIFFIN
Reserved

Elnor T. WHITE
Feb 14, 1903
May 20, 1959

Hilda L. BAILEY
Died May 20, 1957

Grave unmarked

George M. CHAVIS Sr.
Jan 15, 1907
April 22, 1956

Goldie M. CHAVIS
Aug 10, 1906
March 2, 1994

Charles A. SAMPSON
Nov 13, 1894
Feb 4, 1949
Asleep in Jesus
Surrounded by Low
cement wall 14" high

Grave unmarked

Grave unmarked

Lydia C. GRIFFIN
Jan 6, 1884
June 18, 1976

William T. GRIFFIN
April 23, 1887
July 30, 1970

Berdie L. PERRY
Oct 6, 1877
Aug 23, 1957

Jennie JEFFERSON
July 7, 1955

Sarah M. JONES
Feb 2, 1882
Oct 10, 1955

Arleen HOLLOWAY
Died Nov 27, 1955

William A. MILES
Sept 16, 1876
Apr 19, 1964

Grave unmarked

Dwight E. WEST
July 26, 1947
May 9, 1954

Grave unmarked

Grave unmarked

Sallie F. RIDLEY
Oct 31, 1907
Oct 13, 1957
w/o Mark RIDLEY

Edith MOORE
Jan 13, 1918
Dec 31, 1985

Essie B. SCOTT
Feb 12, 1894
May 17, 1968

Grave unmarked

Glady S. MOORE
Born 1930
Died 1952

Percy D. BOONE Sr.
June 11, 1906
Sept 16, 1952

Grave unmarked

George E. GARDNER Sr.
May 29, 1882
Feb 9, 1953
Husband
w/o Rosa GARDNER

Rosa R. GARDNER
Dec 31, 1894
Dec 24, 1981
Wife
h/o George GARDNER

George Edward
GARDNER Jr.
December 5, 1927
August 2, 1972
Virginia PVT US Army
World War 2

Ann WILSON
Died Mar 27, 1958

Emory C. TURNER
1894 - 1982
Name & Date painted on
stone

William FAUNTLEROY
1915 - 1952

Thomas H. WEBB
1899 - 1948

Mary E. SIMON
1861 - 1948

Mary ? SIMON
Aug 14, 1901
Aug 30, 1974

Grave unmarked

Mary TURNER
1893 - 1961

Grave unmarked

Grave unmarked

Grave unmarked

Alice FAUNTLEROY
Feb 22, 1896
Jan 26, 1948

Clara V. PAYNE
Dec 8, 1877
Feb 20, 1959
d/s w/ Louise PAYNE

Louise PAYNE
Aug 25, 1863
May 20, 1947
d/s w/ Clara V. PAYNE

James H. KING
Sept 30, 1887
May 4, 1947

Ethel L. YOUNG
1910 - 1947

Frances THORNTON
1880 - 1957

Freeman SMITH
March 9, 1888
Oct 3, 1946
At Rest

Grave unmarked

Grave unmarked

Grave unmarked

Alonzo CLAYTON
1902 - 1947
Son

Martha CLAYTON
1876 - 1947

Grave unmarked

Grave unmarked

Rosa KNOX
June 8, 1876
June 7, 1988

Inez F. KNOX
May 4, 1907
June 27, 1986

Julia Ann LASSITER
Aug 22, 1915
Mar 31, 1992
The Lord is my Strength
and my Salvation Who
shall I Fear

Robert LASSITER
March 22, 1871
April 25, 1951
Masonic

Leroy G. LASSITER
Oct 7, 1903
June 7, 1977

Lucy ARMSTEAD
Dec 7, 1882
Oct 23, 1971
Surrounded by ground
level cement wall

Robert JETER
Born 1867
Died Dec 10, 1907

Joseph CUFFEE
Died Aug 24, 1946
At Rest

Arnold ANDERSON Jr.
Born Mar 23, 1944
Died Feb 2, 1946
Temporary Metal plate on
stone

Grave unmarked

Eunick D. CARTER
Jan 8, 1895
April 26, 1945

Alex MANN
June 6, 1876
Jan 30, 1945
Father
At Rest
Tall pointed stone broken

Grave unmarked

Grave unmarked

Ramsey C. LINDSAY
April 6, 1906
Jan 30, 1943

Fuphenia _____
1908 - 1945

Foot Marker
S. T. J.

Louise S. MYERS
April 9, 1890
March 17, 1967

Grave unmarked

Sophia S. CLARKE
1881 - 1959
Mother in loving memory

James N. CLARKE
1879 - 1944
Father well done

James H. WILSON Sr.
Dec 18, 1916
April 30, 1996
PVT US Army
World War 2

Pearl WILSON
Dec 25, 1893
Dec 10, 1948
w/ Henry

Henry WILSON
Feb 15, 1882
July 27, 1941
w/ Pearl

Lavinia CUFFEE
Died June 5, 1941
At Rest

Gladys O. HARRELL
Nov 15, 1922
July 24, 1976
surrounded by Iron fence
about 18" high

Lillian H. WHITE
June 8, 1912
Oct 7, 1938
Stone off pedestal

Stone in ground
cannot read

Cement fence 8" high
no graves

Melvin FOUNTAIN
June 20, 1920
Nov 10, 1937

Henrietta JACKSON
July 18, 1889
April 27, 1938
Mother

Carrie E. MANN
Dec 1, 1875
Mar 6, 1942
Mother A devoted
wife and Mother

William H. JONES
Aug 15, 1873
Dec 6, 1942

Cardel YOUNG
Born Sept 4
Stone in ground
cannot read

Georgia Anna SARGENT
Feb 18, 1941
Stone in ground
cannot read

E. S. WILSON
25 Feb 1956
Temporary Metal Marker

Robert N. COOPER
April 5, 1872
Jan 25, 1942

Milton A. PAIGE
Dec 22, 1914
Feb 20, 1942

Mary JONES
Jan 3, 1882
Jan 15, 1961
Mother

Grave unmarked

Grave unmarked

John SARGENT
Dec 24, 1870
Sept 19, 1941
Gone but not Forgotten

Warren L. BLACKLEY
Sept 17, 1925
Aug 31, 1940

Pauline SCARBOR
March 22, 1885
August 24, 1941

Mary E. BAKER
May 15, 1867
In ground
w/o Benjamin F.
BROKENBURR
Stone in shape of cross

Gloria Gates JOHNSON
March 14, 1940
April 5, 1975

───────────────

inside cement wall 12" high

Nicey SAMPSON
Feb 15, 1865
May 29, 1961

Hester S. SMITH
Died Sept 26, 1966

Celestine SMITH
1915 - 1932
Stone shape of Bible

Malinda MOSSON
Died Sept 3, 1937

Harold BRINN
Dec 16, 1904
Sept 9, 1936

Moses ANDERSON
Died Sept 6, 1934
Age 79 years
At Rest

Dinah E. MANN
Mar 2, 1883
Nov 20, 1960

Grave unmarked

"Niece" Elnora A. MERCY
May 7, 1902
Sept 11, 1938

Elizabeth SARGENT
Died Jan 14, 1938
Age 64 years

Jackson W. PAIGE
Jan 29, 1916
June 20, 1938

Mable H. LIVELY
May 17, 1889
May 23, 1960

W. B. REED
No data given

Lewis WILKERSON
1893 - 1974

Ruth SMITH
1902 - 1973

Grave unmarked

Low Cement fence
no grave inside

Harold GATES
July 19, 1905
Oct 14, 1974

Inez A. HARRELL
Died Feb 23, 1960
Temporary Metal Marker

Geneva WILKERSON
Aug 14, 1897
Aug 14, 1988

Kettie B. REED
Born Aug 1876
Died Dec 12, 1920
Age 44 years
at Rest
Wife

Clarence L. SMITH
August 20, 1901
March 31, 1970

Fred SMITH
1901 - 1972

Hilliard BAYLOR
Military insignia
U. S. Navy
No Dates

Henry J. BOYKIN
h/o Mary D. BOYKIN
Born Sept 1, 1861
Died Aug 21, 1932
Father

Mary D. FRAZIER
w/o Henry J. BOYKIN
Born Aug 16, 1874
Died Jan 5, 1928
At Rest
Mother

Dorothea Boykin SELVY
August 13, 1895
September 7, 1988
At Rest

Lena B. JENKINS
w/o Mansfield J. BOYKIN
May 24, 1902
May 3, 1940
At Rest
Mother

Paul L. JACKSON
Apr 23, 1915
Mar 6, 1994

Arthur JACKSON
1884 - 1929
Son
d/s w/ Millie

Millie JACKSON
1867 - 1947
Mother
d/s w/ Arthur

Robert E. JACKSON
Feb 2, 1891
Dec 3, 1975
d/s w/ Anna

Anna M. JACKSON
May 12, 1893
July 21, 1975
d/s w/ Robert E.

Susie SARGENT
June 5, 1895
Aug 15, 1932
Stone off pedestal

Theodore BLACKLEY Sr
Feb 26, 1895
Feb 23, 1933

Patsy KING
Oct 1, 1864
March 10, 1933
Rest in Peace

Minnie G. WILKINSON
Oct 25, 1873
Aug 3, 1951

Lawrence E. WILKINSON
Dec 6, 1874
Sept 28, 1950

Ethel McHERN
1894 - 1976
Temporary Metal Marker

Owen McHERN
No Dates
Temporary Metal Marker

Lucy C. BARROW
June 30, 1891
Jan 30, 1969
She has done what
she could
f/s L. C. B.

John TOLIVER
Born 1871
Mar 16, 1928
Husband
d/s w/ Lura

Lura TOLIVER
May 19, 1876
May 27, 1926
Wife
d/s w/ John
Gone but Not Forgotten

Dennis C. BARROW
March 30, 1899
June 17, 1952
Virginia 801 Pioneer
Inf World War 1

George H. DYKE
March 7, 1909
Aug 6, 1927
Son

James H. DYKE
Oct 3, 1869
April 29, 1955

Mrs Elfred D. DAVIS
Died May 6, 1993
Temporary Metal Marker

Isabella E. STEWARD
Feb 9, 1875
Nov 13, 1926
d/s w/ William H.

William H. STEWARD
Sept 4, 1868
Jan 19, 1941
Their children shall rise up
and call them blessed

Angeline E. STEWARD
Aug 16, 1902
Dec 19, 1977

Ada M. BOWINS
July 9, 1893
June 23, 1932

Jeff BROWN
1889 - 1930
Husband

Ardnella W. BROWN
Mar 16, 1889
Aug 24, 1985

Claude ASKEW
1884 - 1931
Brother

Elizabeth BARROW
Born 1871
Died Aug 30, 1921
Aged 50 years
cannot read inscription

Daniel BARROW
Born May 1867
Died Feb 23, 1937
Age 70 years
Grave unmarked

Walter BARROW
December 14, 1949
Virginia Corpl 540
Engineers

Helen M. DYKE
June 1, 1898
Nov 1, 1925
Daughter

Fannie M. DYKE
May 28, 1878
Dec 6, 1967

Margaret T. McCOY
Died July 28, 1959
Wife

In Memory of
Rosy BEASLEY
w/o H. D. BEASLEY
Born 1881
Nov 18, 1925
At rest

Peter GAYLE
No Dates
Temporary Metal Marker

Nathaniel SIMON
Dec 6, 1876
Nov 27, 1929
Husband

Isaiah SATISFIELD
Died Feb 11, 1939
Gone but not forgotten

Berry COLEMAN
Born Dec 25, 1872
Died Mar 26, 1915 ?

Minnie C. BROWN
Feb 16, 1877
Jan 8, 1960

Grave cannot read

Grave unmarked

Luther W. ROBINSON
Sunken in Ground
cannot read

Katie SIMPSON
Died Jan 31, 1935

Samuel SIMPSON
No Dates

Margaret S. MATTHEWS
Died Oct 9, 1925
Mother
d/s w/ Eva E.

Eva E. MATTHEWS
Died April 19, 1956
Daughter
d/s w/ Margaret S.

Harry W. MATTHEWS
Died July 20, 1958

Rebecca OLIVER
Aug 1, 1893
May 20, 1977

George OLIVER
June 27, 1898
Sept 6, 1956

John H. JONES
Sunken in Ground

Julia W. LASSITER
July 27, 1873
Nov 30, 1944

George E. ECHOLS
July 15, 1922
Alabama PVT 24 Inf.

Dora A. ROBINSON
Died Aug 24, 1939
Sister

Hester ARMSTEAD
Died July 30, 1940
Mother

Samuel KNOX
April 8, 1879
May 17, 1942
Loving Husband
A Benevolent Soul

Elorena CARTER
Mar 22, 1902
Oct 25, 199-
w/o L. A. CARTER
Gone but not Forgotten
Stone in bad condition

Rosetta MILES
Mar 9, 1877
Dec 5, 1925
Mother
Stone in bad condition

Martha WALKER
Jan 12, 1887
Jan 12, 1928
Mother
At Rest

Frances GREEN
April 28, 1909
Aug 5, 1926
A sleep in Jesus

Mary E. BAPTIS
Oct 11, 1888
Jul 31, 1926
w/o J. B. BAPTIS
Mother
Gone but not Forgotten
Headstone in bad condition

Nannie COOPER
Died March 12, 1928
Age 51 yrs
At Rest

Susie C. HORTON
March 17, 1906
March 25, 1928
surrounded by fence 2-3 inches high

Foot Marker
C. J.

Martha JOYNES
Born 1861
Died Sept 11, 1926
A Sleep in Jesus

Joseph WILLIAMS
Born May 2, 1851
Died Sept 23, 1911
Masonic insignia
No pain, no grief, no anxious fears can reach our loved one
 sleeping here
3 foot high pointed monument top missing

Cement fence even with ground
No Grave inside

Cornelious WILLIAMS
Aug 30, 1878
Nov 18, 1924
At Rest (Father)
Stone broken and bad condition

Eliza CRUZ
Feb 28, 1880
Jan 29, 1925
At Rest (Mother)

Mary MILES
Oct 2, 1876
Feb 21, 1924
w/o J. C. MILES
Mother

Leniod S. LACY
Painted on Stone
Surrounded by cement wall

Mary E. MINNS
Jan 3, 1876
Mar 5, 1928
Gone but not Forgotten

Elizabeth JONES
Died Aug 13, 1927
Age 65 Yrs
w/o Edward JONES
Gone but not Forgotten
Stone broken & bad condition

Lavin A. CUFFEE
July 24, 1905
May 12, 1922
d/o J. W. & L. L. CUFFEE
At Rest

Richard HARRIS
Nov 1, 1890
Aug 6, 1922
At Rest
Stone broken

Sallie FITCHETT
1873 - 1924
w/o Dan FITCHETT
Stone in bad condition

Indianna COOPER
Dec 27, 1900
Oct 2, 1918

Margaret SIMPSON
Died Jan 10, 1920
Peaceful be thy slumber

James H. JONES
Mar 18, 1866
Nov 10, 1922
d/s w/ Nellie
Father

Nellie JONES
Sept 9, 1867
Aug 3, 1925
d/s w/ James H.

Norris ASKEW
May 26, 1925
Virginia PVT Vet.
Hosp. 3

Small cement wall
2" high
No Graves

Grave unmarked

Mildred JONES
Mar 192
June 12, 1920

Thomas H. ASKEW
1855 - 1914
Father
d/s w/ Emmeline

Emmeline ASKEW
1893 - 1915
Sister
d/s w/ Thomas H.

Jac ? _____
Died Mar 12, 18xx
Aged 65 yrs
Gone but not forgotten

Gove ? _____
Died Jan 18, 1916
Age 70 yrs
Asleep in Jesus

Joseph Thomas SELDEN
Oct 20, 1876
Apr 14, 1917
Father
Gone but not Forgotten

Jennie SATISFIELD
Born 1859
Oct 1, 1918
Mother
Gone but not Forgotten

Cement wall
Grave unmarked

Pedestal only

Stone Markings only
Thy memory shall ever be
a guiding star to heaven

Smith Cemetery

Cemeteries of the City of Hampton, Virginia / formerly Elizabeth City County

STORES CEMETERY
Fox Hill Road (46) {K - 7}
Behind Benjamin Syms School

The following memorandum for the record was made on April 18, 1983 by P. W. after a call received from Melania Goodman concerning Judith Stores grave: "Melania Goodman and a friend, John Burfield, called this date to report they had found a grave on some property back of Benjamin Syms Jr. High.

The property belongs to Paul Bickford and it is for sale. They are concerned that the grave will be eventually plowed under if something is not done about it.

It is the grave of Judith Stores died in 1886. They were a prominent family in Hampton and owned so much of the property in Fox Hill. Mrs Stores age at the time of death was 77. There is a nice tombstone with an epitaph on it. Paul Bickford will assist in locating the grave for it is hidden under vines, etc.

I talked to Kingston Winget about it, and he had a Horn book telling about the Stores Family. He was a Captain.

Also contacted Beverly Gundry who suggested advertising for descendant of the Stores if they are in the area.   P. W. "

November 1, 1983 a memorandum was sent to Mr Steven L. Kinney, Asst. Director of Planning, City of Hampton, by Mr E. J. Sulzberger, Jr., President Hampton Heritage Foundation, Inc. regarding the Stores Cemetery:

"Subject: Grave site of Members of Capt. William Stores' Family.

It has come to the attention of the Foundation that there are two known graves on the grounds of the W. H. Thomas Estate. They were found by John Burfield when walking through the area several months ago. There are photographs of the site in our files. Judith Stores died in 1886 at the age of 77. The son, John Stores died in 1846 at age of 45 years.

In checking at the City Treasurer's office, it was found that, according to their records, William Forbes pays the taxes on the property. This office wrote Mr. Forbes telling him of the graves. We are interested in having them saved if possible. We have not had a reply to the letter written May 31, 1983. We also wrote "Question Line" in the Times-Herald, asking if there are any of the Stores family in the area, and if so, to contact this office. There have been no replies to this inquiry.

Our concern as a preservation group is, if any of this area is developed, the graves could be plowed under. Capt. William Stores was a prominent citizen in Hampton, and active during the Civil War. We are interested in having the graves saved. We could see that they're well taken care of and protected. It was evidently a burial site near the home."

Acknowledgment: Picture by John Burfield November 14, 1983.

In
Memory of
John STORES
who departed this life
Dec 24th 1846
aged 45 yrs.

Blessed are the dead
that die in thy Lord

Now all thy toils a----
thy suffering and thy pain
who meet on that eternal
shore.
shall never part again

Mrs Judeeth STORES
Died
Jan 28, 1886
Aged 75 years

Emanuell Holy Mother
(rest not readable)

Tombstone of Mrs. Judeeth Stores

TENNIS CEMETERY
Off Dandy Point Road (47) {O - 3}
Grave site is back in woods

This site is believed to be the Tennis cemetery. It is located off Dandy Point Road in Fox Hill and is owned by Horace Spruill who purchased the property some 20 years ago.

The site sits off by itself in the woods so has little undergrowth to remove nor maintenance necessary. Someone years ago protected the marker from being moved by burying it in concrete.

Acknowledgments: Transcribed by Mrs Wm. W. Wyatt (Betty Harper Wyatt) Fox Hill Cemeteries 10 Oct 1984. Mr. David Routten and Mr. Barry Miles visited the site on 6 April 1997. We were escorted to the site by Mr. Spruill's son. According to Mr. Routten, the land was owned by Joshua Tennis.

Joshua TENNIS   (The inscription is carved in natural stone and imbedded in
Departed this life   a slab of concrete, apparently done much later.)
A. D. 1809
Age 74   There are other graves sites marked by field stones.

210   Cemeteries of the City of Hampton, Virginia / formerly Elizabeth City County

THORNTON CEMETERY
Formerly known as "ZION"
Woodland Road off Mercury Blvd. (49) {L - 10}
African American

This site is very overgrown and many more markers will certainly be found beneath the carpet of ivy and trash, if the cemetery is ever restored.

Acknowledgment: Transcribed by S. Keith and Winters 1990's; Darla B. Long for an additional tombstone she uncovered, information and corrections.

Thomas H. HENDERSON
1906-1941
d/s w/Clara J.

Clara J. HENDERSON
1865-1935
d/s w/ Thomas

Morris C.
Son of C H & C J
HENDERSON
May 30, 1909
June 27, 1909
Asleep in Jesus

Elma M.
Dau of C H & C J
HENDERSON
Aug 9, 1892
Jul 13, 1922
Gone but not forgotten

Mother
Alice BROWN
Died Jan 5, 1918
Age 50 Years
rest in peace
(w/foot stone)

Sergt. Geo. STRONG
Co. C. 1 U.S.C. Cav.

A. I. READ
Died 1890

Lettie DANIELS
Died June 28, 1910

Mary E. RICHARDSON
1895 - 1896

In memory of
Mrs Leah YOUNG
Born Dec 25, 1817
Died April 16, 1893
Aged 76 Years
How sweet it will be in that
beautiful land so free from
sorrow and pain

With songs on our lips
and harps in our hand
to meet each other again

Patience JOHNSON
Born 1847
Died May 16, 1907
Rich are the rays which
cannot die with God laid up in
store treasures
beyond the changing
sky, brighter than
golden ore.

Jacob S. KINNER
Died Jul 1891
At rest

In memory of
Sarah J. DRUITT
wife of
Anderson DRUITT
Born Dec 8, 1851
Died May 22, 1902

In memory of
Marus ARMSTEAD
Born 1821
Died Mar 6, 1901
Age 80 Years

Adline
Wife of
James ALLEN
Died July 12, 1897
Age 70 Years
Gone but not forgotten

Sarah Tyson ALLEN
Born Aug 25, 1868
Died Sept 30, 1901
Age 33 Years

Sacred to the memory of
Elizabeth SKINNER
Died Dec 11, 1896
Mother

Sacred memory of
Nathan JACKSON
Died May 4, 1895
Brother

In memory of
Adeline SAUNDERS
Born 1857
Died Apr 6, 1913
Aged 56 Years
Servant of God well done

(foot stone C. A. J.)

Ernest S.
Son of
W. D. & Margaret DIGGS
Died Sept 30, 1908
Aged 33 Years, 3 Mo.

Anna
Dau of
W. & M. DIGGS
Born June 15, 1865
Died Sept 15, 1881
(adjacent grave dug up)

_____ DIGGS
(broken marker name lost)
Died May 2, 1901
Corporal of Co. F
10 Regt. U. S. Vol.

Isaia DIGGS
Born Sept 17, 1869
Died Sept 18, 1909
At rest

Washington DIGGS
Died May 5, 1898
Aged 31 Years
One precious to our hearts
gone the voice we loved is
stilled
the place made vacant in our
home can never more be filled

Margaret
wife of Washington DIGGS
Died May 11, 1890
Aged 52 Years

Washington DIGGS Jr.
Born Jan 15, 1836
Died April 12, 1920
At rest

Mary S. DIGGS
wife of
Deacon Washington DIGGS
Died May 28, 1918
Age 60 Years
At rest

Maggie RAY
Born 1887
July 16, 1906
At rest

Mary BOOKER
Died April 12, 1904
Aged 48 Years
Nearer my God to Thee

Sacred to the memory of
my beloved husband
James T. BANKS
Who departed this life
Oct 9, 1919
Aged 40 Years

Blessed are the dead who
die in the Lord
Anna BANKS
(No Dates)

Mother
India BECKET
Born 1836
Sept 17, 1905
At rest

Mother
Phoebe THOMAS
Born 1835
Oct 9, 1899
At rest

In memory of
Earnest JENKINS
born March 23, 1847
Died Oct 2, 1899
Aged 52 Years
At rest

Rufus BARNES
Son of
Davis & Hattie BARNES
Born Jun 1, 1878
Died Sept 9, 1898

In memory of our mother
Harriett BARNES
Born Oct 6, 1857
Died Sept 22, 1907

Mother
Jane SARGENT
1848-1896
At rest
(adjacent to Pleasant)

Father
Pleasant SARGENT
1836-1892
At rest
(adjacent to Jane)

In memorium
Nancy JOHNSON
Died April 13, 1915
Age 60 Years
Erected by Silver Link
Tent No. 90
asleep in Jesus

In remembrance of
Samuel STEWART
Born Nov 22, 1867
Died Oct 8, 1903
asleep in Jesus
blessed sleep

_____
next three graves is surrounded
by a low iron pipe including
a large urn and bench

Elsie JOHNSON
Oct 25, 1901
Age 116

Bessie GOLDSMITH
Died Jun 2, 1918
Age 28

Eliza PAYNE
Born 1834
Died Nov 19, 1915
Age 85 Years

_____
Next four graves surrounded
by a
low iron fence

Thomas COOK
Nov 5, 1916
Aged 64

In memory of
Cornelia COOKE
Died Nov 24, 1924
Aged 66 Years

Thelma M.
Dau of
M. C. or G. & M. E.
THORPE
Sept 7, 1896
Oct 19, 1896

Elizabeth TURNER
Died Jan 18, 1919
Aged 66 Years
asleep in Jesus

_____

Samuel S. SIMPSON
Died Mar 25, 1904
Age 67 Years

Nelson TURNER
Died Oct 15, 1905
Age 50 Years
Gone but not forgotten

John HUGHES
Died Jul 7, 1912
Aged 61 Years
At rest in the arms of
Jesus I expect to rest in
the bright shining world
on high.

The following is submitted by Darla Long.

Rev. Wm. Thornton and his wife Mrs Ellen Thornton were buried in this cemetery. Their tombstones have not been found.

Burial of Ellen THORNTON
9 May, 1902
Ordered by St. Lukes
(Catharian Smith Comm)
extras on coffin, embalming
ordered by her husband
Rev. Thornton
(live Sugar Hill)

Rev. Wm. THORNTON
burial May 16, 1909
by Masonic Lodge #13
extras on casket, embalming,
carriages by his daughters,
extra paid live Fox Hill Road,
Phoebus, died May 11.

The following markers have been uncovered by Darla Long.

Henry ARMSTEAD
Born Dec 1853
Died Apr 28, 1903
Age 50 years

Moses CLAYTON
June 1, 1876
Jul 21, 1915

Virginia A. WILSON
Born May 17, 1871
Died Sept 6, 1896
Age 25 years 3 mos 19 days
"Blessed are the death
which die in the Lord"

Daisy GARNETT
Died July 21, 1902
Age 20 years

Neolus A. JONES
Born 1889
Died March 27, 1915
Age 26, years

Maggie RAY
Born 1887
Died July 16, 1906

Kittie ELDER
Died Sept 17, 1913
"Stone erected by
Mrs Dorothy Jordan"

Alonzo J. WALKER
Died May 5, 1913
Age 42 years

Ida DIGGS
Born June 15, 1865
Died Sept 15, 1881
dau of W. & M. Diggs

Tombstone of Morris C. Henderson and Emma M. Henderson

TUCKER CEMETERY
Formerly Susla and/or Little Zion
Sharon Court (89) {E - 9}
African American

History: At entrance of the Cemetery is a sign, "Tucker Cemetery 300 Years". This cemetery was also known as Susla (sometimes called Little Zion Cemetery).

Acknowledgment: Transcribed by Barry W. Miles on 4 April 1997.

Father
Richard WRENN
1849 - 1924
at rest
f/s No Data

Hiram WRENN
died Nov 27, 1912
Age 66 Yrs.
at rest
surrounded by stones
about 4" high

Richard WRENN Jr.
1891 - 1921
at rest

Robert ANDERSON
died Sept 10, 1960
Temporary Metal Marker

Mother
Susan PARKER
1859 - 1919
at rest

Simon PARKER
s/o W. W. & E. W.
Parker
July 28, 1894
Oct 15, 1918
at rest
f/t No Data

Simon PARKER Sr
1842 - 1911
at rest

Ella PARISH
1871 - 1911
at rest
f/s No Data

James William TUCKER
Dec 19, 1909
Jan 12, 1970

Stone, No Markings

Stone, No Markings

Stone, No markings

Gladys PEGRAM
May 14, 1935
April 1, 1983

Emanuel TUCKER
June 26, 1912
Jan 22, 1979

Alexander TUCKER Sr
May 21, 1907
Feb 10, 1997

Mary E. TUCKER
born March 5, 1856
died June 18, 1904

Stone No Markings

Mary
w/o Randolph WALKINS
died June 5, 1915
Age 27 Yrs.
Gone to a Brighter Home
where grief cannot come

Alice G. GREEN
1918 - 1974

Mrs Mary A. TUCKER
No Dates

Stone No Markings

Stone No Markings

Stone No Markings

Graves in Woods and
Brush

William BRAXTON
born Dec 1863
died June 16, 1905

Everlina P. WARD
born Oct 25, 1885
died Aug 12, 1906
cannot read inscription

Stone & f/s
No Data

_____ DOUGLAS
December 23, 1905
October 17, 1964

Richard DOUGLAS
June 22, 1901
November 28, 1952

Jessie WILLIAMS
died Aug 27, 1952

Garret GRANGER
born Aug 12, 1879
died July 24, 1958

Vault No Markings

VAUGHAN (CLOVERDALE) CEMETERY
Doolittle and Ames Street (50) {G - 2}
On grounds of NASA

The following is from the Work Progress Administration of Virginia Historical Inventory, March 12, 1937, by Mrs Jacobs. This cemetery is about a half mile from the house. There is an acre of land in the cemetery, with square gray stone posts seven inches wide on each side and five feet high, set about fifty feet apart, all around it, with a hole through the posts so that a chain could be run through them, but the chains have been taken away. A road which goes by the back of the field, runs through the north corner of the cemetery. It has grown up with weeds and briers, and cows are allowed to graze there; no one takes any interest in it. There are many graves here with markers which have only the initials on them; no dates of any kind to tell anything about them. Some of these graves must have been enclosed with a brick wall, as a brick wall extends above the ground about a foot on top of which is laid the inscription slab.

Acknowledgments: Transcribed by Mrs Eleanor Jacobs, Elizabeth City County, Virginia under the WPA on March 12, 1937. Property was owned by Mr. Howard Sinclair Collier at that time. Transcribed by Barry Miles on 2 May 1997, property is now owned by NASA. The tombstones are very unique, they look like over size chess pieces. The distances given above do not appear to be very accurate.

Sacred
to the memory of
Isabel VAUGHAN
Daughter of
Robert E. & Lavina C. VAUGHAN
who was born
on the 15th day of August 1846
and died on the 18th day of October 1853
Aged 7 Years and 2 Months
(this grave was enclosed in a brick wall)

To our Mother
Mrs Ariadne VAUGHAN
who was born in Mathews
County Sept 26, 1796
and departed this life
Feb 12, 1854
Aged 57 Years 4 Mos & 17 Days
This monument has been erected
by her children as a tribute
of affection to their Mother.
(This is a beautiful white
Marble Slab)

Albert Tallen
son of Geo. B. & Anna JONES
Born Dec 12, 1858
Died April 25, 1859
God blesses in an early death
And takes the infant to himself
(This is a granite stone and lays down flat,
and instead of being bricked up, has granite
blocks up to the stone that lays on top. In
the corner of the stone; J. D. COOPER,
Norfolk)

Sacred to the Memory of
James M. VAUGHAN
Who was born in Gloucester
County Mar.11, 1787
and departed this life at his residence in
Elizabeth City County, October 10, 1850
Aged 63 Years & 4 Months
This monument was erected
to his memory by his widow
and children

Blessed are the peace makers
for they shall be called
the children of God.
Matth. 5th Chap. Vrs. 9.

(this stone is about ten feet high, gray
marble placed upon a base four by six
inches of gray stone about five inches thick.
This stone is in the center of the cemetery)

E. B. CHILES
October 22, 1825
May 8, 1854

Ed. B. CHILES
1861 - 1908

V. Montrose
His wife
1857
E. V. CHILES
1828-1908

(This is a large family size
gray stone monument)

Wm. T. HENDREN
Oct 2, 1827
Aug 16, 1862

Henrietta V. HENDREN
April 5, 1832
Feb 15, 1899

James V. J. HENDREN
infant son of
Wm. T. HENDREN and
Henrietta HENDREN
Born Sep 23, 1851
Died Aug 15, 1852
He dwells where the
fields can never fade
Where night comes nor the
day is dawn
Where the Glory of God is
Sun and the shade
Is the shadowing wing of
the cherubim.

(This stone is four feet long and two feet
wide, marble, on the bricked up grave
which is about one foot out of the ground)

Sacred
to the memory of
James M. VAUGHAN, Jr.
Son of James M. & Ariadne VAUGHAN
Who was born on the
28th of June 1840
Died Sept 30th, 1853
This stone is dedicated to
his memory by his brother and sister.

(This is a flat slab on top of a
foot of brick, where the grave was
brick walled)

In Memory of
Catherine P.
Daughter of
James & Catherine VAUGHAN
and beloved wife of
Caleb MELSON
to whom she was married
Dec 15, 1824
was Born in Mathews Co., Va.
Mar 4, 1798
and Died in Norfolk City
Sept 22, 1872
Sincere in her attachments and faithful in
the discharge of duty her death has
occasioned sorrow to many friends and a
pang of anguish in the heart of her
surviving companion with whom for more
than 47 years, a period marked with
untiring devotion and affection, she has
happily lived.
We resign her spirit unto the
keeping of a merciful Savior.
footstone C.P.M.

Jas. Robert VAUGHAN
Born June 25, 1848
and departed this life
Jan 8, 1852
Aged
3 Yrs 6 Months, 14 days.

The above was the beloved son
of Robt. & Lavina C. VAUGHAN

This Monument is erected
to the memory of
Elizabeth T. SMITH
wife of
Wm. S. SMITH
of CELEYS
in Elizabeth City County.
She was born in Mathews
County, in the year of 1796 and
died at her residence in this
County December 1857.
Asleep in Jesus far from thee
Thy kindred and their graves may be
but thine is still a blessed sleep
From which none ever wakes to weep.
f/m G.J.S. & W.S.S.

(Stones of another VAUGHAN family)

Wm. R. VAUGHAN
May 28, 1827
Sept 28, 1889
f/m Wm.R.V.

Mary A. VAUGHAN
March 2, 1826
March 31, 1893
f/m M.A.V.

Walter R. VAUGHAN
Nov 17, 1860
June 10, 1861

Robt. H. VAUGHAN
Jan 12, 1855
March 28, 1863
f/m R.H.V.

Bernard C. VAUGHAN
Sept 11, 1870
April 12, 1875
f/m B.C.V.

Wm. S. SMITH
1798
June 14, 1863

Geo. J. SMITH
Jan 16, 1836
Jan 16, 1864

George VAUGHAN
April 25, 1867
April 5, 1890
f/m G.V.

(This is a large granite stone and
extends about five feet above
the ground.)

Some think that the CELEYS buried
their dead here, as this was a part of their
land, but there are no stones
to verify that fact,
although there are many unmarked graves.

WATTS CEMETERY
Overton Drive (52) {H - 7}

W. Samuel Watts   1859 - 1947

The area where the grave site is located is shown on the E. A. Semple map of the 1880's. At that time the land was owned by the Watts and the Wray land was adjacent. It seems normal for both families to be buried at this site.

Located between Numbers 4 and 6 on Overton Drive in the Riverdale section of Hampton.

The Watts Cemetery is presently in a trust maintained by Cummings & Hatcher Law Firm. The cemetery is surrounded by a chain link fence and is well maintained. On a visit to the site on 17 May 1997 by Barry Miles, there were only three stones.

Acknowledgment: Cemetery information was submitted by Thelma P. Savage of Hampton and Published in the Virginia Genealogical Society Quarterly Bulletin, Volume VII, No. 1, January 1969 and April 1969. Also read by Steve Keith or Tim Winters (date unknown).

This tribute of pure affection is given by
his wife
To the memory of
Geo. Walker WATTS
who was born May 1811
and died after a short but severe illness
at the Sweet Springs in Virginia
August 13th 1853
Rest in Peace

The inscription on the grave reads
"Thou gainest peace with Him who made
thee bound the shield of faith in Christ full firmly o'er
the breast that when its pulse was still,
the soul might pass unshrinkly, unreluctant,
unafraid into the fulness of the light
of heaven. M. B. Burcher

W. Samuel WATTS
1859 - 1947

Louisa Ham WRAY   Died 1904

WEST CEMETERY
West Queen Street (53) {H - 10}

Margaret West wife of Benj. West, Cemetery founder

Location: One half mile from Hampton High school on West Queen Street in back of the Grist Mill housing development, formerly McDonald's Nursery Field.

Background: Benjamin West (1780-1836) was the founder of the cemetery. A plat which bears the date of December 8, 1880 was prepared by E. A. Semple of the Old Family Graveyard which shows the land of Geo. B. West with the Family Graveyard. The plat shows the graveyard in the center surrounded by the lots of Geo. B. West, John West, Wm. Jones, Robt. Hogg, G. Topping, John Saunders, Jno. Barnes, Wm. Mooring, R. A. Davis, Robt. Davis and Wm. Turnbull. The graveyard was circled with eight foot road. The entrance, with a gate, was between the property of Robt. Davis and Wm. Turnbull. Reference is made to a deed from Book 1, Page 331.

On page 15 of the book, "When the Yankees Came" by George Benjamin West (1839-1917) and edited by Parke Rouse, Jr., the following is stated by Mr. Rouse in his notes on chapter 1: "Parker West had a second farm at New Market in Elizabeth City County, near the intersection of West Queen Street and Briarfield Road in Hampton, referred to in this chapter as the burial place of Sarah West, the author's sister, who died in 1844 of the measles and whooping cough." George Benjamin West was the son of Parker West. The relationship of Parker West to Benjamin West, founder of the West Cemetery, is not known.

Acknowledgment Transcribed by Miss Thelma P. Savage of Hampton, Virginia and published in the Virginia Genealogical Society Quarterly Bulletins, Volume VII, No. 1, January 1969 and No. 2, April 1969, Steve Keith on June 20, 1990, and Barry Miles on June 7, 1997.

SGT. William Hogg Confederate Veteran

Infant
daughter of
W. W. & Janie HOGGE
born July 14, 1899
died Sept 28, 1899
Sleep on sweet babe and
take thy rest.
God called thee home he
thought it best

Louise Howe
daughter of
W. W. & Janie HOGGE
born May 28, 1901
died Oct 23, 1902
Little Darling was here --
flower (cannot read)

William HOGG
1840 - 1897
SGT Co K 32 Va. Inf
CSA
CSA Marker

Frances HOGG
1844 - 1901
CSA Marker

John T. HOGG
April 3, 1871
July 7, 1946
d/s w/ Mamie L.

Mamie L. HOGG
Oct. 2, 1895
April 6, 1907
d/s w/ John T

Robert T. HOGG
1838 - 1915
Capt Co. B. 115 Va.
CSA (Mil)

Margaret Mouring HOGG
March 21, 1852
February 12, 1938

Jesse Hope HOGG Sr.
Feb 13, 1879
May 29, 1963

Emily Lewellyn HOGG
Aug 12, 1888
Oct 26, 1974
Wife of Jesse Hope Hogg Sr.

William T. PATRICK Sr.
January 18, 1876
December 22, 1961
footstone

Sallie West PATRICK
February 18, 1882
March 20, 1961
footstone

PATRICK Monument

McDonough PATRICK
born Sept 30, 1869
died July 12, 1916

Margaret Ann MALLICOTTE
1849 - 1927
Wife of Thomas C. PATRICK

Thomas Jefferson PATRICK
died in Warwick Co. Va. 1883

Charlie A. WEST
Aug 4, 1887
Aug 25, 1892

George B. WEST
Mar 15, 1890
Apr 27, 1892

Mary O. WEST
Aug 2, 1893
June 15, 1894

Caxton A. WEST
Apr 9, 1886
July 20, 1886

Bessie W. WEST
Oct 17, 1879
Sept 14, 1882

Lena S. WEST
Oct 17, 1878
Oct 15, 1879

John W. WEST
June 14, 1855
Nov 28, 1923
d/s w. Molly M.
f/s Father

Molly M. WEST
Feb 21, 1855
Jan 3, 1922
He giveth his beloved sleep
d/s w/ John W.
f/s Mother

The following 4 graves
recently moved.

John Hubert WEST
Aug 4, 1884
Jan 5, 1945
d/s w/ Frances S.
f/s Father

Frances S. WEST
Aug 5, 1888
June 3, 1966
d/s w/ John Hurbert
f/s Mother

Caxton Royster WEST
Aug 23, 1909
Feb 9, 1973
Father
In Loving Memory

Edwin Staples WEST
Feb 28, 1919
Dec 23, 1985
In Loving Memory

WILLIAM BRYAN WEST
VIRGINIA HAYWOOD
Monument

Cemeteries of the City of Hampton, Virginia / formerly Elizabeth City County

William Bryan WEST
June 15, 1896
December 17, 1982
d/s w/ Virginia Haywood

Virginia Haywood WEST
November 22, 1888
December 2, 1967
d/s w/ William Bryan

Lucille E. ASHE
July 5, 1894
Jan 27, 1932
Wife of Z. A. Ashe
At Rest

Louzetta ADAMS
1879 - 1937
d/s w/ William T.

William T. ADAMS
1869 - 1935
d/s w/ Louzetta

next three on same stone

Hattie L. TURNBULL
born June 9, 1877
died March 26, 1900
Just as the morning of her life
was opening into Day
The young and lovely spirit
passed from earth and grief
away

Marker of Spanish American
War 1898 - 1902 Philippine
Island, Puerto Rico, USA,
Cuba
(In front of Hattie Turnbull
Marker)

Walter TURNBULL
born Jan 6, 1898
died April 1, 1898

Eugene Royal TURNBULL
born Sept 3, 1896
died March 31, 1890
(rechecked error on stone)
Sleep on

foot stone broken off

Annie HOWARD
died Aug 24, 1885
aged 4 mos 12 days
At rest

Sacred to the Memory
William TURNBULL
born April 1828
died August 1915

Sacred to the memory
Margaret Ann TURNBULL
born March 27, 1871
died July 4, 1896

Allen A. TURNBULL
Jan 25, 1910
March 29, 1978

Geo. W. TURNBULL
born May 23, 1831
died Nov 2, 1879

Elizabeth Eudora DAVIS
born Feb 26, 1842
died Dec 30, 1921
Loving wife of James A.
DAVIS
She lived for others and died
for her Loving Savior who she
loved
f/s E.E.D. at rest

James Allen DAVIS
born Dec 1, 1851
died March 11, 1925
CSA Marker
f/s J.A.D.

Ellanora DAVIS
born Mar 21, 1867
died Sept 24, 1888
Asleep in Jesus

John W. DAVIS
June 30, 1865
April 16, 1954
d/s w/ Mary Ann

Mary Ann DAVIS
Nov 30, 1871
Oct 23, 1959
d/s w/ John W.

Robert A. DAVIS
1834 - 1907
Co. B. 3 Va. Cav.
CSA Marker

John W. WILLIAMS
1835 - 1917
Co. B. 3 Va. CSA
CSA Marker

J. T. EDWARDS
born Feb 8, 1853
died Oct 31, 1935
d/s w/ Cora D.

Wife
Cora D. EDWARDS
born Sept 25, 1857
died March 9, 1937
d/s w/ J. T.
DAR Marker

Sarah Page EDWARDS
Sept 12, 1885
Jan 16, 1955

In Memory
Margaret
wife of
Benj. WEST
who died January 12, 1830
aged 50 years

Robert DAVIS
born Feb 9, 1810
died Oct 20, 1888
at rest

Benj. WEST
born June 19, 1780
died June 12, 1836
Founder of Cemetery

In memory of
Ann WEST
wife of
Arther WEST
who departed this life
January 24, 1833
aged 34 years

f/s R. R.

f/s P. R.

BUCHANAN Monument

Floyd Linwood BUCHANAN
Sept 23, 1893
Dec 7, 1957
f/s

Estelle Barnes BUCHANAN
Aug 26, 1901
June 26, 1955

BARNES Monument

William M. BARNES
Aug 6, 1873
Dec 19, 1927
f/s

Virdie E. BARNES
Nov 18, 1881
July 18, 1933

Thomas B. BARNES
Feb 17, 1873
May 28, 1952

Sarah Jane BARNES
May 24, 1850
April 13, 1947
wife of John BARNES

Thomas Edward Reid
BARNES
Dec 8, 1952

Baby BARNES
1916

Infant son of
Mr. & Mrs. T. W. BARNES
July 12, 1942

Thomas Wesley BARNES
Feb 24, 1917
Apr 16, 1985

Dorothea Newman BARNES
Oct 4, 1920
May 17, 1994

Emma John BARNES
Sept 2, 1880
Dec 7, 1966

William H. BARNES
Aug 16, 1919
Aug 13, 1970
Father

Willard H. BARNES
1944 - 1978
Temporary Metal Marker

John BARNES
1832 - 1880
Corp Co. K 32 Va Inf
CSA Marker

Mollie E.
Daughter of
W. P. and Mary E. MORROW
born July 25, 1859
died Aug 20, 1860
stone damaged

Elizabeth SAUNDERS
Jan 30, 1792
died Jan 3, 1819

Thomas SAUNDERS Jr
born Sept 12, 1854
died Oct 10, 1854

William H. SAUNDERS
born Feb 15, 1858
died Nov 19, 1863

Sarah A. SAUNDERS
born April 6 1831
died Jan 2, 1857

John Seatney SAUNDERS Sr.
April 20, 1823
August 10, 1899

Oliver T. SAUNDERS
born April 20, 1844
died Aug 4, 1885

Hannah
wife of
Wm. R. TOPPING
was married Apr 28, 1824
died Jan 14, 1854
AET 56
inscription cannot read

Garret TOPPING
June 27, 1828
Jan 8, 1909
d/s w/ Martha
f/s G. T.

Martha TOPPING
March 20, 1827
Oct 7, 1881
d/s w/ Garret
f/s M. T.

Thomas SAUNDERS Sr.
born Jan 10, 1792
died Feb 16, 187x

Martha Susan TOPPING
Aug 9, 1889
Sept 26, 1890

Mother
Hanna Jane
wife of
W. H. MATER
born Aug 17, 1854
died March 23, 1893

Sarah E.
wife of
Charles BUTLER
born Dec 23, 1849
died May 20, 1909
aged 59 yrs 4 mos 27 days

Florence T. BURCHER
June 6, 1895
Sept 19, 1973
"She at rest in Heaven"

Henry Sellie TOPPING
June 2, 1885
Jan 20, 1961
"Earth toiling ended. Heaven begun"

John Wesley TOPPING
born Sept 10, 1851
died Jan 4, 1922
Father
at rest

Lucetta TOPPING
born Sept 20, 1885
died Dec 18, 1916
Mother
at rest

John Raymond TOPPING
May 25, 1909
June 19, 1941

John G. TOPPING
Aug 13, 1874
Nov 14, 1930
d/s w/ Nettie Landrum

Nettie Landrum
wife of
John G. TOPPING
Nov 12, 1874
Nov 6, 1930
d/s w/ John G.

Melvin D. TOPPING
Aug 21, 1887
May 15, 1982

Mattie S. TOPPING
Sept 17, 1892
Nov 18, 1981

Elizabeth Saunders, William Saunders, Jr. and William Saunders
The WPA listed this cemetery as Saunders Cemetery on Lake's Farm.

WILLIAMS PIT LANDFILL
Big Bethel Road (91) {B - 5}

There is only one tombstone at the present site in the City of Hamptons landfill on Big Bethel Road. The Cemetery's name has not been found. Very little information has been found on this cemetery. It is possible this is an African American burial site. From the appearance of the cemetery, it appears that there are other graves without tombstones or markers. The site is now owned by the City of Hampton, Mr. Williams owned the land when this grave was discovered. He would not let the site be disturbed.

Acknowledgment: Barry W. Miles for transcription and picture.

Richard H. HAMILTON
Nov 26, 1897
Oct 21, 1913
In heaven

Richard H. Hamilton

WINDER - GARRETT CEMETERY
Wythe Landing Road, NASA (54) {F - 1}

Above ground vaults of Miss Louisa E. Haller & Mrs. Mary H. Winder

The E. A. Semple map of 1880's shows the area where the cemetery was located on the John Winder Farm and Chesterville Farm.

Located on Wythe Landing Road, NASA property, Lunar Landing Site, inside a chain link fence. There is one tall monument about 8 feet tall and two above ground vaults.

Acknowledgment: Transcribed on December 28, 1994 at NASA, by Ernest Lee Culler with help from John Mouring, Master Planner of NASA.

In Memory of
R. R. GARRETT
Born Jan 1, 1810
Deceased Jan 13, 1855
Age 45 Years
This Spirit Rests in the Arms of the Redeemer

On the right side of the monument are these inscriptions:

Laura GARRETT
Born Sept 15, 1842
Deceased Oct 2, 1846

Under this is another inscription:

Susan A. GARRETT
Born May 29, 1845
Deceased Aug 15, 1846

To the right of this monument are two above the ground vaults, with inscriptions:

In Memory of
Miss Louisa E. HALLER
First Daughter of
Mary H. WINDER
Age 41 Years
Departed this Life
February 19, 1849
Her Spirit is at Rest

In Memory of
Mrs. Mary H. WINDER
Wife of
Dr George H. WINDER
Departed this Life
March 3rd 1845
Age 55 Years
To Know Her was to Love Her

Out side of the fence, to the right are several depressions which may have been other graves, but there are no markers or anything else.

DESTROYED CEMETERIES
CEMETERIES NOT LOCATED
CEMETERIES GRAVES MOVED
CEMETERIES WITHOUT TOMBSTONES

The following Cemeteries may or may not exist. Most of the locations of these Cemeteries have been identified, as best as possible. In most cases it is evident that there were graves at the sites. Several have not been located, but the site of the cemetery is usually directly related to the ownership of the land. In some cases the owner is known, but still the site has not been identified.

FIRST METHODIST CHURCH
Wine Street (56) {J - 10}

The First United Methodist Church, Hampton, Virginia: A Historical Sketch by James P. Welch, Chairman, Records and History Committee. This historical sketch was presented at a meeting of the United Methodist Episcopal Historical Society of the Peninsula District, Virginia Conference, at First United Methodist Church, Hampton, May 15, 1969.

Mr. Welch gives much history of the development of Methodism in Hampton area. If you are interested in the development of Methodism in Hampton it is recommended that this sketch be researched.

The main interest of this researcher is the First Methodist Church Cemetery. A deed on file in the records of Elizabeth City County in the Hampton Court House shows that on February 7, 1811, a Mrs Elizabeth Margaret Mallory, "for and in consideration of one dollar," deeded to a group of trustees on the east side of Wine Street in the old town of Hampton a lot on which to build "a place or house of worship for the use of the members of the Methodist Episcopal Church in the United States of America". Reference: Old Deed Book 33, Records of Elizabeth City County, pp. 317-319. This lot was the first known building site of the present First United Methodist church of Hampton. That a church was in fact erected on the site is evidenced by an entry in the Journal of Bishop Asbury when he made a second visit to Hampton in the year 1812. Reference: Journal of Francis Asbury, Vol. 11, p. 695. War broke out with the British in June of 1812 and it is not known if the Methodist Church suffered similar depredations as St. John's.

It is not known how long the church occupied its building on the east side of Wine Street, but even after a church building was no longer located there, a Methodist graveyard for many decades occupied part of the site. When the area was acquired by the city of Hampton for use as a parking lot, bodies in the last remaining graves were transferred to other locations in the early 1950's.

It was reported by Mr. Luther Alexander that the graves were moved to Oakland Cemetery, on Pembroke Avenue.

There is an extensive history of the church building and rebuilding, the burning of Hampton in the Civil War, and the reconstruction years to 1969, when the historical sketch was written.

From the Daily Press June 16, 1971, Cemetery on Wine Street:

Is there a record of a church and cemetery that at one time was located by the old A&P store in Hampton. If so, whatever became of them and is there a listing of the persons buried in the cemetery and what was done with the tombstones that marked the graves? --Mrs D.C.S.

In the article; The Chairman of the Records and History Committee of First United Methodist Church of Hampton give us a wealth of information on this old church and cemetery. Here's the story--"In the year 1811, a Mrs Elizabeth Margaret Mallory sold a piece of ground at a location on the east side of Wine Street to a group of trustees of the Methodist Episcopal Church for the sum of one dollar on which to build a place or house of worship for use of members of the Methodist Episcopal Church in the United States of America.

"A church was built on the location within a year or so after the lot was purchased Feb. 7, 1811. We know there was a church at this location in March the following year because Bishop Francis Asbury noted in his journal, 'On March 5, Thursday, 1812, I preached in the new brick house, Hampton.'

"Apparently the cemetery of this church had been more or less abandoned by the beginning of the present century, because by World War 1, according to the memories of members of the First United Methodist Church, most of the tombstones had disappeared.
"Efforts were made over a lengthy period to dispose of the property. The church owned the land until November 1941, and in the fall of 1941, the City of Hampton brought a friendly condemnation suit to acquire the land for a parking lot which they did Nov. 5, 1941. The City of Hampton paid the church $4,000 for the property.

"There are extensive back-up papers in the Hampton Court House on this suit saying that as early as 1919, the church's Official Board had undertaken to remove to other repositories 'all remains of persons interred in the lot, ' Frank C. Reese, undertaker, was engaged by the church for this. Some of the remains, to my understanding, were taken to Oakland Cemetery on Pembroke Avenue and some to St. John's Episcopal Cemetery.

"A complete listing of persons buried in this cemetery is not available. When the town of Hampton was burned during the Civil War, many local records were destroyed by fire."

ASBURY CEMETERY
Fox Hill (69) {unknown}

This cemetery was on Mr. Luther L. Alexander's list. He states that this cemetery was not found. In the William and Mary Quarterly Volume 14, Series 1, TOMBSTONEs IN ELIZABETH CITY COUNTY, Miss Thelma Savage of Syms-Eaton Museum, Hampton, Virginia, submitted the tombstone inscriptions, also sent the names of the following family cemeteries and locations which have no stones:
Asbury Cemetery, located in Fox Hill. Exact location of the Asbury Cemetery has not been found.

FREDERICK BARNES CEMETERY
Southall Landing and Main Sail Drive (3) {O - 6}

On 31 December 1996, Barry Miles met with Mr. David Routten. Mr. David Routten is very familiar with the Fox Hill area of Hampton, Virginia. Because of his knowledge in the land records and his job with the City of Hampton, he knew the families that had resided in the area where the cemetery was located. The land was developed in the early 1980's. Due to Mr. Routten and the Barnes family's involvement, the cemetery was not destroyed during the development of this area to residences. Today the site is marked and identified as the Barnes Cemetery.

Mr. David Routten has studied the land records and believes this Cemetery is next to the cemetery of the Watts and Routten families. The Routten family owned the land before the Barnes family, and he believes the Barnes Burial ground is next the Watts/Routten Burial ground. On 6 April 1997, Mr David Routten and Barry Miles visited the site of this cemetery. It is marked with a sign, Barnes Cemetery 1825. Mr. Routten says this is incorrect, because the Barnes family did not own the land until about 1830.
Reference: Elizabeth City County (now City of Hampton,) Old Plat Book 1, page 67. On November 8th, 1830, Thomas Watts to Parker Barnes 100 acres, more or less.

WILLIAM BEAN CEMETERY
Silver Isles Boulevard (67) {O - 6}

Mr. David Routten believes this cemetery was at the intersection of Silver Isle Boulevard and Woodburn Drive. It has not been located; therefore is placed under the destroyed list.

CONFEDERATE CEMETERY
At end of Pembroke Avenue, Buckroe Beach (55) {O - 8}

This Cemetery is now washed away. Its location was at the end of Pembroke Avenue, at Buckroe Beach. From the Syms-Eaton Museum Horn Book Series No. 17, November 1976: "She (Mrs Margaret Dobbins Herbert) opened the first Buckroe Beach boarding house for summer guests in 1883, and shortly after, a bathhouse and a dancing pavilion were constructed. The area was still somewhat isolated, not to say eerie, in the early 1880's. Confederate entrenchments could still be seen, and during northeast storms, waves uncovered coffins in an abandoned Confederate cemetery. Mrs Herbert's boarding house stood near the present-day Atlantic and Herbert Streets and ...." From the above information the exact location cannot be determined, but it substantiates the existence of the cemetery.

HAMILTON CEMETERY
Bloxom's Corner, Fox Hill (16) {M - 6}

The Hamilton Cemetery was located in the area now in the vicinity of Allendale Drive. On 15 May 1997, Mr. George Peake said it was on the property of Mr. Robert Clark Peake. The land came through his wife's family named Watson. Mr. George Peake said the graves were moved when the area was being developed. He said that they did not tell anyone where the graves were moved. A Confederate soldier's grave was found in this area. Mr. Fletcher Johnson told Barry Miles on 14 May 1997, that nothing is left of the cemetery. Also, Mr. Johnson said this property was the Hamilton Farm. On the A. E. Semple map of the 1880's, it shows the families of Watson and Peek owning the land.

HAWKINS CEMETERY
Lighthouse Drive (57) {P - 4}

There is indication of a cemetery behind the house. There are several sunken sites, and this land is the highest in the area, which would be consistent with selection of a site on the highest spot on the owner's property. Mr. David Routten, says the land was one time owned by James Hawkins. Location of the Hawkins property can be seen on the E. A. Semple map done in the late 1880's.

HUBBARD/GUY CEMETERY
Beach Road and Sharon Bass Court (58) {N - 5}

The site of this cemetery was identified to Mr. Routten by E. N. Routten who owned the land and operated a chicken farm there. Today there is a small shed on the site on Brian Road just off Beach Road. There are no stones or signs of a cemetery today.

LEWIS CEMETERY
Pine Lane (62) {N - 5}

The site of this cemetery has not been clearly identified. The property south of Pine Road was owned by William Lewis and his wife, Elizabeth Lewis, prior to January 2, 1802 when it was conveyed to John Guy. James N. Dunton, born March 8, 1850 and died May 15, 1887 was buried at this cemetery and later reburied at Clark Cemetery. Information from Mr. David Routten.

MALLORY CEMETERY
Beach Road and Silver Isle Blvd. (27) {N - 6}
Northwest Intersection

This is where Mr. David Routten believes the Mallory Cemetery was located. The land was once owned by the Mallory Family.

MASSENBURG CEMETERY
Between Union and Lincoln Street (70) {J - 10}

From the Daily Press (21 May 1969) Pre-Civil war Cemetery Posing Problem for Hampton's Redevelopment Authority.
During the development of a lot by the Hampton Redevelopment Housing Authority, a pre-Civil War Cemetery was discovered: A twenty onefoot square plot of land enclosed by a three foot high brick wall in a portion of land considered sold to HRHA in a court insurance sale.

Although no tombstones are visible today, the small plot is reported to have been a family cemetery at one time, according to Hampton Culture Heritage Committee. The land lies approximately 400 feet from King Street on the south side of Union Street, between Union and Lincoln Street. Two Brick columns, dated 1842 mark the entrance facing King Street.

One tombstone was found. It reads:

Judith B. MASSENBURG
1842

An early court record of a deed transfer dated Jan. 2, 1840, reveals that the small plot of land was set aside for a family burial ground when the land was deeded to one Jefferson B. Sinclair, who purchased it from a Dr. Edward Camm and wife, Eliza Jane Massenburg Camm.

In a map of the land by William Ivey, surveyor of Elizabeth City and Warwick County shortly after the Civil War, the cemetery plot is drawn to present day size and recorded set aside as a cemetery by Camm and his wife.

On a later map, in 1880 by E. A. Semple, surveyor for Elizabeth City County, the cemetery is not drawn or even made reference to. This could mean no one was actually buried in the plot, according to an HCHC spokesman.

The mystery of the cemetery is further clouded by the sale of land in the longest court case on record in Hampton, where Jefferson B. and Georgian Sinclair sought, after the Civil War to discharge their debts by selling off property in Elizabeth City County to meet their obligations. The court record with Mr. Jefferson B. Sinclair continued from 1869 to 1906.

The outcome of this situation should be followed by any one researching the Massenburg family.

MOORE CEMETERY
LAFB (Old Moore Farm) (85) {G - 3}

The following information is from the Works Progress Adnimistration of Virginia Historical Inventory. The research was done by Mary Bullifant of Hampton, Virginia, on December 22, 1936. " This grave is in the family lot of what was formerly the old Moore farm, now a Goverment Reservation, C. C. C. Camp."

The grave of Col. John Moore was moved to Oakland Cemetery on Pembroke Avenue. The grave is located in section 4 of the cemetery.

Col. John MOORE
22 Va. Inf. 1861 - 1865
Born 1824
Died 1865

The listing in the inscriptions of Oakand Cemetery is as follows:

John MOORE
Co I 32 Va Inf.
C. S. A.

PEMBROKE FARM GRAVEYARD
Pembroke Avenue and Patterson Street

THIS IS THE SAME CEMETERY AS THE 3RD CHURCH
OF ELIZABETH CITY PARISH

POOLE CEMETERY
Grundland Drive (63) {O - 2)
West of the Nike Site.

The Poole Family owned about 300 acres in 1793. In the deed, land was set aside for a cemetery. The deed reads 50 acres, which surely must be a mistake; maybe 0.5 acres. The area thought to be the cemetery is directly to the west of the Nike Site, just outside of a chain link fence. This area was investigated, by David Routten and Barry Miles, 6 April 1997, but no indication of a cemetery could be found. This area is covered with very heavy undergrowth and the grave sites could not seen. Reference: Old Deed Book 34, page 179, Robert Pool to James Latimer Sept 10, 1794.

POOR HOUSE FARM CEMETERY
Woodland Road and Woodside Drive (64) {L -7}

Woodland Road was originally known as Poor House Road. We spoke to one of the local residents on Woodside Drive. He stated that his aunt and uncle owned the land that encompassed the site for the Poor House Cemetery. He remembered as a young boy seeing the sunken graves. Today there are houses built on the site. It is not known if the houses are built directly on the site or next to the cemetery site. The E. A. Semple map of the late 1880's shows the Poor House being located on what is now Woodside Drive.

POST CEMETERY, FORT MONROE
Fort Monroe, Virginia (88) {N -11}

The following information is from the Works Progress Administration of Virginia Historical Inventory. The information was compiled by Mrs Eleanor S. Jacobs on March 3, 1937.

Location: Follow Route #60 out of Phoebus to Fort Monroe, continue on Ingallis Road; this you enter and follow until you come to Fenwick Road which is about 1/4 mile. Turn west on Fenwick Road and the site is at the end of this road.

Historical Significance: The first cemetery at Fort Monroe started about 1819 and was known as the "Pine Forest", a narrow strip of land next to the beach northwest of the fort and joined the Buckroe Farm. This proved to be an objectionable site because here was the Post Cemetery containing the bodies of all the soldiers and others who had died at Fort Monroe during more than half a century, which has long since been abandoned. The Post Cemetery remained at the northwest of the ridge of sand hills north of the fort, above the Mortai Batteries. It had been used to inter those who died at the Hygeia Hospital. In the years immediately following the war, many of the bodies were removed and the cemetery abandoned, despite the fact that it had an estimated capacity of ten to fifteen thousand graves. This cemetery continued until early in 1860, when it was deemed necessary to have this strip of land to build batteries upon as protection for the fort. These bodies were moved to the Hampton National Cemetery just being started by the United States Government. There are no records to show just when this movement was begun. The Anti-Air-Craft Guns now stand there.

It is said that some of our foremost military men were buried here and no one knows and probably never will know who these were.

References: Major Robert Arthurs's History of Fort Monroe, pages 88, 131 and 139.
    Coast Artillery School Print Shop.
    Coast Artillery School Library.

On August 13, 1937 the following research for the Works Progress Administration of Virginia Historical Inventory was done by Ashby A. Welch of Phoebus.

Location was same as report above.

Historical Significance: Here the simple resting ground, sometimes spoken of as the "Pine Forest Cemetery" were interred all of the remains of soldiers, officers and their immediate relatives. There were also bodies of persons who had died at the old Hygeia Hospital.

When the War Between the States began it was realized that the cemetery land was needed so that batteries could be built for the protection of the fort. Over ten thousand bodies were disinterred and moved over to the Hampton National Cemetery.

It is said that some of our greatest military men were buried there.

My Grandmother, the wife of Captain William Adams, was buried there, but my grandfather had her body removed to St. Johns Cemetery in Hampton, Virginia.

Sources are same as above.

The Map of Elizabeth City Co. Va. from actual surveys by E. A. Sample, Wm. Ivy and C. Hubbard and platted by E. A. Sample, Civil Engineer and County Surveyor, copyright Dec 22, 1892, shows the U. S. Cemetery location.

JOSEPH ROUTTEN CEMETERY
Beach Road and Willow Road (24) N - 4}

This site has only a few graves, one being Mr. Joseph C. ROUTTEN and several babies, according to Mr. David Routten. The graves are next to Beach Road.

SAUNDERS CEMETERY
Saunders Road
Presently West Queen Street

This is now the West Cemetery.

The following information is from the Works Progress Administration of Virginia Historical Inventory. Research was done by Mary Bullifant, Hampton, Virginia, on September 7, 1937.

Only two grave inscriptions were recorded. The Saunders are the earliest settlers of Elizabeth City County.

Location: John Lake Farm, 1 1/2 miles west of Hampton, Virginia on Sawyers Swamp Road, (Big Bethel Road) 500 Yards north of the road. The John Lake Farm can be seen on the Semple Map of Elizabeth City County

The Saunders Cemetery is the same as the West Cemetery at Salter Creek off North Queen Street. The two graves listed by Mary Bullifant are in the West Cemetery.

Thomas SAUNDERS
Born January 1790
Died Feburary 16, 1840

Elizabeth B. SAUNDERS
Born January 30, 1792
Died January 5, 1845

MARTHA SAVAGE BURIAL GROUND
Inlandview Drive (78) {G - 10}

Mr. Kenneth Quinn, saw this grave prior to development of this area. After construction he went back and asked what happened to this grave. The response he received was, "What grave. We did not see any grave." The grave was mother of Teagle Savage:

Martha SAVAGE
born ------
died circa 1852

Cemeteries of the City of Hampton, Virginia / formerly Elizabeth City County

JAMES SMITH CEMETERY
Between Wind Mill Point and Dandy Point Road (10) {N - 2}

Mr. Douglas Smith, son of James Smith, indicated that his mother and father were buried at the site. His mother's maiden name was Hopkins. Location of the Smith property can be seen on the E. A. Semple map of Elizabeth City County done in the late 1880's. Information from David Routten.

JOHN SMITH CEMETERY
Betweeen Wind Mill Point and Dandy Point Road (22) {N - 3}

These sites are believed to be in the wooded land between the roads listed above. This area has been investigated by Mr. David Routten, but he has not found any grave sites. Mr. Routten said the following persons are buried at this site. Ref. Deed Book 2 at page 281, date March 24, xxxx
Elizabeth City County, now City of Hampton. The location of the Smith property can be seen on the E. A. Semple map of Elizabeth City County done in the late 1880's.

Margaret Elizabeth Irongonger SMITH
born Sept 8, 1829 York Co. Va.
died Dec 30, 1889 Elizabeth City Co. Va.

John H. SMITH
born _____
died _____

TENTS LODGE CEMETERY (ISRAELITE)
Easterly Avenue (79) {J - 8}
Behind Langley Square Shopping Center

From Mr. Luther L. Alexander's records of October 2, 1987, "No one has been buried in this cemetery and the Lodge is in the process of having the land reclassified to open land.

JAMES TOPPING CEMETERY
Roger Avenue and Buckroe Court (59) {N - 7}

Mr. David Routten says this cemetery has been destroyed.

JOHN P. L. TOPPING CEMETERY
Wallace Road (60) {N - 4}

This site is just behind Mr. David Routten's home. It is behind the last house on the west side of Wallace Road at it northerly terminus. There is no evidence of the cemetery today. Mr. David Routten remembers the tombstone sin the middle of a field when he was young. The following information on the tombstones was passed to Mr. Routten by Mrs Evelyn Wallace Becker, who purchased the land and built a house on the property. Mrs Evelyn Wallace Becker transcribed the information from the tombstones.

Alice J. TOPPING
daughter of P. L. TOPPING &
Sarah H. TOPPING
died Sept 10, 1853
age 4 months and 7 days

In Memory of
John TOPPING
son of J. P. L. & S. H. TOPPING
died Sept 30, 1843
age 3 months and 28 days

Ann TOPPING
wife of John P. TOPPING
died July 18, 1849
age 60 yrs.

In Sacred Memory of
Margaret TOPPING
daughter of John P. L &
Sarah H. TOPPING
died Dec 18, 1840
age 4 yrs.

(Note: This John P. TOPPING
must have been the father of
John P. L. TOPPING,
herein mentioned,
from David Routten)

In Memory
Thaddeus TOPPING
son of John P. L. TOPPING and Sarah H. TOPPING
died March 15, 1853
age 14 yrs, 2 months, 18 days
"How happy every child of grace,
who knows his sins forgiven,
This earth he cries is not my place,
I seek my place in Heaven"

ROBERT TOPPING CEMETERY
Hall Road and Foxgate Way (65) {O - 5}

This site is behind a large field on the east side of Hall Road in a group of pine trees. It is not accessible. Land is closed by owner. There are graves but no tombstones with markings. Information from Mr. David Routten.

UNKNOWN BURYING GROUNDS
Bowing Avenue (76) {J - 6}

Daily Press 5 March 1970.
"Three young boys playing discovered a hole in the ground. They thought they had found a cave and started digging and found a Cast Iron Casket. The casket was the shape of a human. "Solidly covered with rust, the artifact is about six feet long, 12 inches deep and about 20 inches wide at the shoulders, narrowing at the neck and head and the lower torso. It was surrounded by brickwork and buried about two feet below the surface.

Twenty rusted bolts hold the frame together, around the sides from head to feet, forming a top and bottom. Five more bolts hold a face plate in position, with hinge at the top so the face cover can be opened. Handles at the feet, waste and head provide lifting points for six pallbearers. There is a flat portion in the lower chest area, possibly a name plate at one time. It weighed about 100 pounds.

Other depressions in the ground in the vicinity of the coffin discovery indicate the possible presence of others."

Different opinions were offered, but it was never determined who was inside the casket. It was from a family with means, because of such a ornate casket. The casket was reburied by the City of Hampton and the location was not given.

WALLACE - TENNIS CEMETERY

This is the same cemetery as the Hansford Cemetery. See Hansford Cemetery.

C. WRAY CEMETERY
Location not found

This cemetery was on Mr. Luther L. Alexander's list of Cemeteries and Grave Sites in the City of Hampton. We have not been able to find it's location. This researcher believes that the Wray and Watt Cemeteries are one and the same. The Watts' and Wray had adjoining land, (see the Semple map of the 1880's) The families intermarried and there is a Wray buried in the Watt Cemetery.

WOOD CEMETERY
Wood Lane (68) {B - 6}

This grave site is reported by Mr. Mack McDonald, the current resident in the old Wood homestead. Graves are located in a group of trees, adjacent to an old wooden shed, about 25 yards from the McDonald house. There are no existing markers, and no signs of the graveyard except a slightly elevated area of the ground.

Acknowledgment: W. S Keith for compiling information. Mrs C. W. Purcell, Elwood Wood, Kenneth Wood and John William Jones for providing information. Site visited by Barry Miles on 4 January 1997, and Mr. Mack McDonald informed him that he had learned that there was a slave cemetery in the woods at the end of Wood Lane to the right (same side of road as the McDonald house and gravesite). These woods were part of the original Wood Plantation which was several thousand acres.

The following are reported buried in the Wood Cemetery.

William WOOD

Elizabeth Jones WOOD

Jessie PARKER

Elizabeth JONES

John William JONES

Baby COPELAND

From the WOOD family Bible and the Hampton Health Dept.

William WOOD
Born 29 Dec 1812
Died 2 Nov 1902

Elizabeth Susan Jones WOOD
Wife o William WOOD
Born 1825
Died 24 May 1908

Elizabeth Wood JONES
Born 2 June 1905
Died 25 Oct 1905

Jessie F. PARKER
Born 25 Feb 1872
Died about the age of 12 Years.

CEMETERIES NOT IN THIS BOOK

The following Cemeteries are not included in this book. After each entry there is an explanation why they are not included.

THE FOURTH CHURCH OF ELIZABETH CITY PARISH
ST. JOHN'S CHURCH, HAMPTON
1728 - PRESENT
West Queen Way (39) {J - 10}

The fourth church of Elizabeth City Parish was completed in 1728. The Parish is the oldest Parish in continuous service in America. The church building has changed considerably because of the tragedies of war. It was twice under the control of the British, in the Revolutionary War and in the War of 1812. The church was severely damaged in the War of 1812. It was destroyed again in 1861 during the Civil War. The citizens of Hampton set fire to the town to keep it from falling into the hands of the Federal Forces. It was restored again to its present day structure.

The tombstone inscriptions of the St. John's churchyard were published by the Hugh S. Watson, Jr., Genealogical Society of Tidewater Virginia (Tidewater Genealogical Society) in 1975. The original transcriptions were by the Reverend John B. Bentley. The book was prepared for publication and indexed by William L. Litsey, a member of the society, now deceased. The oldest interment in the churchyard is the eighteenth century site of Captain Willis Wilson who died in 1701.

Cemetery Inscriptions
St. John's Church
Hampton, Virginia

A copy of this book is in the Hampton Public Library, call number; V975.541 H189g.

CLARK CEMETERY
Beach Road, Fox Hill (8) {N -5}

The Clark Cemetery was complied and published by the Fox Hill Woman's Club. A copy is in the Hampton Library, call number; V975.541, C547c.

In the 1850's the Clark family selected the site for a graveyard. The site was the highest point in the 60 acres of John H. Clark property. John H. Clark purchased from Michael P. Guy by deed dated March 15, 1855.

EBENEZER BAPTIST CHURCH CEMETERY
171 Semple Farm Road (81) {D - 3}

The Board of directors for the Ebenezer Baptist Church denied the request for the Tidewater Genealogical Society to transcribe the tombstones in their church cemetery.

HAMPTON MEMORIAL GARDENS
HAMPTON VETERAN MEMORIAL GARDENS
Butler Farm Road and Airborn Drive (17) (20) {E - 6}

These Cemeteries have over nine thousand grave sites. If the owners will allow the transcription of the grave markers, this will be the subject of a future publication. The Hampton Memorial Gardens was know as Carver Memorial.

HAMPTON NATIONAL CEMETERY
County Street (18) {L - 11}

The Hampton National Cemetery has over ninteen thousand interments. This Cemetery was officially established in 1866, though burials from the Hampton Military Hospital were made dating from 1862. By November 1868, there were 5122, graves of which 475 were unknown. Of this number only 62 were non-military. By this date remains had been brought to this cemetery from Ft. Monroe, Big Bethel in Elizabeth City Co. (the first significant battle sites of the Civil War in Peninsula, Virginia), Jamestown, Craney Island, Deep Creek, Norfolk, Portsmouth, Blackwater in Norfolk Co., Smithfield, Suffolk and Cherry Stone in Northampton Co. There are 272 Confederate graves, 26 German and 5 Italian WWII POW's graves and remains of 29 German servicemen recovered when U-85 went down off the coast of Virginia in 1942.

Inquires may be made of the Chief, National Cemetery Supervising Office
U.S. Army
2800 South 20th St.
Philadelphia, Pa. 19101

The Tidewater Genealogical Society will request the Chief, National Cemetery Supervising Office, to see if they will provide a copy of the listings if available. If not available they will request permission to record the inscriptions. This is a very large future project, and will require the dedication of several individuals.

MOUNT OLIVE BAPTIST CHURCH CEMETERY
Big Bethel Road and Joynes Road (86) {D - 11}

The Pastor of Mt. Olive Baptist Church denied the request of the Tidewater Genealogical Society to transcribe the tombstones in the church cemetery, which is located just a couple lots from the church on Joynes Road.

OAKLAND CEMETERY
1009 E. Pembroke Avenue (31) {L - 9}

The Oakland Cemetery was published by the Oakland Cemetery Association in 1994 under the title "Identified Grave sites of Oakland Cemetery, Hampton, Virginia. The call number at the Hampton Public Library: V 975. 5412 Id2g. Oakland cemetery should not be overlooked by any one doing genealogical or historical work in Hampton. Many graves from other cemeteries were relocated here. Graves have been moved from Lattimer Cemetery, "Airville Farm", Hollier Family Cemeteries on Langley Field, 1st Methodist Church Cemetery on Wine Street, and possibly others.

PARKLAWN MEMORIAL PARK
North Armistead Ave. and Downy Farm Road (32) {F - 7}

This is a very large managed cemetery which could be a complete book. It is not the intention of this endeavor to incorporate large managed cemeteries. By checking with the cemetery offices the desired data can usually be obtained.

PENINSULA CHAPEL MAUSOLEUM
Butler Farm and Airborne Drive (33) {E - 6}

Peninsula Chapel Mausoleum is also a managed cemetery and information can be obtained from the cemetery office.

PLEASANT SHADE
Shell Road (33) {E - 13}

Pleasant Shade is also a very large managed cemetery with about 12,000 interments. The transcriptions must be the subject of a future book. Pleasant Shade Cemetery was merged with Holly Grove Cemetery.

VETERANS ADMINISTRATION
Harris Avenue (90) {K - 11}

Veterans Administration Cemetery is at the entrance of the Hampton, Virginia, Veterans Administration Medical Center. There are only 20 to 25 graves in this small cemetery. It is surrounded by a nice hedge and is well maintained by the U. S. Government. It is under the control of National Cemetery Management.

The plaque states that the interments are veterans of the Spanish American War. There is one stone that commemorates a veteran of the American Mexican War.

This cemetery is not recorded in this book because it is under the control of the U. S. Government and the National Cemetery Administration, and is documented at their office in Hampton, Virginia.

SLAVE CEMETERIES

This section has caused much concern because most of the information cannot be verified in records. The information has mainly come through verbal recollections of individuals. Usually someone remembers that some older person told them that there was a slave cemetery at some location. With this in mind and that authenticity may never be verified, we will list ones that have been brought to our attention. Please use this information with the greatest of care.
Tidewater Genealogical Society

WOOD PLANTATION

In a visit to the Wood Cemetery on Wood Road, we spoke to Mr. MacDonald. He informed us that the Wood Plantation contained several thousand acres, and that he had heard there was a Slave Cemetery at the end of Wood Road to the right in the woods. Barry Miles, January 1997.

DOWNEY FARM

In reference to the Nelson Ballard Grave, Mr. Kenneth Quinn, remembered Mr. Soure hearing an elderly black man, Mr. John Walters, saying he had seen people buried at the same site where Nelson Ballard is buried. Mr Walters grew up on the Downey Farm. Mr. Quinn said that Mr. Sourse stated that these people were buried in their underwear, because a suit of clothes was so expensive, and they could not afford them.

SLAVE CEMETERY
Woodland Road and Hampton Golf Course

The following correspondence was made on 15 June 1984.

To Mr Steve Kinney, Asst. Director, Planning Dept., from Charles E. Smith, Cultural Programs Supervisor, Recreation Dept. Subject (Soil sample/bone discovery).
"After having spoken with Mr. Barnhill of Law Engineering, who assured me that the bones are human, we have continued our research here which indicates the following: 1) There are strong indications of at least one burial site for black people, **not necessarily slaves,** is in this area. 2) That the burial site or sites is in close proximity of a known cemetery with marked graves. 3) That the bodies were arranged without pattern, placed in shallow depressions.

Because of this information I would consider this an actual burial ground with the likelihood of discovering more and more bones through any further investigation. I would recommend that we leave the area undisturbed."

Thank you for consulting us in this matter.

Reply:
Steve Kinney Called June 14, 1894 requesting validity to information that the site of a proposed water tower at Woodland Rd. and the gulf course (18th hole), next to a marked & maintained cemetery, is a slave burial pit.

On Old Black man, admitting to the age of "90's", spoke to workmen and said as a young boy his father would take him to the area and say that's where slaves were put when they died. They weren't buried, just placed in shallow depressions and covered over."

Index

———
- Baby 149
- Chamberlin's Man 4
- Cyrus H. 60
- Elizabeth 3
- Elvira 60
- Fuphenia 200
- Gilbert 3
- Gladys Helene 125
- Gove ? 206
- H. S. 197
- Hillary 34
- Jac ? 206
- James 3
- John 3
- June 13
- Marcan 54
- Nicholas 3
- Peeter 4
- Phil 48
- Sandra Atalie 125
- Thomas 3
- Warren 59
- William 56, 183

AARON
- Harry J. 162
- Lillian B. 162
- Pearl Franklin 168
- Robert Lee 168

AAROW
- Minnie Fisch 105

ABEL
- Joseph Alex 124
- Morris E. 117
- Rebecca 124
- Rosa R. 117

ABELKOP
- Benjamin 105
- Sarah 105

ABIDELL
- Sallie L. J. 134

ABRAHAM
- Alec 98
- Etta Toby 113
- Meyer 124
- Morris 104
- Rose I. 124
- Sophie Brady 104

ABRAMS
- Thelma 101

ACKERMAN
- Fannie 106
- John 106

ACOIEHUT
- Henry Kendall 78

ADAMS
- Amanda N. 83
- James M. 83
- Louzetta 225
- Matilda 48
- William T. 225

ADDISON
- Rachel 50

ADELSON
- Eva Levine 168
- Phillip 168

AERY
- Catharine E. 74

- Clara T. 79
- William A. 79

AIKEN
- Esther B. 75
- Esther Burl 24

AKERMAN
- Alfred 94

ALBOUY
- Ceorcia H. 26

ALEXANDER
- ——— 150
- Charlotte T. 47
- W. C. 70

ALLEN
- A. P. 68
- Adline 211
- Carnelious 21
- George P. 192
- James 211
- Martha Knox 195
- Sarah Tyson 211

ALLINSON
- Andrew 3

ALSTON
- Marion L. 194

ALTON
- James 84

ANDERSON
- Arnold 200
- Ernest Sr. 13
- G. A 69
- Geo. D. 59
- Gertrude 150
- Ira 55
- James N. 55
- Jeanette H. 85
- Lena 13
- Lillian 55
- Matilda E. 59
- Moses 202
- R. M. 55
- R. M. 55
- Reaver 150
- Robert 215
- Robert L. 85
- Thomas K. 38

ANDREW
- Anthony 3

ANDREWS
- Thos. H. 68
- W. G. 69

ANKER
- Goldye 115
- Irving 127
- Moses 127
- Samuel 115

ANTHONY
- Beatrice N. Hill 198
- Raymond B. 198

ANTHONY-JONES
- M. Elizabeth 191

ARBS
- Ellen 192

ARCH
- Benjamin 113
- Eva 113
- Kenneth 113

ARCHIE
- Effie Jo 196

ARENOV
- Abe 108

ARMESTRONGE
- Jocky 3

ARMFIELD
- Sarah E. 52

ARMISTEAD
- Alexina 31
- Daniel 31
- Elizabeth M. 182-184
- Louisa M. 17
- Moss 182, 183
- Samuel 17
- Westwood S. 17

ARMSTEAD
- Elizabeth 57
- Henry 213
- Hester 204
- Lucy 200
- Marus 211
- Sadora 57

ARMSTRONG
- Daniel W. 77
- Louise G. 83
- Samuel Chapman 77

ARNER
- David M. 159
- Fannie Brown 159
- Selma Elsie 159

ARONOFF
- Bertha Newman 115
- Isidore 115

ARONOW
- Fannie 105
- Issac 105
- Louis B. 159

AROTZKY
- Sarah 104

ARROLL
- Herman 118
- Raymond J. 120
- Sarah Farnk 118

ASENSTEATER
- A. J. 102

ASH
- Juanita C. 194
- Lenard 28
- Marion V. 34
- Otis 31, 32

ASHE
- Lucille E. 225
- Z. A. 225

ASKEW
- Claude 203
- David D. 191
- Ella 195
- Emmeline 206
- Lillie 147
- Norris 205
- Thomas H. 206

ASTOR
- Julius 111
- Rae 111

ATKINS
- Bertha E. 23
- Celestyne 29
- Ida Binga 29

Index

Lloyd 193
Nellie R. 198
Olivet C. 23
William E. 51
AURBACH
Abraham 93
Norman 97
AUSTAIN
Moses 95
AUSTIN
Annie S. 53
Clare Lipman 165
Harry Jac 165
Haywood L. 53
Junius P. 29
AUSTRAIN
Abraham 93
Belle 95
AVERA
Charles 173
Charles 173
Hannh 173
Ursula Copland 173
BACKUS
Winfield 25
BAILEY
Alice V. 51
Arthur R. 53
Elnora 28
Henry 33
Hilda L. 199
J. 151
James 49
Josephine 33
Kate J. 49
Robert 26
Sarah 53
Sarah 146
BAILY
Clara 151
BAKER
Bennie 25
David 97
Elmer A. 193
John 3
Mary E. 201
Sarah 98
Viola Collings 38
Walter B. 192
Willie 25
BALL'S
Robert 3
BALLARD
Isaiah 29
Nelson 19
Thomas 29
BALSER
Ben B. 118
Joe 118
Louis 105
Marvin Tubin 93
Max 100
Miriam 93
Miriam D. 118
Mollie 100
Nathan 100
Neil Morton 93
BANDY

Margaret 195
Martha C. 13
Roland 195
BANE
Susie 34
BANKS
Andrew 52
Anna 212
Annie 48
Augustus 50
Clarissa D. 85
Curtis 48
Curtis 150
Dixie C. 76
Earnest 150
Elizabeth 57
Fannie L. 53
Frank D. 76
Frank Dean 75
Frank Gibson 76
George 78
James T. 212
Jennie 26
Jennie Polan 108
Katrina L. 85
Lewis E. 85
Louisa 77
Mary C. 25, 26
Orpheus Marshall 76
Phillip 24
Rosa 57
Sol Harry 108
Susie T. 75
Sylvester W. 85
Wm. 57
BANRIDGE
Frances Johnson 189
BAPTIS
J. B. 205
Mary E. 205
BARBER
Ann 3
George R. 29
BARGER
Isidore 100
Sarah 100
BARKERS
Evelyn 27
Junius 27
BARKS
Charles 26
BARLETT
Alexander 27
BARMER
Mary M. 150
BARNES
Annie E. 134
Baby 226
Col N. G. 21
Davis 212
Dorothea Newman . . . 226
Emma John 226
Harriett 212
Hattie 212
Infant son 226
John 21
John 226
Julia 21

R. 69
Roscoe T. 21
Rufus 212
Sarah Jane 226
Thomas B. 226
Thomas Edward Reid . 226
Thomas Wesley 226
Virdie E. 226
Virginia B. 21
Willard H. 226
William H. 226
William M. 226
BARNWELL
William 32
BARON
Abraham Louis 124
Edgar 110
BARR
David 197
Ruth J. 197
BARRER
David N. 196
BARRETT
Harris 55
Janie Porter 55
May Porter 55
BARROW
Blanche 13
Daniel 203
Dennis C. 203
Elizabeth 203
Lucy C. 203
Walter 203
BARTLETT
Allen 28
Clearington Augustus . . 78
Harriet B. 78
BASS
Milton (Johnny) 121
Sarah C. 121
BASSETT
Andrew W. 48
C. S. 48
Ida Elaine 58
Infant sons 48
Pearl B. 48
BASSETTE
A. W. E. 3rd MD 32
A. W. E. Jr 32
A. W. E. Sr 32
Burl 32
Burl 60
C. S. Dr. 33
Edward E. DDS 32
Fanny 60
Ida E. 32
Pearl B. 33
Phoebe Estella 32
Undine Davis 32
BATES
F. 67
BATTEN
David F. 34
George M. 25
Junius T. 52
Lewis 3rd 26
Olara 25
Sarah 146

Index

BATTERSON
- Lena F. 169
- Sidney A. 169
- Zella M. 169

BATTON
- Noris B. 29

BAYKEN
- B. B. 68

BAYLOR
- Hilliard 202

BEACH
- Charles 194
- Mabel 196

BEAMON
- Cora Miller 81
- James R. 38
- Rosa 37
- Sherman 37

BEAN
- W. J. 69

BEAR-BIRD
- Benjamin 77

BEASLEY
- H. D. 204
- Rosy 204

BECKER
- Benjamin 169
- Jack A. 116
- Jennie 106
- Louis 106
- Maxine Daniels 169
- Milton S. 120
- Rossye Nachman 102
- Sidney 112

BECKET
- India 212

BECKHAM
- B. 67

BELL
- James E. Jr 31
- William David 122

BENDIGE
- Edward 3

BENEN
- Elisa Faye 171

BENJAMIN
- John 52
- Rosetta 52

BENNETT
- Margaret 28

BENTHAL
- Harver H. 193

BENTHALL
- Gwendolyn 192

BERGER
- Lena 94
- Pearl Neustein 127

BERK
- Albert 161

BERLIN
- Daniel 166
- Fannie M. 166

BERMAN
- Celia 94
- Jack 119
- Joseph J. 97
- Minnie 103
- Phillip 169

- Sol 103
- Yetta S. 169

BERRY
- Llewellyn M. 83
- Nancy 39

BESKIN
- Esther Felstein 103
- Joseph 99
- Lena Fisch 99
- Theodore H. 103

BEST
- James Moses 33

BETTS
- Charles Wilson 75
- Laura 73

BEWBRICKE
- John 3

BILLUPS
- Annie 62
- Braxton 142
- Caroline 62
- Laura 142
- Laura V. 83
- Lewis 62
- Maria 47

BINDER
- Celia H. 119
- Charles 119
- Deborah Gellman 110
- Edwin Jacob 110
- Hannah A. 116
- Israel 104
- Jake 104
- Katie D. 99
- Meyer J. 99
- Monte L. 160
- Robert D. 109
- Rose K. 109
- Rose M. 119
- William 112
- William 112

BIRGE
- Grorge A. 39
- Sadie E. 39

BLACK
- Abraham 116
- Alex S. 27
- Betty P. 118
- Henry S. 193
- Joseph G. 116
- Lucy Ida 77
- Rebecca L. 116

BLACKLE
- Sarita E. 192

BLACKLEY
- Clementine H. 14
- Mr. 196
- Theodore 203
- Warren L. 201

BLACKLY
- Sarah A. 62

BLACKMAN
- Benjamin 103
- Dora 103
- Leon M. 113
- Mauachia 98
- Sarah 113

BLAKE

- Amada B. 198

BLAND
- Addie 198
- Emily 191
- Harry 149
- Walter J. 198

BLANKENSHIP
- S. 69

BLANTON
- Harold Curtis 74

BLECHMAN
- Benjamin 163
- E. David 163
- Eva 96
- Frank O. 163
- Julius 96

BLIZZARD
- Myrtle V. 26

BLOCH
- Gertrude 161

BLOCK
- Ethel Fox 114
- Irving 114
- Maurice L. 114

BLODGETT
- Margaret Loring 73

BLOOM
- Joseph 109
- Leba 109

BLOXOM
- G. 67
- John 42
- Susan 42

BLUE
- Bruce 23
- Helen R. 23
- Lucy A. 59

BLUE-PIPE
- John 78

BOAZ
- Hattie H. W. 151

BOLLING
- Edward A. 79
- Georgia A. 79
- Mary Florence 28
- Rosco Howard 75
- Venus Ann 50

BOLTON
- Dowling M. 86
- Lorraine W. 86

BOOKBINDER
- Fae M. 161
- Hyman J. 119
- Minnie M. 119
- Robert Allen 161

BOOKER
- Betty 184
- Francis 25
- George 184
- George E. 58
- Georgia B. 15
- John 184
- Lillie E. 58
- Marian S. 58
- Mary 212
- Richard 184
- Samuel Eugene 58

BOONE

Index

    Clarence C. 31
    Effie L. 196
    Evelyn 14
    Janie M. 31
    Jessie M. 194
    Katie 25
    Percy C. 192
    Percy D. 199
    Polly 14
    Raleigh 13
    Rosa M. 14
    Walter T. 196
BOOSE
    Lucy 53
BOOTH
    Jennie Dee 79
    Kate Lewis 32
BOTTS
    John Minor 80
BOWDEN
    John 51
    Lillie 49
    Sarah 59
BOWINS
    Ada M. 203
BOWMAN
    A. L. 142
    Mayme V. 81
    Peter E. 81
BOXER
    John 3
BOYD
    Collins 14
BOYKIN
    Alice V. 14
    Daisy B. 13
    Henry J. 202
    Infant 151
    Lavinia 194
    Margaret 13
    Naomi W. 37
    O. P. 151
    Ogden P. 37
    Victor L. 14
BOYKINS
    Arthur 14
BOYLE
    Charles 67
BRADSBERY
    Joseph L. 29
BRAKTON
    Pricilla 33
BRASLOW
    Myrtle Blanche Shoaf . 159
BRASWELL
    Riley 197
BRATCHER
    Willis 146
BRAVERMAN
    Isaac 96
    Sarah M. 96
BRAVNSTEIN
    Rose 100
BRAXTON
    Mattie M. 151
    Myrtle B. 151
    William 215
BREGMAN

    Dorothy Kruger 159
    Irwin 159
BRENER
    Rose 98
BRENNER
    Benjamin Fred 121
    Dorothy Kruzer 115
    Hyman 115
    Jacob 107
    Milton David 122
    Rose 107
BREWERTON
    H. W. 67
BRIDGES
    Henry 3
BRIGGS
    Caroline 145
BRIGHT
    Elizabeth 47
    George E. 32
    Hannah 47
    Sarah 24
BRINKLEY
    Rosa 25
BRINN
    Harold 202
BRISCO
    Grace 197
BRISTOE
    N. P. 70
BRITT
    Alexander 70
BROADFIELD
    Chas. 37
    Chas. 37
    Geo R. 37
    Margaret 37
    Richard E. 31
BROCKWOOD
    Geo. 68
BRODBANKE
    Thomas 3
BROKENBURR
    Benjamin F. 201
BROMBERG
    Celia 100
    Rebecca 118
    Samuel 118
BROOKER
    Arthur 33
    Frank 14
BROOKS
    Cutberd 3
    Essiex 37
    Mary L. 40
    Stewart 26
BROUT
    Albert T. 165
    Sara F. 165
BROWN
    A. L. 36
    Alice 211
    Ardnella W. 203
    Bessie Reyner 110
    Bishop 75
    Chaney 56
    Charles S. 24
    Edith 75

    Emma 36
    George A. 53
    Georgiana 148
    Ida Ester 106
    J. 69
    Jeff 203
    John 49
    John 49
    John H. 149
    John W. 86
    Joseph P. 28
    Joseph W. 150
    Josephine D. 191
    Laura 145
    Lenora 149
    Leon D. 110
    Lois Sheppard 82
    Louise Bassette 32
    Minnie C. 204
    Monroe Reyner 110
    Montrose T. 86
    Nathan 58
    Noralicia Montrose 14
    Renaud 74
    Russell 146
    Sarah 58
    Solomon 99
    Thomas N. 53
    Virginia 33
    Walter R. 82
    William 168
BROWNE
    Thomas 3
    Weston 4
BRYAN
    Carter 90
BRYANT
    Adeline V. 23
    Catharine 55
    Fanny 48
    James E. 23
    Mary L. 55
    Simon 48, 55
BUCHANAN
    Estelle Barnes 226
    Floyd Linwood 226
BUCK
    Edward 77
    Son 75
BULLOCK
    Kether 24
BURCHER
    Florence T. 227
BURDEN
    Ivy M. 84
BURELL
    Sallie 48
BURGE
    Susan A. 179
    William D. 179
BURGER
    W. 70
BURKE
    Ruby M. 85
BURKLEY
    Geo. F. 50
BURLE
    Timothy 3

Index

BURLOCK
    Carl Linwood 125
BURNELL
    William N. 28
BURNHOUSE
    William 3
BURNS
    Alexander 125
BURRELL
    Sallie 145
    William H. 38
BURROUGHS
    Lee W. 36
BURTON
    Chas. E. 49
    Nancy 49
    Nora 194
BUSH
    John 4
BUTLER
    Charles 227
    Charles 227
    Eva S. 159
    Irene 198
    Jesse T. 198
    Sarah E. 227
BUWEN
    Thomas 3
BYRD
    Herbert L. 34
    William 26
CAFFEE
    Charles Wallace 40
    Sarah Anne Elizabeth . . 40
    Stanley J. 40
CALHOUN
    Amelia 39
CALLIS
    Marie J. 196
    Mary Ann 49
    Robert 27
    Virginia 194
CALLOWAY
    Fred 27
CALM
    Annie N. 62
    Robert 62
    Velvet Lorriane 13
    Willie 62
CAMPBELL
    A. 68
    Charles W. 195
CANNADY
    Archer F. 80
    Mary Lelia 80
CANNEY
    Louise 191
CAPLAN
    Arthur B. 123
    Rose F. 123
CAPLON
    Joseph 124
    Michael 124
CAPLOW
    H. L. 99
    Rose 99
CAPPEL
    Morris 98

CAPPS
    Cathrin 3
CARDWELL
    Mary W. 31
CAREY
    Elen 50
    John H. 33
    Mamie K. 28
    Rosa 14
CARLTON
    Alice B. 198
CARMEL
    David 127
    Ethel 107
    Frank Joseph 105
    Harry A. 105
    Irvin 94
    M. J. 107
    Macy Milton 121
    Melvin M. 121
    Miriam Belle 105
    Percy 105
    Rose Lee 121
    Sarah K. 105
    Sarah Lena 105
CARNES
    J. R. 181
    Joseph 181
    Susan R. 181
CARPER
    Harriet 57
CARR
    Mammie 47
CARROLL
    D. 67
CARROW
    Bennie 30
CARSON
    Ella H. 23
CARTER
    Albert J. 80
    C. H. 47
    Charles H. 33
    Elizabeth Beth 34
    Elorena 204
    Eunick D. 200
    Hattie J. 33
    J. Stanley 85
    James S. 85
    Jamie 196
    Julia T. 85
    Maggie 27
    Margaret 47
    Martha 36
    Martha S. 80
    Newton 24
    Richard F. 26
    Vivian W. 196
    Willie J. 52
CARTTER
    Edmond 3
CARY
    Ellen 146
CASEY
    Leon 195
    Sallie 195
CELEYS 219
CHAIET

    Rachael 124
CHAMBERLIN
    James 4
CHAMBERLINE
    Frances 3
CHANDLER
    Eliza 32
    Andren 36
    Annie R. 31
    Cecil 27
    Colonett 141
    Eliza 141
    Elizabeth 146, 147
    Hannah 32
    Hattie B. 32
    Hattie E. 55
    James H. 55
    John 193
    John F. 31
    Junious S. 56
    Junius S. 24
    Leander 52
    Louisa 57
    Luke 57
    Luke Jr 31
    Lymas 141
    Nymrod 141
    Rebecca 36
    Rebecca 49
    Rufus 25
    Ruth 32
    Samuel 31
    Thomas A. 55
CHAPMAN
    Alice 24
    J. M. 68
    Keenley 62
    L. J. 67
    Sarah 40
    William H. 49
CHARITY
    Harold R. 197
    Williams 30
CHARLOT
    David 28
CHATMAN
    Lillian R. 30
    Peter 150
    Peter T. 147
    Verdell W. 84
CHAVIS
    George M. 199
    Goldie 195
    Goldie M. 199
CHEATHAM
    Amanda Peele 82
    Ludd Nelson 82
CHELTON
    Rebecca Young 39
CHENAULT
    Oliver B. 37
CHENG-YANG H U S 80
CHERNOCK
    Louis 125
CHESLER
    Sarah 160
CHESNEAU
    Dorothy 159

CHEYNE
    Happy 89
CHIDES
    V. Montrose 217
CHILES
    E. B. 217
    E. V. 217
    V. Montrose 217
CHIRSTIAN
    Edna A. 150
    Osborne 152
CHISMAN
    John H. 56
    Junius 50
    Marion 50
    Mary Z. 55
    Sarah 50
    William 50
CHISWELL
    H. J. 67
Chrisenus
    His Child 3
CHRISTIAN
    Edward 142
    Elizabeth 194
    Ernestine T. 23
    Fleming 25
    Harriett W. 23
    Harry 23
    Laura 142
    Nora A. 23
    William E. 142
CHRISTY
    Elmo Saylor 82
    Nellie Pierce 82
CHUDD
    Otenia L. 51
Cisely
    a maid 3
CLAIBORNE
    Eleanor 195
    Ethel D. Wainwright . . . 73
CLAIR
    Maude Phillips 29
CLAPP
    Cecily C. 23
    Clifford Jr. 23
    Henry L. Jr. 23
    Henry M. 23
    Mary S. 23
    Rita B. 23
CLARK
    _____ 148
    Andrew G. 33
    Bennie 62
    Elnora H. 149
    J. D. 67
    Nealie 62
    Robert C. 62
CLARKE
    James N. 201
    Mamie Lee 192
    Margaret 60
    Sophia S. 201
CLAYTON
    Alonzo 200
    J. 67
    Martha 200

    Moses 213
CLAYTOR
    Ora V. 194
CLINE
    Annie L. 193
CLOUTZ
    James M. 69
COHEN
    Abraham 98, 101
    Alfred 116
    Annie 94
    Charles 111
    Fannie E. 94
    Florence Kapp 116
    Harold "Dooley" 120
    Harry 109
    Helen 101
    Hyman 124
    Ida 95
    Irvin 120
    Isaac 95, 102
    Katie Kurzer 120
    Milton 110
    Minnie 121
    Minnie S. 123
    Mollie 109
    Morris 101
    Nathan 101
    Rebecca 103
    Rose Gordon 124
    Sarah 103
    Sigmund 110
    Simon 109
COIN
    Shirley Nachman 122
COLE
    Estell Rollins 149
    Joseph 71
COLEMAN
    _____ 145
    Berry 204
    Eunice Minkins 146
    Glender N. 151
    Mary 145
    Minnie L. 193
    William T. 151
COLES
    Aubrer E. 83
    Eva Roberta 75
    James Egbert 75
    Lucy C. 79
    Robert Allen 79
    Rosa Belle 79
COLLIS
    James 3
COMBS
    Alvin 27
    Edith 27
    Indiana R. 51
    Lilliam R. 51
CONEY
    Alva 194
    Lucy 24
CONN
    Abraham 99
    Allen S. 158
    Archie M. 110
    Ellis 170

    Eva 161
    Julius 170
    Lillian 161
    Minnie 109
    Minnie Meyhr 110
    Rose J. 110
    Sarah Bertha 99
    Simon 109
CONNON
    Esther Meyhr 110
COOK
    Clinton 33
    Daniel 76
    J. B. 69
    Thomas 24, 212
    Woodson W. 33
COOKE
    Cornelia 212
    Garland A. 85
    George 3
    Mary Anne 85
    Phillip 4
    Rosetta M. 188
COOPER
    Audrey B. 85
    Blannie V. 198
    Ednora Mae 81
    Indianna 205
    Isadore W. 106
    J. D. 217
    Jack 192
    Joseph T. 198
    Lena W. 198
    Margaret 53
    Mary 181
    Mary Wilkins 163
    Mittie Ann 52
    Morris Samuel 106
    Nannie 205
    Risha 96
    Robert N. 201
    Rose Harris 106
    Sara R. 106
    William M. 52
    William M. 85
    Wm 53
COPELAND
    Baby 243
    Fannie 145
    Wm. H. 39
COPLAND
    Bessie Rose 167
    Moses Peter 167
COPPEL
    Eva 94
CORBIN
    J. W. 150
    Alfonso 148
    James 148
    Leonard O. 13
    Leonard O. 14
    Malcolm 26
    Mary V. 148
    Patsy 13
    Virginia Brown 82
    Wardell 148
CORNELL
    Louisa 62

Index

CORNEY
    Jane 62
CORNICK
    Thomas 49
CORTELL
    P. 111
COSBY
    Minnie 197
COTTON
    Dorothy P. 84
    Nannie B. 81
    Queen A. 81
COULLING
    James D. 17
    James W. 17
    Mary Susan 17
    Nancy 17
    Nancy Todd 17
COURTNEY
    Myrtle B. 151
    Vernon M. 151
COX
    Edward M. 69
    Martha 145
CR____
    Agnes 48
CRACKING-WING 77
CRAMER
    Sol 104
CRAWFORD
    Elijah 26
    Ida J. 167
    Pinkey 26
CRITTENDON
    Andrew E. 60
CRODELL
    S. I. 69
CROELL
    Dennis 75
CROSS
    Anna Laura 74
    John W. 74
    Mamie Levin 170
CROW
    William Little 75
CRUISE
    W. S. 68
CRUM
    Robert Eugene 122
CRUZ
    Eliza 205
CUFFE
    Martin 3
CUFFEE
    J. W. 205
    Joseph 200
    L. L. 205
    Lavin A. 205
    Lavinia 201
CUNDIFF
    G. W. 68
CURLE
    Thomas 9, 10
CURTIS
    Beula Davis 43
    Charles H. 52
    Mary Ellen 52
    Mary L. 53
    Robert H. 53
CUTHBERTSON
    Wm S. 70
DABNET
    John A. 28
DABNEY
    Beulah J. 31
    Deller 146
    Mary E. 26
    Rosa 24
DAEZIEN
    Janette Copeland 78
DAGGS
    Wm. H. 57
DALE
    Frank 59
DAMERON
    Bridgett 3
DAMSKY
    Jacob B. 124
    Rosa B. 124
DANCE
    J. Arthur 62
    Mamie A. 62
DANDRIDGE
    M. Euphon 8
    Wilson 8
DANIEL
    Annie D. 29
    C. L. 141
    infant son 141
DANIELS
    Elizabeth J. 196
    Lettie 211
DAVID
    Goldie Rubin 158
    William Rice 158
DAVIDSON
    Dave 94
    Maxwell Mickey 160
    Rachel 94
    Sarah 94
DAVIES
    Elizabeth 3
    William 3
DAVINSON
    Jennie 104
DAVIS
    Abraham 30
    Alice West 43
    Andrew 54
    Charles 47
    Charlotte F. 75
    Clarence A. 195
    Collis Huntington 81
    Don A. 78, 80
    Don Andrew 83
    Elfred D. 203
    Elizabeth Eudora 225
    Ella Nora 225
    Ethel D. 83
    Frances 54
    Fred D. 55
    George J. 75
    Hannah 88
    Harry 147
    Henry 62
    Infant Daughter 78
    Isabella 76
    J. 69
    J. L. 69
    James Allen 225
    James S. 50
    John W. 225
    Josephine 147
    Julin 27
    Lennie S. 80
    Liza 195
    LouiseBarbour 81
    Mary Ann 225
    Millie 56
    Nannie W. 55
    Philip P. 43
    Reda Samuels 125
    Robert 225
    Robert A. 225
    Rosa E. 50
    Rose P. 30
    Sallie N. 33
    Thomas 4
    Thomas 56
    Thomas H. 56
    Victoria 191
DAWNS
    Ethel Frazier 28
DAY
    Carrie 25
DEAN
    Benjamin F. 50
    Emma 50
    Hattie V. 195
    Julia J. 50
    Martha V. 37
DEANE
    Emily Chadsey 79
    Marion Colvin 79
DEBRICK
    Elanora 24
    Montre 24
DENNIS
    Alice E. 51
    Bernard 195
    Cornelious 24
    J. R. 69
    James W. 191
    Lawrence E. 191
    Oscar 198
    Plesant 145
    Raymond 152
    Robert 145
DEVENPORT
    Dorsey 49
DEYONG
    Simon 118
DIAMANT
    Abbot Robert 166
DIAMOND
    Anna 101
    Harry Charles 122
    Joseph Bernard 108
    Phyllis L. 122
    Tillie Rebecca 108
    Zilpa Greenspon 119
DIAMONDSTEIN
    Leon Elias 123
    Tillie S. 123

Index

DIAMONSTEIN
- William 163

DICKERSON
- Peeter 4

DICKINS
- Ruth 85

DIGGS 211
- Anna 211
- C. H. 56
- Deacon Washington . . . 212
- Emma K. 32
- Frank H. 51
- Hattie S. 30
- Ida 213
- Isaia 211
- John Henry 31
- M. 211
- Margaret 211
- Mary 51
- Raymond 48
- Seretha Ann 33
- W. 211
- W. D. 211
- Washington 211
- Washington Jr. 212

DILLARD
- Moses 146
- Roy H. 39

DIXON
- Eunice Congdon 74
- Harvey 175
- J. M. 68

DONAHUE
- S. R. 68

DOOR
- Frank 76

DORN
- Samuel 158

DOUGLAS
- _____ 215
- Richard 215
- Walter C. 81

DOWE
- Esther 188

DOWNEMAN
- Mary 4

DOWNES
- William 3

DOWNING
- Mariah 62

DRELICK
- Moses 95

DRESSER
- Lydia F. 76

DREW
- Clara V. 191
- Fredrick 33
- Mattie S. 15

DRUCKER
- A. Louis 163
- Loraine Blechman 163

DRUITT
- Anderson 211
- Laura E. 195
- Sarah J. 211
- Walter T. 195

DRUMMOND
- George 173

- George F. 40
- Julia Ann 139
- Susan Howell 173

DUDLEY
- M. P. 68

DUPPER
- Edward 3

DUTTON
- Benson L. 84
- Infant 73
- Josephine B. 84

DYKE
- Fannie M. 204
- George H. 203
- Helen M. 204
- James H. 203

EAGLE
- Walter Little 76

EAGLESON
- Frances M. 84

EASTE
- Richard 4

EBB
- Maretha "Marie" R. . . . 83

EBES
- Thomas 4

ECHOLS
- George E. 204
- Royal 54

ECORUPTAHA 78

EDRICK
- F. __ 56

EDWARDS
- Adeline W. 25
- Cora D. 225
- J. W. 225
- Laura 25
- Necie 25
- Sarah Page 225
- Thomas 48

EIBELL
- A. F. 75

EISENMAN
- Arthur F. 163
- Hattie W. 162
- Louis 162

ELAM
- Lucy H. 31

ELBRIDG
- William 3

ELDER
- Kittie 213

ELEY
- David 36

ELKINS
- Wm. 67

ELLENSON
- Harry 110
- Hilda Scoll 116
- Louis 116
- Mary D. 110
- Polly D. 122
- Robert 122
- Rosalind Stern 121
- Samuel Leon 121
- Sol 162

ELLIOTT
- Albert 145

- Emily H. 32
- Emma 27

ELLIS
- Bernard 126
- M. A. 68
- Sally S. 126

ELSBERG
- Blanche S. 159
- Edward 159

EMMET
- Emuel Holloway 23

ENCONTRE
- Francis R. 78

EPPS
- Azarina L. 38
- Pauline D. 31

EPSTEIN
- Benjamin Louis 112
- Bessie M. 94
- Charles 111
- Etta Leah 99
- Ida 97
- Ida K. 111
- Jack Kanter 127
- Jacob Robert 99
- Marlel Phillip 122
- Maurice 165
- Monnie 99
- Morris Aaron 112
- Rose Lipman 165
- Sarah Carmel 112

ERLACH
- Elias 107
- Infant 93
- Jake 170
- Lena 107
- Lewis H. 115
- Maurice 93, 158
- Rose C. 93

ESTES
- Alexander 75

EVANS
- Ella Lockhart 80
- Estella M. 75
- John H. 75
- John Scott 80
- Laura Alice 198

EVERETT
- Mary A. 13
- Richard 13

EVERETTE
- Sylvester 193

FAIRFIELD
- Charlotte 74

FAISON
- Mancil R. 148

FALK
- Nalalie 107

FAMILANT
- Davis 114
- Leon Albert 117
- Lillian Newman 120
- Milton J. 120
- Sophia 114

FARBER
- Barney 161

FARRAR
- John 3

Index

FAUNTLEROY
    Alice 200
    William 199
FEARNE
    Henry 3
FELDMAN
    Lou 107
    Shirly L. 107
FELSTERN
    Annie 97
FELTHAM
    Sarah K. 74
FELTMAN
    Matthew B. 171
FENIGSOHN
    David 118
    Esther H. 118
    Eva 118
    Julius S. 118
    Sol 118
FENTON
    James 3
    Mr. 4
FIELDS
    Carrie B. 52
    Catherine W. 54
    George W. 54
    Margaret 50
    Martha A. 54
    Maude Pierce 38
    Robert T. 53, 54
    Sallie B. 54
    Victor Hugo 73
    W. O. 67
    Washington 54
    William Louis 81
FINCH
    Jas. H. 130
    Jas. Henry C. 130
    Laura F. 130
FINE
    William 117
FINEMAN
    Charles 127
FINK
    Israel 122
    Julius 93
    Sidney J. 122
    Sophia 122
FIRE-CLOUD
    Armstrong 77
FISCH
    Benjamin 103
    Dora Goodman 112
    Goldie Epstein 103
    Jacob 112
    Louis 95
FISH
    Charles 97
    Hannah Pika 97
FISHER
    Ida 114
    Israel Kaiman 113
    Jack David 125
    Kate Weger 125
    Sadie 126
FITCHETT
    Robert C. 191
    Sallie 205
FITCHETTE
    Addie 194
FLAKOWITZ
    Sam 126
    Sara 126
FLAX
    Charles H. 76
    David Edward 121
    Jennie Gold 119
    Morris H. 119
FLEETWOOD
    Dercy 197
FLEMING
    Garie 13
    Hugh 191
    Mary E. 191
FLICK
    Anita Butler 159
    Walter 159
FOLEY
    David 69
FOLIOTT
    Elizabeth 88
FOLKOWITZ
    Pauline 105
FORMAN
    Benard 109
FORTUNE
    John 36
FOSTER
    Ezekiel 28
    Ronald E. 27
    Willis E. 27
FOUNTAIN
    Melvin 201
    W. 15
FOWLER
    Ernest H. 33
    J. 68
FOX
    Baby 171
    Bernard "Bucky" 167
    C. J. 69
    Estol W. 120
    Hannah M. 127
    Joseph 24
    Joseph R. 160
    Lilian Curtis 43
    Phillip 127
    Sada L. 160
FOXX
    Ethel Harrell 84
FRANCES
    James H. 47
FRANCIS
    Daisy 195
    Dora 34
    Frances 50
    Mary A. 33
    Mary Susan 33
FRANK
    Eugene 117
    Harry 117
    Irvin 118
    Jacob 107
    Joe 93
    Jules R. 161
    Lilyan M. 117
    Nettie 93
FRANKEL
    Helen Nachman 102
FRANKLIN
    Joseph 94
FRAZIER
    Mary D. 202
FREELAND
    Albert A. 73
    Emma Booth 75
    Margaret Booth 73
FREELOW
    Daniel 77
FREEMAN
    Alma Ray Ruben 120
    Daisy 13
    George W. 38
    Margta 27
    Mary 52
    Mildred T. 73
    Rebecca 38
    William A. 73
FRENKEL
    David 108
    Eva Rosenstein 125
    Flora 108
    Jacob 125
    Siegfried 125
FRIED
    Fannie 101
FRIEDBERG
    Ray 95
FRIEDLAND
    Frank 106
    Frank 106
    Grunne 97
    Ida 106
    Martin D. 124
    Sidney 124
FRIEDLANDER
    Sarah 114
FRIEDMAN
    Ben F. 167
    Ernest 120
    Herman 101
    Joseph 112
    Louis 119
    Minnie 125
    Mollie 96
    Samuel 96
    Seymour 117
    Sol 125
    Sol 105
    Stanley R. 119
    Vivian 105
    Zeporah 100
FRISLE
    Margery 3
FRISSELL
    Hollis Burke 76
    Julia Dodd 77
FRUZELAND
    Jacob 69
FULHAM
    Thomas 3
FURLOW
    Mary Ann 197

Index

FURST
- Mollie 107

GAINES
- Allie L. 85
- Seymour J. 85

GAMM
- Cornelious 60

GARDINER
- Alexander 49

GARDNER
- Edward 51
- George D. 51
- George E. 199
- George Edward 199
- Rosa R. 199

GARNER
- Catharine 36
- Jennie 164
- Lillie Baskin 164
- Selwyn C. 164
- Shirley Kruger 164
- Stanley Solomon 164

GARNETT
- Daisy 213

GARRETT
- Laura 230
- R. R. 230
- Susan A. 230

GARRICK
- Edward 166

GARRIS
- Mamie E. 12

GASKINS
- Ben. J. W. 152

GATES
- Harold 202

GATHRIGHT
- Chas. D. 57
- James 57

GATLEING
- Thomas 21

GAUNTLETT
- William 3

GAVETT
- John 3

GAYLE
- Christine 26
- Peter 204

GEALES
- William 3

GEARY
- James 68

GELLMAN
- Bertha 113

GERBER
- Florence S. 167

GETSUG
- Mollie Paster 127

GIBBS
- Henry 49
- J. S. 68
- Norah 52

GIBSON
- Fannie M. 81
- William O. 75

GIDDINGS
- McGee 71
- William 71

GILBERT
- Ida Cooke 75

GILLETT
- Richard 3

GILLIARD
- Bertha L. 85
- Joseph W. 85

GILMAR
- Eleanor A. 81

GITLES
- Pearl L. 121

GLASSMAN
- Hirsh 94

GLAZER
- Edythe S 127

GLEASON
- Frederic D. 74

GLENN
- Mary 191

GLOVER
- Willie T. 85

GLUCKSTEIN
- Minnie 98

GODUTI
- Kathy Mirmelstein 165

GOFF
- Sarah A. 75

GOLD
- Martin A. 158

GOLDBERG
- David 94
- Esther Rachel 104
- Ethel 101
- Ida 100
- Ida T. 113
- Isaac Morris 113
- Israel B. 100
- Jacob 124
- Marilyn Levin 165
- Mollie Fingerman 170
- Morris 110
- Rebecca 101
- Sara Levy 113
- Solomon H. 113
- Virginia B. 124

GOLDEN
- Joseph Aaron 126
- Leon N. 24

GOLDMAN
- Ada 160
- Jack David 161

GOLDSMITH
- Bessie 212

GOLDSTEIN
- Albert Maurice 103
- Bertha Heimlich 109
- Emanuel 117
- Esther 117
- Esther G. 161
- Ethel Conn 118
- Gertrude Klaft 114
- Irving F. 161
- Isadore 111
- Jacob Henry 126
- Max A. 126
- Milton Stanley 118
- Morris 111
- Myer Joseph 109

- Rose Nachman 103
- Ruth Cohen 116
- Sadie F. 111

GOLOMBIK
- Leonard 126
- Lillian 126

GOLUB
- Celia Lavender 118
- Samuel Keva 118

GOOD-ROAD
- Eva 77

GOODCHILD
- Richard 3

GOODEN
- Laura Louise 142

GOODMAN
- Abe F. 111
- Harrison 191
- Mollie J. 108
- Morris J. 108
- Simon 114

GOODWIN
- Marcellus 68
- Thos. 68

GORDEN
- Narris 103
- Rachel 103

GORDON
- F. B. 93
- Annie 105
- Ben 93
- Benjamin 122
- Bennie Bernard 103
- Bernard 93
- Bernice Slavin 162
- Bertha 93
- Bertha 102
- Charles 106
- F. B. 93
- Frances 93
- Hanna Cohen 170
- Jack A. 170
- Jennie 122
- Joseph 119
- Katie 113
- Leo Ike 93
- Nathan 103
- Pauline 103
- Sam 119
- Sam 106
- William 102
- Wm. 93

GOTTLIEB
- Morris S. 125

GRADY
- C. J. 68
- Frank L. 81
- Mary S. 81

GRAFF
- Alan Myron 102
- Bernard Z. 100
- Dorothy 102
- Ellis Joseph 100
- Jeannette Mintz 100
- William A. 100

GRAINE
- Delores 98
- Florence 98

Index

GRANGER
    James 98
    Garret 215

GRANNICK
    Jonas 126

GRAVES
    Lauvinin Sykes 14
    V. 181

GRAY
    Ellen F. 51
    John H. 51

GREEN
    Alice G. 215
    Bessie Hawkins 75
    Daniel 120
    Frances 204
    Harry Aaron 102
    Jack 117
    Josephen 102
    Marian Morewitz 117
    Percy J. 26
    Robert C. 78
    Sarah 102
    Sarah Peake 48
    Tena 25

GREENBERG
    Anne P. 116
    Arthur S. 116
    Rebecca Carmel 112

GREENSPON
    Emanuel 120
    Fannie 96
    Isaac 110
    Lillian S. 119
    Max William 110
    Minnie 110
    Reuben 119
    Rose Shimkowitz 110
    Solomon 98

GREGORY
    David 69

GRIFFIN
    Alonzo 192
    Charles 198
    James 199
    Lydia C. 199
    Marjorie 198
    Richard 3
    William T. 199

GRINSTEAD
    William 54

GRONER
    Fannie 95

GROSS
    Faye G. 160
    Harry David 160
    Jacob 99
    Pearl 98
    Rebecca 97
    Victoria 193

GRUNWALD
    Eugene John 159

GUILL
    Charles 70

GULSTONS
    Chad. 3
    infant 3
    uxor 3

GUTHRIE
    Jas. L. 69

GUY
    Adolphus 71
    Catharine Snead 71
    Charles 71
    George W. 42
    Jno. T. 71
    John T. 42
    John Thomas 71
    Lucy Belle 71
    Margaret Ann 71
    Martha Ann 71
    Mary 71
    Mary E. 42
    Mary Elizabeth Cooper . 71
    Nancy P. 42
    Sophia 71
    Thomas 71
    Whitney 3
    William Hopkins 71

HABITHAN
    Carl A. 78

HALE
    Frederick 75

HALL
    Daisy M. 63
    Ida B. 14
    Isabella 63
    Joseph H. 63
    Katie M. 62
    Lucilla J. 63
    Lucy J. 63
    Romeo C. 62
    Thomas 3

HALLER
    Louisa E. 230

HALPERIN
    Anna 108
    E. S. 97
    Hanna Rebecca 97
    Jacob 98
    Jennie 101
    Joseph L. 108
    Morris Herbert 122
    Sarah 97
    Sarah 97

HAMILTON
    Richard H. 228

HAMMOND
    Rosa 26

HAMPTON
    Elnora 196
    William 196

HANDELSMAN
    Mary 100
    Morris M. 100

HANDFINGER
    Adam Shawn 171

HANKIN
    Lena 117

HANSFORD
    Charles 88
    Hannah Davis 90
    James 87, 89, 90
    James D. 89
    John 88, 89
    Missoura 89
    Richard 88
    Thelma Ironmonger 91
    Thomas 88, 90

HARDY
    Ella 195
    Maggie 194

HARMICLE
    J. R. 69

HARMON
    Kate 192
    Sara 54
    Thomas 54
    Thomas 54

HARRELL
    Gladys O. 201
    Inez A. 202
    Martha 192
    Wilton 192

HARRIS
    Aaron H. 106
    Beatrice H. 198
    Bettie E. 62
    Charles H. 24
    Clara B. 49
    Delia 21
    Diana 62
    Earl B. 27
    Edgar 32
    Eva L. 106
    Fannie 29
    Farley P. 59
    Ida M. 34
    James B. 33
    Jennie Freeland 73
    John 70
    Laura E. 62
    Leonard P. 122
    Lucy 24
    Richard 205
    Sarah Parker 33
    Viola B. 36
    William 142

HARRISON
    ____ 52
    Artelia V. 193
    Nannie 192
    Raph 3
    Russell L. 84
    Thomas 26

HART
    Helen Santa Cruz 79
    William S. 81
    William Stephen 79

HARTFIELD
    David 26

HARVEY
    Michael 25

HARVIE
    Samwell 3

HASSEBANK
    F. 67

HAUSMAN
    William Albert 182

HAWKINS
    Blanche D. 150
    Jurline 28
    Rebecca 189

HAWLEY

HAYES
- Jesse 77

HAYES
- Martha B. 21
- Susie J. 79
- Truly W. 79

HAYNES
- C. E. 67

HAYWARD
- Elizabeth 30

HEILBERG
- Sybil 166

HENDERSON
- C H 211
- C J 211
- Clara J. 211
- Elma M. 211
- Ernest 151
- Ernest Courtney 151
- Lillian C. 151
- Minnie B. 31
- Morris C. 211
- Thomas H. 211

HENDIN
- Samuel 120

HENDREN
- Henrietta V. 218
- James V. J. 218
- Wm. T. 217, 218

HENNESS
- Elizabeth 175

HENRY
- Jas. 62
- Samuel 14

HERBERT
- Arthur W. 34
- Esther A. 47
- John 47
- Mary 57
- Pascow 130
- Robert John 57
- Rosa A. 58
- Susie 28

HERMAN
- Sadie Rubin 111
- William 111

HERSHFIELD
- James M. 116
- Miriam Scoll 116

HERZEKOW
- Harry 107
- Louis 94

HEYMAN
- Peter 9, 10

HEYWARD
- Edward 30

HICKCOCKE
- Capt. 3

HICKMAN
- Loolah 137
- Martha 137
- Mary E. 51
- Nanni 137
- Sarah 137
- Susan L. 137
- William 137
- William I 137

HIGGINBOTHAM
- Joseph Shafter 81

HILL
- Volena Gale 81

HILL
- Carl McClellan 76
- Charles H. 34
- Dallis 25
- Edward 4, 48
- Harriett M. 82
- Mary M. 34
- Mary S. 28
- Simon S. 49

HILLIARD
- Gregory 3
- John 3
- John 3

HILTON
- Solomon 192

HIPOYA
- Grorge Norcross 78

HIRSCH
- Karen Wilks 123

HOCHMAN
- Harry 125

HOFFMAN
- Benjamin 126
- Michael 108
- Tillie 108

HOGES
- Bessie G. 194

HOGGE
- Emily Lewellyn 224
- Frances 224
- Infant 224
- Janie 224
- Jesse Hope 224
- John T. 224
- Louise Howe 224
- Mamie L. 224
- Margaret Mouring ... 224
- Robert T. 224
- W. W. 224
- William 224

HOLLAND
- Alpha B. 81
- J. W. 67

HOLLARD
- Esther 23
- Roland S. 23

HOLLIER
- Ann 131
- Frances 131
- Mattie 28
- Simon 131

HOLLINS
- James F. 67

HOLLOWAY
- Arleen 199
- George 195
- Jessie Marie 23
- Josephine 25
- William S. 60

HOLLY
- Alphonsus 78

HOLMES
- Henry 68
- Samuel 60
- Thomas 62
- Willie 59
- Wm. S. 62

Wm. T. 62

HOLTSCLAW
- G. H. 67

HOLZSWEIG
- Bessie 107
- Fannie B. 108
- Israel 99
- Julius 93
- Louis 108
- Meyer 107
- Morton Isaac 94
- Philip 108
- Rose 108
- Sarah 96
- Sidney 111

HOLZSWIG
- Milton 109

HOOKER
- Cob 28
- Daisy W. 28

HOOSMAN
- William Albert 183

HOPE
- Cecil 30
- Cora 34
- Eva T. 23
- Hattie 147
- Mary L. 30
- Rosa Celestine 49

HOPKICKE
- William 3

HOPKINS
- J. H. 69

HOPSON
- Carrie L. 188
- Leon T. M. 151
- Sallie A. 32

HORNIS
- Elizabeth 146, 149

HORSALEY
- William Albert 183

HORTON
- Alfred 75
- Susie C. 205

HOUGHTON
- Jennie 73

HOUSE
- M. C. 68

HOUSEMAN
- William A. 184

HOUSER
- Oscar H. 80

HOWARD
- _____ 53
- Ann Lepearl 53
- Annie 225
- Beulah W. 84
- Catharine 58
- Comfort 53
- Fannie T. Ash 53
- Gabbie 15
- Henry 26
- James 58
- Mary Louise 75
- Morphelia 33
- Nat 53
- Robert 148
- Thomas J. 53

Index

Thomas J.	53
Violet	80
W____	53

HOWE
- Albert 76
- Elizabeth Wingate 76
- Harriette W. 76
- Harry Dresser 76
- Isaac 73

HOWELL
- James 173
- James E. 173
- Margaret 173
- Mrs James E. 173

HOWERTON
- Ethel M. 37
- Mary B. 39
- Ruth J. 37
- W. R. 39

HOYLE
- Elizabeth Sampson 32

HUBBARD
- Ethel L. 14
- James C. 14
- Oliver Joshua 75

HUDGENS
- Samuel 70

HUDGINS
- Morris W. 198

HUDSON
- R. M. 69

HUFFMAN
- J. R. 69

HUFFY
- Mr. 3

HUGHES
- John 213
- Melvin L. 28
- Saluda 77
- Samuel 76

HUNSHER
- Sonya Binder 160

HUNT
- Benjamin 67

HUNTER
- Donald 24
- Thomas 4

HUNTHILTON
- Pearl 26

HURWITZ
- Charles 170
- Sadie 170

INGE
- Frederick D. 73

ISHAM
- Caroline S. 80
- Charles S. 81

ISLER
- Patsy 14

JACKSON
- Anna M. 203
- Arthur 202
- B. B. 68
- Davie W. 54
- Eva M. 49
- Florence B. 54
- Florine 197
- Henrietta 201
- John 4
- Jules F. 84
- Lillie 147
- Louise Sykes 14
- Lulan 197
- Martha 62
- Maurice S. 84
- Millie 202
- Millie 203
- Myrtle Palmer 80
- Nathan 211
- Nathaniel E. 14
- Olga T. 54
- Ora W. 192
- Paul L. 202
- Robert 34
- Robert 192
- Robert E. 203
- William 24
- Willie 21
- Y. 47

JACOBS
- A. 69
- Harry 125
- Lydia A. 28
- Sam 102
- Walter P. 39
- Yetta 102

JACOBSON
- Gitela L. 166
- Joseph W. 166

JAFFEE
- Elizabeth Lichtenstein 168

JARVIS
- Beulah H. 55
- Curl H. 55
- Josephine 32
- Roxanna E. 55
- Shirley S. 55

JEFFERSON
- Jennie 199

JEFFRESS
- Josephine E. 38

JENKINS
- Alexander 39
- Earnest 212
- Edward H. 14
- Grace 195
- Lena B. 202
- Lillian C. 39
- Lizzie A. 38
- Luster 193
- Raymond 192
- Sarah 196
- Thelma 192

JENNINGS
- Claudis 191
- Vivian 27

JETER
- Robert 200

JETT
- Horace 89, 90
- Martha 196
- Missoura Hansford 90, 91
- Robert 89, 91
- William 91

JINKS
- John H. 79

Nancy Nather	79

JOHNS
- Ehel Tynes 34

JOHNSON
- ____ 150
- Alberta 188
- Alice 147
- Alma L. 85
- Artelia C. 134
- B. F. 134
- Betty M. 29
- Catherine 134
- Clara 188
- Clara B. 188
- Clemetine H. 149
- David 134
- E. 39
- Edward 189
- Eliza 188, 189
- Elnora P. 23
- Elsie 212
- Fannie 49
- Frances 189
- Francis 21
- Fredinand V. 85
- Georgiana 149
- Gloria Gates 201
- Harrison W. 188
- Helena M. Wainwright 73
- Hollis F. 188
- Ida Bell 145
- Isaac 188, 189
- Isabelle 25
- Lewis 188, 189
- Lillie 145
- Mary 147
- Mary B. 83
- Mary E. 39, 134
- Mary F. 27
- Montaque 188
- Nancy 212
- P. M. 69
- Patience 211
- Priscilla 189
- Rebecca 189
- Samuel 188
- Samuel E. 51
- Samuel R. 134
- Sarah 62
- T. W. 68
- W. H. 39
- Walter P. 49
- William H. 62
- Willie 189

JOHNSTON
- Charles H. 33

JOLLIE
- Baby Boy 197

JOLLY
- Eliza 63
- Elizabeth 63
- W. M. 63

JONES 183
- Albert B. 13
- Albert Tallen 217
- Althea Harris 54
- Anna 217
- Benjamin F. 14

Bettie 150	**KAPLAN**	Minnie 104
Carrie 53	Edwin I. 112	**KINNER**
Edmond 150	Esther 170	Jacob S. 211
Edward N. 84	Joseph M. 100	**KIRBY**
Elizabeth 243	Kate 98	Martha 50
Elizabeth 205	Milton 126	**KIRSNER**
Elizabeth Wood 244	Moses 97	Fannie B. 107
Esther 40	Reba Morewitz 112	Harriet Weger 100
Frank 13	Samuel I. 167	Hattie 120
Geo. B. 217	Sarah R. 98	Isaac 107
George 3	**KAPLIN**	Jacob 99
George L. 192	Flora 101	Raymond B. 107
George W. 60	Harry 101	**KLEIN**
Harold 14	**KATES**	Joseph 104
James H. 205	Charles 161	**KLESMER**
John H. 204	Rena Nachma 161	Irving 121
John William 243	**KATZ**	**KNEIP**
Joseph Julian 54	Rudolph Aaron 161	Pearl Lichtenberg 169
Julia 13	**KATZENBERG**	**KNETTEL**
Lena Young 195	Esther G. 160	Louis 68
Leola Johnson 188	**KAUFMAN**	**KNIER**
Lillian B. 83	Brunette E. 163	W. W. 68
M. 68	Maurice C. 163	**KNIGHT**
Margaret S. 82	**KEFFIE**	John 3
Mary 201	Elaine Evans 80	**KNOWLES**
Mary Booker 184	William H. 80	Isarell 3
Mildred 206	**KEINNSTON**	**KNOX**
Nellie 205	Thomas 3	Inez F. 200
Neolus A. 213	**KELLOGG**	Rosa 200
Nora 47	Hattie 76	Samuel 204
Richard 13	**KELLY**	**KOPELSON**
Richard H. 13	E. 67	Sheldon 169
Rosa 150	**KEMACK**	**KOPLON**
Saphonia 37	Daniel Leon 127	Charles M. 104
Sarah M. 199	Phyllis Goodman 127	Esther L. 104
Susie D. 31	**KEMP**	Rita Faye 107
W. H. 69	Albert 146	**KOVACS**
W. Herman 194	Allen M. 195	William 111
Walter S. 82	Christopher M. 86	**KRADITOR**
Warren Thomas 84	George M. 195	Charles 121
William 3	Harrison 25	Shirley S. 121
William H. 201	Howard S. 86	**KRAMER**
JORDAN	Joseph B. 27	Benjamin 107
Eliza Ann 36	Lillian W. 86	Daniel 115
Emily A. 38	Percy L. 28	Donald B. 117
Henry Bailey 74	**KENNEDY**	Florence H. 115
Josephine 37	Elizabeth 77	Ida Berman 115
Roxanna 24	Elnora 29	Mike L. 115
William Albert 37	Lizzie 47	Rachel 107
Wm. Elmore 49	Lucy 36	Toby 116
JORDON	Thomas 36	**KRATZER**
Jesse J. 198	**KENT**	Angelina Watkins Tennis 90
JOYNER	J. E. 69	Callie 89
Agie B. 21	**KERBEL**	**KRESSEL**
JOYNES	Rudolf 103	Kate Sarah 127
Martha 205	Sarah Nachman 103	**KRUGER**
JULIUS	**KESSLER**	Amanda Willis 59
Florence V. 193	Yetta 106	**KULMAN**
JUNIFER	**KEY**	Bertha J. 111
Sam'l 38	C. H. 69	David 111
KALBFLEISH	**KHIGER**	Harvey Joel 111
John 67	Anna 171	Ida 100
KANTER	**KING**	Issac 104
Celia Epstein 121	James H. 200	Minnie 119
Max Joseph 121	Mary E. 47, 63	**KURZER**
KANTOR	Patsy 203	Bella A. 126
Emma Satisky 123	Percilla 63	Bernard W. 126
Murray 123	**KINLAND**	Henrietta 117

Index

- Julius 117
- Morris 115
- Philip 111
- Razel 115
- Rose S. 115

LaCROSSE
- Ida Estelle 75
- John Francis 73
- Lillian Wallace 73

LACY
- Leniod S. 205

LAMBERT
- Sammuell 4

LANCASTER
- Paige Irving 81

LANCFORD
- Hattie B. 192
- John 194
- William M. 196

LANE
- E. W. 69
- James E. 69
- Sara 80

LANGLEY
- Daniel 15
- James R. 195
- Jennie S. 15

LANGSTON
- Katie 198

LASSITER
- Isaac 13
- J. J. 67
- Julia Ann 200
- Julia W. 204
- Leroy G. 200
- Robert 200

LASUTE-WHITE-BACK 78

LATIMER
- Almora S. 135
- Charles W. 155
- Elizabeth 135
- George 135
- Kay R. 82
- Martha 135
- Mary Jane 155
- Matthew 135
- Thomas 137
- Virginia R. 155
- William 137

LATTIMORE
- Delia E. 29
- Edward M. 29
- Hattie Daggs 57
- Mary 23
- Nannie L. 49

LAWS
- Frank 52
- John Bril 52
- Matilda 52

LAWSON
- Ellen 59

LAWYLER
- Sallie Law 15

LAZARUS
- Etta 110
- Harry 127
- infant son 94
- Robert 96

LEACOOK
- Margaret 33

LEADER
- Earl D. 158

LEANER
- Robert 3

LEDERMAN
- Joseph 104

LEE
- Andrew 69
- Berna 93
- Charles H. 51
- Ethel L. 51
- James G. 50
- Lucy A. 51
- Martha 150
- Mary B. 27
- Mary Elizabeth 56
- Rosa S. 193
- Sprigg 51
- W. C. 67
- William L. 51

LEGUM
- Edith Nachman 161

LEIBOWITZ
- Annie T. 95
- Max 95

LEIFER
- Leo 126

LENETSKY
- Jacob 95

LERNER
- Margaret Ann 169
- Robert W. 161
- Shirley Kruger 161
- Simon 169

LEVI
- Goldie M. 111
- Harry 111

LEVIN
- Abraham J. 102
- Augustus 100
- Benjamin 105
- Chanah 104
- David 104
- Edna M. 119
- Esther Garfield 165
- Florence P. 116
- Harry 166
- Joseph M. 105
- Leo W. 116
- Milton 170
- Minnie L. 165
- Paulin 102
- Sarah 104
- Sarah A. 105
- Wolfe 102

LEVINE
- Herman 104
- Ida 104
- Isadore I. 117
- Meyer 119
- Sarah R. 117
- Yetta C. 119

LEVINETZKY
- Sarah 95

LEVINSON
- Belle Reva 160
- Bessie Lazarus 113
- Celia 96
- Charles Abraham 113
- Elizabeth M. 96
- Gilbert Ben 160
- Isaac J. 96
- Jerome 160
- Julian Leonard 123
- Max 96
- Rosa 96
- Rose Mae 160
- Sarah 95
- Sarah Ida 99
- Sol Phillip 160
- Sylvia Sevy 160

LEVITT
- Abraham 99
- Louisa V. 56

LEVITT-KRUGER
- Lynn 161

LEVY
- Anna E. 101
- Anna F. 94
- Benjamin 114
- Florance 93
- Goldie Peltz 116
- I. 95
- Ida 97, 107
- J. B. 102
- Jacob 107
- Kreine 97
- Maurice B. 127
- Maxwell 116
- Nathan Joseph 114
- Racheal Lena 109
- Samuel 101
- Sophie 102
- Theodore Barney 109
- Wolfe 100

LEWCOVITZ
- Henry 99

LEWELLEN
- Fannie D. 138

LEWIS
- Jane 71
- John 134
- John Wesley 83
- Louis 115
- Martin Luther 71
- Mary B. 36
- Mary Cole 71
- Mary Sue 134
- Roscoe E. 81
- Ursula Fleming 83

LICHT
- Clara B. 116

LICHTENBERG
- Henry 100
- Rose 100

LICHTENSTEIN
- Esther 170
- Julian 170

LIEBERMAN
- Anna S. 123
- Morris H. 123

LINCOLNE
- Capt. 3

LINDSAY

J. 68
Ramsey C. 200
LINDSEY
William 192
LINKRAMM
Annie I. 93
LIPMAN
Annie S. 164
Bernard L. 165
Isaac 164
LIPSCOMB
Lucille 31
Willie 31
LIPSCOMBE
Edward T. 84
Julian H. 85
Louise T. 85
LIPSCOME
Leroy 192
LIPSITZ
Alex 167
Rose Schwartz 168
LIPSOCMBE
Lucy S. 85
LIRMAN
? Myer 93
LIVAS
"Ace" Henry Lewis 73
"Coke" Alice Smith 73
LIVELY
Abraham J. 149
Horace A. 147
Horsit 146
John L. 55
Kisiah 141
Mable H. 202
Rosett B. 141
Susie J. 149
LIVINSON
Benard L. 121
LLOYD
D. Blanche 38
Mary 47
Richard 47
Ruppert A. B. 38
LOCKE
John 3
John 3
LOGAN
Susie S. 30
LONG
Alberta 32
LOREN
Nathan 112
Rebecca 115
Sam 115
LOVE
Jefferson 193
LOVETTE
Maria 49
LOWE
Dora R. 108
Lucy 197
LOWENSTERN
Lee 159
Sidney 159
LUCIOUS
B. 69

LUCOTT
William 3
LUFSEY
Catharien Willis 173
Iris Burnell 173
LUKOWITZ
Rachel M. 97
LUPER
Josephine Toliver 151
LUPO
William 3
LUSTER
Clayborn 24
LYLES
Clifford Ermine 40
Iola W. 36
William E. 36
M. S. P. 77
MAHPLYA-MANI 78
MAJOR
Joseph 149
Mary 149
Sadie Roberta 59
MAKER
Mina 24
Nina 24
MALINA
Elizabeth Gordon 169
Max Herman 111
MALLICOTTE
Margaret Ann 224
MALLORY
William 54
MALNICK
Abraham 101
Raymond D. 101
Rose 101
MALONE
Anna 147, 152
MANLEY
W. L. 69
MANN
Alex 200
Alice J. 194
Carrie E. 201
Celestine A. 197
Dinah E. 202
Ettrula R. 197
Louis 95
Marim D. 80
Walter S. 197
William S. 80
William S. 198
MANTEL
Judah 123
MARKOFF
Bessie E. 118
MARKOWITZ
Marion M. 120
MARKS
Harry 170
Helen B. 21
MARROW
Charles H. 27
MARSHALL 184
Charle 3
Charlie L. 32
Estelle 32

Leolia 191
Lucy 47
Marie L. 26
Ruth 47
MARSHBURN
Rita Armstead Echols . 198
MARTIN
Alice H. 194
James F. 68
MASON
Alfred C. 63
Alva L. 146
Elizabeth 3
Georgie 63
John T. 139
Lina R. 47
Lucinda 145
William H. 145
Winnie 53
MASSELL
Fannie M. 96
Herman 96
Irvin R. 163
MASSENBURG
Ann 184
MATAN
Zelda 116
MATER
Hanna Jane 226
W. H. 226
MATTHEWS
Eva E. 204
Harry W. 204
Howard 194
Margaret S. 204
McClellan R. 191
Minnie A. 191
Susan 150
MAUEN
Arlean J. 51
MAY
Rosa Hutchins 82
MAYER
L. 97
MAYO
Nannie 48
MAYS
Lucy 78
MAZAKUTE
Simon 77
MAZZEL
Zachary Dane 171
McALISTER
Henry Adam 79
Mary Brandon 79
McALLISTER
Willie 82
McAULEY
M. 68
McCLENAHAN
John 68
McCLOUD
Cora L. 13
McCOY
J. F. 67
James 76
Mabel B. 30
Margaret T. 204

Index

Walter T. 30
McDONALD
    Annie 27
McEWEEN
    J. 68
McGEE
    Peter 67
McGHEE
    Nancy B. 84
    Samuel C. 84
McGINNIS
    J. B. 67
McHERN
    Ethel 203
    Matilda Cooper 52
    Owen 203
    Sarah 63
McMURRAY
    R. 68
McNAIR
    Julia H. 29
McNEAL
    Bobbie Jean 13
McNICHOLS
    Doris C. 74
MEARS
    Albert 140
    Edward 140
    Edward W. 140
    G. J. 140
    James L. 140
    Sally L. 140
    Tha--t 140
MEDICINE-BULL
    Virginia 77
MELAMED
    Moses 162
MELSON
    Caleb 218
    George 139
MELTON
    Martha 36
MELVIN
    Horace W. 73
    Johnelle K. 73
    Mary Elizabeth 48
MERCER
    James 67
MERCEY
    Alice M. 197
    Elnora A. 202
MERLEY
    John H. 56
MERRELL
    E. A. 69
MERRITT
    Jerome 14
    Jessie E. 15
MEYER
    Adolf 108
    Annie Levy 108
    Rebecca 96
MEYHR
    Aaron 98
    Goldie 97
    Harry A. 112
    Mary 106
MICHAELSON

Eva 106
Fanny 98
Issac 98
Joseph 97
M. 106
Rosa 97
MIDDELLTON
    Henrie 4
MILBURN
    Kate Wms. 55
MILEMAN
    John 4
MILES
    Clara M. 191
    Fred 24
    J. C. 205
    Mary 205
    Mary J. 80
    Rosetta 204
    Samuel C. 193
    William A. 199
    William H. 31
MILFORD
    Thos J. 68
MILLER
    Ada N. 80
    Ann 103
    Annie 52
    Eliza A. 55
    Katie 111
    Mary Charles 37
    Robert B. 80
    Samuel 126
    Samuel C. 55
MILLS
    Charles P. 31
    Charlie 33
    Emma S. 36
    James 78
    May 78
    Sarah 78
    Susie 78
MINER
    Leigh Richmond 79
MINFOFF
    Ida 123
    Jack 123
MINKING
    John H. 52
MINKINS
    Bettie V. M. 81
    Bickford E. 81
    Emma 31
    George M. 30
    Mary A. 146
MINNS
    Corrine 197
    Mary E. 205
MINTER
    A. 67
MIRMELSTEIN
    Abraham Benzion 95
    Betty Joanne 164
    Dora B. 165
    Ellis B. 165
    Etta Beck 95
    Fannie Binder 96
    Florence B. 165

Grace B. 164
Isaac 165
Louis B. 96
Rebecca 95
Robert 164
Rona Becker 165
Samuel A. 95
Samuel H. 164
MITCHEIL
    Frank 23
    Irene B. 23
    William H. 23
MITCHELL
    Addie V. 14
    Albert 29
    Alfred 14
    Alphonso 14
    Beatrice 198
    Eli 197
    Forest 13
    Garfield 14
    James 29
    Oliver 26
    Oliver 27
    Richard 29
    Robert 14
MONDEN
    George W. 28
MONEGHON
    Wm. 69
MONROE
    Carrie 25
MONTAQUE
    Dorothy 193
MOODY
    Chery 62
MOONVES
    Sylvia Freed 165
MOORE
    Charles H. 31
    Edith 199
    Eleanor J. 84
    Eliza S. 74
    Esther M. 193
    Glady S. 199
    John 236
    Mary E. 29, 138
    Reginald Q. 74
    Sylvius S. 84
    Thomas E. 49
MORE
    James 4
MOREWITZ
    A. H. 94
    Cecelia 168
    Dora 94
    Harry A. 168
    Herbert 158
    Jacob L. 166
    John A. 94
    Louis 158
    Rachel 106
    Reba B. Dorf 164
    Rose E. 94
    Ruth August 166
    Sallie Rome 166
    Samuel Maurice 164
    Samuel Solomon 106

Sarah W. 168	Goldie Greenspon 115	Mary J. 147
Thomas D. 164	Harry J. 96	Rose E. 146, 152
MORGAINE	Harry L. 96	NICHOLS
Robert 3	Herbert 162	Prince E. 194
MORGAN	Hilda M. 118	NICKCOTT
Christopher 33	Ida Richman 102	Hugh 3
Dora 25	Ida Solomon 162	NIXON
Jean Lazarus 110	Irvin E. 112	Wm. 69
Maurice 104	Isaac 98	NOARD
MORGENSTERN	Isadore E. 120	David 121
Kenneth 162	Joshua 97	NOBLE
Rosaline L. 162	Louis 102	Thomas 78
William 162	Marx 103	NONN
MORGON	Max E. 113	Goodwife 3
Sibill 4	Myer 99	NORTHCUTT
MORITZ	Rachel 103	Emmaline 14
Ludwig 107	Sadye C. 96	Geo. D. 14
Selma 107	Sarah 96, 97	NORTHERN
MORRIS	Simon 118	Bessie S. 28
Abraham 96	Sol 162	NOTTINGHAM
Alfred 106	William 115	Ernest 147
Amelia 106	NEADHAM	NUNN
Anna 106	Lucy 47	S. L. 69
Ellen 37	Thomas 47	NURSE
Hannah 96	NEELY	Harold 145
Lillian C. 99	Phyllis E. 194	Martha W. 145
Mark 106	NEIHOUSE	O'HARITY
O. W. 69	Anshal I. 121	Alanda R. 188
Phillip 99	NEILSON	OAKLEY
Russell T. 194	Herman N. 74	Jas. 68
Sadye Meyhr 106	NEISSER	ODIS
Sophia 106	Eugenie Spingarn 168	Morris 94
William 106	NELSON	OFSA
MORRISETTE	Charles A. 81	Jacob 109
John T. 78	Edward W. 31	Minna Schugam 109
MORROW	Elizabeth 37	OGLESBY
Lillian 192	Fred A. 38	M. O. 69
Mary E. 226	Hamlin 81	OLDFIELD
Mollie E. 226	Johnson 40	Elizabeth Jett 91
W. P. 226	Julin W. 81	OLIVER
MORTHCUTT	Lola M. 59	George 204
Mattie L. 37	Nettie R. 38	George T. 146
MOSELEY	William T. 36	Rebecca 204
Mary Jane 30	NETTLES	OLSHANSKY
MOSES	Gertrude 25	Charles 114
Julia M. 83	NEVIAS	OMAR
William H. 83	Ethel 109	Julie 29
MOSKOWITZ	Morris Jacob 117	ORR
Bernard 93	Rose Klein 111	Naomi E. 32
David Aaron 108	NEVILL	ORRELL
MOSSON	John 9	Mary O. 48
Malinda 202	NEVILLE	OSBORNE
MOTON	John 9, 10	John W. 31
Robert R. 79	NEWBY	Walter M. 191
MOUND	Elva Mae 196	William A. 195
Milton Norman 162	Oscar E. 193	Willie L. 191
MYERS	NEWMAN	OSER
Louise S. 201	David L. 105	Abe E. 93
NACHMAN	Ethel 104	B. M. 95
Abe 96, 161	Marih A. 48	Beryl Morton 95
B. 97	Mordechai Heshil 99	Dorothy Dora 93
Ben D. 99	NEWSOM	Edith G. 93
Benard 102	Louise B. 192	Hannah R. 95
Benjamin 103	NEWSOME	Harry 93
Charles 102	Watt D. 60	Louis E. 93
Chave Esther 97	Willie R. 60	Sylvan 93
Ella C. 99	NEWSON	OWENS
Esther Scoll 102	Mary 146	Angle B. 73

Index

Evelyn 25
Mattie B. 73
OXMAN
Harry 101
PACKER
Arlene H. 188
PAGE
Callie M. 195
PAIGE
Aurther 63
Buster 63
Ethel Webb 33
Jackson W. 202
Milton A. 201
Rachel 63
PALMER
Edward Nelson 81
Lutrelle Fleming 80
Richard R. 55
V. A. 68
Viola Goin 81
PARISH
Ella 215
Thomas 68
PARKER
E. W. 215
W. W. 215
_____ 50, 52
Addison 50
Dean 50
Eli 28
Ellison 50
James L. 50
Jessie 243
Jessie F. 244
John E. 50
Lady A. 50
Lillian 149
Margaret 50
Nancy 51
Pearl Lewis 158
Rachel 50
Ruth M. 50
Sidney Zalak 158
Simon 215
Susan 215
Theodore 13
Walter 149
William 150
William S. 50
Willie 47
PARKINS
Thomas 3
PARKINSON
Dorothie 3
PARKS
Clinton R. 85
PARSON
Jacob 47
PATERSON
Lillie E. 198
PATRICK
Hanna 26
Millie R. 33
Sallie West 224
Thomas C. 224
Thomas Jefferson 224
William T. 224

PATTERSON
Belle F. 54
James Z. 53
Jesse W. 30
Julia C. 30
PAYNE
America 39
Americus 152
Clara V. 200
Eliza 212
Louise 200
PAYTON
Harry R. 32
Henry 3
Martha E. 32
PEADEN
Annie 24
PEAKE
Ernest T. 48
Frances M. 196
Mary 48
Sarah A. 48
Thomas 48
PEAR
Benjamin A. 102
Jennie 113
PEARSON
Susie G. 198
PEEDEN
Florence A. 40
Raymond 27
Thaddeus H. 39
Viola M. 40
PEELE
Elizabeth 150
PEGRAM
Gladys 215
PEKARSKY
Leah Peltz 116
Morris 116
PELSANT
Sampson 3
Walston 3
PELTZ
Abraham J. 109
Alfred D. 93
Anna 117
Beatrice S. 127
Freidel S. 95
Gertrude D. 163
Goldie 93
H. David 163
Harry 117
Harry E. 95
Henry M. 93
Mary Stein 127
Mollie B. 117
Morris B. 117
Nathan 117
Phillip W. 127
Sarah Rifka 109
Sarah S. 93
Walter L. 117
PENNICK
Nannie A. 52
Orine M. 28
PERKINS
Frances 47

Herbert A. 83
Joseph 151
Phillips 146
Sadie Lee Marchant 83
PERLOWITZ
Sol A. 170
Wilma Roberts 170
PERRY
Berdie L. 199
Blair B. 30
Elsie S. 103
Isaiah B. 84
Izie F. 30
Vera E. 84
PERZEKOW
Goldie 114
Harry 114
Henry 111
Julian Newman 120
Nathan Louis 120
Sarah 107
PESKIN
Annie 106
Philip 106
PETHAM
Lucy A. 54
PEYTON
_____ 29
John 141
PHELPS
Obed 76
PHENIX
George Perley 77
Maria Stevens 77
PHILLIPS
Ben 154
Benjamin 154
C. 186
C. P. 186
Carlton L. 155
Carlton Latimer 155
Caroline E. 154
Col J. 186
Col. J. C. 186
Cora 155
E. Curle 154
Elijah 154
F. B. 154
George 154
Hattie Moseley 30
Helena G. 149
Ida 109
Ida Elizabeth 186
J. M. 55
James Mitchell 155
Jefferson C. 154
John 3
John Mallery 30
Joseph 154
Joseph Manley 30
Lola 155
Margaret 154
Mary C. 154
Mary E. 55
Mary Jane 155
Mary Jane (Lattimer . . 155
Rebecca 154
Samuel Latimer 155

Index

PICKERING
- Samuel W. 155
- Samuel Watts 155
- Sarah E. 155
- Sarah Knox 194
- Solomon 149
- H. 68

PIERCE
- Alberta 26
- Beatrice J. 80
- John B. 80
- Louisa 48
- Thelma B. 14

PIGROM
- Agnes 151

PINNER
- Edward 13
- Ethel E. 14
- Mills 39

PLASTER
- Michael 67

PLESANTS
- Curley 148
- James 148
- Lucy 148
- Richard 148
- Sadie 148
- Sherman 148

PLUNKETT
- J. D. 69

PODOFF
- Samuel 127

POINDESTER
- C. 58

POLAN
- Arthur 108
- Robert M. 108
- Sadie M. 108

POLE-ANT
- Tyrrell 76

POLISH
- _____ 94
- Hadaso 94
- Hyman Davis 94

POLLACK
- Mary Farber 161

POMERANZ
- Charles 94

PONDEXTER
- Estella 31
- Samuel 31

PONTON
- Button 150

POORE
- Innocent 3

POPPER
- Esther N. 167
- Nathan N. 167

PORTER
- Annie L. 29
- Emma R. 27
- Ida 40

POTTS
- Fannie Oser 112
- Julian T. 112
- Michael 112

POWELL
- Albert 26

PRATT
- Nick 78

PRESCOTT
- Margaret 145

PRESLEY
- Frank 147

PRESSEY
- Franklin 28
- Mary A. 59
- William 63

PRESTON
- Hattie W. 194

PRETTY-HAIR
- Mary 77

PREVILLE
- Arthur Joseph 124
- Mildred Samuels 124

PRICE
- George W. 49
- John H. 52
- Margaret 49
- Nell Hudgins 89

PRIMAKOW
- Mynne F. 169

PRINCE
- Eva Sidney 155

PRITCHELL
- Mary A. 197

PRITCHETT
- Bessie L. 195
- Carrie 142
- Clyde 30
- Henry 142
- J. 142
- Julia Thelma 193
- Lousiana 142
- Maggie 142
- Martha A. 194
- William A. 194

PURCELL
- Mary C. 198

PURDY
- Robert S. 49
- Valeria 33

PURFOY 184

QUICK
- Eliza 74

QUIVERS
- Agnes H. 193

RABINOWITZ
- David Michael 166

RADIN
- Benzion 109
- Sarah Rebecca 109

RANDAL
- Louisa 148
- Samel 148

RANDALE
- William 192

RANDALL
- Agnes 54
- Eliza 147
- Lawson S. 81
- Mary 54
- Niza L. 81
- Peter L. 54
- Wm. 54

RANDOLPH
- Lucous 28

RANSOME
- Matilda 52

RARIDAN
- Daniel 67

RAWSEY
- W. 69

RAY
- Alfred H. 193
- D. 68
- Maggie 212
- Maggie 197, 213

RAYSOR
- Mamie Latimer 81

READ
- A. I. 211
- James C. 76

RECANT
- Ethel H. 127

RED-BIRD
- Mary 77

REDDING
- W. 69

REDGROSS
- W. P. 59

REDWOOD
- Amy 146
- Edith 150
- Mary 146

REED
- Hattie 23
- J. W. 68
- Kettie B. 202
- Robert 23
- W. B. 202

REICHMAN
- Bertha 98
- Jennie 101
- Nathan 101

REID
- Bernice C. 13
- Jonathan B. 21
- Mae Beamon 80
- Sarah E. 21
- Walter M. 29
- William Thaddeus 80

REISFIELD
- Abraham M. 99
- Millie 99

RESNICK
- Lillian 109

REVIER
- Vincent L. 170

REYNER
- Harry 103
- Joseph 103
- Sarah 103

REYNOLDS
- Betty 63
- J. D. 69
- J. S. 67

RHODES
- R. S. 67

RICE
- Benjamin Solomon ... 115
- Eleanor Lundy 85
- Frances L. 115
- Helen I. 126

Index

J. D. 68
Julian Meyer 115
Margaret Ethel 100
Mary Rose 115
Robert Aaron 85
William S. 126
RICHARDS
    Lewis 197
    William 3
RICHARDSON
    A. K. 70
    Clara S. 191
    Emma 40
    Georgia L. 30
    Hattie 14
    Helen P. 191
    James 29, 142
    Margaret 142
    Mary E. 211
    Paul J. 30
    Rose 26
RICHMAN
    Abraham 112
    Esther 121
    Gertrude 112
    Joe 121
    Lillian Senie 112
    Louis Joseph 112
    Paul 169
    Ruth 169
    Sade Kirsner 107
    Sarah 112
    Sheri Gayle 112
    William 112
RICKS
    Eli 53
RIDDICK
    Geraldine Lewis 82
    Harold 150
    John 150
    John 83
    Mamie 150
    Mamie 84
    Sadie 54
RIDLEY
    Mark 199
    Sallie F. 199
RIIBNER
    Cillie 167
    Leopold 167
RILEY
    Annie E. 59
    Chas. E. 56, 59
RIOS
    Francesoa 77
RITAER
    Goldier 98
RITNER
    Sam 111
RIVERS
    Anthony E. 54
    Frank 21
    Mary 21
RIX
    Eliza G. 74
ROBBINS
    George B. 33
ROBERSON

Camaliel 76
J. Henry 48
ROBERTS
    Emma 114
    Ida Gordon 114
    Robert 114
    Violet 151
ROBERTSON
    L. W. 68
    Susan 63
ROBERTTS
    Christo 3
    William 3
ROBINSON
    _____ 60
    Adrianna Williams 73
    Andrew W. 57
    Blanche 73
    Catharine 60
    Charles 73
    De Russey 56
    Dora A. 204
    Edward V. 23
    Elizabeth Harris 52
    Ethel 196
    Frederick Jay 73
    Henry 8, 48, 56
    Henry 48
    Henry B. 57
    Inez B. 23
    J. Henry 56
    John 57
    John H. 149
    John J. 57
    Johnnie 30
    Julia J. 57
    Lettie 48, 56
    Lossie Tanner 55
    Luther W. 204
    Mary 8, 53
    Milie 60
    Mitchell B. 57
    Peter 47
    Queen V. 58
    Rosa 51
    Saria E. 145
    Viola 30
    W. H. 53
    Wesley 58
    William H. 84
    Willie E. 196
ROCKLEY
    Raph 3
ROGATZ
    Ethel Gottlieb 125
    Lillian 170
    Nathan 170
ROGERS
    Frances 115
    Hyman 115
ROLLINS
    Envie 150
    Nannie 149
ROSE
    Josephine 196
ROSENBALT
    David 97
ROSENBAUM

A. 162
Dora W. 163
Nathan 163
Nellie 100
ROSENBLOCH
    Jacob 94
ROSENBLOTH
    Mary 103
ROSENFELD
    Boris 159
    Irving 126
    Lisa U. 159
ROSENSTEIN
    Bertha 104
    Nathan 112
    Samuel 112
ROSENWASSER
    Hyman 122
ROSS
    Jessie Shadrack 24
    Rose W. 163
    Roy 163
ROTGIN
    Louis 164
ROTHENBERG
    Lesliebeth Diamant ... 166
ROTHMAN
    David 127
    Esther Jacob 127
ROTHSCHILD
    Meyer 95
ROUSLEY
    William 68
ROUTTEN
    Annie Laura 175
    Clifton E. 177
    Edward T. 179
    Henry P. 177
    J. J. 175
    James E. 177
    Joseph C. 238
    Louisa E. 175
    Matha A. 177
    Missouri F. 179
    Richard P. 177
    Sarah L. 177
    Spencer S. 179
    Thaddeus L. 175
    Wm. C. 175
ROWE
    Benjamin F. 71
    Louisa 71
    Thomas 71
ROY
    Frenchie 151
    Inez B. 148
    James A. 193
    Winnie 54
ROYAL
    Joseph 78
ROYSTER
    Purnell 28
RUBEN
    Belle Brenner 109
    David H. 120
    Frank 105
    Isaac 105
    Joseph Milton 120

Index

Rebecca	105
Sarah	105

RUBENSTEIN
- Aubrey Abraham 160
- Yetta 97

RUBIN
- David B. 113
- Gertrude 162
- Jack 162
- Joseph 104
- Rachel 104
- Yetta Fisch 113

RUDISIL
- Jacob 67

RUEGER
- Fannie 119

RUFF
- Ernestine 191

RUGGLES
- Harold L. 74
- Ruth T. 74

RUSSCIA
- Fanny 48
- Karl 48

RUSSELL
- Chaney 24
- Gladys L. 57
- Harriett 26

RUTKIN
- Maynard Leroy 160

SACFAN
- Leon 111
- Rose Mirmelstein ... 111

SACHS
- Bertha 167
- Henry R. 167
- Ida Sear 167
- Kate W. 167
- Louis 167
- Melvin L. 167

SAGMAN
- Sidney 161

SAMET
- Lotta Reyner 110
- Michael 110
- Rose 94

SAMPSON
- Alice Goode 32
- Ben, Capt. 32
- Charles A. 199
- Mary 76
- Nicey 202
- Peter 13

SAMUEL
- Goldie 104
- Rose 98

SAMUELS
- Ester 101
- Fred Edward 123
- Harris 104
- Joseph 125
- Tillye Satisky 123

SANDERS
- Sam 118
- Sara W. 160
- Sarah Levy 118

SANDERSON
- John 3

John	3

SANDFORD
- Esther 26

SANDLER
- Alfred H. 123
- Bessie M. 123
- Fanny 97
- Jacob 125
- Rosa Fega 125

SANDWELL
- Daniell 3

SANTA CRUZ
- Alexander 79
- Calixta 76
- Maceo A. 81
- Mary Alston 79

SARGENT
- Edgar A. 197
- Eliza A. 193
- Elizabeth 202
- Franklin 196
- Georgia Anna 201
- Hattie B. 21
- Jane 212
- John 201
- John H. 197
- Pleasant 212
- Richard 21
- Ruth 197
- Ruth Jackson 13
- Susie 203

SATCHELL 30
- Evelyn L. 31
- Julia Chandler 30
- Spencer 30

SATISFIELD
- Isaiah 204
- Jennie 206

SATISKY
- Aaron 113
- Dave 124
- Dora S. 100
- Elsye 123
- Ida 124
- Louis 102
- Marcus 158
- Maurice 124

SAUNDERS
- Adeline 211
- Alfred 38
- Beryl Leon 126
- Elizabeth 226
- Elizabeth B. 239
- Ida Warren 125
- Isadore A. 117
- John Seatney 226
- Lena 37
- Oliver T. 226
- Raymond 192
- Rose Hattie 117
- Sarah A. 226
- Sophie Samet 126
- Thomas 239
- Thomas 226
- William H. 226

SAVAGE
- Albert 25
- Estelle J. 30

James H.	30
John	33
Sarah	49
Sarah E.	30

SAVARPKS
- Enoch Conklin 78

SAVILLE
- Harry 104
- Raphael A. 120
- Sophia H. 104

SAWELS
- Martha Toliver 24

SAYON
- Belany 77

SCALES
- Delores 196

SCARBOR
- Pauline 201

SCHAIRWITZ
- Samuel 96

SCHEINMAN
- Gertrude 114
- Morris S. 114

SCHER
- Joseph Frank 108
- Josephine 108
- Kay Andrea 164

SCHLEY
- Herman 124

SCHLOSSER
- Daniel 163

SCHNEIDER
- Moses 168
- Rose 168
- Shulamith 168

SCHOENBAUM
- Ray 166

SCHONFIELD
- Bertha 116

SCHTAMF
- Frank 121

SCHUGAM
- Albert Mintz 109
- Irving 109
- Jack 109
- Rose Segal 109

SCHUSTER
- Samuel B. 168

SCHWAB
- Florence (Folla) ... 122
- Joanie 122

SCHWARTZ
- Ben 169
- Bessye Solomon 162
- Julia Roslyn 119
- Morris Wolf 162
- Nathan 119
- Sarah 98
- Tobias H. 98

SCHY
- Dorothy Jane 127

SCOLL
- Dora 95
- Irvin L. 93
- Meyer 95
- Mina Devera 98
- Ruth E. 93
- W. 95

Index

SCOTT
- Baby Boy 80
- Bettie 63
- Charlie L. 32
- Clarence Oscar 74
- Essie B. 199
- Etts 151
- Frederick Conklin 83
- Georgette A. 38
- Helen 77
- Inez Fields 83
- Lucy S. 36
- Mary A. 51
- Mary J. 146
- Mollie L. 31
- Norma Boisseau Armistead 82
- Samuel J. 51
- Stonewall Jackson 74
- William L. 31
- William T. 31

SCRIVENS
- Nora F. 40
- Robert 40

SEAR
- Abraham 107
- Bessie 101
- David 102
- Edyth Arch 121
- Kieve 121

SEARLE
- Brigett 3

SEAY
- Wallac 142

SEDGEWICK
- William 25

SEGALIN
- Ethel 99

SEGALOFF
- Anne Burack 166
- Bess M. 166
- Charles L. 166
- William 166

SEIDMAN
- Anna A. 122

SEIGEL
- Jean C. 111

SELDEN
- Elizabeth 191
- Joseph Thomas 206

SELDON
- Grace E. 191
- James T. 191

SELTZER
- Dora W. 160
- Hyman 160

SELVY
- Dorothea Boykin 202

SEMPLE
- Emily Booker 184

SENSTEATER
- Mary A. 100

SERASKY
- Estelle T. 119
- Phillip 119

SERVANT
- Thomas 3
- Thomas 3

SEXTON
- Alfred 51
- Jennie S. 51
- London 51

SEYMOUR
- L. Dwight 78
- Lucy Ann 78

SHAFFER
- Max 93

SHAPIRO
- Beckei 96
- Charles 123
- David Herman 99
- Jennie Klesmer 111
- Max Bernard 99
- Mollie 103

SHARF
- Alex 98
- Fannie J. 104
- Julia Reichman 126
- Macy Morris 126
- Max 104
- Rosie 94
- Thomas 105
- Yetta 105

SHARP-HORN
- George 78

SHAUITT
- Corinne Jacobs 127
- Maxine 127

SHAW
- Alex 34
- Elsie Simpson 29
- W. S. 67

SHAWEL
- Albert 126
- Annie R. 118
- Max W. 118
- Sarah Fox 121

SHEARRIN
- Annie 13

SHELTON
- C. B. 181
- C. S. 181
- Charles C. 181
- Claud B. 181
- E. 181
- G. S. 181
- J. 181
- James 181
- Jane E. 181
- L. V. 181
- Liliee 181
- M. 181
- Mary G. 181
- N. 181
- W. L. 68
- W. N. 181

SHEMER
- Lillyan A. 122

SHERMAN
- Cornelius W. 86
- Goldie J. 125
- Sarah E. 96
- Shirley C. 86

SHERR
- Norma R. 93

SHIELD
- Dora 24

James T. 24

SHIELDS
- Dr. S. R. 17
- Elizabeth 59
- Elizabeth S. 17
- Frank L. 31
- G. S. 17
- Howard 17
- Minnie B. 194
- S. R. 17
- Washington 194

SHIMKOWITZ
- Annie 113
- Esther Kemp 98
- Louis 113
- Minnie 108
- Morris 98
- Sam 108
- Simon 98

SHININGHOUSE
- Caroline 37
- Henry 37

SHIVER
- Abner 67

SHOEMAKER
- Wm. 69

SHORTS
- Cornealious D. 58
- Rev. T. H. 58

SHRIBER
- Dora Gordon 114
- Martin 114

SHWERDLOFF
- Rachel 98

SIDEL
- Werner 56

SIEGEL
- Abraham 107
- Benjamin 108
- Cecella 162
- Fannie 105
- Henry 119
- I. 105
- Infant 93
- Irwin "Teasy" 108
- Isaac 118
- Israel 162
- Jennie Berger 119
- Mary 121
- Mary 93
- Molly Esher 98
- Nathan 110
- Sam 121
- Sam 93
- Sarah 110
- Sarah E. 94

SILVER
- Abraham 107
- Benedict 94
- Hyman 107
- Minnie 107
- Sarah T. 97

SILVERMAN
- Freda 123
- Lena G. 166
- Reuben 123
- Samuel Jerome "Nubby" 166

SIMMONS

SIMMS
- C. 69
- Geo. W. 50
- S. 67

SIMNELL
- John 4

SIMON
- Henry Toliver 13
- Mary ? 200
- Mary E. 199
- Nathaniel 204
- Raphael 58
- VirginiA E. 12
- William 94

SIMONS
- J. E. 70

SIMPKINS
- Alice Greene 13

SIMPSON
- Daisy 13
- Elizabeth 192
- Katie 204
- Margaret 205
- Mary 197
- Ophelia 32
- Samuel 204
- Samuel S. 212

SIMS
- Asa C. 83
- Ethel C. 83
- Scott G. 75

SINCLAIR
- Atwell E. 186
- Carrie 186
- Carrie P. 186
- Chetwyn E. 186
- Elizabeth S. 186
- G. K. 186
- Georgana Wray 186
- George Keith 185, 186
- Ida Phillips 186
- James C. 186
- Jefferson B. 186
- Mamie E. 186
- Roy Lee 186
- T. A. 186
- Thomas A. 186

SISICO
- Viola 34

SKIMKOWITZ
- Leah 100

SKINNER
- Elizabeth 211
- Louise 148
- Queen Victoria 148
- Richard A. 148

SLATER
- C. 68

SLAUGHTER
- Betsy Ann Hodges 39
- Wm. 70

SLOANE
- Edythe Nachman 122

SMALE
- Hugo 3

SMITH
- Eugene T. 34
- Stephen 32
- A. B. 67
- A. Mitchell 55
- Annie E. 57
- Annie Eliz. Willis 173
- Arthur B. 58
- Baby Girl 149
- Beatrice Stevens 28
- Bennie 97
- Bettie M. 55
- Booker 67
- Celestine 202
- Charles 56, 59
- Claiborne A. 63
- Clarence A. 82
- Clarence L. 202
- David Gershom 114
- Edith Elizabeth 73
- Elizabeth 54
- Elizabeth T. 219
- Ella 56, 59
- Fred 202
- Freeman 200
- Geo. J. 219
- Gideon Edward 82
- Gracie A. 49
- Harry Sol 123
- Hattie Madison 58
- Henry 141
- Hester S. 202
- Hyman 97
- Isham 76
- Jack E. 114
- John H. 240
- Johnny 189
- Joseph 114
- Josephine Elizabeth 74
- Julius 94
- Junious 51
- Leon Morris 122
- Lillian P. 82
- Marcus 63, 114
- Margaret Elizabeth Irongonger . 240
- Martha R. 50
- Mary Ann 194
- Mary E. 63
- Mary T. M. 82
- Maude Holloway 23
- Mildred George 82
- Paul A. 193
- Robert M. 55
- Robert S. 55
- Robert W. 50
- Rosa 29
- Rosetta 197
- Ruth 202
- Samuel Jr. 23
- Samuel T. 50
- Tena 97
- Theresa Sims 85
- Thomas 3
- Verlenia Sampson 32
- Vivien Lipscombe 84
- Warren T. 50
- William F. 25
- Wm. S. 219
- Yetta Gross 114

SMITHERS
- Harry C. 57
- Maria 57

SMITHSON
- E. L. 69

SNEED
- Wm. 54

SNITZ
- Esther 94
- Fannie 103
- Isidore 103
- Max E. 110
- Simon 110

SNOBOWED-HEADW
- Lora 77

SNYDER
- Albert R. 122
- Dorothy 123
- Esther N. 122
- Joseph 123

SOLDINGER
- Harold 162

SOLOMON
- Jacob 95
- Max 97
- Susan 98

SOLTZ
- Esther Gillel 124
- Esther Rebecca 97
- Soloman 124

SPAPIRO
- Ethel B. 124
- Saul 124

SPARKES
- John 3

SPARKS
- William 38

SPARTLEY
- Eliza 145
- Mary E. 145

SPENNIE
- Alta G. 74
- Edward H. 74
- Susie Rix 74

SPICKARD
- Sam'l 68

SPIGEL
- Bertha Fisch 95
- Bertha Stern 168
- Frederick A. 166
- Goldie Garner 164
- Harvey 164
- Helen J. 167
- Isaac A. 168
- Jack S. 167
- Leroy M. 166
- Morton W. 166

SPINDELL
- Mary 116
- Sam 116

SPIRN
- Sidney 114

SPOONER
- Harry 124
- Rose 109
- Shirley 111

SPRATLEY
- Caroline 47
- Charles 193

Index

	Mary E. 193	
	Sylvia 57	
SPRIGGS		
	Ellen J. 47	
St. ALTON		
	James 84	
STACEY		
	baby girl 90	
STADLIN		
	Frances E. 125	
STAMFORD		
	John 4	
STANLEY		
	Estelle B. 14	
STARKS		
	Isabell Johnson 188	
STATEN		
	Elizabeth 28	
STEIN		
	Benjamin 101	
	Joseph 101	
	Max 126	
	Molly 101	
	Morris N. 120	
	Robert 101	
	Sarah 101	
	Susan Roth 101	
STEINBERG		
	Sadie Hochman 125	
STEPHEN		
	Louise N. 58	
	William D. 58	
STEPHENSON		
	James 142	
STERN		
	Emma Moritz 117	
	Joseph 116	
	Ludwig 117	
	Rachel 168	
	Siegfried 168	
	Walter 167	
STEVENS		
	Harriet Mason 78	
STEVENSON		
	Emma J. 60	
	P. B. 60	
STEWARD		
	Angeline E. 203	
	Isabella E. 203	
	William H. 203	
STEWART		
	Dorothy 52	
	Fannie M. 29	
	M. C. 52	
	Preston 24	
	S. E. 52	
	Samuel 212	
	W. G. 51	
	W. H. 52	
	Willis H. 29	
STINNEFORD		
	Jessie S. 74	
	Leroy H. 74	
STONE		
	F. M. 69	
STONEY		
	Juliet E. 79	
	Ralph S. 79	

STORES		
	John 208	
	Judeeth 208	
STRASSNER		
	M. Frances 84	
	William R. 84	
STREET		
	Betty 104	
	Joan Goldie Levy 108	
	Samuel Jacob 119	
STRONG		
	Sergt. Geo. 211	
STROUD		
	Annie Laura Fleming ... 82	
	Lamar Alexander 82	
	Rosa L. 197	
	Roscoe 196	
STURMAN		
	Sol 169	
SUGERMAN		
	Al Abe 119	
SUGG		
	Mary E. 37	
SUMMERS		
	Mary Erlach 116	
	Milton 116	
SUTTON		
	Queen E. 60	
SWAN		
	Laura 145	
SWEET		
	David 68	
SWELL		
	Victoria Lee 52	
SYKES		
	Edith Laura 192	
	James 14	
	Junious 14	
	Lillie S. 14	
	Rebecca 146	
	William H. 195	
TABB		
	Laura E. 26	
	Peter E. 24	
	Phillip 47	
	Thomas 58	
TAFT		
	Elouise Phillips 30	
TALBOT		
	Edith Armstrong 77	
TALIAFEROR		
	Mattie 56, 59	
TALIAFERRO		
	Henley 26	
	J. J. 26	
	S. A. 29	
TANNEN		
	Joseph S. 120	
TANNER		
	John 67	
	Lossie 55	
	Rebecca 55	
TARLTON		
	Annie 36	
	Lena F. 195	
TARPLET		
	Pauline 25	
TARRAGANO		

	Celia 108	
	Nissim Raphael 98	
TASUNKA-WASTE		
	Joseph 78	
TAUSIG		
	Dora G. 164	
TAYLOR		
	____ 82	
	Ada S. 83	
	Albert 149	
	Alice M. 193	
	Arthur 25	
	Bessie Luster 47	
	Clarence 24	
	J. 67	
	J. G. 21	
	J. H. 21	
	J. W. 151	
	Jasper 3	
	Margaret 193	
	Mary 23, 27	
	Mildred G. 23	
	Oliver G. 83	
	Rachel 50	
	Sallie B. 198	
	Virginia W. 81	
	Willie Anna 53	
TEICHMAN		
	Sol Gilbert 159	
	Sylvia Marian 159	
TENNIS		
	Angelina Watkins 89	
	Benjamin 89, 90	
	Casandra Bunting .. 89, 90	
	James 89, 90	
	John 91	
	Joseph 90	
	Joshua 209	
	Paul A. 91	
	Tribulation 90	
TERRY		
	David H. 81	
	Janie I. 81	
	Leona 197	
	William E. 197	
TESSLER		
	Bessie L. 117	
TESSMANN		
	Gesien M. 79	
	William M. O. 79	
THOMAS		
	Beatrice R. 38	
	Bettie 39	
	George 57	
	Horace 39	
	James 63	
	Johnnie 25	
	Josephine 28	
	Martin H. 80	
	Phoebe 212	
	R. G. 69	
	Tommie 26	
	William 25	
THOMPSON		
	Andrew 9, 11	
	Ida B. 83	
	Wendell L. 83	
	William 3	

William Hale 82
THOMSON
    Mr. 4
THORNTON
    Albert 25
    Arthur B. 58
    Ellen 213
    Frances 200
    Harold W. 26
    Joseph 39
    Maria 50
    Mary T. 27
    Matthews 29
    Samuel D. 27
    Wm. 213
THORPE
    M. C. or G. 212
    M. E. 212
    Thelma M. 212
THORSTON
    Marion Grant 82
THRUSTON
    Otis S. 196
THURGOOD
    Jennie 48
TOLIVER
    Andred 49
    Bennie 27
    Charles 195
    Cynthia 23
    George 33
    Helena H. 59
    John 203
    Lena W. 25
    Lura 203
    Mamie L. 25
    Susan 57
    Susie 50
    Warren 56
TONKINS
    Olive V. Stewart 51
TOPPING
    Alice J. 241
    Ann 241
    Garret 226
    Hannah 226
    Henry Sellie 227
    John 241
    John G. 227
    John P. 241
    John P. L. 241
    John Raymond 227
    John Wesley 227
    Lucetta 227
    Margaret 241
    Martha 226
    Martha 226
    Martha Susan 226
    Mattie S. 227
    Melvin D. 227
    Nettie Landrum 227
    P. L. 241
    Sarah H. 241
    Thaddeus 241
    Thaddeus 241
    Thomas 226
    Wm. R. 226
TOUBERT

Nathan 102
TOWNSEND
    Martha 13
TRAVIS
    Emma T. 193
TRENT
    Daniel E. 80
    T. D. 70
TROY
    Isaac 27
TRUHART
    Armistead W. 38
    Fannie 38
    Granbville T. 38
    W. 36
TUCHMAN
    Mollie E. 103
TUCKER
    Agie Chapman 63
    Alexander 215
    Charles 26
    Emanuel 215
    James William 215
    Mary A. 215
    Mary E. 215
TULL
    John W. B. 80
    Phoencie L. 80
TUMER
    Merritt 24
TUNSTILL
    A. H. 68
TURK
    Hebert 105
    Ray 105
    Thelma 105
TURNBULL
    Allen A. 225
    Eugene Royal 225
    Geo. W. 225
    Hattie L. 225
    Margaret Ann 225
    Walter 225
    William 225
TURNER
    Adell H 23
    Corrine M. 191
    E. 48
    Elizabeth 212
    Emory C. 199
    Laura Miller 74
    Mary 77, 200
    Matilda 148
    Nelson 212
    Thomas Wyatt 74
TYAS
    Henry 21
TYGER
    Eva Session 84
    Waders Jack 84
TYNES
    Charles A. 34
    Elizabeth A. 34
    Lucie Brooks 51
    Toney 34
TYSON
    Rosetta 193
UNDERWOOD

Mary Virginia 89
UNGER
    Allen N. 166
    Daniel 107
    Rose 110
    William 110
Unknown 43
UROUHART
    Daisy 27
VAN BEVERHOUD
    Albert E. F. 74
VAN HORN
    Charles Robert 74
VANISON
    Sarabheterson 76
    Theodore V. 75
VANN
    David J. 191
    Mary J. 194
VAUGHAN
    Ariadne 217
    Bernard C. 219
    Catherine 218
    Catherine P. 218
    George 219
    George W. 50
    Isabel 217
    James 218
    James M. 217, 218
    Jas. Robert 218
    Lavina C. 217, 218
    Mary A. 219
    Robert E. 217
    Robt. 218
    Robt. H. 219
    W. H. R. 219
    Walter R. 219
VIA
    T. L. 67
VINSON
    Fannie 27
    Robert 148
VINYARD
    J. H. 69
VOGEL
    Benjamin 119
VON McRAE
    Russell 34
Von SCHILLING
    Nannie 184
WACHTEL
    Hattie 169
    Joseph 169
WAINWRIGHT
    Jessie Cornelia 73
    John Henry 79
    Mary Chaney 79
WALKER
    Alonzo J. 213
    Annie Hamm 83
    Barney 149
    Edna C. 29
    Emmal 152
    Frissell C. 83
    John E. Sr. 29
    Martha 59
    Martha 204
    Mary M. 192

Index

WALKINS
- Milton 58, 59
- Sarah 48
- Ulysses E. 192

- Mary 215
- Randolph 215

WALLACE
- David 134
- James 8
- James 90
- James C. 134
- James W. 87
- Mary J. 134
- Mrs. James 90
- Peter 52
- Peter P. 52
- Roseanna 134

WALLER
- Arthur N. 33

WALTER
- Evan 141

WALTHER
- Frederica 75

WANT
- Harry 168

WARD
- Anna 194
- Annie C. 31
- Bertha 101
- Eugene 188
- Everlina P. 215
- Folrence 188
- Johnson 188
- Lavina 188
- Leon E. 188
- Louis 101
- Mary R. 188
- Pearl. L. 188
- Richard T. 188
- Tainma V. 188
- Theodore A. 194

WARREN
- Alphonso 82
- Elizabeth 197
- John C. 192
- Pauline 82
- William 196

WASH
- Ida Cooper 27

WASHINGTON
- A., Mrs. 33
- Allen 75
- Annie 75
- Catherine 32
- Coleman 151
- Eddie 33
- Hattie 32
- John H. 33
- Julia 31
- Ludwool Lee 49
- Mabel 31
- Maggie 24
- Mary B. 47
- Mary E. 191
- Mary Frances 47
- Mary J. 29
- Peter 54
- Rebecca 32

- Selena 54
- Susan 56, 147
- Tiberis 145
- William 48

WASSERMAN
- Gertrude 168

WATERS
- Leonard R. 158
- Sylvia B. 158
- W. J. 69

WATFORD
- Cashes 141
- Elnora 141
- Thomas 141

WATKINS
- Ada E. 27
- Elmore 27

WATSON
- Frank Lee 26
- James 25

WATTS
- Albert 141
- Bettie 141
- David 34
- Dollie 141
- Geo. Walker 221
- George 34
- Janne Estelle 141
- Richard 57
- W. Samuel 221

WEAVER
- Elizabeth 36
- Raymon B. 58
- Rhoda Anna 58
- William B. 58

WEBB
- Ann 53
- Elijiah 63
- Jackson 53
- Jackson 53
- Thomas H. 199

WEBSTER
- Arleann M. 195
- Lillian 30
- Maddie A. 27

WEGER
- A. Sol 124
- Jenny F. 112
- Lenp Sinker 124
- Maurice A. 112
- Meyer L. 99
- Rose Bess 100
- Sarah 99

WEINBERGER
- Morton Emanuel 95

WEINER
- Benjamin 168
- Isabel C. 168
- Louis S. 169

WEINSTEIN
- Allen D. 158
- Anne 126
- Bessie 111
- Ellis I. 111
- Jerald 127
- Julius 167
- Morris 167
- Sophia 167

- Zelda E. 158

WEINSTOCK
- Bernard M. 159

WELCHMAN
- Christopher 3

WELLS
- Andrew 69
- Coleman 28
- M. F. 69

WERBLOW
- Alfred 120
- Hayman 101
- Hilda 120
- Isadore 120
- Rebecca 120

WERNHAM
- Lillian A. 59
- Sarah A. 59
- Thomas 59

WERTHEIMER
- Edgar B. 164
- Maud Garner 164

WESSERMAN
- Eva Gordon 113
- Joseph 113

WEST
- Ann 226
- Arther 226
- Benj. 225
- Bessie W. 224
- Caxton A. 224
- Caxton Royster 224
- Charles A. 224
- Dwight E. 199
- Edwin Staples 224
- Frances S. 224
- George B. 224
- Henry 3
- John Hurbert 224
- John W. 224
- Lena S. 224
- Lucy J. 54
- Margaret 225
- Mary O. 224
- Molly M. 224
- Samuel H. 196
- Virginia Haywood 225
- William Bryan 225
- William H. 54

WESTBROOK
- Mattie 193
- Samuel 198

WETHERSBY
- _____ 4

WHEELOCK
- Fred D. 73
- Fred T. 82
- Matilda T. 73

WHIPS
- Emma 77

WHITE
- Amanda 60
- Barton 75
- Corodius 26
- Elnor T. 199
- Hazel 53
- Helen Ray 104
- Hester 27

Infant 75
J. M. 68
John 47
John H. 60
Joseph 48
Joseph P. 76
Lena Jason 73
Lillian H. 201
Lorenzo C. 81
Louisa 53
Martha J. 47
Mildred Jeanette 79
Missouri 75
Missouri F. 75
Nathaniel 196
Nayton 94
Nicholas C. 198
R. L. 53
Samuel 95
Tamer 49
William 4
Zula Patterson 79

WHITECOTTON
Harriet L. 160

WHITMAN
John A. 67

WIESEN
Marvin Arthur 158

WIFFE
Richard 4

WIGGEON
Caleb 64
Comfort 64

WILDHORN
Louis 113

WILKERSON
Mathaline A. 33
Geneva 202
Lewis 202

WILKINS
Benjamin E. 163
Mary E. 39
Pompie 13
Ruth B. 163

WILKINSON
B. 67
Lawrence E. 203
Minnie G. 203

WILKS
Abe M. 113
Joseph W. 113
Leon 123
Rachel 113
Rosalie S. 113
S. 94
Seymour I. 158

WILLIAM
Fannie 33

WILLIAMS
A. E. 68
Addie 30
Alma M. 82
Alvin 15
Annie B. 53
Beatrice 193
Catherine B. 51
Charles H. 82
Clara 191
Cornelious 205
Edward 40
Edwards 33
Eleanor 30
Freddie 59
George 52
Gladys M. 149
Hartin L. 53
Jacob 31
James S. 24
Jessie 215
John M. 13
John W. 225
Joseph 205
Louise H. 33
Lucile W. 84
Maceo T. 82
Madeline 195
Martha B. 47
Mary E. 28, 55, 57
N. 53
Pinkey 52
Rebecca 53
Robert 21
Samuel S. W. 28
T. W. 53
Thaddeus 53
Thaddeus 146

WILLIAMSON
J. 181
Nannie S. 181

WILLIS
Baily 173
Catharine Lawson . . . 173
Harold 173
John 173
Josephine Booker . . . 196
Laural L. 52
Lottie Mae 173
Pete 173

WILLOUGHBY
J. P. 67

WILSON
Ann 199
Clementine 28
E. S. 201
Edna 62
Fannie 56
Fannie E. 48
Helen J. 38
Henry 201
J. 69
James H. 201
Jessie J. 25
John J. 26
Joseph 32
Joseph 150
Katie 150
Katte 149
Lena B. 193
Leonidas E. 38
Pearl 201
Richard 32
Tony 25
Virginia A. 213

WINBURN
John W. 15

WINDER
George H. 230
Mary H. 230

WINDHAUS
Mary Elizabeth 74

WINSTON
Emily Jane 151
Frank C. 151
Frank C. 37
Lillian W. 151
Lillie B. 37
Martha Hill 151
Melvin S. 151

WINTERFALL
Thomas 3

WISE
Ella 30
Henry 28

WITHER
Symon 3

WOLF
Dora Rosenthal 169
William S. 169

WOLSHIN
Bob Davis nee 125
Israel 125
Rose G. 125

WOOD
Elizabeth Jones 243
Elizabeth Susan Jones . . 243
Samuel 67
William 243

WOODARD
Rosa 54
Sandy 54

WOODEN
J. W. 68

WOODMAN
Theodore H. 126

WOODY
Ida H. 53

WOOLDRIDGE
James M. 70

WOUTTEN
Hadrach 43
Margaret 43

WRAY
Arthur 26
Bertha 51
Edward 49
Georgianna 185
Hattie S. 33
John Henry 51
Louisa Ham 221

WRENN
Hiram 215
Hiram 215
Richard 215

WRIGHT
Annie Austin 26
Effie Payton 28
Ella M. 29
G. W. 68
James Herbert 27
John 3
Mary L. 48
Sarah Janette 49
Thomas H. 25
W. D. 68

WYCHE
- Addie 83
- Elliott 83
- Lucy J. 37
- William A. 38

WYNN
- Columbus 54
- Ernest L. 34
- Mary 54
- Sarah 54

YEARBY
- Charlett 145
- Hyrm 145

YELLOW-HAIR
- Edyth 77

YOUN
- J. C. 67

YOUNG 21
- Adelaide B. 82
- Agnes E. 196
- Alexander 28
- Beatrice P. 148
- Cardel 201
- Charles William 81
- Clarence A. 82
- Colia B. 195
- Estelle 21
- Ethel L. 200
- Frances 31
- Laura 49
- Leah 211
- Marshall Delaney 39
- Nancy 36
- Thomas White 82
- Walter E. 36

YOUNGER
- A. J. 70
- John W. 28

YOUNT
- Luther 68

ZERNES
- Richard L. 169

ZILBER
- Gertrude M. 105
- William M. 105

ZWERDLING
- David 123